FANNY MENDELSSOHN

A portrait of Fanny Mendelssohn by her husband, Wilhelm Hensel, inscribed
Berlin 1836. Private collection.

Fanny Mendelssohn

by

Françoise Tillard

TRANSLATED BY CAMILLE NAISH

AMADEUS PRESS
Reinhard G. Pauly, General Editor
Portland, Oregon

Translation of this book into English was assisted by a grant from the French Ministry of Culture.

On the jacket: Undated portrait of Fanny Mendelssohn, drawn by her husband Wilhelm Hensel shortly before her death. It was engraved by Eduard Mandel in 1847. Mendelssohn Archiv, Staatsbibliothek, Preussischer Kulturbesitz, Berlin.

ISBN 0-931340-96-9

Printed in Singapore

AMADEUS PRESS
The Haseltine Building
133 S.W. Second Avenue, Suite 450
Portland, Oregon 97204, U.S.A.

Library of Congress Cataloging-in-Publication Data

Tillard, Françoise.
    [Fanny Mendelssohn. English]
    Fanny Mendelssohn / by Françoise Tillard; translated by Camille Naish.
        p.   cm.
    Includes bibliographical references (p.   ) and index.
    ISBN 0-931340-96-9
    1. Hensel, Fanny Mendelssohn, 1805–1847. 2. Women composers—
Germany—Biography. I. Title.
ML410.H482T513 1996
786.2′092—dc20
    [B]   95-17336
                                                                        CIP
                                                                        MN

For Liouba,
my great grandmother,
who graduated from the Leipzig Conservatory in 1905

Contents

CONTENTS

Illustrations follow page 176

Preface

That the canon of excellence in western art music includes no female Bach, Beethoven, or Mozart has long been used as an argument to shore up the bastion of innate male superiority. Even in mid-Enlightenment, Jean-Jacques Rousseau wrote to d'Alembert: "Women, in general, possess neither artistic sensibility . . . nor genius." As for women's creativity in music, Havelock Ellis, that tireless postulator of the sexual norm, observed in 1894 (forty-seven years after Fanny Mendelssohn's death), "There is certainly no art in which they have shown themselves more helpless," adding that their lack of musical achievement was proof of their biological inferiority.

In fact, until the past several decades a dismaying quantity of books on music have either failed to mention those women, like Fanny, who did manage to compose, or else relegated them to footnote status in discussions of their more famous brothers and husbands. What better way could there be to redress centuries of neglect than with *Fanny Mendelssohn*—the first full-length study in English of this fascinating personage—composer, pianist, and one of the most accomplished and discerning musical personalities of her day?

Françoise Tillard does not attempt to impose a new musicology but carefully examines Fanny's life and works in their historical context, drawing extensively from the observations of contemporaries and from Mendelssohn family documents. Tillard creates an absorbing view of life in Berlin during the late-eighteenth and early-nineteenth centuries, from the optimistic, egalitarian climate of the *Auf-*

klärung to the conservative, sometimes racist nationalism of the nascent Prussian state striving to assert itself in the wake of the Napoleonic invasion. She situates Fanny and Felix in the German classic tradition and against the backdrop of German Romanticism, with all its generous ideals and noble enthusiasms—not forgetting the passionate contradictions of a movement that embraced both mystical Catholicism and liberal republicanism, love of nature and freedom and stolid bourgeois virtue.

A significant portion of the narrative is devoted to the attitudes and obstacles that affected Fanny's destiny. Fanny's personal domestic duty, as defined by her father and brother, is linked by Tillard to the larger questions of cultural assimilation and the destiny of German Jewry. So imperious does this duty seem that one cannot really wonder that she chose to follow it; indeed, one wonders if the passiveness and self-doubt for which women composers are often criticized was not, in Fanny's case, the result of her having internalized, almost as a matter of pride, the restrictions to which she felt subject. Above all, Françoise Tillard strikes a credible blow for the principle of equal opportunity. Reconstructed from the evidence of letters, the childhoods of Fanny and Felix Mendelssohn offer rich material. The words "equally gifted" recur as a leitmotif for the adolescent Fanny and her soon-to-be-famous younger sibling. Tillard proceeds to show what happens when two equally talented, equally trained youngsters receive vastly different levels of professional encouragement.

It is a testament to the devoted efforts of interested musicians and scholars that many of the compositions by Fanny Mendelssohn mentioned in this book have been extracted from the relative obscurity of libraries, archives, and private collections and are now available in printed form and on compact disc or cassette. Fanny's Trio in D Minor—probably her best-known work—has appeared in several recorded versions, including one on the Harmonia Mundi label featuring Ms. Tillard at the piano; several of Fanny's songs are also included on this disc. To mention several others: two quartets have been recorded on the Troubadisc label, and two volumes of solo piano pieces are available in recordings by Liana Serbescu on CPO. Fanny's unaccompanied choral works, including *Nachtreigen*, have appeared on small German labels, Bayer and CPO. The prestigious Sony Classical company has issued a disc of piano music for four hands by the Mendelssohns, including three pieces by Fanny; in the accompanying notes David Montgomery observes that "In some ways Fanny was the more adventurous of the two composers. . . . Occasionally her melodic writing reveals traits similar to her brother's, but her harmonic and structural sense was entirely personal." Yet Montgomery advises against comparing Fanny's four-hand music with Felix's; for all their affinities in life, he adds, they were "remarkably different as musicians."

Despite Montgomery's warning, we can't help but notice a certain contrast in the way brother and sister titled their works, apparent in two of Fanny's more ambitious compositions. Recorded live in 1984 in Cologne by CPO, Fanny's oratorio of 1831, scored for orchestra, chorus, and soloists, represents her most far-reaching endeavor in a large genre. Yet its title is of an almost abstract modesty: whereas Felix's two oratorios, *Elijah* and *Saint Paul*, are firmly identified by their titles with strong biblical personalities from testaments old and new, Fanny's title, *Oratorio on Biblical Themes* is dry and neutral by comparison. Similarly self-effacing is her Overture of 1832, her one full-scale orchestral work, rescued from oblivion in 1992 by the Women's Philharmonic Orchestra and recorded by Koch International. In striking contrast to the more literary titles Felix bestowed upon his overtures, *Ruy Blas, Fair Melusine, A Calm Sea and a Prosperous Voyage*, and *Fingal's Cave*, Fanny's work is simply entitled Overture. Although it was not unusual at the time for overtures to remain untitled—or at least, to bear titles that reflected nothing more than the circumstances of performance—Felix's more evocative appellations imply a specific, dramatic orientation of the listener before the music ever begins. It is sad that at the time of composing her Overture, Fanny quite possibly had little expectation of its acquiring listeners at all. Painstakingly reconstructed by a member of the Women's Philharmonic, the Overture's score does nevertheless engage the listener in a private world, does nevertheless open onto private, mysterious horizons. Despite Fanny's evident symphonic potential, her talent was left to mature virtually in private, a talent of which David Montgomery further declares: "Only the lack of compulsion (or perhaps opportunity) to publish more often seems to have prevented her skills from developing to match those of any major European composer of the day."

Camille Naish
Santa Fe, 1994

Introduction

In *A Room of One's Own*, Virginia Woolf ponders the hypothetical fate of an imaginary sister of Shakespeare. Innumerable difficulties would doubtless have beset her, all so insuperable she would probably have killed herself in despair.[1] Humorously, Woolf raises the question of female creativity, a question some in earlier centuries dared answer by remarking that a woman could never be a genius. Thanks to Fanny Hensel, such conjecture becomes superfluous: Felix Mendelssohn's sister did not commit suicide; she led a happy life and did a great deal of composing.

Fanny was born in Hamburg in 1805 and died in Berlin in 1847. She was four years older than her brother, the composer Felix Mendelssohn Bartholdy. The two children studied music together, and their friends considered them equally gifted. Fanny, however, never described herself as a professional composer or musician; she had to be content with house and family for a career. There is nothing new about that, and ordinarily it would not be worth mentioning—especially because Fanny did not shrink from her domestic role, apparently filling it with pleasure. What does interest us, on the other hand, is that Fanny never let herself be turned away from music. To be sure, she had the good fortune never to experience financial problems, and to marry a man who, though not musical himself, encouraged her to compose. Yet Fanny always felt the weight of the interdiction uttered by her father, reiterated later by her brothers Felix and Paul: no self-respecting woman indulges in public creativity. Accordingly, Fanny indulged in private creativity. While her brother pursued a career in public, Fanny pursued one in private, arranging fabulous concerts in her salon and making maximal use of the marginal means at her disposal. Thus she was able to manifest her gifts as a pianist and her talent for organization and conducting, whether orchestral or choral—abilities in which she was her brother's equal. But she did not stop there. When circumstances pressed her to keep quiet and no one took her compositions seriously—Felix least of all—Fanny continued to write music.

We are indebted to her for some four hundred works. Most are in manuscript form, respectfully preserved in the Staatsbibliothek Preussischer Kulturbesitz in Berlin. Fanny was almost forty before she dared take the step of making her private work public, publishing a few notebooks of piano pieces and some lieder. After her death, Felix had two other notebooks and a trio published, bringing the total up to eleven opus numbers. Since 1980 these notebooks have been reedited; at the same time, material still slumbering in the German state archives or belonging to descendants of the Mendelssohns is gradually being rescued from oblivion.

Naturally, I would never have undertaken this project had I not loved Fanny Hensel's music. But Fanny should not be treated as a misunderstood genius, partly because Fanny herself did not really tackle life head on, did not complete her life's work, and never reached her full potential. Above all, however, the notion of genius belongs to a world of masculine concepts that do not include female creativity. In the French Robert dictionary, the entry for *génie* or genius notes that what was termed "innate aptitude, or natural disposition" in the seventeenth century ("Those chosen for different tasks, each according to his genius," as La Bruyère puts it) subsequently came to mean a "superior aptitude of the mind that lifts a man above the common measure and renders him capable of creations, inventions and undertakings which seem extraordinary or superhuman to his peers." A *man*, naturally. Beginning in the eighteenth century, a term had to be found that could endow artistic labors with a magical air. This corresponded to the philosophical legerdemain of viewing men as the principal agents in procreation.[2] For reasons both symbolic and practical, it was evidently important to keep women at home and protect the patrilineal family. Here were two equally gifted children, one authorized to pronounce himself a creator in the eyes of the world while the other was enjoined to keep quiet, or at least to speak softly, no matter what her talent or desire. What perils it would cause society if a woman openly described herself as creative!

The relationship of women to musical composition varies from era to era according to the value granted the idea of creativity. Whenever music remains a spontaneous phenomenon that vanishes as soon as the piece ends, and when written scores are proportionately rare, then composition is not really separate from musical performance. And when composition forms part of a person's upbringing, in the sense that he or she has access to a musical education—or simply to an education[3]—then well brought-up men and women "compose," or rather, produce "madrigals" on poems conceived for particular occasions. The techniques of composition are not very complicated and bear more resemblance to a particular knack than to inspiration. Our idea of composition does not readily apply to these spontaneous endeavors, in which writing plays so small a part. The Italian baroque set great store in improvisation: can one really say that a cadenza is composed? Not really: it is sung, played, but improvised. Francesca Caccini, Barbara Strozzi, and other female Italian singers or virtuoso players were nonetheless inventive, as their work required them to be; there have always been women to "make" music. We tend to project our own convictions into history: women are not creative; therefore they have never been creative. The rediscovery of Élisabeth Jacquet de la Guerre, among others, has contradicted this tenet; perhaps, as Virginia Woolf remarked, we shall presently perceive that Anonymous is a woman.[4]

The question of women's creativity arose when musical composition was written down. In the late eighteenth century, when publishing prospered, composition turned into thought and works belonged to a creator who gave them his name—a man's name. At that point, women composers were seen as trained monkeys.

Fanny therefore could not belong to the "genius" category thus defined as masculine. Felix, who was very fond of his sister, agreed to publish a few of her works under his own name. He did not conceal the fact, and nobody found it unusual.

Felix and Fanny: F Major and F Minor (F in Dur und F in Moll).[5] This major–minor dualism dates from the beginning of our rational,

Cartesian period. As children, we are taught that the minor mode is an old lady, Miss Minor, not as strong as Mr. Major, and that the added leading tone is a little cane to support her in life. Thus the diversity of modes, or rather, the fickleness of rules, established Mr. Major and Miss Minor. Clarity and regularity belong to the major mode, whereas the minor mode is invested with every ambiguity—ascending major sixths, descending minor ones—inherited from the medieval fear of the Devil. Three halftones instead of two: how unbalanced, how perverted, how sensual! Let's not forget that in the fourteenth century Guillaume de Machaut was excommunicated for over-indulging in halftones.

This distinction between major and minor, between light and darkness, recurs at every turn in the lives of the two twinlike Mendelssohn children—despite the four years' difference in their ages. Felix is handsome, Fanny is ugly; Felix goes traveling, Fanny stays at home; Felix has a public persona while Fanny cultivates a private one.

A taste for antithesis was particularly suited to Prussian society after 1810. After the Napoleonic invasion, the collapse of Prussia, and the dismantling of the Holy Roman Empire, everything had to be refashioned, preferably by following a course antithetical to that of the preceding period. Admiration for the French Revolution gave way to hatred for the French; the cult of feeling replaced the cult of reason; pan-Germanism took the place of universalism. In the stampede, freedom of thought and a measure of sexual emancipation gave way to prudishness and to confinement within family life. The royal couple of Friedrich Wilhelm III and Queen Luise aroused the admiration of such Romantics as Novalis and Kleist. The queen's death engendered a cult wherein the struggle against Napoleon blended idealistically with respect for the family and the prizing of conjugal love, exalted in Beethoven's *Fidelio* as the first step in the pursuit of liberty. From the top to the bottom of the social ladder the model established by the royal family recurred. Politics had disappeared: there were only family cells, proclaiming by their structure allegiance to the monarchy. In other words, nothing was happening in Prussia; history belonged to some other portion of the world, such as France or England. Even if something did happen, it couldn't be reported: there was no freedom of the press, no constitution. The beginning of Fanny's diary, in 1829, forcefully describes this suffocating state: Prussia inside, the world outside. This was a far cry from the Berlin salons of the *Aufklärung*, that brief period of Enlightenment in which society was happily diverse, with aristocrats and members of the new middle class, including Jews, mingling together, and free discussions on every conceivable topic. The nineteenth-century Biedermeier salon had the privilege of performing good music, and must be forgiven for its insipid bucolic poetry, since that was the sole language permitted. Not by accident did the greatest German poet of that time, Heinrich Heine, flee to Paris!

But why would a talented woman agree to stay at home? Obedience to social pressure would certainly be one reason. Civilized beings must play a role that allows them to identify with those around them, and women did not live alone in the nineteenth century, any more than they traveled alone—unless they absolutely had to. This state of affairs would last until the First World War. Despite her talent, Fanny conformed to the general rule, which in her case offered many advantages. The mistress of the house was much esteemed in the Mendelssohn family, and mothers were revered as idols. In addition, Fanny's personal reasons had to do with the very particular rules governing the Mendelssohn clan.

Fanny's paternal grandfather, the German-Jewish philosopher Moses Mendelssohn, had left the ghetto, braving poverty and the disapproval of both Jewish and Christian communities in his quest for learning. The fame he acquired gave his family a special and enduring renown, but also endowed it with a moral duty. When social pressure gradually constrained almost every member of the family to convert, this duty only became more pronounced. A Jew has constantly to prove that he is "good"; a converted Jew must prove that he is even better. Fanny's father, Abraham, gave up banking when he became a Christian. Felix wrote no operas, thus never entering that world of compromise and money. As for Fanny, she was a model wife and mother, zealous in fulfilling all her family duties—and these were numerous in an age when diseases spread rapidly and the sick were cared for at home. But what was especially remarkable was that intellect had no gender in the Mendelssohn home. Thus the two daughters, Fanny and Rebecka, were fortunate in having access to knowledge and culture that made them privileged women who could not have wished for a better lot in life. If they accomplished something, the feat was judged on its own merits, without being subject to "feminine" criteria. If Fanny wrote music, then it had to be good. This, however, was not her role, and music must not distract her from her true duties.

As a child, then as an adolescent, Fanny devoted herself to music with such ardor that Felix came to detest all idea of competition for the rest of his life. Then the rug was pulled from under her when she had to leave the field entirely to Felix and learn how to run a house. She was allowed to choose her husband, the painter Wilhelm Hensel. This was fortunate for her because she had been afraid that marriage would constitute a dramatic break from the past, but the day after their wedding he sat her down at the piano and put a sheet of manuscript paper in front of her. She had a son, Sebastian, who grew up surrounded by his father's paintbrushes and his mother's musical scores. Sebastian set himself the task of writing down the Mendelssohn family memoirs; had he not done so, no study of these exceptional personalities would be feasible. In the midst of all her family tasks, Fanny arranged and rehearsed her Sunday concerts, composed music, and wrote letters to her brother and her friends. The total number of letters written by the Mendelssohn family as a whole is colossal; those from Felix to his family alone amount to more than nine hundred.[6] Perhaps influenced by this pictorial and epistolary environment, Fanny's compositions often assume the character of sketches, or of a musical diary. Shorter musical forms—lieder, melodies for piano, and études—abound in her manuscript notebooks. Longer forms, such as sonatas or cantatas, are rare, and she wrote only one solo orchestral work.

Fanny displayed a typically feminine failing, carefully inculcated and maintained: lack of self-confidence. It takes a certain self-assurance to engage in work that requires so many days of patience, and to overcome the necessary alternation of frenzy and discouragement. To our late twentieth-century eyes, sketches possess as much charm as the grandiose effects dear to the nineteenth century, and Wilhelm Hensel is known and esteemed more for his rapid pencil sketches than for his paintings.[7] While it is certainly pleasant to imagine the Hensels simultaneously dashing away with pen and brush, we may also feel some regret that Fanny did not devote herself entirely to music from early youth on. Her most polished work, the Trio in D Minor, was composed a few months before her death and attests to what she was capable of; how sad she did not forge ahead sooner!

Nonetheless, the work she did leave behind is both powerful and individual. Fanny composed quickly and her sketches, as I term them, are lively and inspired. In the space of a few pages, never abandoning her improvisational style or flaunting her technique, Fanny was able to make her own voice heard, without the slightest trace of pedantry. Her meeting with the artists at the Villa Medici in Rome brought her the strongest encouragement she was ever to receive. In 1839 the Hensels embarked on a journey that Fanny had dreamed of all her life: they spent three months in Rome, from February to May 1840. Among the artists then in residence there were the composers Gounod and Bousquet, the painter Dugasseau, and their mentor Ingres, the director of the Académie de France in Rome; all were ecstatic over Fanny's talent, especially Gounod. Fanny showed them a side of German music they had hitherto not known, drawing on her remarkable memory and playing all of Bach, Beethoven, and her brother Felix's works. She also played her own compositions for them, and their admiration knew no bounds. Thus for the first time in her life Fanny was fêted and encouraged in the way she deserved. Compositions flowed effortlessly from her—there was certainly no lack of inspiration. But the Hensels' subsequent return to Berlin was terribly hard for Fanny. Only several years later, egged on by her young friend Robert von Keudell and pressed by the publishing houses of Schlesinger and Bote und Bock, did she decide to publish a few works, which were encouragingly well received by critics. Fanny was leading a life she loved, a life that made her happy and enabled her to make others happy too, when she died suddenly on 14 May 1847 while rehearsing for one of her Sunday concerts. As if unable to go on living without her, Felix died with equal suddenness on 4 November that same year.

To attempt the biography of any single member of the Mendelssohn family is something of a gamble. Not only does the author become passionately interested in each of them in turn—and they constitute a numerous clan–but the Mendelssohns only conceived of themselves in relation to other family members. In writing about Fanny Hensel and bringing her to life, I could find no better way of proceeding than to describe the people she loved and situate this little world in its context. Above all, the Mendelssohns were a family and a clan. Fanny gradually became the heart of this clan, and with her death it rent asunder.

CHAPTER ONE

Moses Mendelssohn

A central figure of the Berlin Enlightenment, Moses Mendelssohn (1729–1786) created his own destiny as well as his own name. Born on 6 September 1729, Fanny's grandfather was originally known as Moses, son of Mendel Dessau, after the name of the small town where his family lived. Mendel was a teacher in the rabbinical primary school and, despite his great poverty, was determined to pass on all his knowledge to his son. Either his erudition was minimal or Moses possessed exceptional ability, for family legend has it that at the age of five he was as learned as his father.[1] At that point Mendel entrusted him to the Rabbi Fränkel, a man distinguished in this Jewish community for his intellectual freedom and his knowledge. Poverty forced Moses to become a traveling salesman, wandering from village to village with his wares packed on his back. But when Fränkel was appointed *Oberrabbiner* (head rabbi) in Berlin, young Moses, then aged fourteen, decided to follow him, knowing Fränkel was his only means of gaining knowledge. He entered Berlin through the Rosenthal Gate, the entrance reserved for Jews.[2] When asked "What is your business?" he is said to have answered "I have come to learn."

Moses needed incomparable mental strength to make such a decision for he was alone and penniless. His physical strength was negligible: he was small and hunchbacked—he probably had rickets. For seven years he lived in abject poverty. Fränkel obtained work for him as a copyist, which would not have covered his upkeep had not several wealthier fellow Jews—Fränkel among them–occasionally provided him with food. His psychological condition was no easier. Jews were only tolerated in Berlin if they had money, and the Jewish community could thus only sustain a small quantity of poor. This community was ruled by Polish rabbis who permitted only Hebrew and Yiddish to be spoken; German was utterly forbidden. In this way the rabbis maintained their own power. For Moses, however, the German language was not simply a means of emerging from the ghetto: it represented access to science, knowledge in general, and ultimately philosophy. He therefore started learning it in secret as soon as he arrived in Berlin. Discovery would have resulted in his being expelled from the city. A truly self-educated man, he absorbed everything he encountered—mathematics, dead or living languages, and above all philosophy. Only history bored him: since he was not a citizen, how could history concern him? His difficulties lasted until 1750 when, at the age of twenty-one, he went to work for Bernhard the silk merchant. Bernhard engaged him as his children's tutor, then as an accountant; toward the end of his life he made Moses his partner. Thus Moses acquired the independence he longed for, enabling him both to feed his family and to read and write as he saw fit. After a youth like his, the course of his future life was clear: he must help his fellow Jews to emerge from their physical and moral wretchedness and enter into German civilization as Germans. Moses was actually the first person to assert this double identity and call himself a German Jew. Returning to Palestine did not seem feasible; rather, he wanted German culture itself to be a promised land for Jews. He translated the five books of Moses, the Psalms, and the Song of Songs from Hebrew into German. His goal was to make German accessible to Jews and to restore to the Germans a poetic text freed of its mysticism and tendentious aspects. He did not have time to translate the entire Old Testament, as had been his wish.

With his friend the dramatist Gotthold Ephraim Lessing (1729–1781) and the publisher and bookseller Friedrich Nicolai (1733–1811), Mendelssohn exerted a decisive influence on German literature. Even before Lessing published his *Hamburgische Dramaturgie* (1767–1768)—articles that praised Shakespeare while excluding French dramatic models—the two friends had contributed to the *Literaturbriefe* (Letters about Literature), which sought to free German authors from the imitation of the French that they found ridiculous. Moses even criticized Friedrich II for writing his *Poésies diverses* in French. This was an extraordinary act of courage on the part of a man whose own situation was far from stable, and it was equally remarkable for a Jew to be defending German culture.

Naturally, Moses provoked bitter controversy among fanatical adherents of both religions, but he also aroused enormous enthusiasm among philosophers and enlightened persons. Mirabeau wrote of him: "A man thrown by nature into the midst of a debased horde, born without any kind of wealth . . . , has reached the level of the greatest writers to appear this century in Germany."[3] Robert Badinter describes how Moses's ideas influenced the French Constituent Assembly during discussions concerning the emancipation and citizenship of Jews.[4] Moses had become the champion of Jewish civil rights and integration.

His intelligence and brilliant conversation won him as many friends as did his writing. His taste for discussing ideas freely and without prejudice is reflected in his *Phaedon*, a book that earned him the nickname of the German Socrates.[5] An admirer, Johann Kaspar Lavater (1741–1801), unwittingly made Moses the center of an unpleasant public altercation. Lavater was a Swiss Protestant theologian who invented physiognomy; he thought that a person's character could be judged by facial features. Opining that the essential goodness of Moses's face could only be manifest in the features of a Christian, Lavater publicly charged Moses in 1769 to give his reasons for being a Jew, or else to convert. The unthinking Lavater did not realize he was jeopardizing Moses's right to remain in Berlin. As a philosopher, Moses could not possibly admit that any one religion could contain a universal truth. In his play *Nathan the Wise* (1779), Lessing gives an idea of how his friend may have replied: the sultan Saladin requires Nathan—whose character is based on Moses—to disclose which of the three revealed religions was the true one. Caught in a situation as delicate as that of Moses, the Jewish Nathan tells the sultan a parable. A miraculous ring, which gave whoever owned it the power of being loved by all, was handed down from father to son. It came about that a certain father could not decide which of his three sons, all of whom he loved equally, should inherit the ring. He arranged matters so that each of the sons inherited an identical ring. When he died, a dispute arose. Called in to decide the question, a judge ruled that none of the three rings was the true one, since none of the three brothers knew how to make himself loved by the other two. It was, however, each brother's duty to keep the ring their father had bequeathed him out of love. The original ring had probably been lost. Perhaps the father had grown weary of the tyranny of one sole truth?[6]

Nathan-Moses won the fight honorably, and even showed a touch of humor. When another would-be converter named Teller addressed the following poem to him:

> You do believe in God the Father,
> Believe therefore in his Son.
> After all, you give credit to children
> Although their father is still alive!

Moses, wittily continuing to equate the granting of faith with the granting of financial credit, replied:

> No, indeed, I would not be so foolish as
>   to make a loan to the son;
> The father is immortal!

Moses Mendelssohn believed strongly in tolerance, and for that reason favored the separation of church and state. He did not obtain the *Schutzbrief*, or letter of protection authorizing him to reside in Berlin, until 1763. The Marquis d'Argens wrote a letter to Friedrich II, supporting his request with these words: "A philosopher who is a bad Catholic hereby begs a philosopher who is a bad Protestant to grant a favor to a philosopher who is a bad Jew. There's too much philosophy involved in all of this for reason not to side with my request." Mendelssohn expressed a wish to have the privilege extended to his descendants, but it took until 1787 for Friedrich Wilhelm II to extend it to Moses's widow and children.[7]

All these particulars are found in *The Mendelssohn Family*, the book written by Fanny's son Sebastian—a true memorial to his parents, compiled in 1879. Modern researchers quibble with Sebastian, claiming that on various points he seems to lack accuracy. No doubt he does, but that need scarcely concern us. Sebastian never knew Moses and was just a small child when his grandparents died. The family legend was narrated to him mainly by his mother, and that is precisely what interests us. Of course, he did possess an enviable quantity of firsthand documents. Yet his admiration for this exceptional ancestor was given him by Fanny, who had herself been brought up to respect this man of courage and intelligence. Moses Mendelssohn's religion was founded on reason, tolerance, and fidelity to oneself and those one loves. These values were even reflected in the family's aesthetic sense: Fanny and Felix both received a musical education distinguished by a rigorous study of earlier composers, particularly earlier German composers such as Bach, Handel, and Gluck. This background did not impair the fluidity of their musical language, which was always elegant and immediately comprehensible, like the conversation of a well-bred person. The influence Moses had exerted on his descendants was probably more intellectual than musical, although his taste for mathematics and chess was not unrelated to music. Pride in the name of Mendelssohn went hand in hand with a firm belief in the absolute power of thought, reason, and knowledge. As Heinrich Heine (1797–1856) remarked with customary irony in these lines from "Atta Troll":

> Hört es, hört, ich bin ein Bär,
> Nimmer schäm' ich mich des Ursprungs,
> Und bin stolz darauf, als stammt' ich
> Ab von Moses Mendelssohn!

> (Hear me, hear, I am a bear,
> Not ashamed at all of my forbears;
> I'm as proud of them as if descended from
> Moses Mendelssohn!)[8]

Fanny, alas, could boast with certainty of being descended from Moses, for like him she was hunchbacked. Most of Moses's immediate descendants experienced the same rapid, painless death he had met. He died on 4 January 1786.

CHAPTER TWO

Fanny Mendelssohn's Ancestors

THE DAUGHTERS OF MOSES MENDELSSOHN

From his marriage to Fromet Gugenheim, the daughter of a Hamburg merchant, Moses had three daughters and three sons: Brendel, Recha, Joseph, Henriette, Abraham, and Nathan. According to Sebastian, he took great pains with his children's education—which means that he took great pains to educate his sons. Should Moses have shown himself to be more intelligent than Rousseau? Sophie could learn only what would please, comfort, and prove helpful to Emile. Such was the law of the universe, the order of nature, no more to be questioned than the laws of harmony, with their major and their minor modes. Girls were subject to men as minor was to major: even savages knew that! The Mendelssohn boys, particularly Joseph —for the others were still small when Moses died—received philosophical, biblical instruction from their father; they had a tutor, Herz Homberg, and learned Latin, Hebrew, German, and science. The girls were given the education of a rather intellectual Sophie: housekeeping, music, drawing, modern languages including German. Their father ruled them with despotic power. Despite his advanced ideas, he arranged marriages for Recha and Brendel—who were only thirteen at the time—without asking their opinion. Both would later divorce their husbands. Henriette never married at all.

The late eighteenth century was nonetheless favorable to the minor mode, for it was during the *Sturm und Drang* period that the greatest number of pieces in a minor key were written. Rational argument and a desire to learn promote a measure of emancipation. During the 1780s in Berlin, a literary movement was launched in the salons of "beautiful Jewish daughters" such as Henriette Herz and Rahel Levin (later Rahel Varnhagen), who were close friends of Brendel Mendelssohn. Henriette de Lemos had also been married young (at fifteen) to the celebrated physician Markus Herz. But while Markus surrounded himself with scientists, the young and pretty Henriette assembled a circle of friends—Schleiermacher and the Humboldt brothers among them—with whom she discussed literature and sentiment. It was here that Brendel, wife of Simon Veit, met Friedrich von Schlegel (1772–1829), for whom she subsequently abandoned husband, family, and fatherland. Less attractive than Henriette, Rahel Levin was bent on listening to and understanding the psychology of the friends who came to her house for tea; here, in her mansard-attic salon, Prince Louis-Ferdinand met Pauline Wiesel. It seems that in Berlin—a city expanding in the heart of a dying Holy Roman Empire—some sort of outlet or free zone was necessary, and since the idea of social exclusion was obviously absurd in Jewish salons, aristocrats mixed freely with bourgeois and Jews. The one criterion was a common taste for conversation. Given this freedom of language and behavior, women were demanding something entirely new in Germany: the freedom to love and choose whom they pleased.

Brendel Mendelssohn (1764–1839), who had married the man her father chose, banker Simon Veit, changed her given name to Dorothea. She pursued this logic of independence until it led to scandal. Approximately half the Jewish women accepted in polite society divorced the husbands who had been imposed on them; however, they came from rich families and remarried into the impoverished Prussian aristocracy.[1] But Dorothea chose to share the destiny of a penniless literary man. Simon Veit behaved rather well toward her, leaving her an allowance and custody of the younger of their two sons, Philipp, on condition she did not remarry. Dorothea and Friedrich spent the rest of their lives asking their friends and families for money or a job. Dorothea did translations[2] and wrote a novel, *Florentin*. Friedrich von Schlegel—who was, among other things, an excellent literary critic[3]—meanwhile pursued money and success. Hoping to obtain both he published *Lucinda*, the story of their love affair. In it he described his passion for Dorothea and their amorous frolics as bluntly as he dared. Not only does it boast descriptions of torn clothes, seductive physical charms, and ardent embraces, but Lucinda is bold enough to make known her desire, to call for and make love in every conceivable position. The medical books of the time did not recommend this, but Friedrich and Dorothea had either not read them or found them ridiculous.

The society of that time was incapable of understanding the couple. With the exception of Schleiermacher, even their closest friends were shocked and showed it. The daughter of the model for *Nathan der Weise* as the heroine of a pornographic novel: it was inconceivable. To complete the scandal, she was Jewish, ugly, and ten years older than her lover. Unfortunately the novel was a financial disaster: everyone discussed it, but nobody had bought or read it.

Dorothea converted to Protestantism and married Friedrich von Schlegel in Paris on 6 April 1804. After a life of travels and material vicissitudes she underwent a second conversion, ending her days in Frankfurt as a bigoted Catholic and dying in the house of her son, the painter Philipp Veit.

Moses arranged for his second daughter, Recha (1767–1831), to marry Mendel Meyer, son of the banker Nathan Meyer, of Mecklenburg-Strelitz. Meyer served as a court Jew, or *Hofjude*, a Jew allowed to share in the court life as a diplomat, banker, or the like. Recha, too, divorced her husband and became headmistress of a girls' school in Altona,[4] then lived in Berlin until she died. Recha was known as a woman of intelligence but very fragile health.

The situation of the youngest Mendelssohn sister, Henriette, was as difficult as her father could have feared knowing that she was unmarried. Moses left very little to his family, and his widow, who had only the slenderest means, had to leave Berlin and return to her family in Hamburg. Henrictte lived for a while with her mother, then decided to take off on her own—a decision dictated by necessity. She became a governess and set out for Vienna. According to Jean-Jacques Anstett,[5] Henriette's first task as a governess was to perfect the education of Henrietta, daughter of Fanny von Arnstein (1758–1818).[6] Disliking the conservative atmosphere of Vienna, she remained there for only two years before moving to Paris in 1801 to join her brother Abraham, a clerk in Fould's Bank. Fould either rented or lent her a pavilion adjoining his apartment building in the rue Bergère, where she opened a boarding school for girls. Henriette accepted children aged seven or more, not necessarily of Jewish faith since she had an assistant who could give them a Catholic education.[7]

In 1812, Henriette became a governess again and spent the next thirteen years attending to the education of Fanny Sébastiani, daughter of Count Horace Sébastiani, a former general of Napoleon. This clever officer continued his career during the Restoration, becoming a deputy, a minister, and finally a marshal. Henriette therefore lived very grandly—not that she was much impressed by this. She tried to obtain from her charge the same good results her Berlin sister-in-law obtained with our Fanny, but in vain. Although extremely nice, the young Parisian was a society girl and had set her sights on a fashionable marriage. Fanny Sébastiani was to die the same year as Fanny Hensel, in 1847—but in vastly different circumstances: she was murdered by her husband, the Duke of Choiseul-Praslin, peer of France, who committed suicide in prison rather than appear before the court. This scandal reflected badly on the government of Louis-Philippe—which was accused of having encouraged the duke's suicide—and contributed to its disfavor. Education cannot guarantee everything. Henriette did not live to witness her student's tragic end. She returned to Berlin in 1825 after Fanny Sébastiani's marriage, living on the pension of 3000 francs per year that General Sébastiani had granted her.[8] Henriette died a good Catholic, like her sister, on 9 November 1831.

Could these two women, Dorothea and Henriette, have been role models for Fanny Mendelssohn? Fanny was thirty or forty years younger than her aunts. One might have hoped that during this lapse of time female emancipation would have taken such leaps and bounds that Dorothea's sexual liberation and Henriette's financial independence would have provided models for Fanny to emulate. But when she met her aunts they were charming old ladies, cultivated and interesting but entirely well-behaved, who had found in Catholicism the "little cane" they needed (see Introduction). The nineteenth century was sailing full steam ahead with its conservative ideas.

FANNY'S PARENTS

Henriette was very close to her brother Abraham, who was a year younger than his sister and a clerk at Fould's Bank. One of her dearest friends was Lea Salomon, granddaughter of the court Jew Daniel Itzig (1723–1799), and a member of one of Berlin's most privileged Jewish families. Henriette succeeded in convincing her brother that he should try to marry Lea.

The Hohenzollerns' policies concerning Jews depended, as everywhere else, on their own interests. The Brandenburg March, or region, had been forbidden to Jews since 1573—that is, ever since the court Jew Lippold, treasury director for Elector Prince Joachim II (1505–1571), had been accused of poisoning the prince and seducing his mistress, Anna Sydow. Lippold was tortured, racked, and torn into pieces, and all Jews were expelled from Brandenburg. Lippold's good name was restored shortly thereafter, but the Jews did not regain the rights they had previously enjoyed.[9] A century later, in 1670, the need to repopulate a country decimated by the Thirty Years' War (in which Brandenburg had lost one-third of its inhabitants) prompted the Grand Elector Friedrich Wilhelm (1620–1688) to bring fifty Jewish families from Vienna, where the Jesuit views of the Spanish wife of Emperor Leopold I had led to their expulsion.[10] The Grand Elector did not invite just any families, but only those possessing a fortune of at least 10,000 thalers—money he needed to revive trade and to finance his wars.[11] These families were given a *Schutzbrief*, or letter of protection granting them the right to reside and to do trade, mostly in the textile and clothing industries. After 1700, a collective tax was levied on the community, which its leaders (eight *parnassim*) were charged with collecting. There were, of course, enormous social differences between the Viennese Jews or those who had managed to obtain a *Schutzbrief*, and all the others. The former began frequenting the Christian aristocracy, leaving behind their Jewish customs and assimilating into the society around them. Even so, the Jewish community remained extremely close-knit; contacts with fellow Jews from other towns proved commercially and financially rewarding, bringing a certain advantage to the fact of being Jewish.

The edict of 1731[12] regulated and greatly reduced freedom of commerce: the intention was to protect the country's newly established factories by reserving for them the right to work on raw materials. Jews found themselves limited to a few areas of trading: jewels, a certain type of cloth (cattun), one or two kinds of hide (sheepskin, calf leather), coffee, and tea. The poorer among them dealt in shoddy goods, used clothing, horses, and money changing.

This regulation was certainly intended to protect the traditional corporations, but also to push rich Jews to invest in factories and banking. Poor Jews could only leave and try their luck elsewhere. In 1737, the number of Jewish families "tolerated" in Berlin was set at 120. Although all newly arrived families had to be able to declare a fortune of 10,000 thalers, a father could include two of his sons in his letter of protection on condition that the first son possessed the sum of 1000 thalers and the second, 2000 thalers. Daughters were not taken into account.

In 1750 the "enlightened" ruler Friedrich II—who on ascending to the throne in 1740 had decreed that every subject in his states must *nach seiner Fasson selich werden*, find his salvation in his own way—promulgated an edict forbidding Jews from any craft that might endanger the profits of the burghers. "A law worthy of cannibals," wrote Mirabeau in his *De la monarchie prussienne sous Frédéric le Grand* (Prussian Monarchy under Frederick the Great, 1787).[13] A distinction was introduced between *ordentliche Schutzjuden*, ordinary protected Jews, whose privilege extended to their children, and *ausserordentliche Schutzjuden*, or extraordinary Jews, permitted to remain in the country during their lifetime but whose children had no alternative but to leave unless they managed to obtain the protection of a *Schutzjude*—as did Moses Mendelssohn when taken under the wing of the *Schutzjude* Bernhard.

Clearly, Friedrich II was using the Jews to fill his own coffers. He had the minimum fortune raised to 15,000 and then 20,000 thalers, and finally sold off the second son's privilege for the round figure of 70,000 thalers.

On the other hand, Friedrich needed the *Hofjuden* or court Jews far too much not to exempt them from the general rule. Minting money—a privilege granted the bankers Gumpertz, Itzig, Isaac, and Ephraim—and financing various factories constituted services to the Prussian royalty too precious not to be rewarded, and the rewards usually consisted of social benefits. In 1761 Ephraim, Itzig, and Abraham Markuse received a general privilege for themselves and their children, one that granted them the same rights as Christian merchants. And in 1791 Daniel Itzig became the first Prussian Jew to receive a patent of naturalization, making him, his entire family, and his descendants the equal of the burghers in His Majesty's States.[14]

These *Hofjuden* were actually the only partners Friedrich II could find who understood and supported his financial plans. After 1753, the sovereign first sought the help of Berlin merchants, who refused him either from prudence or lack of imagination. Perhaps the bourgeoisie of a small town like Berlin, which had only expanded recently, simply did not possess the awareness or lofty vision of a Hanseatic city such as Hamburg, or of a city with a strong commercial tradition such as Leipzig. Friedrich II then appealed to foreigners, but neither the Italian Calzabigi nor the Dutchman Clement were bankers.[15] So Friedrich finally turned to the Jewish bankers of Berlin. The city's bourgeoisie, which could afford to be timorous, had neither their contacts nor their spirit of enterprise.

Daniel Itzig and Moses Mendelssohn: they represented two completely different ways of obtaining the keys of the city. From his marriage to Miriam Wulff, Daniel Itzig had five sons and eleven daughters, a considerable kinship for Lea Mendelssohn. His children were given an education which proved that money was no object to Daniel. One of his daughters, Franziska or Fanny (1758–1818), married the banker Nathan Arnstein. They went to live in Vienna, where Fanny brilliantly continued the tradition of Berlin salons. Another daughter, Sara (1761–1854), also married a banker, Samuel Levy; she had a salon in Berlin and was a harpsichordist of repute, taking part in concerts at the Singakademie. Bella, or Babette (1749–1824), married Levin Jacob Salomon and won a place in the history of music for leaving a copy of J. S. Bach's *Saint Matthew Passion* at the bedside of her grandson, Felix Mendelssohn, on Christmas night in 1823. The Itzigs were great admirers of Bach and his sons, sponsoring their works and helping the sons in times of need.

When Moses Mendelssohn died, his children's situation was not particularly secure. The three boys looked for jobs. As we know, Abraham settled in Paris in 1797 and went to work at Fould's Bank on the rue Bergère; he frequently saw his sister Henriette, who lived and taught on the nearby rue Richer. Abraham became a Parisian and Francophile, swearing never to return to Berlin, that dusty provincial town. Henriette, however, displayed little enthusiasm for her brother's professional situation, which she deemed too dependent on the whims of his boss. She thought his future in Paris might rapidly be jeopardized, if only for political reasons. Thus she arranged for him to meet her friend Lea Salomon, a perfect young woman in every respect; not only was Lea intelligent, she was *highly* intelligent and extremely well brought up. She spoke and wrote French, English, Italian; musical, like everyone in her family, she played the piano and sang; her wit and social talents were manifested in her apposite but never-wounding repartee. Though not a classic beauty, Lea had black, expressive eyes, a sylphlike waist, and a sweetly modest air. She read Homer in Greek, but was far too modest to praise herself for that. She sketched admirably, showed an aptitude for economical housekeeping—and to top it all, she was rich![16] Ever the loving sister, Henriette had to sing her brother's praises, which was not too difficult. Abraham met Lea in Berlin and was accepted by the young woman and even by her mother—who was nonetheless not thrilled at the idea of her daughter marrying a simple clerk. Much later, Lea would write to her future son-in-law in these words:

Above all, do not accuse me of selfishness or greed, my dear, sweet, insolent young man! Otherwise I shall have to remind you that I married my husband before he had a penny. But at least he had an income, albeit a very modest one, from Fould's Bank in Paris and I knew he could earn a lot of interest with the fortune I was bringing him. Admittedly, it did not suit my mother's ambition to see me marry a clerk, and that is why Mendelssohn had to enter into partnership with his brother: their prosperity, thank God, dates from that time.

In Lea Salomon's family one married the banker, not his clerk. With the dowry she had, Lea could have even envisioned marrying into the Prussian aristocracy, like many of her female cousins. She showed that this was not what she had in mind. In any case, Abraham was now in a position to launch himself in business with capital in his name, even if it was his wife's money, and he and his brother Joseph became partners.

Abraham's elder brother, Joseph Mendelssohn (1770–1848), was certainly the financial leader of the family.[17] Moses had had the time to educate him personally, since Joseph was sixteen when his father died. He was not really able to choose his profession: he would doubtless have preferred a career in science, but that option was forbidden to Jews. In the years following his father's death he worked as an accountant in the Itzig Bank, until its bankruptcy in 1796. In addition, Joseph had founded his own bank the previous year, on the Spandauer Strasse in Berlin. At that time, this was just a small business he directed with Moses Friedländer, son of David Friedländer, Berlin's first Jewish city councilor.[18] This partnership was broken off in 1803, when Joseph took his brother Abraham as partner. Abraham gave up life in Paris to marry Lea, with all the advantages the match offered. The following year, the two brothers founded another bank in Hamburg—Brothers Mendelssohn and Company—and went to live there; they did not, however, close down the Berlin office,[19] which remained in the family until liquidated by the Nazis in 1938.

The mighty Itzig Bank goes bankrupt, and the brothers Mendelssohn open up their own: two signs of these turbulent and changing times. Indeed, several private banks began to flourish in Germany in the late eighteenth century, while the older court banks slipped into the background. From 1790 until the end of the Napoleonic era there was—for obvious social, political, and economic reasons—a change in the commercial system, necessitating a new style of bank.[20]

In Cologne, Düsseldorf, Krefeld, Elberfeld, Berlin, Hamburg, and elsewhere, Jewish and Christian merchants abandoned commerce, turning from the transfer of wealth or loans against security to specialize in banking instead. From the beginning of the French Revolutionary Wars until the Wars of Liberation (1813–1815), the French occupation did not simply signify freedom or oppression, but also the need for capital and liquid assets. During these years, the Oppenheim and Warburg banks sprang to life in Cologne and Hamburg respectively, even as the Mendelssohn Bank was flourishing.[21]

Thus did Abraham Mendelssohn, a young banker of twenty-eight, marry Lea Salomon on 28 December 1804 and settle in the free city of Hamburg, the largest port in Germany and second largest port in Europe. The marriage promised to be very happy, with the young couple setting up house in some disorder, as is not infrequent. When her dear "sister" Henriette asked for a description of their home, Lea wrote back:

It's frantically untidy, *à dire le vrai* [to tell the truth], like the most eccentric student's dwelling . . . the comforts of Berlin are out of the question here, and when I contemplate my *remue-ménage* [disorderly household] I can scarcely believe I'm really married. This change of state is normally accompanied by the magical appearance of hordes of pots and pans, of chandeliers, of mirrors and mahoganies: a bewitching vision I have thus far had to do without, in my *chez-moi* [home]. . . . Order will only come of chaos when we move to the country, where we've been offered a pretty house with a balcony, on the river Elbe, very close to Neumühlen.[22]

Sebastian Hensel tells us that it was in this house, known as Marten's Mill, that Lea gave birth to her first three children: Fanny Caecilia, born on 14 November 1805; Felix, born 3 February 1809; and Rebecka, born 11 April 1811. Lea's first thought when Fanny was born was to look at the baby's hands, and she declared delightedly that the infant had fingers suitable for playing Bach fugues, *Bach'sche Fugenfinger*.[23]

Abraham's business was going extremely well. The blockade imposed by Napoleon in 1806 forbade importation of the manufactured goods and colonial commodities that Europe needed—sugar, coffee, cocoa, goods for dyeing, cotton—and that England sold to the continental countries. For its part England needed the oils, wines, and wools of southern Europe, and also imported corn and wood through the Baltic ports. Hamburg thus became the center of a vast network of smuggling that greatly benefited the Mendelssohn brothers—and the French authorities as well who were "compensated" at the border. But in January 1812 a new French governor arrived; realizing they had been found out, the Mendelssohns, disguised, fled by night to Berlin,[24] where Lea was able to bring to bear her connections with the French ambassador.[25] It is an amusing picture: these two rich bankers and their respectable wives, fleeing with their children like thieves. Joseph's two sons, Benjamin and Alexander, were seventeen and fifteen respectively, and probably adapted to the situation quite well. But the three smaller children probably posed a few problems during the escapade: Fanny was six at the time; Felix, almost three; and Rebecka, only a few months old. History does not inform us how they were disguised, and it is rather surprising we do not know more about this epic adventure. Naturally, fear of censorship prevented them from boasting about it in their letters; yet after 1815 pens and tongues could have been loosened. Perhaps the Mendelssohns were afraid of appearing irresponsible, or of awakening curiosity about how they really became rich!

CHAPTER THREE

Berlin: Back to Their Origins

"I don't know whose idea it was to stick a town in all this sand, but they say it's a town with 159,000 inhabitants."[1] Written in 1806, this observation by Stendhal still reflects the view of every traveler passing through Berlin: the soil of the Brandenburg March is astonishingly infertile. Berlin is purely a product of political will. To turn their city into a European capital, the Hohenzollerns did everything they could during the seventeenth and eighteenth centuries to attract a qualified work force from France or Bohemia—mostly Protestants driven from those regions by religious persecution. After the Thirty Years' War, the suburbs, which had been burned down to protect the city, were rebuilt along more rational lines. The plans of Unter den Linden were drawn up in 1647 by the architect Memhardt, who died around 1678. In 1685, fourteen thousand Huguenots were absorbed into the Brandenburg March, six thousand of them in Berlin alone. They moved into the most recently constructed districts such as Friedrichswerder, Dorotheenstadt, or Friedrichstadt. The Huguenots continued to flock there in vast numbers, which is why a Französische Strasse, or French Street, still exists in Berlin.

The town continued to develop in the best interests of its rulers, who controlled the population and rents, and organized lodging, transportation, and supplies. Berlin grew steadily in size, extended by several suburbs: Spandauer Vorstadt, Königstadt, Stralauer Vorstadt, Cöpenicker Vorstadt, and Sebastianskirche (which became part of

Luisenstadt after 1801). At the same time, churches were built throughout the city.[2] When the emperor made Friedrich III, Elector of Brandenburg, into a "Prussian King" known as Friedrich I, the vast territories of which Brandenburg and its capital Berlin were only a part adopted the generic name of Prussia.[3] The royal family erected monuments appropriate to this new dignity: the Academy of Fine Arts (1696), the Academy of Science (1700), and the Arsenal (1696); they also transformed the royal library and castle. In 1695 the architect Nering began another castle in Lietzow, one to which Queen Sophie Charlotte lent her name; later she gave her name to the whole district: Charlottenburg. Under King Friedrich Wilhelm I, known as the Sergeant King, Berlin continued its planned development and three public squares were constructed at the ends of the three most important streets of new Berlin: the Square, at the end of Unter den Linden; the Octagon, at the end of Leipziger Strasse, and finally the Roundel, to the south of Friedrichstrasse.[4]

Friedrich II did not transform his town radically, but when he died in 1786 it had grown from ninety thousand inhabitants in 1740 to 150,000, including the garrison. The cultivated image of this monarch was confirmed by the construction of a prestigious opera house opened in 1742, and by a royal library situated opposite (1775–1780). The Gendarmenmarkt—the most prestigious square in the new Berlin—was conceived as an architectural ensemble with the French Theater occupying a place of honor between the French and German cathedrals. Friedrich Wilhelm II, who was Friedrich II's nephew and successor, found time in his eleven-year reign to have the famous Brandenburg Gate erected (1788–1791). In 1789 street names began to be indicated by signs, houses by numbers, and the more important thoroughfares were illuminated at night.[5]

His son, Friedrich Wilhelm III, who became king in 1797, had the misfortune to endure a Napoleonic invasion. After the battles of Jena and of Auerstedt (14 October 1806), Napoleon and his troops entered Berlin on 27 October and occupied it until December 1808. The court fled to Königsberg, remaining there until 1809. The treaty of Tilsit, ratified on 8 July 1807, dismantled Prussia and turned it into a vassal state of France. Years of appalling wretchedness ensued: the occupying forces helped themselves to whatever they wanted while hunger and disease spread rapidly. The Francophilia hitherto shared by well-educated persons decreased enormously, and enthusiasm for the French Revolution was transformed in many minds into a general rejection of anything France had to offer, including civil rights and freedom of thought. The German Holy Roman Empire, which was in the last stages of degeneracy, was certainly not worth weeping over. But in destroying it with his reforms Napoleon had thrown out the baby with the bath water, thus creating a bitterness and hostility to France that formed the basis of pan-Germanism.

Everything that had once contributed to the enlightened atmosphere of Berlin during the *Aufklärung* had now vanished into thin air. Prince Louis-Ferdinand—the poetic musician who admired Beethoven and the Jewish salons, and who was the model for the Prince of Homburg—died in 1806 at the battle of Saalfeld. With him Germany lost the symbol of social classes blending harmoniously in the name of ideas and of art. The nation's hopes took shape again around the royal couple of Friedrich Wilhelm III and Luise—that ardently patriotic queen who in 1810 died of grief at her country's defeat. Because of all these factors, the nation's attempt to recreate its identity was accompanied by a conservatism that prevented reforms already begun from being fully carried out. So complete was the disaster that it soon fostered a vigorous reaction: the statesmen Stein and Hardenberg[6] actually managed to impart an air of modernity to Prussian social structures. Serfdom was abolished, as well as feudal obligations and forced labor. Landed aristocrats nonetheless retained their estates and the right to administer justice; Prussian squires once again distanced themselves from the social advances of the *Aufklärung.* Bourgeois and peasants, however, now had the right to own land, and guilds were abolished. Generals Scharnhorst and Gneisenau succeeded in rebuilding the army. The plan to create a parliament was not fulfilled, but at least towns were able to elect their own municipal councilors.

Berlin was divided into 102 districts,[7] with a supreme magistrate chosen by the district representatives. The last of these important reforms occurred in 1810 when Wilhelm von Humboldt founded Friedrich Wilhelm University, selecting Prince Heinrich's palace as its home, on Opera Square. This university became the cultural center for all Germany—thanks to the teachings of the historian Niebuhr, the legal scholar Savigny, and the philosopher Fichte, whose *Discourse to the German Nation* (1807–1808) launched the foundations of pan-Germanism.

≈ 38 ≈

The Mendelssohns returned to Berlin in this atmosphere of cultural revolution—but it was difficult to know whether this atmosphere was progressive, reactionary, or both. As Jews, what rights would they have to live in Berlin? Being a granddaughter of Daniel Itzig, Lea had the "privilege," but what rights would her children have? What, indeed, had happened to the "privilege" after Napoleon's reforms? And finally, what had happened to the Jews and their supposed assimilation?

Bent on modernizing Prussia, Chancellor Hardenberg issued a decree on 11 March 1812 emancipating Prussian Jews: "Jews and their families presently residing in our States and in possession of general privileges, patents of naturalization, letters of protection, and concessions are considered inhabitants and citizens of Prussia."[8]

The edict contained no restrictions, or rather, did not limit access to administrative functions or military service. Since guilds had been abolished, all crafts were now theoretically open to Jews, as they were to everybody else.

The year of the edict was also the year in which Paul Mendelssohn, fourth and last of Lea's children, was born.

There is an essential difference between a law voted in the name of a nation, as was the emancipation of the Jews in France in 1791, and an edict emanating from personal power. The emancipation of Jews in Prussia was consequently associated with French oppression and despotic power, since Prussia was at that time a vassal state of France. That Prussian liberation movements sometimes expressed themselves in radically anti-Jewish ways is reprehensible but perhaps explainable in this context. Founded in 1811, the Christlich-deutsche Tischgesellschaft (German-Christian Assembly), whose ranks included many intellectuals—Heinrich von Kleist, Clemens Brentano, Friedrich Karl von Savigny, and Johann Gottlieb Fichte, among others—nonetheless denied membership to Frenchmen, philistines (that is, those they considered materialists), Jews, and women. To this society's credit, it did dissolve itself in 1813, believing that its goals had been attained.

When racist opinions are expressed by minds of such high caliber, they contain a stupefying, pathological element that can only be explained in terms of the aggression their authors felt had been perpetrated on them. Resolutely noble, Prussian, and Romantic, the German-Christian Assembly completely rejected the eighteenth century.

First of all it rejected the French, on political grounds; then it rejected philistines, the "classical" rationalists who, as Brentano put it, "scorned popular holidays, old legends, and everything growing grey in out-of-the-way places, sheltered from contemporary insolence";[9] next it rejected Jews, "tools of the Enlightenment," who owed their freedom to the French.[10] Last of all, it rejected women, whom the *Aufklärung* had in some measure liberated and who were thus excluded from the German-Christian Assembly. Hannah Arendt has pointed out that it even held its meetings at lunchtime, thus differing from the tea time of Jewish salons. Women and Jews were rejected together. Jews were also criticized for their cosmopolitanism, which was considered a factor in the Prussian defeat.

Even so, there were some remarkable aspects to the assembly's functioning. The member charged with addressing the topic of a meeting had to present it first in a serious manner, then in an ironic one. This self-criticism was characteristic of their Romanticism, and distanced them from any temptation to think like philistines—materialistically, or in a one-sided fashion. According to them, rational thought offered only one version of things—the materialist one. Romantic irony, however, allowed them to grasp the world in all its profundity and diversity. Women, Jews, and Frenchmen symbolized the cult of Cartesian reason, of the material world, and the triumphal growth of cities. It should not be forgotten that these Prussian squires were defending the interests of their class, that of the great landed gentry.

The linguistic aberrations of the German-Christian Assembly are nonetheless horrifying. The society's secretary, the fine poet Clemens Brentano, once wrote that Jews were like "flies, the last traces of the Egyptian plague." And in 1793 Fichte opined that Jews needed "to have their heads cut off and other ones substituted, which would not contain a single Jewish idea. To protect ourselves from them, I see no alternative but to conquer their promised land and send them all back there."[11]

These anti-Jewish opinions found an immediate echo in the speech of certain Jews. Rahel Varnhagen, for example, wrote in these terms to her brother: "The Jew, that's what needs to be stamped out in us: this is a sacred truth, even if it costs us our lives."[12]

A small Jewish minority attempted to bring about change within the community. In 1799 David Friedländer[13] wrote an anonymous book in which he proposed teaching German rather than Hebrew in Jewish schools and purging prayer books of any wish to return to Palestine.

At the other end of the scale, afraid of losing Judaic identity, Eduard Gans (a friend of the Mendelssohn Bartholdys), Moses Moser, and Leopold Zunz founded the Verein für Kultur und Wissenschaft der Juden (Association for Jewish Culture and Knowledge). The goal of this association was to rethink Judaism so that it could become a way of life in the modern world without losing its roots. The association disappeared in 1824.[14]

The greater part of the Jewish community remained attached to traditional religious and professional forms, and did not concern itself with other problems. The Mendelssohns no longer had anything to do with this community. Having inherited the ideas of the French Revolution, Abraham may have thought, like Johann Jacoby (1805–1841), that Jewish emancipation could only come about in a state based on law. He may even have considered, as did Gabriel Riesser (1806–1865), that German democracy, Jewish emancipation, and German unity were all part of the same ideal.

Of Moses Mendelssohn's six children two remained Jewish, two converted to Protestantism, and two to Catholicism. Refusing to accept that there was only one valid religion and only one truth, Joseph Mendelssohn and his wife Henriette[15] clung to Judaism. They did so out of conviction, fidelity, and independence of mind.[16] The same held true for Recha, who had probably nothing to gain by converting. Henriette and Dorothea—both possessed of eminently Romantic souls—chose Catholicism, whereas Abraham and Nathan, who had connections with the Prussian state, opted for the Evangelical faith. This, too, was partly dictated by conviction but also by practical considerations and a desire to be assimilated.

Converted or not, in 1813 the Jews could still believe in the possibility of real assimilation. An opportunity to prove their patriotism was provided by the Prussian Wars of Liberation. All Prussian subjects who were old enough to fight enlisted in the new Prussian army. The Mendelssohns were no exception: Moses's youngest son, Nathan (1782–1852), and Joseph's oldest boy, Benjamin (1794–1874), took part in the fighting.

Dorothea delved into her maternal inheritance (Fromet Gugenheim had died in 1812) to equip her son Philipp Veit,[17] and her brothers, who did not usually allow her to touch her slender capital, made no objection in this case. Fanny's future husband, Wilhelm Hensel, also risked his life for his country. Abraham Mendelssohn financed two battalions, which earned him an appointment to the Berlin city council. Christians and Jews were of a single mind: Germany. To have fought for one's country distinguished individuals or families for several decades thereafter.

The Mendelssohn Bank also made handsome profits from the war, and Hardenberg's chancellery taxed it accordingly. In 1812 the Mendelssohns, who figured among the twenty most important houses in Berlin, paid an initial forced loan of 15,000 thalers; several months later, they paid another 25,000 thalers. In 1813 they imported forty thousand muskets from Austria in the space of nine or ten months, at a cost of 8 thalers per musket. This provided them with ample means for showing their generosity and patriotism. By 1815 the Mendelssohn Bank had become one of the six or seven largest in Berlin; it moved from the Poststrasse to the Jägerstrasse, next to the imposing Gendarmenmarkt, in the center of prestigious Friedrichstadt. Henceforth the Mendelssohn Bank would keep the same address: 51 Jägerstrasse, where it stayed until "Aryanized" in 1938.[18]

THE CONVERSION

Where did Abraham Mendelssohn's family live during their first few years in Berlin? Two addresses have come down to us, despite some uncertainty concerning dates. The Mendelssohns lived for some time at 48 Markgrafenstrasse (now 40 Wilhelm-Külz-Strasse), near the Gendarmenmarkt, in the house of Johann Jakob Staegemann, a priest who was also their friend. They left this home in 1820 at the latest; Staegemann died on 20 March of that year. Their house of refuge—perhaps as soon as they arrived in Berlin and in any case after 1820—was the house of Lea's mother, 7 Neue Promenade in the Spandauer Vorstadt, near the fortifications and opposite the Garnison Kirche. A letter written by Henriette Mendelssohn to her niece Fanny on 15 October 1820 attests to the move: "It will be rather tiring for your father to have to walk to Jägerstrasse twice every day, but perhaps that will be good for his health." Abraham had therefore chosen to live at some distance from his place of work—a thirty-minute walk, for bridges were few and far between.[19] The house was relatively small. According to Manfred Kliem, grandmother Salomon must have lived on the ground floor, and since there were renters on the second floor, the only space remaining for the Mendelssohn family would be the *Beletage*, or "noble" floor. Since the house was about thirty meters long, the Mendelssohns' apartment would probably only have comprised four rooms—not much for a family of four children, with servants appropriate to their station. Manfred Kliem thinks that the social climate of this street better suited converted or assimilated Jews such as the Mendelssohns. In any case, the Neue Promenade was scarcely representative of contemporary society in Berlin: hardly any officers or functionaries lived there. On the other hand, almost every house contained at least one Jew; out of fifteen families of merchants, eight were Christian and seven Jewish. At a time of growing antisemitism in Berlin, this district must have constituted a zone of mutual tolerance where neighbors knew and accepted one another, where children played together in the street, and the different social classes were in constant contact.

The problem of whether to convert tormented the generation of Abraham and Lea Mendelssohn. Considerable time had elapsed since they had left the ghetto and become culturally assimilated with the Christians, through language, customs, music, and literature. They felt no solidarity at all with the Jewish community that was still attached to its language and traditions; if anything they were rather ashamed of it, like Rahel. This can be seen from a letter Lea wrote to her friend G. Merkel, dated 26 August 1799:

Itzig has finished his studies in Wittenberg and has been here for several weeks. What will you say when I tell you he has converted to Christianity? Being in the town where Luther was born and in the holy place where he did his teaching had an effect on him, and he could not resist the temptation of being baptized beneath the image of this great man, thereby putting himself under his protection. In taking this step he has saved his soul while earning a more temporal benefit: he will soon obtain a post within his field of study. Unfortunately this will probably be in Poland, and I rather doubt that his onerous responsibilities there will leave him enough perseverance and patience to stay faithful to his choice. I cannot tell you how much I hope he will do so, for the majority of apostates have until now behaved so despicably or at the very least, so thoughtlessly, that they have brought a kind of discredit to conversion that brands even the best of them. If someone of spotless character were to convert, faithful to his intentions and diplomatic in behavior (for it is unfortunately behavior that influences most opinions)—someone who would offer an example worthy of respect—then he would dispel much of this all-too-justified assumption. It would be a blessing if we could dispense with all this hypocrisy. But given the desire for a more elevated occupation than that of merchant, and the prospect of those many affectionate friendships which induce young people to befriend other members of a religious community, there is really no other option.[20]

In this letter, Lea recorded the first conversion to occur in her family. The young man in question was her first cousin Isaak Elias (1780–1849), son of Elias Daniel Itzig (1772–1818) and Marianne Leffmann. Isaak Elias converted in 1799, immediately after the death of his grandfather, Daniel Itzig, adopting the more Christian first names of Julius Eduard.[21] He became director of judicial police and was a friend of the poets Zacharia Werner, E. T. A. Hoffmann, and Adalbert Chamisso. Chamisso borrowed several of his personal traits for the character of Peter Schlemihl. Itzig was also very close to the ideas and men of the German-Christian Assembly, and became a proselyte for his new religion. In 1818 he added an *H* to his last name—probably, remarked Heinrich Heine ironically, because Hitzig sounded "Heiliger" (holier). Julius Eduard's sisters also converted, early in the nineteenth century. One of them, Henriette (1775–1831), married Nathan Mendelssohn, Abraham's youngest brother, which implies that matrimonial possibilities were rather limited among assimilated Jews of this milieu.

Julius Eduard went to enormous lengths to convince those around him that his conversion was sincere, but apparently failed to convince his cousin Lea. She did not marry a converted Jew—that would have been too easy. How, in her own conscience, could she have justified taking such a step? She married a man who shared her sentiments. Abraham and Lea could not convert as long as "public opinion" might hold that they had done so from self-interest. Their children, however, were another matter. Which religion should they choose for them?

At this point a new character enters the story: Lea's brother Jacob Salomon, who was baptized in 1805 and took the name of one of his properties, Bartholdy, near the river Spree. Like Lea, Jacob Bartholdy (1774–1825) was a child of Levin Jacob Salomon and Bella, daughter of banker Daniel Itzig. In 1779 the banker had bought the farm of Bartholdy, situated close to Berlin in what was subsequently known as Luisenstadt. Jacob studied in Halle and Berlin, spent several years in Paris, and traveled in Italy and Greece. He fought against Napoleon in the Austrian army in 1809, and in 1813 entered Hardenberg's chancellery. He accompanied Hardenberg to Paris, London, and the Congress of Vienna. In 1815 he was appointed consul general in Rome, and in 1818, Prussian attaché for commerce at the court of Tuscany. A great patron of the arts, he supported both painters and scholars. Among other Bartholdy commissions was a room of his Roman villa, la Casa Bartholdy, decorated with frescoes by painters Peter Cornelius, Wilhelm Schadow, Friedrich Overbeck, and Philipp Veit[22] (Abraham's nephew). In 1822 he organized an exhibition at the Casa Bartholdy[23] for the visit of the Prussian king, Friedrich Wilhelm III.

Like Abraham, Jacob had spent part of his youth in Paris. Among the liberal ideas he returned with was the belief that one should not connect religion with a form, but rather with a morality. His opinions concerning his nephews' and nieces' education and religion were anything but equivocal, as can be seen in this letter to Abraham:

You say you owe it to your father's memory—do you therefore think you've done something wrong, in giving your children the religion you consider best for them? In fact this is a way for you and all the rest of us to pay tribute to your father's steps toward true enlightenment. He would have acted as you are doing in regard to your children—perhaps as I have acted in regard to myself. One can remain faithful to a religion that is persecuted and oppressed; one can yoke one's children to it, as to a lifelong martyrdom—as long as one considers it the sole path to salvation. But as soon as one no longer believes that, then such conduct becomes barbarous. I would advise you to take the name of Mendelssohn Bartholdy, to distinguish yourself from the other Mendelssohns. This would be especially agreeable to me, because it would be a means of remembering me through the children, and that would cause me heartfelt joy. You would thus attain your goal without doing anything unusual—for it is customary in France, as everywhere else, to add one's wife's family name to one's own.[24]

The cosmopolitan Bartholdy had no qualms in attributing to Moses Mendelssohn ideas that Moses had spent his life rebutting. Jacob was nonetheless aware that his own conversion had put him in the bad graces of part of his family; his mother even went so far as to disown him, and only forgave him thanks to the intervention of her favorite granddaughter, Fanny Mendelssohn. But in 1812 Bella, too, adopted the name of Bartholdy; ever since the decree of emancipation, Jews had been required to take a patronymic family name. Instead of calling themselves—for example—Moses, son of Mendel, they now had to be known as Moses Mendelssohn. So Bella then decided officially to take her son's name, Bartholdy—but without converting.

Abraham and Lea did not have their children baptized at birth. Were they perhaps not totally convinced? Who could tell how society might change? Perhaps, conquered by the patriotism of the Jews during the War of Liberation, anti-Jewish prejudices would diminish, and all the professions would become accessible without restriction? Perhaps the word *Jude* would cease to be an insult?

Reality, alas, intervened in the form of this *votum*, or vow, issued by the Prussian Ministry of Finance in 1816:

It would be desirable not to have any Jews at all in the country. We must tolerate those we already have, but at the same time we must try constantly to render them as inoffensive as possible. The conversion of Jews to the Christian religion must be facilitated, and all civil rights must be linked to their conversion. But as long as a Jew remains Jewish, he cannot obtain a position in the State.[25]

The question had answered itself. In 1816 the Mendelssohns were living at Pastor Staegemann's house, and the pastor baptized the four children in utmost secrecy on 21 March in the Jerusalemkirche where he officiated. Needless to say, nobody dared tell their grandmother, who must certainly have found out somehow or other, as her will later indicates. As for Abraham and Lea, they took advantage of a trip to Frankfurt in October 1822 to convert, far from prying eyes. They added Bartholdy to their name, as Lea's brother Jacob wished, but without hyphenation: Abraham wanted the extremely Jewish "Mendelssohn" to disappear entirely with the next generation, and hoped the family would become entirely Christianized, keeping no visible traces of their origins. His children did not carry out this wish. Abraham had given up his activities at the Mendelssohn Bank the preceding year; perhaps he had already foreseen this retirement when he took refuge in the Neue Promenade. His relationship with his brother Joseph had become difficult: either Abraham's retirement posed problems, or else his conversion and altered name had put a barrier between them. A third, more likely, possibility is that Abraham had a difficult disposition, for he was terribly punctilious and frequently awkward in his business dealings. Whatever the case, the ostensible purpose of his retirement was to educate his children.

The success of the conversion did indeed depend on them, especially the two eldest, Fanny and Felix. When Fanny was confirmed in 1819, Abraham, who was in Paris at the time, sent her the following letter:

My dear daughter, you have taken an important step in life, and while as a father I congratulate you with all my heart, today and for your whole future life, I feel obliged to speak seriously to you about certain matters we have never discussed before.

Does God exist? What might God be? Is part of our life eternal, and does it continue to exist after the other part has died? If so, where? And how? I don't know the answer to all this, and that is why I have never taught you anything on the subject. I know only that there is within me, within you, and within all human beings an eternal attachment to what is good, true, and just, along with a conscience that warns us and brings us back to the right path when we stray from it. I know, believe in, and live in this faith; it is my religion. I could not teach it to you and nobody can learn it, for each of us carries it inside himself, unless he knowingly and intentionally abjures it. That you will not abjure it is guaranteed me by the example of your mother, whose entire life has been devoted to duty, love, and good deeds—the personification of this religion. You grew up in it under her protection, constantly contemplating and unconsciously imitating those qualities that give a person value. Your mother was, is, and shall remain for a long time—my heart tells me so—your providential guardian, just as she is to your brothers and sister and to us all; the star that guides us on life's path. When you contemplate her, when you measure the immense kindness she has shown you, in a constant spirit of sacrifice and devotion, then your heart will soar with gratitude, respect, and love, and your eyes will fill with tears: thus will you feel God, and be pious.

That is all I can tell you about religion, all I know of it, but it will remain true as long as a human being exists, just as it has been true since the first man was created.

The form in which your tutor in religion presented it to you is historical and, like all human doctrines, subject to transformation. A few thousand years ago the Jewish form was dominant, then the pagan one; today, the Christian form predominates. Your mother and I were born into Judaism, through our parents; we were raised in it and, without having to change that form, have managed to follow God inside ourselves and in our consciences. We raised you and your brothers and sister to be Christians because that is the form of belief of most civilized people and because Christianity contains nothing that can turn us from the good; on the contrary, it can show you the path of love, obedience, acceptance, and resignation, if only through the example of its founder, recognized by so few and followed by still fewer.

In professing your faith you have accomplished what society required of you: you can say that you are Christian. Now you must be what your human duty requires you to be: truthful, faithful, good. Toward your mother and— I have the right to demand this too—your father, be faithful and devoted unto death. Be unceasingly attentive to the voice of your conscience, which may be dulled but never silenced, and thus will you attain the highest happiness that may be given you on earth: harmony and peace with yourself.

Thereupon I press you to my heart with all my fatherly tenderness, and I hope always to find in you a daughter worthy of your mother. Farewell, and ponder my words.[26]

Fanny must have been overwhelmed by this letter. What an impression it must have left in her mind: God, religion, and faith are "within" the human being and a mother bears them like a child. Abraham establishes the mother as humanity's model and makes her the object of an almost divine cult—perhaps rather unusual in a Christian. Fanny owed it to herself to follow this model to the letter and to become the female version of the "spotless character," the one "faithful to his intentions" of whom her mother spoke in 1799. It was Felix's duty to be the masculine version, and the two would become irreproachable converts. The Mendelssohn parents did what they thought best.

The year in which this letter was written, 1819, saw a wave of pogroms sweep through Germany. In Berlin this *Judensturm*, or "storm on Jews," took the form of vandalism and insults directed at the Jews. Varnhagen von Ense relates how a member of the royal family, meeting young Felix at a castle, found no better way to greet him than "*Hep, hep, Judenjung!*" (Get the Jewish boy!)—the traditional incitement to a pogrom.[27] The Mendelssohn children all had a Semitic air about them. In a sane society they might possibly have managed to forget their origins, but as it was, they were reminded of them so often that they never disavowed them.

CHAPTER FOUR

Education

Born on 14 November 1805 in Hamburg, Fanny was thus the eldest of the Mendelssohn Bartholdy children. For four whole years she had her parents' love all to herself. Lea in particular paid great attention to her children's education. She started them playing the piano as soon as possible, five minutes at a time, gradually extending practice periods as soon as the child was willing. When Lea embarked on the musical education of her second child, Felix, Fanny held a solid lead which she maintained for some years. Two child prodigies, one after the other—Lea could certainly congratulate herself on the efficacy of her instruction. The last two children, Rebecka and Paul, though not endowed with such exceptional talents as those of their older siblings, did possess real musical ability; perhaps discouraged, however, they never attained the level of the other two. In any case Fanny felt responsible for the small group and played a large part in the musical development of her younger brother Felix.

In addition to the instruction given by their mother, Fanny and Felix took piano lessons. The first of these were given in Paris by Marie Bigot in 1816. Chancellor Hardenberg had charged the Mendelssohn bankers with recovering the war damages that France then owed Prussia. The Mendelssohns engaged only the best teachers for their children: Marie Bigot (1786–1820) was a famous pianist who had lived for many years in Vienna. Joseph Haydn reportedly told her that she played his music as if she had composed it herself, and

Beethoven was apparently so impressed with her reading of the "Appassionata" sonata that he later presented her with the manuscript.[1] After returning permanently to Paris, Madame Bigot devoted herself to teaching. She did so to support herself and her husband, whom the Napoleonic invasion had driven from his job as librarian to Count Rasumovsky in Vienna, since French subjects were no longer welcome there. The Mendelssohns were long astonished at the scant attention paid by this frail woman to her physical and emotional health.[2] Henriette Mendelssohn wrote from Viry on 15 October 1820, after the pianist's death: "She was an extremely cultivated woman who possessed rare abilities. Unfortunately, she also possessed too much willpower. Thus the arduous and exhausting kind of existence she obstinately continued to lead certainly shortened her life."[3] This cannot have struck little Fanny as a particularly encouraging example of a woman subsisting from her art. If Fanny ever was curious about Marie Bigot's financial independence or her career as a pianist or a teacher, she must have asked herself some serious questions: women who worked were apparently subject to illness and depression. Fanny and Felix, moreover, never had another female teacher.

Henriette's position in General Sébastiani's household might seem far more enviable, but she herself described it as a gilded cage. Henriette had servants and carriages at her disposal, yet spent most of her time confined to the company of a rather dull young woman—in many ways, a perfect stranger to her—and could only envy Lea's situation: all this must have been perfectly apparent to a child as intelligent as Fanny.

Abraham valued his family above all else. He detested being separated from them and considered nothing too good for them. Traveling with children was nonetheless far from simple: on the way back from Paris the youngest child, four-year-old Paul, was left behind at a relay station and recovered later on the highway. What a trauma for the entire family! Felix wrote to his aunt: "If it hadn't rained, we wouldn't still have our Paul."[4] We know from family correspondence that Lea did not like to leave her home, which is understandable, but because of this her daughters missed several opportunities to see the world and enrich themselves intellectually. The journey to Paris was thus a huge stroke of luck for Fanny and Rebecka.

On the way back to Berlin, the Mendelssohns passed through Frankfurt, thus giving the children an opportunity to meet their aunt

Dorothea Schlegel. Until the death of their mother Fromet in 1812, Dorothea's relations with her brothers and sisters had been rather strained: her siblings were exasperated by her scandalous life, her extremist opinions, and her incessant demands for money. The War of Liberation, however, had probably helped to smooth out their differences. An excellent musician, Dorothea had the pleasure of hearing her niece and nephew play works by her favorite composers, Bach and Handel, on the piano. Dorothea had remained a Berliner in her musical tastes. She spoke with admiration of their playing, which evinced "strength, speed, precision, and expressiveness" to an incredible degree; Felix played "with genius, Fanny with a virtuosity that defeated all understanding."[5] The children met Dorothea after she had come to the end of her peregrinations and returned full of wisdom and piety to the bosom of her "natural" family: the family was the only possible place for a woman. Both Dorothea and Henriette furnished living proof of that.

On their return to Berlin, Fanny and Felix took lessons with pianist Ludwig Berger (1777–1839). An excellent musician from Berlin who had studied with Clementi and Cramer, Berger gave numerous concerts throughout Europe (Saint Petersburg, Stockholm, London) before resettling in Berlin. Although a virtuoso like his masters, Berger had also been influenced by John Field, and his playing possessed a more sentimental touch that heralded the Chopinesque style of the Romantic piano. His own works went far beyond the framework imposed by the Clementi school: he composed some lieder (among them, *The Beautiful Maid of the Mill* on texts by Wilhelm Müller), a piano concerto, piano sonatas, and studies that must have influenced Fanny and Felix in their compositions for the piano. Berger had returned to Berlin in 1815 and lived there until his death in 1839. He gave up public performance in 1817 because of a neurological condition in his arm.[6]

The two children's pianistic education was based far more on the study of the great masters than on a purely technical approach to the instrument. Bach, Haydn, Mozart, Beethoven: nothing but solid values there. Clementi and Cramer formed part of the daily regimen. When Fanny complained about the dearth of exercises written for the fourth and fifth fingers, her father, who was in Paris at the time, wrote back to tell her that according to Marie Bigot she would find everything she needed in Cramer:

Bigot says it's not owing to a dearth of exercises, but to a lack of application if your two fingers—or anybody's fingers—won't follow the others. Every day you must spend part of your practice time watching your fingers and pressing down firmly with them, quite mechanically, without thinking of the music or the interpretation or anything else. There are plenty of pieces in Cramer written for these two weaker fingers; you simply have to play slowly and be sure you press down with them firmly. That is how, with a great deal of patience, she has obtained the best possible results: equal strength in all the fingers. I'm telling you this to encourage you.[7]

Ludwig Berger, friend of Clementi and Cramer, would certainly not have contradicted this advice. Full of good intentions, Felix wrote exercises for her. This shows how seriously Fanny's piano playing and musical studies were taken: she already played extremely well, but in the Mendelssohn household the acceptable level had to exceed mere virtuosity. The young girl showed an amazing musical memory, and at the age of thirteen she surprised her father by playing, by heart, all twenty-four preludes of the first book of Bach's *Well-Tempered Clavier*.[8] Henriette, who always remained a presence even when she lived in Paris, cried out in admiration, though not without expressing some reservations:

I was amazed and dumbfounded at Fanny's heroic achievement in learning 24 preludes by heart—and, dear Lea, by your own perseverance in making her study them—and only recovered use of my tongue to inform everybody of this huge success. Having extended to you both my undivided admiration, I must, however, admit that I find the undertaking worthy of blame: the effort required is too great, and could have become dangerous; the extraordinary talent of your children must be guided and not forced. But Papa Abraham is insatiable, and the very best is only just good enough for him. I can imagine him watching Fanny play, inwardly content and satisfied, but parsimonious in his praise. The children will nonetheless notice very quickly that they're his pride and joy, and will not take his stoic air too seriously.[9]

Henriette perhaps did not realize that a talent such as that of the Mendelssohn children itself influences the teacher, who has no need to force it—on the contrary. Poor Henriette could not imagine asking Fanny Sébastiani to muster up one quarter of the concentration required for such an effort. Despite her gifts as a teacher, Lea could not have obtained such prowess from Fanny had not the little girl herself possessed the necessary strength and will.

With her fingers that were "suitable for playing Bach fugues," Fanny received in early infancy a Lutheran baptism of musical culture. Through Lea and her family, Fanny and Felix Mendelssohn descended from the spiritual father figure of German music, Johann Sebastian Bach—perhaps a larger factor than that of being Jewish or Christian. Figuratively and literally, Fanny and Felix Mendelssohn held in their hands the thread of western musical tradition. Their great-aunt, harpsichordist Sara Levy, scorned the notion of conversion: what was the point of it? Only under protest would the Mendelssohn children call themselves Bartholdy.

At this point Fanny was the child prodigy, more so even than Felix. Her mother taught her the piano, her father listened to her playing, and both parents were all the more demanding since she was living up to their expectations. Surrounded by such love, Fanny had grown up with the illusion that she was accomplishing something—had been able to think it really mattered to her family if she developed her talent to its full potential. Beginning in 1816 or 1817, she maintained a highly serious correspondence with her aunt Henriette, who was still in Paris, and with her uncle Jacob, then in Rome.[10] These intelligent and cultivated adults sent Fanny letters that prove how highly they regarded her. Jacob Bartholdy owed her more than he might to a simple, nice little niece, for Fanny had persuaded his mother to forgive him. Even as a small child, Fanny could not bear squabbles; one day, when she had played the piano particularly well, Bella Salomon asked her what reward she would like. "Forgive Uncle Bartholdy," replied Fanny. She could not have been more than twelve at the time, and it is quite something to imagine this child reflecting on questions of religion and tolerance, ready to brave her grandmother's wrath. We do not know if Fanny had herself been baptized a Lutheran when she sought Jacob's pardon. If this episode with her grandmother took place after 1816, Fanny was in fact soliciting her own pardon while asking for her uncle's. Be that as it may, the little girl appears to have been extremely serious, and this was not to everybody's taste. On 2 March 1818 Fanny's cousin, Rebecka Meyer, wrote to her friend Rosa Herz (who was also a relation: Betty Meyer was the daughter of Recha, Abraham's elder sister, while Rosa Herz was the granddaughter of Abraham Gugenheim, father of Fromet who had married Moses Mendelssohn):

Abraham is here. He has wonderful children, especially the three youngest. I think Fanny is the only one you know: she is the least pretty, and a bit too precocious for now (*etwas stark altklug*), but if she develops within herself, she may become truly attractive, for she's very intelligent. Felix has the looks of an angel and is a veritable musical genius; Beckchen looks like Marianne Saaling and is adorable when she speaks; Paul, the youngest, is the handsomest, most mischievous, most enterprising fellow I can imagine.[11]

Evidently the charming, frivolous Betty Meyer and the serious, reflective Fanny Mendelssohn did not get on too well. Admittedly, the Mendelssohn character was not particularly easy. Abraham Mendelssohn could be extraordinarily grumpy. Henriette wrote to her niece on 30 December 1821,[12] apologizing for the undeserved reproaches she had addressed to her in a previous letter: "I don't remember what I said to you, but I know how the Mendelssohns can be when they're in a bad mood—or rather, I know how incapable they are of resisting that mood. Are you afflicted with this hereditary ill too? I do hope not!" In later life Fanny certainly possessed the attraction of intelligence, as Betty Meyer had hoped, but she was never either graceful or pretty. This did not prevent those close to her from loving her as she was—*schroff*, as Clara Schumann was to put it, which means direct and even abrupt. Yet although she took after her father, Fanny never let her various bad moods weigh on those around her. Though serious, she was also very active, full of verve, energy, and ideas, which constituted her *joie de vivre*; far from weighing people down, she swept them into action.

The life led by the Mendelssohn children was not in any case conducive to frivolity. The cult of reason on which their religion was based had become a cult of knowledge. Their parents left nothing to chance as far as their instruction and the development of their talents were concerned. In 1818 the musician Carl Friedrich Zelter was hired to teach composition to the two eldest, and in 1819 the young philologist Karl Heyse (1797–1855) was engaged as the children's tutor in general subjects, including science. With Berger, they comprised a superb trio; it was as if parents of this day and age had engaged, for example, Michel Serres, Pierre Boulez, and Radu Lupu (or in American terms Noam Chomsky, Aaron Copland, and Leonard Bernstein) to educate their children. The violinist Henning came to give Felix lessons and Professor Rösel taught them to draw landscapes—an area in which Felix excelled. Rebecka learned Greek out of affection for

Felix; he found this language dull, but her company consoled him. In fact Rebecka, known as Beckchen, proved herself the linguist of the group—and also the singer, for she had a lovely voice. In his recollections of young Felix, the actor Eduard Devrient wrote:

Their mother, a woman of great intelligence and culture as well as an alert mistress of the house, was constantly engaged in sewing or in reading while at the same time supervising her children's studies with implacable firmness. It was for this reason that activity became an absolute necessity for Felix. His mother kept him at her feet in her own room, obliging him to do rather boring exercises at Rebecka's little desk. One morning when I was visiting his mother, he came to join me in the anteroom with a slice of bread and butter, which entitled him to take a moment from his work; we chatted for longer than it takes to eat a slice of bread, whereupon a quick word from his mother, "Felix, aren't you doing anything?" (*Felix, tust du nichts?*) recalled him to order and he fled into the room behind.[13]

A formidable mother indeed, wanting irreproachable children against whom the charge of apostasy could not be levied. The effects of her severity stayed with Felix throughout his life; all his friends were struck by his nervousness and restlessness. The young Mendelssohns lived at an intellectual pace which would have been intolerable for less gifted children.

When he was eleven Felix wrote a parody of an epic poem in three cantos, entirely in verse and modeled on Goethe's *Achillëis* of 1808. Felix called his poem *Paphlëis* and recounted the exploits of his younger brother Paul, nicknamed Paphlos, hero of the Neue Promenade. In it Paphlos describes his daily life to his companions in arms:

I wake at five and sit up in my bed
To see if Felix has woken from his slumber.
If he has not, I quickly sprinkle him with water
And pull off all the blankets that are keeping him warm.
If he won't get up, I shout encouragements at him,
And then he wakes and gets dressed as fast as he can.
As for me, I stay in bed until Herr Heyse wakes me.
Why should I rise so early? I find sleep very healthy.
Now this you must know: I have a splendid voice.
That is why, as soon as Herr Heyse's calls have roused me,
I sing a song of morning that I myself compose,

Decorated with fifteen B-flats, and many As.
But it is hard to keep silent, and Herr Heyse frequently beats
   time.
So then I rise, and have a Latin lesson.
Pah! A mere trifle! At eight Caesar comes
To give me a lesson of calokagathiatugraphy.
("Caesar?" murmured Pinne, "I did not know he taught
   calligraphy.")
At nine I take my breakfast with due unction,
Toil a bit at Latin, learn in it a good deal of Greek.
Then at ten I bake a crown of roast apples,
Do calculations with my father, which give me a headache;
But at eleven I play the cello, with my powerful bow.
Sometimes terrifying caterwaulings are heard.
Fraülein Benicke plays the piano, Flix [sic] scrapes away
At his fiddle; and I play the cello. Often a fourth arrives
And sits in the courtyard, playing a guitar and whistle.
All the neighbors stop and listen, but we do not stop;
We would never give up an iota of our rights.[14]

The day continues with history, geography, German, Greek mythol-
ogy, French. . . . The two boys were entitled to some physical education, but after a timetable like that the happy little seven-year-old
Paphlos became a difficult adolescent and a taciturn adult.

   Fortunately there were four of them, enduring all this "training."
The tone was set by Fanny, who had been the first to face their parents' exacting demands and their anguish at having to change religion. No wonder the children felt linked by a strong bond. It must
have been a great source of joy for young Fanny to watch Felix growing up beside her—a little boy who understood all her feelings and
with whom she could share her love of music and play at being
Mummy and piano teacher. To begin with, her own role cannot have
decreased: she continued to be the hyper-talented little girl who
played the piano, which was all the more important in that she served
as a model for Felix. That boys were destined for a more active social
role cannot yet have been apparent in a family where the mother possessed so much power. On the contrary, it must have alleviated the
burden of a weighty love.

   From the texts of the lieder Fanny composed in her childhood, it seems she learned French, Italian, and English. All her liturgical works are in German, implying she did not learn Latin.[15] Moreover, she admitted to having no special gift for languages;[16] this field was reserved for the particular talents of her younger sister Rebecka. Fanny's curriculum thus appears less intense than Felix's, but we may trust Lea not to have left any of her children "doing nothing." Like Rebecka, Fanny had to learn how to run a house, embroider, and sew. And in the Mendelssohn household, even the domestic arts had to be of the highest standard. Henriette continued to comment on this education from afar, not without envy: she simply could not obtain truly satisfying results from Fanny Sébastiani. There is, of course, a question of relative aptitude, but that could only prove vexing to this professional educator:

I received your sumptuous purse a few days ago, and then the letters from you and your mother immediately afterward. Heartfelt thanks for sending both. The workmanship of the purse is extraordinarily fine, as is the choice of colors. I have no idea, my dear child, how in the midst of your studies and with so many serious and diverse occupations, you can still find time to undertake so difficult a task and carry it out so carefully. You take after your mother! She has always had that ability, and thanks to her you have it too. If only Fanny Sébastiani possessed the tiniest part of your industry and talents. Compared to your mother, I must surely be as poor a model as Fanny is a poor student compared to you. You were right, dear Fanny, to be astonished that she should choose poetry so full of moralizing and chill reason. She was so happy to be sending you this poem that I let her do it. Anything to do with music is a book closed with seven seals for her![17]

The Mendelssohn children were raised in the bosom of their family, without going to school. Although the boys received a different education from the girls, all were expected to attain the same degree of excellence, which could give an appearance of equal treatment. Their mother's role was so important that her position must have seemed enviable. Fanny and Rebecka did not fully realize that they would later remain confined to their homes, devoted to domestic life, and that their personal development would halt in adolescence.

CHAPTER FIVE

Zelter and the Singakademie

Beginning in 1818 Fanny and Felix took lessons in composition from the celebrated Berlin musician Carl Friedrich Zelter (1758–1832), thereby becoming even more clearly affiliated with J. S. Bach. By enrolling the young Mendelssohns in the Singakademie, a famous Berlin institution, Zelter placed them in the mainstream of tradition. The Singakademie played such a large part in the two young people's lives that its cultural importance must be explained and included in their story.

A mason's son from the outskirts of Dresden, Zelter had learned his father's trade, had become a master in it, and had taken over the business after his father died in 1787. It was only in 1815 that he left the Berlin masons' guild: even then he is known to have had a house at 13 Brüderstrasse. This occupation, however, was not detrimental to his music. He was initially trained as a violinist by Märker, L. George, and Johann Christian Schulz,[1] and in 1779 became a member of the Döbbelin Theater Orchestra where his performances included operas by Benda. In 1786 he played first violin in a performance of Handel's *Messiah*, conducted by J. A. Hiller.

Despite the mixed reception accorded an early attempt at composition (it was praised by Marpurg but criticized by Kirnberger), Zelter did not become discouraged and persisted in asking the church musician Christian Friedrich Fasch for composition lessons until the master agreed to give them. Between 1784 and 1786 Zelter thus received 168 lessons. When in 1791 the Singakademie was founded to maintain the tradition of composers from preceding centuries, Zelter immediately became an active member.

It is customary for musicologists to claim that the work of Johann Sebastian Bach was left in the wilderness for almost a century, from the time of his death until his supposed rediscovery in mid-nineteenth century. In regard to Berlin, the claim is utterly unfounded. Admittedly, the "fashionable" music composed in the eighteenth century did not correspond at all to the criteria of the past; nevertheless a series of musicians did keep the Bach tradition alive in their hearts and music, beginning with the composer's own sons. Such was the case of Carl Philipp Emanuel (1714–1788), who lived for many years in Berlin; and also of Wilhelm Friedemann (1710–1784), the oldest of Bach's sons, who also lived in Berlin, from 1774 until his death. This latter was considered the greatest organist in Germany, the only one to keep the family tradition going; his students included the harpsichordist Sara Levy, who was Fanny and Felix Mendelssohn's great aunt. Carl Philipp Emanuel,[2] Bach's fifth and most celebrated son, successfully studied law before becoming harpsichordist to the Crown Prince of Prussia, the future Friedrich II. He remained in the king's service until 1768, when he succeeded his godfather Telemann as musical director in Hamburg—a post he held until his death in 1788. Thanks to Bach's sons we have most of Johann Sebastian's manuscripts—thanks also to the numerous pupils to whom the Cantor of Leipzig passed on his knowledge. The most famous of these was Johann Philipp Kirnberger (1721–1783), who studied with Johann Sebastian from 1739 to 1741.[3] Thereafter he held various positions as a teacher and musical director until 1750. In 1752 he became a violinist in the Royal Chapel of Berlin, and from 1754 was professor of composition and Kapellmeister to Princess Amalia of Prussia—herself a composer and a remarkable musician.[4] His numerous theoretical works (for example, the *Kunst des reinen Satzes*, or "Art of Pure Composition," 1774–1779) give an excellent idea of what Johann Sebastian Bach's teaching must have been like. There was no more enthusiastic admirer of the Leipzig master than this industrious musician with his fine critical sense.

His colleague Johann Friedrich Agricola (1720–1774) was an organist before becoming royal Kapellmeister and a composer in Berlin; he, too, had studied harpsichord, organ, and composition with Johann Sebastian Bach. He was, however, more inclined toward opera than sacred music. If we conclude this list of Bach's students with the names of Fasch and Zelter, we must admit that during the last third of the eighteenth century the old master had an extraordinary colony of admirers in Berlin.

Christian Friedrich Fasch (1736–1800) played an essential part in keeping the tradition alive. The son of the Kapellmeister of Zerbst, he studied violin, organ, harmony, and composition with his father. In 1756 Franz Benda recommended him to King Friedrich II whose usual accompanist, Carl Philipp Emanuel Bach, wanted an assistant.[5] Friedrich II did in fact play flute concertos and other solo works for flute every day—at least until he became absorbed in the problems of the Seven Years' War (1756–1763). Fasch did not have to violate his own tastes, which centered on sacred music, for his appointment was extended, and, having little else to do, he was able to devote himself to studying the old masters. Most notably, he copied a mass for sixteen voices presumably by Orazio Benevoli (1605–1672)[6] which Reichardt had brought back from Italy. This gave him the idea of composing a similar mass himself, with sixteen voices, but where would he find singers to perform such a project?

Even if he had been brought up in the Bach tradition and had received the support of the above-mentioned colleagues, a church musician such as Fasch maintained a concept of music that was no longer fashionable. Sacred music does not exist for itself, but by definition adheres to a moral and ethical context. Kirnberger railed against "the tangible expression of raw nature in art,"[7] whereas the Berlin *singspiel* or lied, like comic opera, tended on the contrary to depict human emotions as "naturally" or "obviously" as possible. Two diametrically opposed concepts meet head-on here, and even if one has no intention of deciding between them one must admit that a singer trained only to interpret ariettas with simple melodies would be lost when confronted with the second or third voice of a chorus by Johann Sebastian Bach, or by any other baroque composer. Fasch found no suitable singers in Potsdam or Berlin, either among the royal singers or the school choirs. He therefore decided to rehearse his own students, beginning with twelve singers in the house of the Privy Councilor Milow, on Leipziger Strasse. In April 1791 they rehearsed in the home of Privy Councilor Pappritz's wife; beginning on 24 May 1791, they moved on to Frau Voitus's house at 42 Unter den Linden, where for the first time an attendance sheet was drawn up, comprising twenty-seven names. This date was henceforth considered to be the anniversary of the Singakademie's foundation. After two years the meeting place became too small and the Singakademie was authorized to move into the Academy of Fine Arts (Akademie der Künste) where rehearsals began anew on 5 November 1793.

In September 1791 the chorus gave its first public performance in the Marienkirche. This was also the first time that a chorus of adult male and female voices, with no children's voices, had been heard in concert. In effect, Fasch founded the Singakademie to respond to musical needs, but its development depended on the existence of certain social structures. According to Nägeli, a nation's choral evolution constitutes a step toward self-awareness in that choral achievements provide proof of the efficacy of an action that is simultaneously individual and collective. What could be finer than love for one's neighbor, expressed through so many mingled breaths? "With a hundred well-trained singers, possessed of average voices such as nature gave them, one obtains a well-composed group, symbolic of the majesty of the people."[8] Replacing children's voices with those of adult men and women gave the chorus an even more important social function. On the rational level, one obvious advantage was that this avoided spending years training young boys, only to have their voices break and be ruined in a single night at puberty. A more fundamental, subterranean pressure was emerging as a social force sought to express itself in the very heart of the culture, through religious means. The presence of women in the chorus and among its founding members—Frau Voitus, Frau Sebald, and Frau Dietrich—attests to the dominant role they played in cultural life at the end of the eighteenth century. For a chorus to try to comprise a more accurate representation of society by including both sexes in its ranks signifies the advent of an idea of "naturalness" in art—precisely what the aesthetics of Fasch and Kirnberger rejected. Musical life is so constituted that one cannot break with the tendencies of an era at every turn.

As a rule the Singakademie's rehearsals were closed, but curiosity broke down its doors on 8 April 1794 for a first "Auditorium" (audition), and Prince Louis-Ferdinand came in person with several members of the court. On this occasion people from different social categories rubbed shoulders in a manner typical of the period, which was marked by real respect for the artistic world. Beethoven also visited the academy on 21 June 1796.

Fasch devoted himself to the Singakademie with his entire frenzied capacity for work: he assembled all the scores, wrote the separate vocal parts, and conducted all the rehearsals.[9] From 1794 on, the Singakademie not only tackled Bach's motets, but it also studied the *Mendelssohniana*—that is, the thirtieth psalm as translated by Moses Mendelssohn and set to music by Fasch—and the *Davidiana*, from the translation by Luther. Handel was also included in the program.

The choir distinguished itself by another feature, astonishing in that era: it sang and rehearsed *a cappella*, without any instrumental support to ensure the accuracy of its notes. As one onlooker noted: "In the movements already studied, the conductor left the choir to itself. As if it were a single person and with no help from the conductor, the choir proceeded to observe the artistic pauses, the quickenings of tempo, the changes of expression from loud to soft, with a freedom that has earned this institution the admiration both of distinguished connoisseurs and the most profane incompetents."[10]

In 1799, a year before Fasch died, the Singakademie comprised ninety-four members. A founding member and ardent participator from the very beginning, Carl Friedrich Zelter had often replaced his old professor when the latter fell ill during the last years of his life. After Fasch's death, he naturally became director of the choir, conducting the first Berlin performance of Mozart's Requiem on 8 October 1800 in memory of his master. Since its creation, the Singakademie had been an integral part of musical life in Berlin and had responded to current events, such as the death of Friedrich Wilhelm II in 1797; yet Zelter was able to turn it into a veritable institution of steadily increasing importance in Berlin and a model throughout Germany. The chorus rapidly reached a total of 120 singers, and Zelter no longer accepted anyone who had not been recommended or had not passed a strict test. It was a great honor for Fanny and Felix to be accepted in 1820, at their tender ages.

The repertory still consisted essentially of works by Fasch, Lotti, Naumann, Reichardt, Schulz, Durante, Handel, and Palestrina, among others. But above all, it comprised the motets of Bach, which Zelter, like Fasch, never tired of collecting, recopying, and even adapting slightly according to the tastes of the time. Every Friday, beginning on 10 April 1807, Zelter assembled in his home the instrumentalists, amateurs, and students who wished to practice performing in Bach's style. A number of fugues from the *Well-Tempered Clavier* were arranged for string quartet. Sara Levy, sister of Lea Mendelssohn's mother, played there often. The archives of the Singakademie mention Bach's D Minor Concerto on 31 December 1807 and, on 19 February 1808, the fifth Brandenburg Concerto, arranged for pianoforte, flute, and violin, with Sara Levy at the keyboard.

Between 1813 and 1815, Zelter rehearsed the Mass in B Minor, refusing to be discouraged by its difficult entrances. In 1815 he began work on the *Saint John Passion*,[11] and on several passages from the *Saint Matthew*.

Zelter did not hesitate to modify passages in Johann Sebastian Bach which seemed too arduous for the singers and instrumentalists of his time. He also championed music from the past, in his fashion, and wrote lieder which he kept as simple as possible so that they would be easier to remember and in keeping with the text. In so doing he was only following the example of all his Berlin elders, those same church musicians who revered the learned music of Johann Sebastian Bach but who also composed lieder: Carl Philipp Emanuel Bach and Kirnberger, followed by Fasch and Reichardt.[12] In 1808 the ever-active Zelter founded the *Liedertafel*, or "meal with songs," a monthly meeting in which twenty-five members of the Singakademie sang songs of their own composition during the course of a meal. "It is hard for us to imagine a company that can do without song in an atmosphere of joyous comradeship. Only through the words and melody of song do heart and soul approach a point of togetherness. Whether sadness or joy dominate in the song, our hearts always meet; and then a feeling of solidarity pours forth, which presently inspires good fellowship,"[13] wrote Zelter in 1808. This search for elemental feeling in music might appear to contradict the more intellectual cult of counterpoint, but that was not how Zelter saw it. He was deeply attached to the social role of music, perceiving Bach first and foremost as a composer of sacred music, a musician who addressed the whole community. These lessons were duly absorbed by Fanny and Felix Mendelssohn, for whom music was above all a matter of sharing and communication.

Zelter wanted to shape the taste of a nation, but he was equally influenced by the tastes of his time. He claimed he need only answer to

Bach himself for having altered his scores, doubtless thinking he was doing Bach a good turn by introducing his works to a wider audience, and thinking himself sufficiently fond of and familiar with Bach's works to feel sure of what he was doing. Yet certain phrases that Zelter simplified to an extreme degree do not pose the slightest musical problem today; we may legitimately wonder about how tastes have changed. The belief that one is justified in changing an author's thought in order to make it widely known shows how much power had accrued to public opinion, even in the field of music. In the nineteenth century, the view that the passage of time leads to aesthetic progress justified "improving" artistic works.

The Singakademie had been founded to provide musical education for a certain social class. Zelter was strongly motivated by this idea for the musical reasons already indicated; nevertheless, he knew he must provide more concrete reasons if he wanted to obtain support from the state. With the disappearance of choirs of young boys, the *Kurrende*, and of municipal fanfares (*Stadtpfeifereien*), Zelter had in effect witnessed the end of certain forms of "town music." He was forced to pursue his entrepreneurial activities because the post of director of the Singakademie was honorific, with a salary of only 150 thalers per year (200 thalers after 1811)—a sum in no way adequate to support him and his very large family. From 1803 on he was in constant correspondence with the government, trying to persuade it to take charge of musical education. To this end he emphasized not artistic necessity, but rather the beneficial effect of such education on "morals and religion." He did not obtain tangible results until 1809. After the French occupation, Chancellor Hardenberg surrounded himself with men anxious to modernize Prussia. Among them was Wilhelm von Humboldt who, at Goethe's prompting, had Zelter appointed professor of music at the Berlin Academy of Fine Arts. This subsequently enabled Zelter to have musical education institutes opened in Königsberg (1814), Breslau (1815), and Berlin (1822)—institutes for music both sacred and secular. Thus Zelter controlled musical training throughout Prussia and composed a number of lieder and choruses for schools.

Zelter's posthumous fame derived principally from his friendship with the poet Goethe, a friendship that lasted from 1799 until both died in 1832; Zelter survived his friend by only a few months and was the only person to address him with the familiar *du*. He is commonly held responsible for Goethe's estrangement from Beethoven and Schubert, but Goethe himself preferred to emphasize poetry and its message, uncomplicated by music. Their correspondence was published after their deaths and polite society learned truths that shocked many people greatly—especially those who were directly mentioned.

CHAPTER SIX

Dashed Hopes

Fanny and Felix took composition lessons with Zelter, who trained them in the tradition of Bach, Kirnberger, and Fasch. It was an extremely rigorous method, based on models, and was accompanied by multiple exercises in counterpoint and figured bass. Fanny, the eldest, certainly progressed faster than Felix; "as gifted as Felix," as Goethe put it, she also had the advantage of being four years older. They were not one, but two child prodigies. Fanny was happy to expound her knowledge for Felix's benefit, but for the rest of his life Felix felt the effects of this childhood competition, in which he had not had the upper hand. As a result of this quasi-complex, he always avoided competitive situations, as is shown by this letter of 7 April 1838 to the publisher Alfred Novello:

I wish I could send you the wished-for composition of the set of words you sent me; but it is altogether impossible for me to do anything in the way of prize composition. I cannot do it, if I would force myself to it; and when I was compelled to do so, when a boy, in competition with my sister and fellow-scholars, my works were always wonders of stupidity—not the tenth part of what I could do otherwise.[1]

This appealing modesty shows, first, that Felix was extremely sensitive, and second, that he had frequently doubted his own abilities, particularly when compared to Fanny's. Even so, he got into the habit of submitting everything he wrote for her approval, until Fanny eventually begged him to read what she was writing and give her some encouragement.

In fact, the two children's relationship soon reached a turning point. At first it was Fanny, the elder, the "boss," the "Cantor," who showed her little brother what she could do: she was the virtuoso, at once maternal and didactic. She had everything she needed, everything she desired; much, apparently, was given her. But her brother began to grow up, and one can easily see that he was given even more. Fanny, too, benefited from Zelter's composition lessons, but only after Felix was old enough to understand them. The rest of her adolescence is the story of a talent hidden beneath the bushel of another talent.

The first composition of hers that we know, *Ihr Töne, schwingt euch fröhlich!*[2] (Songs, fly joyously away!), was written in 1819 in honor of her father's birthday, 11 December. It is a pleasant song by an extremely gifted girl of fourteen who has thoroughly absorbed her teachers' lessons. The melody and its accompaniment (a light Alberti bass) emphasize the text while staying close to it, with just enough chromaticism and modulations to related keys to sustain the musical interest. Yet it already evinces the spontaneity and melodic inspiration that would always be characteristic of Fanny's style. Both children wrote and continued all their lives to write in notebooks of manuscript paper. Most of Fanny's notebooks are in Berlin, in the Staatsbibliothek Preussischer Kulturbesitz; the very first, however, belongs to a private collection and is inaccessible. Written between 1820 and 1821, it comprises thirty-eight lieder and ariettas in French (six of them unfinished); an arioso with recitative; a chorus; four choral arrangements for four voices; eleven piano pieces; and Colette's aria, "J'ai perdu tout mon bonheur" (I have lost my happiness) from the *Devin de village* (The Village Soothsayer) by Jean-Jacques Rousseau, orchestrated from a piano part. All this work proves that the young fifteen-year-old studied very seriously under Zelter's guidance, her notebook studded with his corrections.

It was thus high time to make her understand her duty, and Abraham, who was spending a year in Paris between 1819 and 1820, set about trimming her wings by epistolary means. It was no easy task to cool her impassioned nature. In the letters he addressed to his daughter, Abraham had at least two essential and complementary things to communicate to her: since Fanny was being confirmed, he spoke first about religion; and since religion was for him morality in action, he spoke next about the manner of life she was to lead. In the name of the religion he had chosen for her, Fanny must devote herself body and soul to her home, to her family, and to her role as a mother. A professional activity was absolutely unthinkable. There was no intent to belittle her talent—it was simply a question of morality.

The Prussian father thus wrote this letter to his beloved child:

Paris, 16 July 1820

Your last lieder are in Viry. I shall fetch them back from there tomorrow, and then find someone who can sing them to me in a tolerable fashion. Monsieur Leo gave me a very imperfect rendering of Felix's most recent fugue; he finds it very good, and written in an authentic, though difficult, style. I liked it very much; it is a major achievement, and I would not have thought him capable of going so far so soon, and of working so seriously, for it certainly requires much reflection and perseverance to write such a fugue. What you tell me in one of your previous letters about your musical urges as compared to his was as well thought out as it was expressed. Perhaps music will be his profession, whereas for you it can and must be but an ornament, and never the fundamental bass-line[3] of your existence and activity. That is why ambition, and the desire to make the most of himself in circumstances he deems important, are forgivable in Felix, for he experiences it as a vocation. It is, however, no less to your credit that you have always shown your good heart and good sense at such moments, and the joy you manifest when Felix wins applause proves that you would have deserved it equally, had you been in his place. Persevere in these feelings and this attitude, for they are feminine and femininity alone is becoming in a woman. . . .

We read your romances yesterday in Viry, and you will be pleased to learn that Fanny Sébastiani sang *Les Soins de mon troupeau* for me, prettily and accurately and with considerable pleasure. I confess I like this lied the best, to the extent that I can judge the others, which were very badly performed. It is cheerful, fluent, and natural—qualities lacking in most of the other lieder, which occasionally stray too far from the text. I like this lied so much I've sung it to myself many times since yesterday, whereas I recall nothing of the others, and it seems to me the first requirement of a lied is to be easily remembered. This does not mean it's commonplace, and the line "Si j'ai trouvé pour eux une fontaine claire" is very well turned, even if it makes too abrupt an ending for the phrase that's immediately joined to the verses of the paragraph "s'ils sont heureux." I strongly advise you to retain this naturalness and ease in your future compositions.

Postscript: Aunt Jette would like you to send her some of your German lieder, when you can.

Aunt Jette, of course, was Henriette Mendelssohn, still charged with implanting some semblance of learning into the dizzy brains of Fanny Sébastiani. The nickname Jette distinguished her from Joseph Mendelssohn's wife, Henriette Meyer, whose nickname was Hinni. The whole family rejoiced in Fanny's talent, and the care taken by Abraham in criticizing her first attempts shows that he had no desire to minimize her talent. His four children were the apples of his eye; he was inordinately proud of them and proved it on numerous occasions. It cannot be said that Abraham wanted Fanny to renounce music as a profession, for renouncing would imply something more active. There was actually no question of her having any profession at all: a woman could have no destiny other than that of being a woman.

As for the morality he preached, Abraham was a victim of the ambiguities inherent in his time. An intellectual descendant of the eighteenth century in France, but also of the Kantian system, Abraham had convinced himself of the universality of public opinion. Natural order was the basis of legal order. His words to Fanny, "the form of belief adopted by a majority of civilized people," certainly came close to what might be called natural religion, or universal religion. The idea of universals proved irresistibly tempting to Abraham's mind and led him to construct a veritable intellectual house of cards, with his children acting as pillars. The problem with this approach was that the concept of what is natural is rarely demonstrable, save through tautology. Why can't a woman have a profession? That's nature. Really? But how is it nature? It is amusing to note that Abraham gives Fanny similar advice in musical matters: he tells her to "remain natural." Music is as sophisticated an art as moral philosophy, but such a thought would have demolished all Abraham Mendelssohn's bourgeois convictions. He must surely have read the *Calendrier musical universel* (Universal Musical Calendar) that appeared in Paris in 1788:

Music is a natural language, devoid in its principle of all convention; this language is a universal one, the same throughout the world. The African Negro, the American Savage, the Oriental all sing as we do: that is to say, what constitutes singing for these peoples also constitutes it for us, and their songs, to which they attach neither bass nor harmonic parts, can be harmonized just as our songs are, because they derive from the same relationship between sounds, relationships established by nature and which man cannot change.[4]

If one applies the same qualifying phrase to religion and morality, "devoid in its principle of all convention," it is scarcely surprising that human beings, supposedly acting in the name of nature, often find themselves trapped in situations that contradict their wishes. Abraham converted his children, convinced that a religion supported by public opinion must contain a universal truth. This universal, natural religion found a privileged interpreter in woman, who played the part ordained for her by nature—the role of mother. If in addition this mother played natural-sounding tunes upon the piano (so natural an instrument!), the world was in its place, its natural order guaranteed by the noble savages of the *Universal Musical Calendar*. In postulating the universality and naturalness of its functioning, public opinion—that groundswell that had overthrown the Ancien régime—brought about the creation of bourgeois morality, the morality that kept women cloistered in the home.

A further contradiction consisted in the Mendelssohns' wanting to live a socially absolute truth while turning their faces inward, toward family, toward their own private world that cultivated the maternal figure and paternal power. As for the "universal," Abraham chose increasingly to protect himself from a world in which anti-Jewish tension threatened to topple his castle in the clouds. After his return from Paris, the family moved to the Spandauer Vorstadt, a suburb; in 1821 Abraham gave up business; and in 1822 he took his family traveling in Switzerland. Finally, in 1825, the Mendelssohns found their definitive refuge at 3 Leipziger Strasse, in a mansion with an enchanting garden (see Figure 9). Cut off from vulgar society and sheltered from antisemitic pronouncements, the Mendelssohn family was able to devote itself to its elitism, to universality concentrated in a microcosm.

The contrast between the appealing notion of naturalness and the complexity of actual structures was as pungent in musical matters as in the social order. In his letter to Fanny of 16 June 1820, Abraham praised the charms of a smoothly flowing melody that was easy to remember; yet on 10 October that same year Fanny and Felix joined the Singakademie where they sang contrapuntal, intellectual music that was hard to remember and whose aesthetic theories, as we have noted, were radically opposed to "the tangible expression of raw nature in art." Caught between these two worlds, the two young Mendelssohns had only their own characters and discriminating ears to

guide them. Whereas Zelter respected Rossini—the most fashionable composer in all Europe, the composer whose melodies represented "natural" music—Fanny and Felix, who were more perceptive
(or had better taste), considered him a charlatan. It was, of course,
impossible not to be influenced by the *singspiel*, by the *tafellieder*
(table songs), by the Romantic quest for the soul of the people translated into song, or by Clemens Brentano and Achim von Arnim's
publication of *Des Knaben Wunderhorn*, but that did not prevent the
two young Mendelssohns from enthusiastically admiring the rugged
and uncompromising music of Ludwig van Beethoven, for whom
Zelter had only moderate esteem. They were wild about *Der Freischütz*, which was first performed on 18 June 1821 in the Schauspielhaus on the Gendarmenmarkt. That same year Spontini, director of
the Hofoper, had much success with his opera *Olympia*, but neither
the pomp and splendor of French operas nor the suaveness of Italian
tunes could totally seduce the youthful Mendelssohns, resolutely
German in their musical tastes. Through Mozart, Haydn, the lied,
and the *singspiel* they had learned all they needed to know about
lightness and fluidity in music, and they could not accept music that
ignored the rules of counterpoint. They liked Bach and Beethoven—
Fidelio received its premiere in Berlin in 1815—and felt solidarity
with the Lutheran musical tradition which, mixed with the nascent
cult of Germanism and popular Romantic lyricism, attained a sort of
apogee in Weber.

Fanny and Felix Mendelssohn thus had the honor of being admitted to the Singakademie with the comment *brauchbar*, "useful."
Felix was first a boy soprano, then a tenor; Fanny always counted
among the altos, a group exposed to every possibility of making a
mistake. At that time the Singakademie had at its disposal soloists of
the highest caliber. They came from the Königliche Schauspielhaus
whose director, Count Karl von Brühl (1772–1837), had attracted
the finest singers of the day to Berlin: Anna Milder-Hauptmann,
Heinrich Stümer, Heinrich Blume, Johanna Eunicke, Joseph Fis-
cher, Carl Bader.[5] They were all specialists in German opera, from
Fidelio to *Euryanthe*, and also sang at the Singakademie which was
then approaching its zenith. Fanny and Felix were certainly not outstanding singers: even though Felix later possessed a fine tenor voice,
he was never a soloist. As for Fanny, no word of praise has reached us
on the subject of her voice—not a good sign. Zelter often had them

accompany rehearsals at the piano, and they took part in his *Freitags-musik*. He must have held them in great esteem to entrust such responsibility to them at such tender ages. In his *Memories of Felix Mendelssohn Bartholdy* the singer Eduard Devrient comments that after 1822 Fanny "let Felix take full prominence."[6] Abraham was not the only one responsible for this: everyone considered it normal to rein in Fanny's enthusiasm, and Zelter did not object. Neither did Devrient, who in this same book had nonetheless written of Felix: "I found his playing extraordinarily dexterous and possessed of great musical confidence, yet it still did not approach that of his elder sister Fanny." This observation dates from 1820. Two years later their roles had been reversed. Had Fanny ceased to play well, had someone stolen her place, or had she finally resigned herself to being relegated to her brother's shadow? Everyone helped her to accomplish this last mutation. All those who wrote down their recollections of the youth of Felix Mendelssohn Bartholdy—Devrient, Hiller, Moscheles, Marx —employ the same formulas. Practically on the same page, one reads: Fanny, the elder, exhibited a talent as remarkable as her brother's, and being older she played even better than he did. Then, in the same breath: Felix's talent received encouragement and praise. Nobody furnishes either explanations or excuses, since these developments were normal.

From then on, it was Felix's destiny that mattered. In any case, even if Fanny had been the sole child prodigy, she would not have had a greater right to choose her profession. It was through Felix that she had access to an outstanding education in music and gathered the crumbs of a musical destiny that could have been hers. But the Mendelssohn parents were already displaying extraordinary broadmindedness in allowing Felix to become a musician. The voice of their social milieu can be heard through Jacob Bartholdy:

I do not fully agree that you should not give Felix a precise profession. His musical vocation, which everybody recognizes, absolutely cannot pass as such. A professional musician[7]—I can't get that into my head. It's neither a career, nor a life, nor a goal; one is no further advanced at the end than one was at the beginning, and one knows it; in fact, one is generally better off at the beginning. Let the boy study as he should, let him read law at the university and begin a career in the government. Art will remain a friend to him and a diversion. As I see things developing, we shall need people who have studied, and this need will be felt even more strongly in the immediate future. If he has to be a merchant, put him to work at once behind a counter.[8]

If the voice of bourgeois morality had been heard out fully, Felix's position would have been scarcely more encouraging than Fanny's. The sentence "Art will remain a friend to him" carries the reminder that a "respectable" man does not marry his mistress. This leads us to consider another aspect of Lea and Abraham Mendelssohn's mentality, one that completes the portrait of their moral constitution: their relationship to money.

As soon as he converted, Abraham gave up his business dealings. Malicious gossips declared that he had no talent for business, further reproaching him for his pretentious and irascible character. Be that as it may, Abraham had to brave the wrath of his brother, who may have been angered either by his resignation or his conversion—it is hard to tell. But Abraham constantly behaved as if he wanted to make people forget his conversion, or at the very least as if he did not wish them to doubt its sincerity. Thus, he distanced himself from business dealings as quickly as he could. Felix's talent offered an unmatched opportunity to show the world a "spotless character, faithful to its choice and diplomatic in behavior, that would constitute an example worthy of respect."[9]

His cultural integration could not have been more complete. In turning to the arts and away from the professions traditionally open to Jews, this son of a Jew placed himself beyond the customary anti-Jewish stereotypes. Felix was never very interested in money: although he did flirt with the idea of composing an opera, his masterpieces were his oratorios.

Benny, the eldest son of Hinni and Joseph Mendelssohn, would face a similar destiny. His tastes did not incline toward banking, and he became a geographer, obtaining a professorship at the University of Bonn. He, too, converted, but whether on account of his origins or wealth—his colleagues were jealous because he did not need to make his students pay to take his courses—he was never fully accepted by his peers, who did not confirm his appointment as an *ordentlicher* (full) *Professor*. According to them he had not published enough. His younger brother Alexander resumed their father's business, as did Felix's younger brother Paul, who also went to work in the Mendelssohn Bank. Converted or not, the Mendelssohn cousins remained very close, both in their concerns and their manner of living. Alexander married Marianne Seeligmann, the daughter of one of Lea's sisters; Marianne was a lifelong friend of Fanny and the last of the Jewish Mendelssohns. Her funeral was the first time that most of the family members present had ever attended a Jewish ceremony.[10]

Joseph and Abraham both accepted their eldest sons' choice of scholarly and artistic professions.[11] They were too intelligent themselves, and too appreciative of intellectual pursuits, not to be proud of them. It is curious to observe that Jacob Bartholdy, patron of the arts, was already part of the "pragmatic" Germany bent on attaining unity.

Felix and Fanny were thus raised according to an ethical system that prized art and morality; moreover, although rich, their parents always valued simplicity. Devrient wrote of their lodgings in the Neue Promenade:

Considering the wealth attributed to Felix's father, the apartment's furnishings appeared almost ostentatiously simple. The tapestries and furniture were quite unassuming, but the walls of the drawing room were covered with engravings of Raphael's *Rooms*.[12]

The Mendelssohns' morality led them to value intelligence and beauty in art, and in their eyes those qualities justified vast expenditures; on the other hand, comfort and luxury seemed reprehensible to them. In a letter to her future son-in-law, Wilhelm Hensel, Lea Mendelssohn insisted on this point: "In bringing up my children I try to accustom them to a simple way of life, so that they are not obliged to marry for money." This was an eminently Romantic vision: the narrow distribution of wealth did not allow much range of matrimonial choice. That, indeed, is evident in this scene from Jane Austen's *Pride and Prejudice* in which the heroine, Elizabeth Bennet, makes fun of the luxurious habits of Colonel Fitzwilliam, the younger son of an earl. Fitzwilliam complains:

"Younger sons cannot marry whom they like."
"Unless they like rich women, which I think they very often do."
"Our habits of expense make us too dependent, and there are not many in my rank of life who can afford to marry without some attention to money."[13]

In the Mendelssohn household, such a scene could never have occurred. Fanny was well aware that:

1. Marriage was her destiny, whereas music never could be.
2. She must not marry for money.
3. She would have to marry a Lutheran.
4. He would have to be a Lutheran who was sufficiently broad-minded to marry a convert. This was by no means generally the case.[14]

If we further consider the aura that enveloped Felix, as an artist, it comes as no surprise that the painter Wilhelm Hensel was her choice.

CHAPTER SEVEN

Wilhelm Hensel

In preparation for the visit of the heirs to the imperial Russian throne—Grand Duke Nicholas and his wife, a Prussian princess—the King of Prussia had organized numerous festivities, including tableaux vivants illustrating Thomas Moore's poem *Lalla Rookh: An Oriental Romance*. The story consists of four verse tales which young Feramors recites to princess Lalla Rookh, herself betrothed to Prince Aliris: *The Veiled Prophet of Khorasan*, *Paradise and the Peri*, *The Story of the Ghebern*, and *Nurmahal and Dschehangir*. It turns out that Feramors is none other than Prince Aliris himself, and everything ends happily. Oriental exoticism justified all manner of splendors, and the Prussian court went to such lengths that the event was indelibly imprinted in everyone's memory. The sets were designed by the painter Schinkel,[1] the costumes by Forbes and Elphinstone, and Spontini had provided the music. The tableaux vivants had been staged by the young painter Wilhelm Hensel. The actors had been chosen for their good looks or their high social position, and the occasion gave rise to a veritable orgy of pearls, precious stones, and valuable weapons. Sebastian Hensel relates that at the end of this enchanting spectacle the grand duchess, who was taking part in it, exclaimed: "Is it really over? Are future times to have no memento of this blissful evening?" Overhearing her remark the king decided to satisfy her wish, with the result that the young man who had so deftly directed these high-born personalities was appointed to paint their

portraits in full splendor, in the costumes and postures of the tableaux. Thus Wilhelm earned himself royal gratitude, a fellowship to
study in Italy, and a subsequent commission for a full-sized repro-
duction of Raphael's *Transfiguration*.[2]

The two sources consulted here—Sebastian Hensel and Theodor
Fontane—differ as to the scene of Wilhelm and Fanny's first meeting.
According to Fontane, Fanny and her family were among the four
thousand guests at the royal festivities, and met Wilhelm on this
occasion. According to Sebastian, the meeting took place at the exhibition Wilhelm organized to show his paintings before they were
shipped to Saint Petersburg. Even if Fanny, accompanied by her family, had also attended the spectacle and already caught a glimpse of
Wilhelm, a studio would seem a more logical meeting place than a
royal palace. Whatever the case, Wilhelm's talent gained him an en-
trée into the Mendelssohn home, and several months later he asked
for Fanny's hand.

Sebastian Hensel rightly points to the surprising elements of this
encounter which led to the union of two such disparate individuals—disparate in character as well as in background and education.
Fanny, of Jewish origin, had known a sheltered, intellectual childhood, constantly in contact with the outside world if only through
the numerous letters exchanged with her aunt Henriette in Paris and
her uncle Jacob in Rome. Wilhelm, on the other hand, represented
the quintessential "German-Christian."[3] He was the son of a pastor
of the Brandenburg region, a man as poor as the region and small
towns in which he successively held office, Trebbin and then Linum.
Wilhelm was expected to attend mining school, but, as he put it, "he
could draw before he could talk"[4] and, despite the opposition of his
parents, thought only in terms of acquiring colors and finding something to paint, thus teaching himself. How different from the prestigious teachers engaged by the Mendelssohn household! In 1811,
when Wilhelm was supposed to leave for Berlin to complete his studies as a mining engineer, his father suddenly died. His mother then allowed him to study painting at the Academy of Fine Arts, where he
nonetheless maintained the independent attitude and behavior of
one who was self-taught. At this juncture the Wars of Liberation
began. Wilhelm, aged eighteen, immediately enlisted and spent three
years in the army. Extremely brave and enterprising, he was wounded
three times, nearly winning the Iron Cross, the highest decoration

awarded those who took part in that war.[5] After the peace treaty was signed he spent some time in Paris, visiting the museums.

On his return to Berlin, Wilhelm weighed his two talents: poetry and painting. The uncertain future of painting was certainly a consideration, as was the future of German painting generally. Economically, things were going badly in Prussia, and in Germany pictorial art did not have sufficient moral foundation—as did music—for the government to contemplate supporting it for social reasons. It was therefore very risky for an artist to think of living by his painting. Notwithstanding the ateliers of masters, painting is by definition a more individual occupation than music. At that time all the arts were beginning to embrace the cult of "genius," which only accentuated the solitary side of painting. The German states were in the midst of a Metternichian reaction and mistrusted these artists living on the fringe of society, who necessarily questioned the social function of art as a tool of power.

From Rome, Jacob Bartholdy complained of being the only patron of the arts he knew, the only one to support young Prussian artists and give them the chance to form a school and show what they could do. Between 1816 and 1817 he commissioned them to paint frescoes in a room of his villa on the Monte Pincio, la Casa Bartholdy. Prussian artists did not have a Villa Medici where they could stay in Rome, as French artists did. They did, however, all live in the same district, the Monte Pincio, and linked by the same ideal they formed a school of painting. They called themselves the Nazarenes because they parted their hair down the middle and let the curls frame their faces, which made them look like Jesus and the inhabitants of Nazareth.[6] Their ideas tended toward the regeneration of art through religion; being in no position to assume a solitary, individual place in society, like Turner or Goya, they chose this means of resolving the question of the social function of art. Johann Friedrich Overbeck (1789–1869) became leader of the movement, and was joined by the brothers Johannes and Philipp Veit (sons of Dorothea Schlegel, thus nephews of Abraham Mendelssohn Bartholdy); Wilhelm Schadow (son of the sculptor who did the Quadriga atop the Brandenburg Gate); Julius Schnorr von Carolsfeld; and Peter Cornelius. Their art could be defined as triumphal post-Raphaelitism mixed with militant Catholicism—characteristics that made certain of their works rather inaccessible to anyone who did not share their opinions.

In fact they all belonged to the Catholic wing of German Romanticism. With its cultivated irrationality, Catholicism probably seemed a more propitious symbol of the rejection of the cult of reason and Enlightenment than did Protestantism. Except for Peter Cornelius—who, having been born a Catholic, proved the most tolerant of them all—the Nazarenes were all converts to Catholicism. There was also a picturesque element to Catholicism which could assume—as in the writings of Clemens Brentano—the form of nostalgia for medieval Germany and for the universal religion of the Middle Ages which had itself borrowed rituals from pagan antecedents. The religious feeling inspired by natural surroundings in Brentano's *Die Chronik eines Fahrenden Schülers* or Eichendorff's *Aus dem Leben eines Taugenichts* was not typical of all forms of Catholicism, but was a component of German Romantic Catholicism that was understandably attractive to painters.[7]

The Protestant Wilhelm Hensel belonged completely to this latter trend. His friends Adalbert von Chamisso, Achim von Arnim, Ludwig Tieck,[8] and Clemens Brentano—who was at one time deeply in love with Wilhelm's sister Luise—not only tried to convince him to devote himself to poetry, but Brentano, Chamisso, and Arnim also tried to convince him to convert to Catholicism. Luise Hensel did convert, and wrote some of the finest lyrical religious poems in the German language. While deciding on a religion, and despite the difficulty of living by his painting, Wilhelm remained true to his art, earning enough to support not only himself but also his mother and sisters by means of various small jobs such as creating calendars and etchings. He pursued his own studies at night, trying to make up for the delay in his apprenticeship caused by the Wars of Liberation.

Wilhelm's meeting with Fanny Mendelssohn introduced a certain confusion into his religious convictions. The letter he wrote from Rome on 1 December 1823 to his sister Luise so fully expresses his aspirations, contradictory feelings, and difficult position with regard to the Mendelssohns that it deserves to be quoted in its entirety:

G.S.J.C.[9]
I sit down to write to you, my dear sister, with the feeling that I am discharging an important debt. I was unable to accomplish anything during the journey, for I was traveling with men whose unbridled jests prevented me from writing, nor did I have my own bedroom, and I have not been able to write here, because at first I had to share my lodging. And then our compa-

triots wanted news of their families, and I could scarcely refuse to look at their work; then again, I have been very drawn to Rome, with its festivals and antiquities. My time has been completely taken up, especially since I had to start work immediately. All the Bavarian and Prussian artists have promised to produce a drawing for the marriage of our crown prince and the Bavarian princess, and I could not exempt myself from this tribute without risking accusations of ingratitude. I have chosen the *Wedding at Cana*, and am forcing myself to take time off from it so as not to miss another day of the mail. I should have done so sooner, of course, but believe me, I say this for myself and am not trying to exonerate myself in regard to you, any more than I'm exonerating myself in my own eyes. I am particularly hesitant about this letter, for I have decided to confide in you and acquaint you fully with what is in my heart, and with my situation. I had previously intended to do so in a verbal conversation, which would have been much clearer and more comprehensive; it would have been too crude to pluck my deepest heartstrings by writing you a letter from Prague that contained traces of haste and excitement. I do not, however, wish to keep a secret from you until I return—and so here it is: I am in love.

This sounds common enough, and you will wonder why I did not long since inform you of something so natural and customary; however, it so happens that the circumstances are so unusual, and the complications so numerous, that I almost despair of giving you a clear idea of them. Nevertheless, I do not wish you to misjudge me, or anyone else. You would certainly recognize this young girl as a sister, if you knew her, just as she has long since come to love you through my descriptions of you. You would be less in tune with the circle surrounding her and the opinions that prevail there. Her parents have only recently been baptized as Christians, and although she herself was baptized in early childhood, she has been brought up in an extremely Protestant manner, has heard many remarks slandering the Catholic church, and naturally had to share the general prejudice against it. She first heard the truth about the teachings of the Church through me, and was far more disposed to admit the injustice done to it through prejudice than I expected from my influence alone. Nevertheless, I tried to resist my increasing fondness for her, for I could not but see that it would be extremely hard to overcome the various difficulties before she could be mine, unless I submitted to the opinions of her family. I confessed my religious convictions to this young girl, and told her that sooner or later they would lead me to a public profession of faith. At least she could thus explain to herself why I did not declare my fondness for her. But some time afterward a moment of distraction drew the avowal from me; she then asked me to speak of the matter to her parents. You can imagine how hesitant I was to do so. I was afraid of having of my own accord to sacrifice my earthly happiness, for I firmly believed that they would ask me about my religion, and I was prepared to fight for the Lord with all my might. But imagine: it turned out quite differently. Her parents never mentioned the subject of religion, and taking this for tolerance, I was happy not to have to do so. I could henceforth hope that God was satisfied simply with my determination to sacrifice myself. Her parents asked only that the matter remain a complete secret, for the young girl's grandmother did not yet know she had become a Christian, and they did not want the old lady of eighty, an orthodox Jew, to take such a sorrow to her grave, given that she had already disowned her son for having converted to Christianity (nor did she know that her daughter had also become a Christian). Naturally they would not wish officially to announce that her granddaughter was engaged to marry a Christian, and I agreed to this condition.

Some time passed in blissful happiness, but late one evening when I was visiting Fanny and her parents, her mother unexpectedly asked me what my religious opinions were, and whether it was true, as people said, that I intended to turn toward the Catholic church. I replied that she had known this for some time, since I had said as much to her daughter before ever mentioning my love; whereupon it came to light that Fanny, counting on calmer times, had not dared say anything to her parents, for fear of setting them against me. The mother's anger then turned against her daughter, and she declared that had she known she never would have given her consent, that it was totally against her convictions to have a Catholic son-in-law, for Catholicism led infallibly to fanaticism and hypocrisy. Imagine what a state I was in! I prayed to God in silence, and asked the mother this question directly: would my conversion have the effect of causing her to withdraw her consent? If so, it would be best to do so now. Fanny had departed in tears into the darkness of a neighboring room. Her father came in to reestablish peace between us, although he shared his wife's opinion, and the result was this: the mother did not wish to appear tyrannical, and if her daughter persisted in her feelings, then she would not separate us forcibly, but she warned me openly that she would do all she could to dissuade her daughter from this union, should I really convert, and that she must for the time being forbid any lengthy tête-à-tête and all correspondence, unless I promised to remain faithful to the Protestant church. I told her firmly that I could not bind my conscience; the one thing I did promise was to reflect further before taking this step, and that if I did take it, I would make it a point of honor to let them know. That was how matters stood when we parted toward morning. What terror I felt on learning that the mother had suffered a nosebleed lasting nine hours the next day, following our violent argument and her own vexation; still, it was touching that she tried to hide this from me—I only discovered it by chance. Naturally, for the first few days, this sensitive topic was not broached, but the mother silently deprived me of any possibility of talking to Fanny by herself.

Eventually I could not stand this any longer and said so to the young girl. Fanny asked me to beg her mother to authorize an interview, for she did not want to transgress her filial duty by speaking to me without her parents' knowledge; her behavior in this would show me how she would one day fulfill other duties. In Fanny's presence, I was so bold as to ask her mother's permission; she refused. So then, with a fierce vehemence that still rings in my ears, her daughter said: "Mother, I shall speak to him!" These words are the rock on which I build my future! I think that, like me, you will respect a person who was thus able to reconcile two such contradictory obligations. As if alarmed by the child's determination, the mother went out without a word, and I had a long and serious conversation with the daughter in which I asked in all conscience if I could count on her no matter what. She solemnly agreed, and also promised to obtain information about the Church, as far as her parents and circumstances permitted. That is how my final days at home passed, with some hardships, but with complete trust in my beloved, a trust that I still feel. Moreover, her father is truly fond of me and I am relying on him when the struggle comes; his is a valiant nature lacking only in one thing. Her mother, who is in other respects a remarkable and intelligent woman, does nonetheless attach importance to worldly position and renown, and is using her fortune to tip the scales. Both parents have written to me regularly, and in a very friendly spirit; they have not, however, allowed their daughter to do so, since I have not for my part abandoned my intention. That is how matters stand; now you know the essentials. Tell me your opinion, freely and openly, and in any case pray for me. . . .

You are Mary, who chose the better part. My own soul resembles the more active Martha; she, too, loves the Lord, but in her own way, and Mary should not scold; she raises herself because Martha is humbling herself. I think you will understand from the preceding account that I am not sacrificing the Lord for the world, whatever they propose, but I feel increasingly that I shall never succeed in leading a tranquil and contemplative life. I must be active and productive in my life; the Lord has given me a golden talent, and I must make it thrive in my own manner. You do the same in your own way, and I am willing to believe that you are the wiser, but I cannot behave otherwise, even if I wished. May God bless us both! It is a great consolation to know you are satisfied with your present situation, and I am equally happy that you are having a beneficial influence upon helpless youths.[10] I shall do all I can to free you from worries; tell me frankly everything you need, and I shall find a way to help. It is a great thing that you have found a truly religious man, please commend me to him, and to his prayers. . . . The Veits send you their greetings; I spend more time with them than with anyone else, but spend most of my time alone. I follow a middle course. I can be more devout in my room than I can in the company of the most pious, except in church. I have spoken several times to Christian Brentano, but am avoiding any intimacy. You know I've always found the Brentanos rather unpleasant on account of their extremism and their reasons for being extreme. This is how Christian appeared here too, but even Overbeck and the Veits, who are certainly religious and devout Catholics, don't want to have too much to do with him. He takes a considerable interest in you and asked me to greet you warmly for him, which I am happy to do, for I have a lot of respect for him and for his aspirations, just as I do for Clemens. In finishing this letter, I'm suddenly worried that it may contain things you cannot or do not understand. It is very hard to describe years of feeling and experience on a few sheets of paper, and to anticipate and answer possible questions. I prefer not to reread this letter as I might not send it if I did. Tell me frankly where my meaning is obscure, and forgive me if you think I am wrong. I have certainly never been lacking in love for you, nor shall I, ever.

May God be with you!

Your faithful brother

Wilhelm

Let the story of my love remain absolutely secret, I earnestly entreat you. Adieu.[11]

Wilhelm did not become a Catholic. Numerous hypotheses may be advanced as to his probable reasons. One of them is mercenary and practical: Wilhelm was the recipient of a fellowship from the Prussian government and as a *Hofmaler*, or court painter, could not afford to profess a religion other than that of his employer. One prince, one religion—that was the rule in Germany. Wilhelm had lived through too much poverty, had struggled too hard in providing for himself and his family, to take the probable loss of his livelihood lightly. If, on top of that, conversion threatened his marriage to the woman he loved—this was too much for one man to bear. Fanny was worth more than a religious form. Wilhelm's letter to his sister is an apology: his sister's influence had been replaced by that of another woman.

Lea's anger may be understood if we remember that she herself had only converted a few months before. Fanny and Wilhelm met in January 1821. Wilhelm had only been living in Rome for a short time when he wrote this letter to his sister in December 1823. Abraham and Lea had converted in October 1822, on their return from Switzerland. Thus Wilhelm had asked for Fanny's hand between this period and his own departure for Italy. It is also possible that the Mendelssohn parents, on the point of converting, pretended to have done so already. In any case, Wilhelm's temptation to become a Catholic could not have occurred at a worse moment. After waiting for so many years in order to groom their image as converts of impeccable morality, they felt that Wilhelm's plan made them look plainly ridiculous. For Lea and Abraham—adherents of a religion based on reason who habitually intellectualized any actions having to do with faith— the idea of having grandchildren raised in what they saw as irrational mysticism must have been utterly intolerable. The tone of Wilhelm's letter reflects the mannerisms and vocabulary of Catholic Romantics. Expressions such as "Praised be Jesus Christ," "Church teaching," "fight for the Lord," and "sacrifice oneself for the Lord" all flowed from the pens of the Nazarenes or of Dorothea Schlegel—persons who were anything but tolerant. Lea's reproaches were not entirely unfounded: the Catholic Romantics ostentatiously flaunted their opinions (what Lea terms "hypocrisy") and showed themselves to be unpleasantly fanatical and proselytical. Dorothea and Henriette both prayed for their brothers and sisters to turn toward the "one true faith," the "sole revealed truth," which proved highly exasperating to those members of the family who had remained faithful to Judaism, perhaps even more so to those who had converted to Protestantism. Dorothea would not rest until she had brought her two sons Johannes and Philipp Veit into the Catholic fold, thus causing considerable sorrow to their father, Simon Veit. Simon nonetheless behaved extremely well toward his ex-wife and two sons, thereby honoring the teachings of his own religion and the memory of his friendship with Moses Mendelssohn. The exalted Romanticism of this brand of Catholicism made its adherents enemies of tolerance— as did their rejection of rationality and respect for family ties in favor of mystical ecstasy.

In view of Wilhelm's imminent departure for Rome, the Mendelssohn parents were justified in fearing the worst. For the Romantics, the pomp and ceremony of the Roman Catholic church was part of the attraction Italy held for them, and they compared the splendiferous ceremonies of Saint Peter's to "golden oranges shining amid dark leaves."[12] There was a saying that "Everyone who visits Rome returns a Catholic," and this was apparently sufficiently true for the Prussian diplomat Niebuhr to call for a Protestant preacher to be sent to Rome, to try to stem the flood of conversions.[13] It would not have been surprising for Wilhelm to have been swept away by this contagious enthusiasm. But that was not entirely to his taste. As he says, he was too active and enjoyed life too much to feel completely at ease in a circle inclined to mysticism. All through his life and in everything he did, faithfulness, kindness, and a sort of childlike, good-natured humor constituted the dominant traits of Wilhelm's character. If he was drawn to poetry, it was because he possessed an unrivaled facility for versification. Theodor Fontane said of him:

He was gay and talkative . . . ; anecdotes, toasts, letters in verse form, occasional poetry—all that was at his fingertips. But he was at his best in spontaneous witticisms, an art he had really mastered and from which he drew his greatest triumphs. He knew better than anyone how to shape poetic inspiration and form epigrammatic puns. He was not a poet, but he could have been called "Wilhelm the Rhymer." If one could retrospectively compile a collection of his sayings, it would be a book of witticisms and anecdotes, and at the same time the record of a person and character typical of the second quarter of the century. It would be difficult to make a selection![14]

A lover of puns among the Nazarenes—after two or three witty plays on words Wilhelm must have felt ill at ease, doubtless preferring to remain alone with his convictions, whatever they may have been. His sister's influence was certainly a determining factor in his intent to convert; far from Luise, not even the splendor of the Roman Catholic church could convince him to risk an action that would have threatened his relationship with Fanny and jeopardized his artistic livelihood.

Fanny's reaction cannot fail to surprise us, just as it surprised Lea and Wilhelm. How could this young girl, raised in the full rigor of Protestant morality, brought up to respect reason and knowledge, agree to contravene her filial duty and enter the foggy realm of mysticism? It was a slap in the face for the Mendelssohn parents; each of their children in turn would make them realize that conversion was not their problem and that they were not going to call themselves Bartholdy. If Wilhelm had converted, Fanny might have followed his example; for all we know, she may have wished to do so. Of course, her decision "to obtain information about the Church" rather than to await a celestial revelation was not an auspicious step toward the irrational; Fanny sets off very badly down the path of blind faith. But her attitude is typical of her generation's Romanticism: the well-behaved young girl who is nevertheless determined to die, or something of the sort, for her love. Even her youth lends her a Romantic air; did not Novalis fall in love with his first fiancée, Sophie von Kühn, when she was only twelve? Sophie died at the age of fifteen; Fanny will not take Romanticism that far. She was, however, a virtuoso, with all the miraculous abilities this implied, and with the growing aura that the nineteenth century was to confer upon that aspect of music. She was a child prodigy, and that term alone could turn a Romantic head; she was also incredibly intelligent and cultivated. Even her ugliness may have made her tragically interesting, for her looks were improved by her magnificent eyes, and painters, it would seem, attach much importance to the eyes.

At the same time, Fanny must have felt that she was reaching a crossroads in her life. At fifteen, a musician of her caliber reaches a certain stage, must either begin a career or mark time—perhaps even regress. Everyone around her intended her to marry, and the differences in the way she and her brother were treated were becoming ever more apparent. One liberty remained to her, even if it was rather an uncertain one: the choice of a husband. She therefore chose someone as unlike Felix and their own milieu as could possibly be imagined. Wilhelm and Fanny differed in almost all respects. When their son Sebastian came to write the Mendelssohn family memoirs, he was still astonished at being the offspring of such a union. But Fanny had already experienced identity with her brother, and knew that the woman is the loser in such pairings; quite possibly she was eager to love and live with an entirely different type of partner. Wilhelm was utterly incapable of distinguishing a major third from a minor one and could not have sung in tune had his life depended on it; he was certainly a sensitive man, but had no ear for music.

The self-portraits of Wilhelm Hensel[15] depict a handsome blond man with pale-colored eyes; one of them shows him sporting a military moustache. Physically, he was the antithesis of Fanny. According to Theodor Fontane:

[Wilhelm] perfectly exemplified that type of man from the March of which old Schadow was the most eminent representative. Theirs were natures that could be considered amphibious, like an amalgam of crudeness and beauty, of spats and togas, of Prussian militarism and classical idealism. Their souls were Greek, their minds in the tradition of Old Fritz,[16] and their characters were those of natives of the March; in most cases their outward appearance corresponded to their character. . . . In Hensel's case all this was balanced out, none of these heterogeneous elements overwhelmed or took precedence over another, and a new design for the uniform of a regiment of guards or a witty remark by professor Gans interested him as keenly as the purchase of a Raphael.[17]

This description dates from 1872 and was thus written after the painter's death in 1861; it was even further removed in time from the period of his engagement. But Wilhelm's personality was not of a kind that undergoes many changes, for faithfulness was one of his dominant characteristics. Thus Fanny married a perfect model of what was later known as an Aryan: a pastor's son, a hero of the Wars of Liberation, a courageous man, self-taught, who could entertain no doubt as to the legitimacy of his place in the German-Christian world. Nor did Fanny doubt the legitimacy of her own place, acquired through intellect: it was a meeting of two opposite poles, for they were made to meet and complement each other. This certainly bore no resemblance to an arranged marriage between two beings of similar origin, wealth, character, education, and taste. Fanny and Wilhelm belonged to the nineteenth century of Romanticism, in which an aesthetic of contrasts and opposites played a greater part than in the century of reason.

Fanny and Wilhelm's engagement must have left them with rather stormy memories. The least that can be said is that Lea was not bent at all costs on finding her daughter a husband, and Wilhelm showed much worth in bearing up under the attack. Witness this letter from Lea to Wilhelm, dated 25 December 1822:

I did not want to spoil yesterday evening's enjoyment by observing to you that I find it improper for a young man to offer his portrait to a young girl, in whatever form it may take. Forgive the matronly aspect of this maternal concern, you who are a tender and respectful ladies' knight. I am returning your friend's poems so that Fanny may again receive them from you, freely and with pleasure, once the accompanying adornment has been removed.[18]

The gift in question was a collection of poems by Wilhelm Müller (1794–1827), whom Wilhelm had met at the house of one of Prince Hardenberg's colleagues, State Councilor Friedrich von Staegemann

(1763–1840).[19] Friends such as Wilhelm and Luise Hensel, Wilhelm Müller, and Clemens Brentano used to gather at the councilor's home with his wife and daughter, the future Hedwig von Olfers. It was there that the cycle of poems *Die schöne Müllerin* originated, in the form of a drawing-room comedy, with Wilhelm playing the miller. Since conversation did not sanction political—thus critical—digressions, a bucolic tone was introduced.

The volume of poems offered Fanny contained Wilhelm Müller's *Waldhornistenlieder* (Songs of the Hunting-Horn Player). Wilhelm Hensel had drawn his own portrait on the title page, immediately beneath that of the poet. Under the title *Seventy-six Poems*, the painter had written another poem, "To Fanny":

> Sei Dir denn zugeeignet
> Was es enthält in sich.
> Und zum Beweis hab'ich
> Mich selber unterzeichnet.

> (Let what this contains
> Be dedicated to you.
> As proof of which
> I've drawn myself below.)

As a specialist in literary puns, Wilhelm had not been able to restrain himself. Through *hab' ich mich selber unterzeichnet*, Wilhelm wants Fanny to understand that he has not only "drawn himself below," *unterzeichnet*, but "signed below," also a meaning of *unterzeichnet*. Thus he added his own name to the love poems the volume contained, in order to readdress them to Fanny. Lea was no fool and grasped this at once. We do not know if the scene Wilhelm describes in his letter to Luise had already taken place, but we may suppose that the young man had asked for Fanny's hand before offering her these poems—anything else would have been most inappropriate. Accepting a portrait was the equivalent of an amorous commitment. Anyone could have opened the volume and guessed the engagement—or else been scandalized.

Fanny plays a key role here. Everyone gravitated round her, projecting their wishes onto her and asking for her love, and yet both Lea and Wilhelm were astonished when she screamed out a need to express herself. Fortunately, she still had her music. She wrote several lieder to texts by Wilhelm Müller—an entirely proper occupation. Wilhelm drew and Fanny composed: verbal communication was only permitted them sparingly.

It was understood that Fanny would not marry for money. By the same token, Wilhelm had to earn money to provide for a future marriage, partly because this was the established custom, and partly to avoid false ideas about his motivation. The Mendelssohn parents never suspected Wilhelm of venality, but the opinion of society did hold some importance for them—especially for Lea, as her future son-in-law points out—and since Fanny was not reputed to be beautiful, they wanted to be able to affirm that Wilhelm was not marrying her for the material comfort she could bring him. Yet Lea Salomon's children were no longer rich enough to live from the interest on their capital; that, at least, is what she later wrote to Wilhelm when he was in Italy.[20]

Wilhelm did eventually leave for Italy. A grant for this journey had been given to him in 1820 by von Altenstein, minister of public instruction and worship, who entrusted him with the task of copying works of art of educational value for the Academy of Fine Arts. His meeting with Fanny delayed his travel plans just as it disturbed his plans to convert. Necessity prevailed. Wilhelm departed in the autumn of 1823, passing through Vienna before arriving in Rome.[21] It was probably in the autumn of 1824, while visiting Schinkel in Rome—Schinkel had already involved Wilhelm in the reconstruction of the Berlin Schauspielhaus—that the young painter was officially commissioned to make a copy of Raphael's *Transfiguration*. According to the account Schinkel gave Minister von Altenstein, "Wilhelm is becoming a new man here; his work is acquiring style and he is losing both his sugary quality and his churchiness." Apparently the Catholic affectations of Berlin were losing their meaning for Wilhelm in the context of a Catholic country.

When Jacob Bartholdy died in 1825 Wilhelm took charge of his affairs, thus rendering the Mendelssohns a great service. In return they paid him an honorarium, besides the financial aid they were giving him. He even proposed transferring the Nazarene frescoes from the Casa Bartholdy to their new dwelling at 3 Leipziger Strasse, but the Mendelssohns found the undertaking too onerous and ostentatious. They kept up a correspondence, principally through Lea, but as far as can be determined no letters were exchanged between Fanny and

Wilhelm. This made Wilhelm so furious and bitter that Lea felt obliged to answer in these terms:

Seriously, dear Mr. Hensel, you cannot really be annoyed that I refuse to authorize an exchange of letters between Fanny and yourself. Have the fairness to put yourself in a mother's position, if only for a moment, and to substitute my interest for yours, instead of addressing me in the most barbarous terms, in your transports: my refusal will then seem natural, fair, and reasonable to you. For the same reason I could not give you my promise, I declare myself firmly and irrevocably opposed to any correspondence. You know that I feel true affection and esteem for you, and that I have nothing against you personally. The reasons which have thus far prevented me from making a decision in your favor are as follows: the disparity between your ages and the uncertainty of your position. A man should not consider marriage until his condition is relatively assured; at the very least, he should not address reproaches to the young girl's parents, who are by nature fitted to consider both him and her, for they possess experience, reason, and composure. The solitary artist is a happy man, for all circles are open to him, he is encouraged by the favor of the court, and the everyday worries of a difficult life are blotted out; he surmounts with cheerfulness and ease the social barriers that different ranks erect; he works as much as he pleases on subjects of his choosing, and makes art his favorite pursuit and principal enjoyment in life; he is the happiest and most joyful being in creation, poetically transported into other spheres! But as soon as familial and material worries seize hold of him all this magic vanishes; he has to work to support his family; the bright delightful colors fade.

I am resolved to raise my children in simple and modest circumstances so as not to oblige them to marry for money, but in parents' eyes a secure means of subsistence and a regular if modest income are indispensable conditions for a life without anxiety, and even if my husband can give a handsome sum to each of his children, he is not sufficiently wealthy to assure their entire future. Your career is beginning promisingly; live up to this promise, make the best use of time and favor, and rest assured that we shall not be opposed to you as soon as you have finished your studies, reached a comfortable situation, and given proof of your mettle. . . . Fanny is very young and, heaven be praised, entirely innocent and free of passion until now. You have no right to engage her in a destructive sentiment and to envelop her, by means of love letters, in an atmosphere quite foreign to her which would cause her to languish, impatient and preoccupied, for several years when at the present time she is blooming healthily, cheerful and free, beneath my gaze.[22]

Free? Everything is relative. Fanny was certainly not free to express her feelings. As for Lea, she was a snob. Her letter nonetheless suggests that the Mendelssohn parents were convinced Wilhelm would not convert. How did they know? Perhaps they had received a favorable report from Schinkel? Or had Wilhelm himself told them? Lea could thus address him an adjusted promise: the only obstacle was Wilhelm's financial position. Lea's wish not to turn Fanny into a mooning dimwit squares well with the solid education lavished upon her; if Fanny began to daydream, it would exclude her from the family circle. This does Lea credit, and shows how privileged Fanny was compared to her contemporaries.[23] Through their intellectual functioning the Mendelssohn parents, still strangers to the Romantic cult of irrational romantic emotion, show themselves heirs of the eighteenth century, even if their morality and concern with public opinion betray their adherence to the nineteenth century.

Throughout this episode Fanny seldom expresses herself, but when she does she is effective and eventually gets her way. Wilhelm appears no less obstinate. If he cannot write to Fanny, he can draw. He is careful not to send Fanny his self-portrait again, but he sends the entire family idealized portraits of Fanny and of her brothers and sister, to Lea's great delight. In particular Lea compliments him on his admiration for Raphael, the absolute painterly ideal in the Mendelssohn family.

CHAPTER EIGHT

Goethe

When Fanny met Wilhelm Hensel in January 1821, she was just fifteen. If, immediately or gradually, her choice settled on him, it was partly because she had no prospects in her life other than matrimony. Unlike Clara Wieck, whose father disapproved of marriage, Fanny's family circle intended her to wed. Abraham's letters indicate that he did all he could to interrupt her musical élan. Lea was more subtle: she did not want to see her daughter acquire a "feminine" sentimentality, and was determined she should keep her intellectual autonomy. While Abraham's letters sought to discourage Fanny, the treatment accorded Felix must have made her feel, more keenly than any words, that she was only a girl.

Felix's destiny was taking shape while the advantages of being the first-born were growing steadily dimmer. In 1821 the small boy was twelve, showed exceptional ability in everything, and played so well that his teacher Zelter decided to introduce him to God's representative in Germany, the poet Johann Wolfgang von Goethe.

It was not without much hesitation that the Mendelssohn parents envisaged a musical career for Felix: had he been less of a genius, they would have sent him to work in a bank or a university lecture hall. If Jacob Bartholdy was energetically opposed to Felix's embracing an artistic career, his own parents were none too sure themselves of the future social status of their boy.

Before Napoleon's arrival in 1806, when Prussian society could still be termed feudal, the distinction between amateurs and professionals meant nothing as far as the artistic value of musicians was concerned. Concerts had not assumed their present-day importance, and the relationship between a concert artist and his listener was a relationship of teacher and student. If the students belonged to a privileged social class, they could become remarkable, even creative, musicians, as did Sara Levy, Friedrich II, Princess Amalia, or Prince Louis-Ferdinand of Prussia. This was in no way prejudicial to their social role, and whether they were men or women had not the slightest importance. They could give concerts but not teach, for a professor is paid money. The professional musician, however, who generally came from a family of musicians (Bach or Couperin, for example) earned only a small amount of money, or even none at all, by giving concerts; playing was included in his functions. It was under these conditions that Carl Philipp Emanuel Bach accompanied Friedrich II and that Johann Sebastian, employed by the town of Leipzig, played the organ at Saint Thomas's Church.

The abolition of feudal privilege changed the status of musicians, who were no longer employed to give lessons to a prince. Henceforth they were obliged to dispense their knowledge more widely, and schools were formed—for example, the Paris Conservatory in 1795. In Prussia, Zelter worked to renew the educational system,[1] creating schools in Königsberg, Breslau, and Berlin. The music teacher gradually acquired a more bourgeois aspect, and concert performers of humble extraction were also allowed to teach. But what about the Mendelssohns?

To permit and even encourage his elder son to lead a musical career showed either great broadmindedness in Abraham, or an ambition that was unusual in his milieu. Hector Berlioz was far less lucky in his father. Posterity has never forgiven Felix Mendelssohn either his money or his social sphere and has unjustly classed him with the dilettantes; yet he was simply marking the beginning of a new era. From the nineteenth century on, a majority of professional musicians have belonged to the middle classes in all countries.

Nevertheless, Abraham hesitated and went to consult the most influential persons of the cultural world to convince himself that "public opinion" was indeed on his side. Since it was difficult to go and interrogate Johann Sebastian Bach about Felix's talent, the Mendelssohns did the next best thing and turned to that other father-figure of German culture, Johann Wolfgang von Goethe (1749–1832). Even during his lifetime Goethe took himself for a god, and did nothing to discourage the cult forming round his name. Hannah Arendt relates how Rahel Varnhagen clung to her role as priestess of Goethe to uphold her cultural identity—she who suffered more than anyone from her Judaism and conversion. The Mendelssohns were far better protected than she was, by virtue of their fortune and the aura of their name. They were asking Goethe for nothing other than his opinion of Felix's talent.

This visit to the poet constituted the first extraordinary event in the young boy's life, the first memorable encouragement. Zelter gave this opportunity to Felix alone. This was also the first time that young Fanny was faced with real discrimination, with flagrant injustice. Zelter took his daughter Doris too, but not for one second was there any question of taking Fanny, who in any case demanded nothing and manifested no jealousy. She was only sixteen, but Abraham had already almost succeeded in breaking her spirit.

During this journey Felix and Fanny began a correspondence that would continue throughout their lives. Marcia Citron records 279 letters from Fanny to Felix, while Rudolf Elvers enumerates more than nine hundred from Felix to his family.[2] The two young people acquired very early on this habit of communicating, which was well-suited to their literary education. Letters of that time had to be carefully written; they were passed from hand to hand, and whoever wrote them knew that the more polished they were, the more they would circulate, not only among the family but also in the town. This was especially true of Felix, for whom every detail was supervised by those around him. Fanny's letters could afford to be more familiar; they were less likely to be criticized. Furthermore Fanny had a long lead in the epistolary domain, just as she had had in music, having already undergone the ordeal by fire with her father when he was in Paris the previous year—not to mention her regular correspondence with her uncles and aunts.[3]

As soon as Felix had left, Fanny fell ill—what a coincidence—and took up her pen:

Berlin, 29 October 1821
I miss you from morning till night, my dear son! and the music especially will not flow without you. Many thanks to friend Begas for having painted your

little face upon the canvas, so naturally it seems to be living here among us.[4]

It's in the order of things that I won't get a single day ahead of you at the Academy, for since yesterday I've been so ill I cannot even think of singing; I'm coughing like a wheezy old woman. Mother is not very well either today, she has a slight cold, but nothing serious.

Is your current Minerva, your Professor Mentor, satisfied with you? I hope (now I'm going to sound like a *Hofmeister*, a major-domo) that you are behaving sensibly and that you are a credit to your *Hausmeisterin*, the mistress of your manners.[5] When you meet Goethe, I advise you to keep your eyes and ears open, and if on your return you cannot tell me every word he uttered, then our friendship will be a thing of the past. Please do not forget to make a sketch of his house, I would like one. If it's a pretty drawing and a good likeness, then you can copy it in my music book. Herr Berger came yesterday evening but I didn't see him, I had to go to bed at seven o'clock. . . .

You haven't told us anything about what kind of instrument Goethe has. Take a good look at his room, for you must give me an exact description of it. . . . In the evening, when the staircase door is opened at tea-time, we often all call out at once: "It sounds as if Felix is coming home." But stay away from us a while longer, it's better that we do without you and that you store up wonderful memories for your future life. On Tuesday another letter will arrive, and until then time will seem incredibly long, as if a whole month had gone by. . . .

I won't go to the Academy during your absence, because in spite of my entreaties the doctor is keeping me at home. My friends there are going to think I'm traveling incognito with you, and Fanny[6] came recently to make sure with her own eyes that I was really here. Adieu, my little Hamlet! Think of me on my sixteenth birthday; you'll have to take a sip of wine in secret and drink to my health, I'm relying on your conscience to do so. I'll take full responsibility for the red rash which may result. Adieu, don't forget that you're my right hand and the apple of my eye, and that without you no music flows at all.

Your faithful, coughing Fanny[7]

Since letters were only collected on certain days, people were able to spend several days writing them and even dispatch them in the form of a small diary, as the Mendelssohns particularly liked to do. In this letter Fanny displays the tenderest of sisterly feelings: she has only good wishes for her little brother. She has already assigned him her powers of observation and learning: "You're my right hand and the apple of my eye." Even before this letter arrived, Felix had written the following descriptive missive on 30 October, from Leipzig:

We left for Kemberg at three o'clock on Monday, after I had spent from 7 to 12 that morning working on my opera. I have already reached the finale, dear Fanni [sic]. . . . We went immediately to his [Dr. Chladni's] lodgings, a one-room apartment that contains his instruments, three cylinder-keyboards and a euphon. (Ask Beckchen what a euphon means.) This room is his bedroom, his studio, and his drawing room. All his tools are there, and in a small cupboard there is a euphon still being constructed. He played us all his instruments. The cylinder-keyboard sounds like a very sweet oboe. The euphon is made of glass sticks which one moistens and rubs with wet fingers; it sounds just like when one rubs a glass bell with one's fingers. You can very well imagine how this instrument sounds, dear Fanny. Then we went to our "feather-beds" and slept—very badly. Professor Zelter complained about the smallness of the bed, Doris about the things populating it, and I complained about the disagreeable feathers. When it was not yet light I felt a hand grasp me gently and draw back my covers. It was the Herr Professor. I asked if he needed anything, if I could fetch him a glass of water or something else? He said, "Oh no, I dreamed you had been stolen from me and I wanted to see if you were still here!!!"[8]

Fanny was not alone in considering Felix the apple of her eye. But only with Fanny did Felix wish to share everything he saw and heard. He was most fortunate in having an opportunity to leave home and learn about the world. In Leipzig he made the acquaintance of the elderly Professor Schicht (1753–1823), one of J. S. Bach's successors as Cantor of Saint Thomas's Church. Felix played him his compositions and visited all the places in which the godlike Bach had slept, composed, lived. Felix showed Schicht the motets he had just composed, and the old musician copied them by hand. Schicht had them played in Saint Thomas's Church, an event related in the *Leipziger Zeitung* and in a letter Lea sent her cousin Henrietta Pereira. Felix also heard a Gewandhaus concert and, for the first time, Mozart's "Jupiter" Symphony played by an orchestra.[9] Perhaps Felix was able to convey to his elder sister what he had learned from old Schicht, but surely there could be no substitute for the benefits that direct experience conferred upon the young traveler. It was at this juncture that Fanny began to lose the advantage she had gained from being three and a half years older than her brother.

She nonetheless continued to play her role as teacher:

Berlin, 6 November 1821

I had intended, my dear son, to write you a long and detailed letter today, but as Father said yesterday, man proposes and the cough disposes. This unwelcome guest has so tormented me for several days that I feel the victim of a violent aggression and cannot do much of anything at all. Just imagine, I haven't played the piano for three days! I cannot, however, refrain from praising your two lovely letters. They were both well-conceived and well-expressed[10] (which was not usually your strong point), and were therefore especially welcome and pleasing.

It's good that you immediately left for Weimar instead of waiting for the festivities at Wittenberg; that gains you some time and you will certainly know how to put it to good use. I'm extremely happy that you've made such progress with your opera, but tell me if the numbers I don't know turned out well. And don't forget to tell me what you played and what met with the most success—you know it's impossible to go into too many details about such things when you're addressing a *sister*. Something of Hummel's teaching should also reach me through you, but verbally, when you get back. . . .

Since one reads in Goethe that praise and criticism should mingle, I cannot help finding fault with two things in your letter, though very unimportant ones. First of all, dear little fellow, you should have consulted the calendar you took out before your departure, and then you would have discovered that there has never been a 32 October, the date given at the end of your letter. Second, one puts the place on the *right* when beginning a letter, whereas until now you've been writing it on the left. These remarks are unimportant in themselves, you won't take them badly since you know they're kindly meant.

I had just closed my letter when *Der Freischütz* arrived. I didn't shout for joy, because I couldn't; I had to croak. If you had been here, we would have spent a pleasant hour with it, but I was all alone and incapable of singing a note, and so felt only half the pleasure. I find Seidler's aria unique, it's very fine. Yesterday they performed *Freischütz* again, it seems it went splendidly. Some news of dazzling novelty: . . . it seems Spontini is once again to be stripped of his power, and everything will go on as it did before. They say the Crown Prince is responsible for this valiant deed. . . .

I'm very curious to see the text from Vienna, which Mother told you about; a sentimental, naive opera wouldn't be so bad, if nicely done in other respects. There would certainly be some pretty cavatinas, choruses with obligatory animal bawlings, and other rarities of that kind. Joking apart, it's a genre I'm very fond of when it's skillfully written. Pails of milk, Swiss ponytails, Alpine cowbells, glaciers in the sunset, homesickness—these are musical, beloved things of which there will certainly be plenty in your new text. And Madame Robert will be charming as the lovesick shepherdess! I tell you, I'm unreservedly delighted. You can also count on Casper to be spurred on by rivalry, and to provide you with a new and very fine text. Then you'll have no further worries for a long time.

Adieu, dear boy, be glad that you're in Weimar, and breathe in Goethe's air wafting all around you. Your finale must be dated by his native city. Admit how happy you are to be living in Goethe's house for a while, and to see him in private with his friend; give the latter my regards, and dear Doris and *bestissimo*[12] Hummel, and continue to love your Fanny.[13]

Felix never found an opera libretto that suited him. He was only moderately encouraged by his childhood attempts. The censorship then dominant in theaters further impoverished texts already weakened by fashion—circumstances not destined to attract an elitist musician to opera. The opera Fanny mentions was in fact a *singspiel, Die beiden Pädagogen* (The Two Pedagogues). It was Henriette Pereira-Arnstein—Lea's cousin and constant correspondent, the daughter of Fanny von Arnstein—who had tried to obtain a pleasing text for her little cousin, though it was not to Fanny's approval. Exceptional and cultivated women surrounded little Felix, coddling him and urging him, from earliest childhood, to push himself further; it was practically their life's work. Writing an opera seems to have been an obligatory accomplishment of a composer. The operatic world, however, was never very appealing: it was a world of intrigue and deceit. Gaspare Luigi Spontini (1774–1851),[14] an Italian musician, had been living in Paris since 1803 when King Friedrich Wilhelm III heard *La Vestale*—Spontini's one successful opera, written in 1807—while visiting that city in 1814. Filled with enthusiasm, the prince had the delighted musician come to Berlin as the general musical director of the Schauspielhaus, where he thus managed to evade numerous financial problems left behind in Paris. In Berlin Spontini nonetheless encountered a formidable opponent in Count Karl Friedrich von Brühl (1772–1837), general manager of the royal theaters in Berlin from 1815 to 1828.[15] Brühl had worked in Weimar with Goethe on productions of the ducal stages, thus becoming the champion of Weimar's German classicism. Brühl brought about a major reform of costumes and sets in Berlin, a reform both significant and costly—comparable to Talma's reforms in Paris—to make theater worthy of the *Aufklärung*. He aimed at realism in depicting both history and folklore. Brühl would have liked Carl Maria von Weber (1786–1826) to be appointed in Spontini's place, and the success of the first performance of *Der Freischütz* at the Schauspielhaus on 18 June 1821 seemed to justify his preference. *Der Freischütz* was the ideal model for German national opera, the work in which nascent pan-Germanism and the idealism of German youth were most apparent. It is clear that the young Mendelssohns identified with this movement, although their teacher Zelter was far less enthusiastic. However, Spontini remained at his post until 1841. The crown prince, later Friedrich Wilhelm IV, embodied the hopes of German youth—until he completely disappointed them. The *Freischütz* editions mentioned by Fanny were vocal scores, published a few months after the premiere; "Seidler" was Caroline Seidler (1790–after 1860), a singer who joined the Berlin Royal Opera in 1816 and sang the role of Agatha ninety-one times before leaving in 1836. Even if Weber was never to assume the importance of Bach or Beethoven for the Mendelssohns, he would mark a significant stage in their development.

Just as Fanny unconsciously quotes Abraham in her letter of 6 November, Felix, in a letter written that same day, makes a joke on the same proverb, *Der Mensch denkt und Gott lenkt* (see note 10):

Weimar, 6 November 1821

Man proposes, the pen disposes. Just as I was wanting to write and scold you for the laziness of your pens, a fine, fine letter arrived which greatly cheered the old "chick." Paul, your face is very handsome and I could draw you one of my "happy" faces too, but instead I will show you them *in natura* in Berlin. Now listen, boys and girls. Today it is Tuesday. On Sunday the sun of Weimar arrived, Göthe [sic]. In the morning we went to church where they performed half the 100th psalm by Handel. The organ is large, though rather weak; the organ of Saint Mary's is more powerful, though smaller. The one here has 50 registers, 44 voices, and one 32-foot stop. I then wrote you the short letter of 4 November and set off toward the "Elephant," where I sketched the house of Lucas Cranach. Two hours later Professor Zelter arrived—Göthe is there, the old Gentleman is there! We immediately went down the stairs to go to Göthe's house. He was in the garden, and appeared from behind a shrub; isn't it odd, dear Father, that the same thing happened to you. He is very friendly, but I don't think any of his portraits look like him. He was examining his interesting collection of stones, which his son had arranged, and kept saying, "Hm, hm, I'm very satisfied." Then I walked in the garden for half an hour with him and Professor Zelter. Then we sat down to eat. He doesn't look 73; more like 50. After the meal Miss Ulrike, Frau von Göthe's sister, asked him for a kiss and

I did the same. Every morning I receive a kiss from the author of *Faust* and *Werther* and two kisses in the afternoon, from father and friend Göthe. Think of that! . . . In the afternoon I played for Göthe for more than two hours, Bach fugues and improvisations. In the evening we play whist and Professor Zelter, who also played to start with, declared: whist means you must shut up. Powerfully expressed! That evening we all ate together, even Göthe, who otherwise never eats at night. Now, my dear coughing Fanny! Yesterday morning I brought your lieder to Frau von Göthe, who has a pretty voice. She will sing them to the old gentleman. I've already told him that you were the one who composed them, and asked if he would like to hear them. He said, yes, yes, with pleasure. Frau von Göthe is particularly fond of them. That is a good sign. He is to hear them today or tomorrow.[16]

In acquainting Goethe with Fanny's songs, Felix proves himself a very nice brother. Frau von Goethe, the poet's daughter-in-law, sang several songs for him including *Erster Verlust*[17] (First Sorrow) so convincingly that the delighted Goethe wrote Fanny a poem and gave it to Zelter, saying *Gib das dem lieben Kinde* (Give that to the dear child):

An die Entfernte

Wenn ich mir in stiller Seele
    Singe leise Lieder vor:
Wie ich fühle, dass sie fehle,
    Die ich einzig auserkor.

Möcht' ich hoffen, dass sie sänge
    Was ich ihr so gern vertraut;
Ach! aus dieser Brust und Enge
    Drängen frohe Lieder laut.[18]

To the Distant Girl

When in my tranquil soul
    I softly sing songs to myself:
How deeply I do feel her absence,
    for I have chosen her alone.

If I could hope that she would sing
    what I so willingly entrust to her;
Ah! from this constricted heart
    joyful songs would tumble forth.

Sebastian Hensel quotes the poem in a footnote, while describing Felix's visit to Goethe. And that is how, until quite recently, Fanny was always mentioned: in parentheses. It must have been obvious that she could hope for nothing better in this world. Why else would she not immediately set the poem to music? Instead, however, she composed another version of *Erster Verlust*.[19] Was this a form of protest?

In the meantime, young Felix continued to enjoy his unforgettable experiences:

Weimar, 10 November 1821
On Monday I went to Madame von Henkel's house and also visited His Royal Highness, heir to the Grand Duchy, who was very pleased with my Sonata in G Minor. On Wednesday afternoon there was a performance of Wranitzky's *Oberon*, a very pleasant opera. On Thursday morning the Grand Duchess, the Princess, and the heir to the grand Duchy came to our house, and I had to play for them. I played from 11 in the morning until ten o'clock at night, with two hours' interruption; Hummel's Fantasy concluded the program. When I went to visit Hummel recently, I played him my Sonata in G Minor which he liked very much, as he did the piece for Begasse and for you, my dear Fanny. I play far more here than I do at home, seldom for less than four hours, often for six and sometimes as many as eight hours. Every afternoon Goethe opens his Streicher and says: "I haven't heard you yet today, play something for me." He sits down beside me and when I've finished (I improvise most of the time), I ask him for a kiss or else give him one. You cannot imagine how kind and gracious he is, any more than you can conceive the wealth this polar star of poets owns in terms of minerals, busts, engravings, statuettes, large drawings, and so on. I don't find him imposing in build, he's no taller than father. But his bearing, language, name—those things are imposing. His voice is incredibly sonorous, he can shout like ten thousand soldiers. His hair is not yet grey, his gait is firm, his speech gentle. On Tuesday Professor Zelter wanted to take us to Jena and thence immediately to Leipzig. . . . (There's a singer in the theater here, Fanny, who is only fourteen; she recently sang a pure, strong and free D in *Oberon* and she can sing an F.) On Sunday evening Adele Schoppenhauer (the daughter) was at our house and once again, contrary to his habit, Goethe stayed all evening. The conversation turned to our departure and Adele decided we should all fling ourselves at Professor Zelter's feet and beg him to let us stay a few days longer. We dragged him into the room and then Goethe began scolding him in a thunderous voice for wanting to take us to a boring old place; he ordered him to keep quiet and obey without a word, to leave us here and go to Jena by himself and then come back. He was so convincing

that the professor agreed to all Goethe's wishes—at which Goethe was assailed on all sides, we kissed his mouth and hands, and anyone who couldn't get near enough stroked him and kissed his shoulders. Had he not already been at home, we would have taken him there, as the Romans escorted Cicero home after his first Catiline oration. Besides, Fräulein Ulrike had also thrown her arms round him and since he's courting her (she's very pretty), all these things together obtained a positive result.

On Monday at 11 there was a concert at Frau von Henkel's house. When Goethe says to me, little one, some people are coming tomorrow at 11, you must play something too, I can't say no, can I![20]

This letter duly made the rounds of friends and acquaintances. Henriette Mendelssohn sent it back with expressions of boundless admiration. What a source of pride it was to have such a budding artist in the family: what generosity, what talent the boy exhibits when he writes! Sanctified by the poet, Felix took pride of place, and thereafter Fanny withdrew definitively into her brother's shadow.

In Weimar, Felix took lessons from the court Kapellmeister Johann Nepomuk Hummel (1778–1837), whom the Mendelssohn family had previously met in Berlin. Hummel thought Felix had made progress since that spring and gave him good advice—the same advice that Fanny wanted to hear about in detail.[21]

Fanny met Goethe the following year, with all her family, while returning from a long trip to Switzerland. Felix was the only topic of discussion, for he had become the center of the group, and the important matter of his destiny was being determined. Sebastian Hensel wrote:

Goethe never tired of hearing Felix when he sat down at the piano and spoke almost entirely of Felix with his father. One day, when he had been angry about something, he himself told Felix: "I am Saul and you are my David; when I'm sad and somber, you come to me and I am cheered by your playing!" One evening he asked Felix to play him the Bach fugue which young Frau von Goethe indicated. Felix did not know it by heart, he only knew its theme, which he developed in a long fugal movement. Goethe was delighted, went up to Felix's mother, took her hands warmly and exclaimed: "This is a sublime child, a jewel! Send him back to me soon, so that I can replenish myself from him."[22]

On the subject of his mother, Sebastian wrote not a word.

Happily for us, Lea wrote to her cousin Henrietta Pereira that Goethe "was very pleasant and friendly with Fanny too; she had to play Bach to him often, and he was extraordinarily pleased with the lieder she had composed to his poems: it always gladdens him to see his work set to music."[23] When Goethe wrote to Felix to thank him for the dedication of his Piano Quartet in B Minor, he finished his letter with these words: *Empfiehl mir den würdigen Eltern, der gleichbegabten Schwester und dem vortrefflichen Meister* (Please remember me to your worthy parents, your equally gifted sister, and your remarkable professor.) That Goethe should join in the consensus shows that Fanny was powerless to express any idea of revolt or injustice: it was as if she had no word for that.

Yet Goethe's approval was not guaranteed in advance. Thus, in 1823, Wilhelm Hensel came to grief, or very nearly, when he met the great man. Zelter had recommended him in these terms: "This young man is leaving for Italy and does not wish to leave his fatherland without having set eyes on you." Wilhelm attempted a portrait of Goethe, without much success. As Felix says, none of Goethe's portraits looks like him. The poet himself affirms this in a letter to Schulz:

Herr Wolff had also expressed a desire to see my portrait painted by this talented young painter, and I was ready to grant his wish. It was, alas, a failure, and I can only explain it like this. Hensel is too accustomed to grasping a likeness in polite society and rendering it in graceful sketches, which is why he didn't pay enough attention to the contours in the present instance, thereby causing me immediate alarm. When he began executing the different parts separately an entirely different being appeared, who bore little resemblance to me. Unfortunately at this juncture Princess Hohenzollern arrived; she distracted him with numerous suggestions and pieces of advice, until even he observed his work with displeasure.[24]

Dated 1 August 1823, the portrait shows Goethe with the large babyish eyes that Wilhelm so affected.[25] The poet's opinion is even more harshly expressed in his correspondence with Zelter:

He, like others, has the beginnings of talent, but what may come of it, no one knows—not God, who is little concerned with that sort of thing—but me, for I've been observing such aberrations for more than twenty years. He, too, has become bogged down in the insipid amateurism of this age, which mistakenly tries to justify its existence by simpering over the fatherland and antiquity and debilitates itself in churchiness. . . .[26]

Fortunately the work Wilhelm did in Rome restored his judgment; fortunately, again, Schinkel's opinion balances out Goethe's. Wilhelm did not seem to possess a quality that Goethe deemed essential: a global vision of things. Felix, however, possessed it to a high degree, and so did Fanny, and this explains Goethe's benevolence toward them. But since Fanny was only allowed to embark on ambitious projects after all manner of restrictions, Wilhelm was probably the one to benefit from this quality of hers. Apart from the sorrow he felt at his wife's death, this may have been one of the reasons behind his inability to produce a great painting after 1847.

CHAPTER NINE

The Journey to Switzerland

Felix celebrated his thirteenth birthday on 3 February 1822. His childhood was thus drawing to an end, and henceforth his parents were less concerned with molding his character than with showing him the world. Abraham had given up banking to devote himself to his children. Lea was going through a most difficult time: the previous year, in July 1821, her fifth child had died at birth. She was forty-two at the time. Her resulting depression can be divined from her brother Jacob's letters and from the anxious remarks of her whole family. The ever-rational Jacob Bartholdy observed that "losing a child is simply a mishap, since there hasn't been sufficient time to grow attached to it."[1] Lea recovered, but Abraham decided his entire family needed a change of scene, and on 6 July 1822 took everyone to Switzerland.

The most visible divergence of opinion between the Mendelssohn spouses concerned travel. Lea hated to leave home, and in order to persuade her Abraham must have resorted to his most powerful argument: the children's education, for Lea attached little importance to her own well-being. From Interlaken, she wrote her sister-in-law Hinni[2] Mendelssohn: "I would, however, like to let you know, in your friendly concern, that I like this wonderland more than I could possibly say, and that it has even reconciled me with my hereditary foe, traveling—which is also my husband's hereditary sin"[3]—indicating what an event this journey was for the whole family, what a huge effort Lea made, and how necessary it was to extract her from her daily routine. The venture was unusual for the time, for traveling was costly and complicated. But the Mendelssohn Bartholdy parents neglected nothing that could form their children's minds or refine their aesthetic sense and teach them to reflect. Fanny was sixteen, Felix thirteen, Rebecka eleven, and Paul nine.

It was a luxury-class journey; besides the family, they took their tutor, Karl Heyse; a Dr. Neuburg; and some servants. At Frankfurt-am-Main two especially charming young women, Julie and Marianne Saaling, joined the group. Sebastian Hensel does not indicate the number of carriages needed, but the Mendelssohn Bartholdys could certainly not avoid appearing rich, even if Lea did try to raise her children unpretentiously. Entranced, Henriette Mendelssohn[4] wrote to her from Paris: "You're not traveling like Bohemians, but in the style of princes who are also artists and poets!"[5]

The trip's first incident occurred when Felix was left behind at Potsdam, everyone thinking he was in a different coach. His absence was eventually noticed at Grosskreuz, the first stop after Potsdam, three miles further on, and Heyse rushed off to find him. Everyone prepared for a long wait of maybe four or five hours, and must have recalled that a similar accident had befallen little Paul when he was four, on the way back from Paris. Traveling with children was anything but simple. It was a fine sunny day, however, and young Felix had set off toward Brandenburg for a long and dusty walk. He had found a little peasant girl to go with him; the two children had cut themselves walking sticks and were marching along boldly when Heyse found them, a mile from Grosskreuz. Felix had not grown tired, apparently excited by the adventure and by the Romantic dream of the *fahrende Geselle*, the "wandering companion." His attitude would have been deemed reprehensible in a girl, unless she was a peasant: *Geselle* cannot apply to women, and has no feminine form. The stray youth's family had only to wait an hour before seeing him return, and everyone was so relieved that Felix escaped reprimand.

The journey continued toward Magdeburg, the Harz, Göttingen, and Kassel, where, thanks to a letter of introduction from Zelter, Felix met Louis Spohr (1784–1859) and played his new piano quartet in the composer's house.

In Frankfurt they saw the musician Aloys Schmitt, who had given the young Mendelssohns lessons during his visits to Berlin. Schmitt made them take part in one of his musical matinées,[6] causing Fanny very mixed emotions:

I had the most nostalgic thoughts of Henning, Rietz, Kelch, Eysold, etc. You cannot imagine how all these good people grated on our ears. First we heard a violinist from Paris named Fémy, a student of Baillot with a big reputation. To tell you the truth, I didn't like him at all. His playing was all limp, watery, and confused, with no sonority, no forceful bowing, no strength. Felix thought so too. Next they accompanied poor Felix's quartet. My sole pleasure consisted in examining the features of those present. Then I had to play something, and don't ask me to talk about that, tell me to be quiet instead.[7] The room was full of Schmitt's friends and pupils, people totally unknown to me; I accompanied very badly and was trembling in every limb! I was so unsettled I could have given myself and everybody else a thrashing, in my rage. To make a fool of myself in front of twenty other pianists! I'll drop the subject, otherwise I'll fly into a rage again. Fémy then performed another quartet and in conclusion Schmitt's youngest brother played some variations he'd composed. Schmitt has collected some fine students in his school: young Eliot from Strelitz was there too, and also Ferdinand Hiller, his favorite pupil, a handsome boy of nine with a free and open countenance.[8]

Ferdinand Hiller, another child prodigy, remained a friend and colleague of Felix Mendelssohn Bartholdy throughout his life. In 1840 he took part in a historic concert in Leipzig in which Franz Liszt, Felix, and Hiller played Bach's concerto for three pianos.[9] He mentions this matinée at Aloys Schmitt's in his memoirs of Felix Mendelssohn Bartholdy: "What impressed me even more than Felix's performance of one of his quartets (I think it was the one in C minor) was the performance given by his sister Fanny, who played Hummel's celebrated Rondo brillant in A Major with true virtuosity."[10] Which goes to show that artists' judgments of themselves should be viewed with caution. On the other hand, Felix and Fanny's aesthetic judgment seems definitively formed at this point. They knew what they did and did not like: they belonged to a school that contravened contemporary fashions and illusions. As a composer, Felix Mendelssohn willingly followed in the direction taken by history, making a thorough study of preceding masters and consciously situating himself in the loftiest and most refined current of western musical tradition.[11]

He took very seriously his responsibilities as a musician toward composers both living and dead, which meant he had to fight some hard battles; he was much pained by mediocrity and by what Goethe referred to as "amateurism," which he encountered on all sides. He would not allow his sister to live through similar afflictions. In Frankfurt in 1822, however, the Mendelssohn family had but one opinion: they despised the Parisian violinist's affectation and his wimpy bowing!

The journey continued through Darmstadt, Stuttgart, and then Schaffhausen. After Zurich, the Mendelssohns followed a most whimsical itinerary: after all, it was a pleasure trip, and they had plenty of time and money. On the way from Vevey to Lago Maggiore, they detoured through Chamonix before returning to Germany. "They say no one has ever planned a journey in this manner," wrote Fanny proudly from Frankfurt. The Mendelssohn family and its retinue visited the Rigi, the valley of the Reuss, Interlaken, Berne, and Vevey and went through Chamonix before returning to Lago Maggiore and the Borromean Islands via the Simplon pass. In October they were back in Berlin.

Fanny was bursting with enthusiasm during the entire journey. She did not miss a single excursion, and Felix wrote: "Fanny scrambles about too, and when she can't reach something on her own feet, she uses the horses and the porters."[12] Like Felix, Fanny addressed laudatory missives to their friends and relatives: Zelter, Marianne Mendelssohn[13] and her mother Hinni in Berlin, and Henriette Mendelssohn in Paris. One feels in these letters that the mountainous landscapes have not been rendered banal, that the precise descriptions of valleys, gorges, peaks, glaciers, sunrises, shepherd's horns, and Alpine bells were courtesies owed to the letter's recipient, who had probably never seen and probably never would see landscapes of that kind. These landscapes had a most romantic effect on Fanny, as if she saw in them a confirmation of her own impassioned character. Indeed, her love of Italy—the *Sehnsucht nach Italien*—was a typically Romantic emotion. From the Saint Gotthard pass, she wrote to her cousin Marianne:

I spent a day, Marianne, a day I'll keep forever in my heart, and will remember with emotion for a long time to come. I entered God's great Nature, my heart trembled with terror and respect; I grew calm again and was observing, on the Italian border, the finest, most gracious, and pleasant scene that man can imagine when destiny cried out to me: so far, and no further! Never, ever have I felt such gratitude toward God, who allowed me to experience this day; such yearning for what was hidden by the mountains; such strong resolve forming in my heart; the combination of these feelings made me shed warm and beneficial tears. I didn't want to write to you yesterday as you don't like me to be too violently emotional. I was impassioned, but I kept my exaltation to myself; I wanted to wait until I felt calmer, but even now my heart swells at the memories of yesterday and this morning, and leaves me no rest. I shall try to give you as orderly a description as I can of everything I saw and experienced.

Yesterday morning at seven o'clock we left Altdorf under a rather cloudy sky and traveled toward clearer skies, toward the South. Leaving Bürglen and the valley of the Schächen on the left, we arrived in the valley of the Reuss, which is flanked by tall cliffs, broad and quite fertile, with walnut trees, other kinds of fruit trees, and pine trees of extraordinary beauty. The road passes near a tower of Gessler and some ancient fortifications of Zwing Uri. On the left are the glaciers of Surenen, Windgalle, Bristenstock, and other snowy mountains and glaciers. Magnificent pastures can be seen on the nearer mountains. Thus, after passing through a perpetually changing landscape, one reaches Amstag, three hours away from Altdorf, at the foot of the Gotthard. That is where the new Gotthard road begins, which can be traveled by carriages for two hours on this side, as far as Wasen; it has been completed on the Tessin side. The road passes through the dynamited rockface, sometimes on the right and sometimes on the left of the Reuss; it is remarkably well constructed, and supported by walls. Daring bridges thrust their arches across precipices. The titanic labor is an eternal monument to the cantons of Uri and Tessin. It's elating to see how human determination can bend the will of nature. After Wasen, the vegetation gradually disappears, the valley narrows steadily, the rocks rise ever more abruptly and the Reuss roars ever more wildly. At Göschenen, the only village on the entire way, the terrifying Göschenen glacier appears to the left of the Reuss; it was the first glacier we saw up close. As soon as one reaches the Schöllenen, the last signs of life and human proximity disappear. You see nothing all around you except rocks rising to the sky, between which the Reuss has carved its awe-inspiring path. Here it loses its torrential aspect and forms a continual, screaming waterfall. With every step one's horror grows, reaching a climax at the Devil's Bridge. Here you find yourself in a circus of rocks that is completely enclosed; before you the terrifying mass of water cascades down several courses, and you travel higher still along a narrow but sturdy bridge. The cutting wind that blows here at night—a glacial wind, they call it; the snowy peaks rising here and there; the dusk beginning to fall in this infernal valley— these elements all add to one's terror. A little beyond this Devil's Bridge is Uri's Hole, a rocky passage of some eighty feet: emerging from this arch, I was almost petrified by the wonder I perceived ahead. A delightful, peaceful valley with luxuriant carpets of flowers, framed by green hills and dotted with a few huts; in the background the gracious village of Andermatt, the Urseren, and on a high point a chapel whose evening bell rang in my direction; to the right the Gotthard, its summit clearly outlined in the sky; to the left the Saint Annen glacier shining with a green light amid the snow-capped mountains. To one side the Furka and its glacier, the Gotthard glacier, and the Crispalt where the Rhine originates. Gone was the savage roaring of the torrent, which flows rapidly but quietly here over the stony ground; gone was every vestige of the horror that had gripped me a moment before. Around me there was only a restful and profound tranquillity which never seemed to leave this peaceful valley. It was an unforgettable impression!

We walked a few hundred paces into the meadows to get a better view of the Annen glacier, but the cold air forced us to return. The only indications of the altitude are precisely the cold air one breathes in, and the infrequent vegetation. There are only a few conifers in the vicinity of Andermatt, but the ground is covered with luxuriant meadows. What one does not see affects the soul no less than one's visible surroundings—the idea of the country that lies behind these mountains, yes, the tangible proximity of Italy, the mere fact that the people of the region have all been to Italy, speak Italian, and greet the traveler with the gentle accents of that pleasant tongue: I found all this immensely affecting. If I had been a young lad of sixteen yesterday, my God! I would have had to fight against committing some great folly. And though on the one hand I felt impelled by a very strong desire to visit Italy, on the other hand I felt a great wish to cross the Furka and the Grimsel and see the valley of the Hasli—a simple journey for us, had we but prepared for it in advance. Throughout the day I had hoped to go back up the Gotthard in the evening, even if I went alone with Dominique (the guide), it's only three hours from the valley of the Urseren, but this wasn't possible, I had to contain myself. That evening, alone in my room, I spent an hour I shall never forget. Yesterday morning I found the departure very hard. I could not accept the idea of leaving this beautiful and pleasant valley and of turning North to that wild horror, of having to bear the torrent's deafening roar. The valley was infinitely charming in the morning light, the little Mariahilf chapel was prettily illumined, the meadows were shining in the dew, the Gotthard raised its head in the pure air; nothing could rival the tranquillity of this matinal solemnity. I cannot tell you how moved I was; and yet we had to turn our backs on all this pleasing gracefulness, return across the dreadful hole toward those savage gorges. But they, too, had lost some of their horror in the clear light of morning; in any case, they made less impression on us than the day before.

I spent part of the journey alone, silently reflecting on what I had seen, which had touched me to the bottom of my soul. From afar I heard the morning bell from the village of Göschenen, its sonority was solemn and beautiful and the glacier behind the village was flooded with the clearest sunlight. I must mention some very beautiful young girls we chatted with in Wasen. The carriage took us home through Bürglen, where we visited Tell's chapel again and the old ivy-covered tower, and where we found the cool shade of the walnut trees most refreshing after the heat. This valley is also singularly beautiful and romantic. Then with Marianne, H. Heyse, and Rebecka, I walked back to Altdorf along a beautiful path.[14]

Walking: a synonym for freedom. In *Fussreise* (Travels on Foot) the Swabian poet Eduard Moerike (1804–1875) describes the excitement and enthusiasm felt by his "dear old Adam," *mein alter, lieber Adam*. In this poem Adam is the veritable incarnation of masculine essence, and even today it is nearly unthinkable for Hugo Wolf's magnificent lied to be sung by a woman. The joy of solitary walking was a pleasure reserved exclusively for men. In *Pride and Prejudice* Elizabeth Bennett shocks the snobbish Bingley ladies and the self-important Darcy by walking across the muddy countryside to be with her ailing sister. Miss Bingley exclaims:

To walk three miles, or four miles, or five miles, or whatever it is, above her ankles in dirt, and alone, quite alone! What could she mean by it? It seems to me to show an abominable sort of conceited independence, a most country-town indifference to decorum.[15]

Peasant women were indeed allowed to walk. The middle classes either shut up their women or did not allow them to go out alone. Even when George Sand, that great and glorious exception, went roaming through the countryside, she was mainly on a horse, and it was only with Simone de Beauvoir that female walking became associated with literary nobility. For Fanny, the desire to walk across the Gotthard could be no more than a dream: "If I were a boy, I would commit follies." Lea confirms as much, writing to her sister-in-law Hinni: "It was on foot that a strong young man could get about here best, and that's why I envy Benny. Felix is thrilled with walking, and imagines he's retracing our path as a foot-soldier. Amid all these delights, Fanny bemoans the fact that the delicious food prevents her from attaining a picturesque air quite impossible here: slenderness."[16]

Unable to dream of roaming through Switzerland on foot, Fanny devoured pastries. Was it a case of bulimia? Could she have felt dissatisfied? Was that the price she paid for being a child prodigy slowly pushed into the shadows? Sharing her bedroom were two extremely entertaining young women, Julie and Marianne Saaling, the daughters of Jacob Salomon, Lea's uncle. In 1812 they had adopted the less Jewish name of Saling (or Saaling). After this trip Julie (1787–1864), who had lost an eye in childhood after a clumsily performed operation, became engaged to the tutor Karl Heyse. They were married in 1827, and three years later had a son, Paul Heyse (1830–1914), who in 1910 won a Nobel Prize for Literature. Marianne, the elder of the two (1786–1868), was famous for her beauty. After the death of her father, she lived in Vienna with her aunt Fanny von Arnstein (1758–1818), née Itzig, who was also Lea's aunt. In 1815, following her engagement to Count Marialva, the Spanish attaché in Vienna, "the beautiful Marianne" converted to Catholicism. Shortly before the wedding the count died, and Marianne returned to Berlin during the 1820s.[17]

The two sisters were very amusing and were the life and soul of any company. Julie was celebrated for her humor and never shrank from a pun; Fanny did not possess that kind of humor, she had been far too seriously brought up, and it suited neither her character of Cantor nor her role as big sister. Her own sense of humor became more evident once she left behind the rapturous emotions of adolescence and saw herself in perspective. Meanwhile, her friendship with the Saaling sisters brought new life to Fanny; with them, she played the part of the younger rather than the elder sister. As she put it:

We laugh incessantly and especially in the evening, before going to sleep (I always sleep with them), they are absolutely unique. Marianne knows people everywhere and wherever she goes is greeted with delight. . . . Our amusement knows no bounds, and if my letter is distracted and incoherent, don't blame me. Our bedroom is a nightmare![18]

Fanny, who had not been brought up to be rowdy, was becoming aware how seductive two brilliant and amusing young women could be. The Viennese salon of Fanny von Arnstein, which Marianne had recently left, descended from the tradition of Berlin salons where people discussed everything, particularly politics—even if, in Fanny von Arnstein's house, sumptuous festivities replaced the intimate atmosphere of Rahel's mansard salon. Fanny von Arnstein preached Jewish emancipation, upheld Prussian independence and pan-Germanism, refused to receive anyone French in her salon, and manifested her hatred of Napoleon in everything she did. The following generation of salons would be more intimate in the Biedermeier style,[19] more inclined to trivial amusements than politics. Although she had the same first name as her great-aunt, Fanny Mendelssohn would never really become a *salonière* in the full sense of the word: she had her own circle, and people often played and listened to music in her house, but conversation there was never an art in itself. Confronted with the conversational ease of her roommates, Fanny began to have doubts about herself and feel insecure. She confided her distress to Aunt Jette, who responded with a letter addressed to the entire family, with these words for Fanny in the middle:

My dearest Fanny, I should have written a letter just for you, your letter certainly deserved as much. But you have better things to do than to be reading me. How grateful you must be to your dear mother for agreeing to this journey, and how loving you must be to your father for having organized it. Be happy and contented, therefore, and if you cannot manage to be really funny, console yourself with this remark of Goethe's: "Life also needs somber-colored leaves in its wreath." Enjoy it fully, and be happy and free of problems, without worrying too much whether you are living life as you should. In a mind as well-prepared as yours, the real effect of such a journey makes itself felt far more slowly than the result of a thermal cure. May God keep you well and happy. I would like to have sent you an absurd dress for the journey, such as people are wearing in Paris this summer. They are actually very wide pleated shirts such as coachmen wear, and are called blouses, being decorated like blouses with colored embroidery at the neck and on the shoulders; they are quite shapeless but are held in place beneath the bosom by a leather belt. You described yourself as being so corpulent, however, that I didn't dare to send one. Fanny Sébastiani doesn't wear such a thing either, for the same reasons, for only the silhouettes of nymphs or little girls are tolerable inside them.[20]

Fanny wavered between uneasiness and excitement. The contradiction between the intellectual and artistic pursuits she'd always been exposed to and the more sober destiny to which she felt confined could only weigh upon an adolescent mind, causing her to seek solace in the pleasures of the table. A further opportunity for her to explode with enthusiasm occurred at the journey's end: after Lake Geneva, Lago Maggiore:

Today I'm writing to you (from Vevey) still in a kind of intoxication! I fancy I have never seen anything more beautiful than this land and this lake. Not only that, but the weather is divine today, and if it keeps up we shall go to the Borromean Islands tomorrow! Just imagine! The Borromean Islands! I thank heaven that the frontier is there, because if we were to go further, I think I could not bear it. It would be too much all at once for my poor human heart. If heaven continues to grant us this fair weather, we shall go on an excursion![21]

Italy! The old German dream of the country where the lemon trees bloom would only become a reality for Fanny some seventeen years later, whereas Felix was sent on educational trips to Paris, London, and Rome long before he came of age. But revolt was not a feature of Fanny's vocabulary; she was among the blessed of the earth and the most privileged of little girls. No other choice existed—as her Aunt Jette remarked—than to be grateful and loving and to compose a lied on Goethe's poem *Kennst du das Land: Sehnsucht nach Italien* (Yearning for Italy).[22]

Fanny would thus project onto her younger brother all her own hopes for the destiny that was denied her. How else could she tolerate the compliments, tolerate being told by Goethe that she was "as gifted as her brother," tolerate the doors that opened and were immediately shut? Henceforth Felix lived the life she had no right to live, and became the focus of her interest, as he did of all the family. And Wilhelm? Their affection dates from this period, and he must greatly have helped Fanny to overcome her adolescent problems. As different from the Mendelssohn family as anyone could wish, he represented a tremendous chance of escape. He made her realize she possessed a charm and destiny that were hers alone. During all their years apart, when the unjustly different treatment of the two children was taking root like a judgment of nature, Fanny knew that someone belonged to her and that she would have a means of escape.

CHAPTER TEN

Felix and Fanny

"They're really proud of each other," said Lea of Felix and Fanny. Sebastian Hensel, who quotes this remark, adds "Free of jealousy, the deep friendship between the two, brother and sister, would continue unclouded until the end of their lives."[1] Naturally, Felix adored and admired this elder sister, and with all her talent and intelligence, she was ready to make any sacrifice for him. His admiration for her would have only been normal. As for Fanny, one may well wonder if an alternative to romantic love or fraternal identification really presented itself—unless it was to smother or drown her little brother in some shady place, an alternative scarcely in keeping with the customs of the time and which, in any case, would not have changed the fact that she was female. To be the alter ego of a young man as talented as Felix Mendelssohn Bartholdy was an enviable position compared to the boredom enveloping the lives of most other girls.

Thus, in 1822, Fanny decided to become her brother's biographer. She wrote:

I have his full confidence up to this point. I've watched his talent developing step by step and have myself contributed in some way to its formation. He has no musical adviser but me, and so does not commit a single thought to paper without having previously submitted it for my perusal. That is how, for example, I knew his operas by heart, before he wrote a note of them.

She then drew up a "catalogue" of Felix's works for that year:

1) Psalm 66 for three female voices, 2) Concerto in A minor for fortepiano, 3) 2 lieder for male voices, 4) 3 lieder, 5) 3 fugues for piano, 6) Quartet for piano, violin, viola, and bass, 7) 2 symphonies for 2 violins, viola, and bass, 8) an act for the opera *The Two Nephews*, 9) Jube Domine (C major) for the Saint Cecilia of Schelbe association in Frankfurt-am-Main, 10) 1 violin concerto (for Rietz), 11) Magnificat for instruments, 12) Gloria for instruments.[2]

But neither Felix nor anyone else thought to write a biography of Fanny mentioning that in 1821 she composed a sonata in F major;[3] in January 1822 a movement for a piano sonata in E major and at least ten lieder; and between 1 and 22 November of that year her first chamber work: a quartet in A-flat major for piano, violin, viola, and cello. Felix's Quartet in C Minor would be his first published work (Opus 1), but Fanny's quartet and the sonata movement had to wait until the 1990s before being published by Furore. It would certainly have been better to ask the composer's opinion before publication, since she probably would have wanted to rework the pieces before offering them to the public. But in 1822 no one was begging or encouraging Fanny to compose, as she was doing for Felix. Quite by chance we learn from a letter Zelter sent Goethe in 1824 that "Fanny has just finished her 32nd fugue."[4] In 1826 Zelter, who had written a lied to a poem by Voss, again wrote to Goethe: "Fanny set it to music too, and since her version was really more apposite than mine, I sent it to his widow." (Zelter was referring to the poet Voss's widow.) What has become of these fugues?

Felix, on whom the hopes of the entire family rested, had no time for anything but work. When he wanted to relax, he did drawings. Seeing the quantity of manuscript paper covered with notes, as well as an opera that was almost finished, Abraham decided to initiate a series of musical matinées in his house, with singers and instrumentalists meeting there on Sundays, as they did at Zelter's home on Fridays. The cost of this undertaking is not indicated in source material, but Abraham was never stingy with culture and education—witness the journey to Switzerland. Thus Abraham engaged musicians from the Royal Chapel so that Felix could hear his compositions, become familiar with the instruments, and learn how to conduct an orchestra. With these musicians, Felix and Fanny played concertos, trios, and a large repertory for piano and diverse instruments. The singers came from the opera and deemed it an honor to perform at the Mendelssohns' home. In particular, Eduard Devrient (1801–1877)—a singer who was a pupil of Zelter— took part in numerous matinées there. He and his wife Therese—an amateur soprano, who also sang at the Sunday concerts—lived for a while in the Mendelssohn house and are the source of much information about Felix and Fanny's childhood. Therese was Fanny's friend, and Eduard was a friend of Wilhelm Hensel. The two young lovers thus confided in them, and although Devrient simultaneously denies and implies it,[5] he and his wife may even have relayed news or letters between Fanny and Wilhelm during their years apart.

Despite the admiration and astonishment Devrient felt as he observed the tiny Felix conducting musicians in his little boy's suit, he nonetheless wrote: "I found his playing extraordinarily dexterous and possessed of great musical assurance, but still it did not equal that of his older sister Fanny."[6] He drew no conclusions from this, ascertained no injustice, any more than Hiller or Goethe had done.

The *Sonntagsmusik*, or musical Sundays, attracted many people, although Bella Salomon's house on the Neue Promenade had little room for an audience. Among the visitors was the famous pianist Kalkbrenner (1788–1849), of whom Fanny noted: "He heard many of Felix's pieces, praised them with taste, and criticized them with amiable frankness. We listen to him often, and seek to learn from him."[7] Both Felix and Fanny were growing accustomed to playing before an audience, and Felix, who now traveled with his father (Abraham took his sons to Silesia in 1823), was also becoming hardened to playing outside his home. On his fifteenth birthday, 3 February 1824, rehearsals began for his opera, *The Two Nephews* (libretto by Dr. Casper). After the first rehearsal an amateur singer proposed a toast to Felix's health; Zelter took him by the hand and said, "Dear son, from this day on you are no longer an apprentice, but a colleague. I make you a colleague in the name of Mozart, of Haydn, and of the elder Bach."[8] This knightly dubbing was celebrated with many lieder and *tafellieder* typical of Zelter's taste. The enthusiasm with which Felix's opera was greeted within his family encouraged him to begin another, *Die Hochzeit des Camacho* (Camacho's Wedding), based on an episode from *Don Quixote*; as always, the entire family egged him on.

In 1824, Fanny and Felix took lessons with Ignaz Moscheles (1794–1870), known as the "prince of pianists," who was then visiting Berlin. Lea had written to him twice in November of that year, asking him to take an interest in her two eldest children.[9] Thus Moscheles had the two youngsters as pupils during that winter and spoke of them with admiration and amazement, completely taken with the family ambience:

I know of no other family like them: . . . This Felix Mendelssohn is already a mature artist, and he is only fifteen! His elder sister, Fanny, who is also infinitely talented, plays fugues and passacaglias by Bach from memory and with admirable precision; I think she may justifiably be termed "a good musician."

Moscheles attended the *Sonntagsmusik* of 28 November 1824, and made note of the program: "Quartet in C Minor by Felix, Symphony in D Major, Concerto by Bach, Fanny, Duo in D Minor for two pianos by Arnold."[10] He also heard the *Freitagsmusik* a few days later on 3 December at Zelter's house, where Fanny played the Concerto in D Minor by Johann Sebastian Bach—the master of the house having shown her the manuscript.

The autumn of 1826 saw Moscheles return to Berlin for another concert tour: he heard Felix and Fanny perform a four-handed version of the very recent *Midsummer Night's Dream* Overture, and among other works by Felix, his Sonata in E Major and Overture in C.[11] Their itinerant professional lives created solid bonds of friendship between student and professor. Moscheles was in London in 1829 when Felix made his first visit to England, and was able to give him some helpful advice. Years later, Moscheles was at Felix's bedside when he died in Leipzig in 1847. Fanny, who was confined to Berlin, had no reason to maintain such a close relationship with the pianist.

Lea invited many people to her salon, which may perhaps have made it hard for her to ascertain the character of several of her guests. Malla Montgomery-Silfverstolpe (1782–1861) was a Swedish woman living in Finland who spent the winter of 1825–1826 in Berlin. On 21 November 1825 she dined at the Mendelssohn Bartholdys' with Henriette Mendelssohn; Wilhelm von Humboldt and his wife; the two Misses Saaling; the knight, von Bremen, who was the envoy from Turin; and, she claims, many others. She found the food extremely

good and the hosts rich and generous, and gorged herself most con-
scientiously. She was fortunate enough to be invited to the Sunday
concert of 11 December and went with Marianne Mendelssohn.
Filled with curiosity, she heard an overture by Felix that she deemed
too noisy. She was further disturbed by the ugliness of Spontini, who
was sitting next to her, and therefore changed seats to hear Fanny
brilliantly perform a Beethoven concerto and a piece by J. S. Bach.
Felix's overture was played again; she thought it might have something to do with *A Midsummer Night's Dream* and liked it this time,
far more than the overture to *Camacho's Wedding*, which was performed next. She did not, however, like the people there. "When
one looks only at the face of Felix Mendelssohn, when he stands up
and conducts the music in so lively and attentive a manner, he is really
handsome and seems to belong to a far more distinguished species
than the rest of his family, but he has a Jewish, rather ordinary profile
and his head is set too close to his shoulders."[12] What an appalling
woman this must have been!

Felix continued to travel, illustrating to what extent traveling is an
obligatory part of a musician's career: through traveling one learns,
meets colleagues and masters, makes friends, exchanges ideas, becomes productive, and measures oneself against others. Each time
he passed through a city, Felix seized upon new scores and scoured
the libraries. In her *Felix Mendelssohn Bartholdy and the Music of the
Past*, Susanna Grossmann-Vendrey relates how the young composer
built upon the knowledge he had acquired through Zelter: first in
Leipzig with Schicht, then in Heidelberg with Thibault, and finally in
London through his own research.[13] Fanny, once again, stayed in
Berlin with what she had learned, and shared in the journeys through
Felix's descriptions.

But this was certainly not enough for her, and she was pawing at
the ground with eagerness when Felix again left for Paris in 1825.
Abraham had to go and fetch his sister Henriette; since Fanny Sébastiani was now the Duchesse de Choiseul-Praslin, Henriette's task was
at an end, and she wanted to return to Berlin. Abraham saw this as an
opportunity to take Felix and expose him to other opinions and a
different musical climate. Zelter had just dubbed Felix knight or colleague, and so it was time to seek further pronouncements: what, for
example, would Cherubini (1760–1842)—the terrifying director of
the famous Paris Conservatory—have to say about the young man's

possibilities? The interview went very well, and Cherubini was even heard to assert: "The boy is rich, he will do well—he's already doing well—but he's too generous with his money, he puts too much cloth into his clothes"[14]—an unheard-of compliment from so peevish a man. For his part the composer Anton Reicha (1770–1836), a student of Haydn and Albrechtsberger, was equally impressed by this very young man's abilities. Abraham could feel reassured, if he still needed to, for everyone agreed that Felix was extremely gifted.

The adolescent in question, however, was more than disappointed by Parisian musical life. He had great difficulty getting used to the fact that outside his home, he would not find the same artistic qualities as those exhibited by his family: he was used to daily conversations with his "equally talented" sister; with his mother, his grandmother, and his great-aunt—all accomplished musicians; with his sister Rebecka, who was a good singer; and his brother, who was an excellent cellist. His entire family loved working and knew how to work. When Felix was a child—even an adolescent—this attitude and these abilities were supposed to be an integral part of a healthy and well-balanced life. But from a musical point of view, Paris was nothing more than a brilliant, not terribly creative showcase. Nevertheless, the big names of 1825 were all gathered there: Sebastian refers to Hummel, Moscheles, Kalkbrenner, Pixis, Rode, Baillot, Kreuzer, Cherubini, Rossini, Paër, Meyerbeer, Plantade, and Lafont. Neither Beethoven nor Schubert set foot in Paris, where coteries, jealousies, and petty meanness sprang up among people who put their personal glory and financial interests well before music. Felix appeared disgusted by this milieu, and stupefied at its poor educational level and mediocre artistic ambitions. His letters are unmercifully critical of the entertainment and musicians, showing all a young boy's zeal and confidence.

On receiving these missives, Fanny flew into a rage. What! Her brother was lucky enough to be in Paris, to be going out every evening, to be meeting the most celebrated musicians of the time, to be seeing and hearing everything, and yet he dared complain? And complain to her, Fanny, shut up in Berlin and dying to come and see for herself what Parisian musical life was really like? Although they never came to an argument, the remarks exchanged by brother and sister were quite vehement.

In her first letters, Fanny literally bombarded Felix with questions:

she wanted to know, understand, relive everything he saw, as if she were there. The Tuileries, the museums, the walks, the visits, the people, the concerts—Felix must describe it all. Given the young man's timetable, this was no mean task. Fanny also thought her brother should make better use of the opportunity to impart information to people. "Don't Onslow and Schuhu Reicha know Beethoven's thirty-three variations on a waltz?" she asked on 4 April.[15] "Since you meet these gentlemen alone in their practice rooms, it should be an honor for you to introduce them to our great compatriot, as scholar and theoretician." Felix replied on 20 April:

You write that I should change into a missionary and teach Onslow and Reicha to love Beethoven and Sebastian Bach. That is what I'm doing anyway, for what good it does. But just consider, dear child, that people here don't know a single note of *Fidelio*, and that they think Sebastian Bach is an old wig stuffed with erudition. I played Onslow the overture to *Fidelio* on a very poor piano: he was beside himself. He scratched his brow, filled in the instrumentation in his head, ended up singing it with me, in his enthusiasm—in short, he went crazy over it. At Kalkbrenner's request I recently played the organ preludes in E and A minor[16] which people found "very sweet"; someone even observed that the beginning of the A minor prelude bore a striking resemblance to a popular duet in an opera by Montigny:[17] it made me see green and blue.[18]

Fanny again protested, on 25 April:

So there! You go to Paris and you don't hear a single decent note, at least not very many; and those of us who've stayed quietly at home are drowning in music. In one week we've had *Jessonda*, *Alceste*, *Samson*, and the *Pastoral Symphony*, for Sapupi is giving these last two pieces the day after tomorrow for his Good Friday (*Busstag*) concert.[19] What do you say to that? What seems clear to me is that your tendency toward nit-picking has developed brilliantly in Paris. My son, your letters are a web of criticism. Marx[20] will be proud of you. I hope that memory will put pink clothes on everything your prejudices are now covering with grey dust: if everything you see were really as bad as that, it would be a pity to have gone on such a journey. . . . You poor Tantalus! To think you see Rode[21] every day and hear no harmony in those spheres! . . . Oh, what fine paintings you must have seen! Why don't you write a single word about them? Or about the public gardens, or the city, or the monuments! It almost seems as if these tiresome musical evenings are killing all your capacity for enjoyment. Now, you'll like the powerful quality of ours all the better, when we attack your symphony in our big vaulted garden room; how I'm looking forward to it![22]

She continues this epistolary torrent on 30 April:

I'm happy that you finally played with a reasonable accompaniment; until now I imagined you starving in the land of milk and honey. Before I forget again, I would like to ask you a question that's been on my mind for a long time, and that I regularly forget whenever I take up my pen: why, amid all these *matinées, diners, soupers,* or other events ending in *er*, have you not played your Sextet? Is there only one person in the whole of Parisian society who can read the alto clef? Dear F., I wish you and Father had your dear mother, wife, daughters, and your own dearest sister there. When I read about your "sensible" pleasures, my mouth waters.[23]

Young Felix does not perceive the desire hidden behind these lines and behind the exclamation "You poor Tantalus!" He writes back on 9 May, almost angry this time:

I was a bit furious with your last letter and I've decided to send you the scolding you deserve. Time, that benevolent god, will soften it and pour ointment on the wounds my burning rage inflicts on you. You talk about prejudice and bias, nit-picking and grouchiness, about lands of milk and honey—as you call this Paris? Think a little, will you? Am I in Paris, or are you? Well, then I should know better than you! Do I usually judge music on the basis of prejudice?—and even if I did, is Rode being prejudiced when he tells me: *It's a musical disgrace here*! Is Neukomm being prejudiced when he declares: *This is not the land of orchestras.* Is Hertz prejudiced when he says: here, the public can't understand or appreciate anything except variations? Are 10,000 other people prejudiced when they protest about Paris! You yourself have so many prejudices that you're less inclined to believe my highly impartial accounts than the pleasing idea you've got into your head, in which you imagine Paris as an Eldorado. Look in the Constitutional: what, other than Rossini, is being played at the Italian opera? Look in the musical catalogue: what is being published, what's coming out, other than romances and medleys? Come here yourself and hear *Alceste*, come and hear *Robin des Bois*, go to a few *soirées* (which, moreover, you're confusing with salons: *soirées* are concerts you pay to attend, and salons are meetings); listen to the music of the Royal Chapel, and after that you can judge and scold me, but not now, when you're bursting with prejudices and are totally blind![24]

Fanny, of course, would have been only too delighted to go there herself.

Without a doubt, Felix was telling the truth about the musical dilettantism in Paris, and Fanny would probably have been no less critical herself. But surely he should have realized how fortunate he was. Should he not have seen that his travels were refining and enriching him and that Fanny, whose talent he recognized as being equal to his own, also had longings equal to his own, which were not being satisfied? While accompanying Henriette back to Berlin, the Mendelssohns stopped again at Weimar to visit their friend Goethe—yet another experience that Fanny would not have.

3 LEIPZIGER STRASSE

Bella Salomon died on 9 March 1824. She had divided her inheritance into three parts: one third, in the form of revenue, to her son Jacob; one third, to be divided among the children of her granddaughters, who were the children of her daughter Rebecka (Josephine Benedicks and Marianne Mendelssohn); and the remaining third was to be divided among the grandchildren of her daughter Lea, who in 1824 had obviously not yet been born! With some justification Lea wrote to her cousin Henriette von Pereira, on 24 April 1824, that she considered herself "entirely disinherited."[25] The Mendelssohn Bartholdys were thus not at all pleased at the prospect of having to buy or rent a house that could have been theirs.

According to tutor Karl Heyse, that same summer at Dobberan—a seaside resort on the Baltic—Felix and Fanny were attacked and insulted by street urchins, who called them *Judenjungen*, or "children of Jews." They had Semitic features, and with the hunched shoulder inherited from her grandfather Moses, Fanny still bore traces of the ghetto. Felix, who was fifteen at the time, managed to defend himself and his sister, but his sense of justice had been sorely tried. Heyse wrote in his diary:

Felix behaved like a man, but as soon as he got home he was unable to suppress his rage and indignation at the outrage that had been done him. That evening these feelings exploded in a flood of tears and wild accusations of every kind.[26]

In 1825 the antiliberal, antisemitic climate in Prussia induced the Mendelssohns to purchase a property that could serve as both a refuge and a world in itself. It was situated at the western end of the Friedrichstadt and a few yards from the Leipzigerplatz, formerly the Octogon. According to Sebastian Hensel, "3 Leipziger Strasse" became an expression that represented the entire Mendelssohn family.[27] The house, which had once been the palace of the von der Reck family, was in pitifully dilapidated condition, but the fairy-tale garden immediately charmed its future occupants. Incredible plans were formed to improve the building; Abraham wanted to add a fourth floor, but the prudent Lea managed to limit him to merely restoring the premises. Part of the palace would have to be rented: not to get some small return from the capital invested in so large a dwelling would clearly be impracticable. Von Reden, the envoy from Hanover, immediately proposed renting the *Beletage*, the "noble" floor, even before the repairs were complete: rarely, indeed, did one find premises that could be so favorably presented. Lea decided to occupy the greater portion of the second floor and to rent the smaller part. Thus there were only two renters, which made the property more attractive in case it had to be resold. This was how the Hanoverian diplomat Karl Klingemann (1798–1862) came to live at 3 Leipziger Strasse and became the Mendelssohn Bartholdys' closest friend. His departure for London in 1827 caused them much grief, but it did prompt the exchange of numerous letters filled with useful information. Klingemann's friendship was a great source of support for Felix during each of his trips to England.

The imposing façade protected a world of greenery and dreams. Behind the house there was a courtyard with a fountain, outbuildings, and stables, completed by what was known as the *Gartenhaus*, or garden house, a garden-facing wing of the mansion (see Figure 10). Lea spent the summer of 1825 there supervising the repairs, while Abraham was visiting Dobberan. She provided her cousin Henriette Pereira with a description of the garden that offers only a minimal reflection of the family's feelings, for they were as attached to it as if it were a living being:

When I open my door, I am completely cut off from the work site and enjoy such peace and calm I could well imagine myself in the country. A whole row of rooms opens onto the garden, which is itself surrounded by other gardens, and that is why one doesn't hear any carriages or see anyone, and why there is no dust; nevertheless, one is just a few yards from the most elegant and lively streets of Berlin, and able to take advantage of all the comforts of city life. In the middle of the garden house there is an extremely large room, large even for Berlin, with an imposing oval cupola resting on pillars. Four steps lead down to the garden, with a view of its paths and clumps of trees stretching away endlessly. In spring, when the foliage is not too thick, we catch a glimpse of a mill outside the city, and would like to keep this view open by cutting down a few trees. We shall have to add everything that embellishes a garden, for until now we have only lime trees, elms, beeches, chestnut trees, some magnificent acacias, shrubs and clearings, a large meadow, and a small farm where a farmer makes his living from twelve cows, providing us with fresh milk and butter. We would like to do some planting for the autumn, but above all improve the banks of flowers and the lawn, without detracting from the antiquity and nobility of the grounds.[28]

All this helped Lea tolerate the length and expense of the restoration, which naturally took longer and cost more than expected! She was sorry to leave the garden house and move into the wing on the street side of the house, even though it had a view of the courtyard. It was at that time rare to own so sizeable a garden in Berlin. The king had bought up all the houses that had gardens; only two others remained. City planning in Berlin was no longer conducted with the rigor and aesthetic sense of the seventeenth and eighteenth centuries; policy inclined toward profit, with no state control of rent or the price of lodgings. Trees were being cut down, the city was growing uglier, and the population becoming poorer. Until the mid-nineteenth century, the world of the Mendelssohn Bartholdys remained an eighteenth-century enclave.

The large room in the garden house was certainly an additional reason for Abraham to proceed with this purchase, despite the anxieties involved. What an ideal setting it provided for the Sunday matinées! According to Sebastian this room, which was covered with frescoes and faced the garden through glass panels, could contain several hundred people. Mendelssohn scholar Michael Cullen is more reserved: according to him, Fanny's son idealized his recollections and the room was only fourteen meters long, seven and a half meters wide, and eight meters high, and would thus have contained a much smaller audience.[29] Nevertheless, it must have been wonderful to play and listen to music in such a setting: what a luxury for Felix and

Fanny to have not only an orchestra in their home, but also a small concert hall. For Felix, this was a means of furthering his studies; for Fanny, it became a way of life and her musical destiny.

The four Mendelssohn children blossomed in this enchanting garden. Henceforth they would all have to be reckoned with, not just the two eldest: in 1825 Rebecka was fourteen and Paul almost thirteen. It had been fairly hard for Rebecka and Paul to grow up in the shadow of such siblings—Paul, indeed, never quite got over it. As Sebastian, the voice of family legend, was to write in 1879:

This was perhaps the happiest period in my grandfather's life. His condition was assured and his life established in one of the finest properties of old Berlin; he had at his side a wife he deeply loved, who was intelligent, refined, and joined to him through the faithfulness of a long union; all his children were evincing immense potential as they grew; Felix had passed the time of hesitancy and was moving steadily toward the loftiest goal a man can attain: a well-deserved artistic reputation; Fanny, although endowed at birth with equal talent, yet wished for nothing other than to stay modestly within the limits Nature has assigned to women; Rebecka was turning into a beautiful, intelligent, and highly talented young girl, whom only the exceptional gifts of her brother and sister had left slightly behind; Paul was capable and diligent, and a fine musician too; all four were healthy in body and mind, and linked by an extraordinary affection. In his house a circle of friends assembled that included the most capable and renowned men living in Berlin, together with the most promising and enthusiastic young people; his house was sought after, known, and loved by the majority of cultured society: that was how Abraham Mendelssohn lived in the year 1826.[30]

Each of them fulfilled a role, and everything went well for the female Mendelssohns as long as they were content to urge on the others. The children were certainly very attached to each other, because they had received an education that set them apart and established bonds of solidarity that would last their entire lives. Throughout their childhood they had risen at five each morning to study together. They had been subjected to the same intellectual pressures and read the same authors: Lessing, Schiller, Goethe's *Faust* and *Werther* (those two "dazzling lights," as Fanny put it), and, like everyone in their generation, Jean Paul (Johann Paul Friedrich Richter, 1763–1825, known as Jean Paul). Rebecka would later write that the four of them were at an age when young people "do not like to see themselves grow older" and "would prefer to die relatively young, as long as it did not take too long."[31] The culture their education had given them blossomed in the splendid garden, turning to poetry. During the summer months, the four young people and their friends were inspired to create charades, witticisms, games, poems, music, and disguises of every kind. A pavilion in the garden contained a constant provision of pens and reams of paper, allowing all present to express themselves and have fun by collecting the funniest and most extravagant ideas. In winter this *Gartenzeitung* or Garden Times became the *Thee- und Schneezeitung*, Tea and Snow Times. The pen-names adopted by the children indicate how merrily they took this change of identity: Fanny Cäcilia Mendbart, Rehbocka Bart, Paul per procura Bart, and Felix Ludwig Jocko Toldy.[32] For a while Rebecka went so far as to sign herself Rebecka Mendelssohn meden Bartholdy—*meden* meaning "never" in Greek.[33] Abraham noted proudly in the Times: "Until now I was known as my father's son; henceforth I shall be known as my son's father." Visiting adults such as Zelter and Alexander von Humboldt also contributed to the paper.

Inspired by the garden, Felix composed one of his masterpieces, the Octet for Strings in E-flat Major, Opus 20, written for the birthday of his friend, violinist Eduard Rietz (1802–1832). The scherzo had been suggested by a passage from *Faust* and expressed "a puff of wind in the leaves and among the reeds"; absorbed in her biographer's task, Fanny noted:[34]

And it was very well done. He confided his intentions to no one but me. The entire piece will be played staccato and pianissimo; the shivering tremulandos, the light flashes of rebounding trills—everything is new and strange, and yet so pleasing and agreeable, one feels so close to the world of spirits, so lightly borne into the breeze that one would like to seize a broomstick, the better to follow the aerial troop. At the end, the first violin flits off as light as a feather, *and everything vanishes.*[35]

One author was particularly suited to the garden, firing the children's enthusiasm and love of play-acting: Shakespeare, who had just appeared in a new translation by Ludwig Tieck and August Wilhelm Schlegel, Dorothea's brother-in-law.

"Here's a marvelous convenient place for our rehearsal. This green plot shall be our stage, this hawthorn-brake our tiring-house; and we will do it in action as we will do it before the Duke," says Quince the Carpenter to Bottom the Weaver. Of all their favorite author's comedies, the children never tired of *A Midsummer Night's Dream*. The text lent itself so well to the decor, and the decor to the text!

After the octet, the garden inspired Felix to write his famous Overture to *A Midsummer Night's Dream*—so well composed, despite his youth, that he made no changes in it when he came to write the incidental music to the *Dream*, twenty years later. Apparently a member of their circle, Adolph Bernhard Marx (1795–1866), was originally behind the work. Marx, a composer and theoretician, was also a well-known music critic of the Berlin *Allgemeine Musikalische Zeitung*. A great admirer of Beethoven, he was also an ardent champion of novel ideas concerning a new descriptive art in music. He urged Felix in the direction of his own firmly held intellectual and musical views, and a masterpiece resulted. Abraham detested Marx, doubtless on account of his ambiguous personality and unbecomingly short trousers, but above all because of his influence on Felix. Marx nonetheless helped Felix and Fanny to refine their analysis of music, with Beethoven as model.

The musical games played by brother and sister were endless and became ever more sophisticated: one would begin composing a piece the other would finish. For Fanny's birthday present, 14 November 1825, Felix gave her Beethoven's Sonata Opus 106 and wrote an accompanying letter in which he imitated the elder composer's handwriting and style. The letter shows how familiar he was with the master's personality, character, and stylistic ruffles; at the same time, it reveals Felix's penchant for playing the clown:

Most respected young lady! News of the service you have done me has redounded as far as Vienna: a fat man with moustaches and a thin one with a Parisian accent, whose names I forget, told me you induced an audience of connoisseurs to listen in a seemly manner to my concertos in E-flat and G and my Trio in B-flat. Only a few people fled, and such success might almost offend me and make me vexed with my works, but the attractiveness of your own playing forms part of this triumph and puts everything into proportion. That people should appreciate my first trios, my two first symphonies, and certain of my youthful sonatas is not extraordinary: as long as one writes music like everybody else and is young, thus mediocre and trivial, people understand and buy it—but I'm tired of that, and I've made music as Herr van Beethoven, and that is why, at my age and in the solitude of my lonely room, ideas cross my mind which are not necessarily pleasing to everyone. When I encounter people who embrace this music of mine, and thus the utmost secrets of my soul; when such persons treat the solitary old man I am in a friendly manner, they render me a service for which I am most grateful. Such people are my true friends and I don't have no others [*sic*]. On account of this friendship I am taking the liberty of sending you my Sonata in B-flat Major Opus 106, for your birthday, with my sincere congratulations. I did not create it to throw dust in people's eyes: play it only when you have sufficient time, for it needs time, it is not one of the shortest!—but I had much to say. If your friendship for me does not extend so far, ask my admirer Marx, he will analyze it for you, and the adagio, especially, will give him ample opportunity. Morever, it is a particular pleasure for me to offer a sonata written not for pianoforte but for the Hammerklavier to a lady as German as you have been described to me.

In conclusion, I am including a bad portrait of myself with this letter, being certainly the equal of other great men in this world who make presents of their portraits: I do not think myself at all a wicked fellow. Therefore keep a pleasant memory of your very devoted Beethoven.[36]

Felix certainly knew how to make Fanny laugh!

Felix no longer took lessons from Zelter, and thus Fanny no longer had a right to them. He was freeing himself from control and beginning to publish his works: three piano quartets, Opus 1, 2, and 3; a sonata for piano and violin in F minor, Opus 4; piano pieces, Opus 5, 6, and 7; and lieder, Opus 8 and 9. Each of the last two sets contained twelve lieder, of which three in each opus had been composed by Fanny: *Das Heimweh* (Homesickness), Opus 8 no. 2, to a poem by Friederike Robert; *Italien*, Opus 8 no. 3, to a poem by Grillparzer; *Suleika and Hatem*, duet, Opus 8 no. 12, to a text by Goethe; also *Sehnsucht* (Nostalgia), text by Droysen; *Verlust* (Loss), text by Goethe; and *Die Nonne*, (The Nun), text by Uhland, Opus 9 nos. 7, 10, and 12. Many years later, after being received by Queen Victoria at Buckingham Palace, Felix described his visit in a letter of 19 July 1842:

While they were talking, I looked through the music on the piano and came across my very first volume of lieder. Naturally I asked the Queen to sing me one, rather than an aria by Gluck; she agreed most amiably, and what did she choose? *Schöner und schöner* (More and More Beautiful), which she sang prettily and in tune, following the rhythm and very pleasingly; it was only after *der Prosa Last und Mühe* (Sorrow and Fatigue of Prose), when the phrase descends toward the D and ascends harmonically, that she sang a D-sharp, twice; I pointed this out to her both times, and she ended up by singing a very accurate D, just where she should naturally have sung a D-sharp. But apart from that mistake it was really very pretty, I haven't heard an amateur sustain the final long G better, more accurately, or more naturally. So then I had to admit that Fanny had composed the lied (this was hard for me! But pride must suffer some constraint), and I asked her to sing a lied that was really by me.[37]

Nothing could be more normal. Mentioning the above episode in his memoirs, Sebastian Hensel wrote a little footnote about *Italien*: "One of my mother's lieder that appeared under Felix's name." He adds neither explanation nor excuse. Had not Dorothea Schlegel also published under her husband's name? Wasn't it recognized and accepted in the nineteenth century that a woman had to stay at home, only appearing in public if escorted, preferably by a man? Anxious to have some of his beloved elder sister's work heard, Felix was happy to combine it with his own. He had quite a choice, because at that time Fanny had already composed more than a hundred lieder.[38] This was always her favorite domain, and whereas Felix had a tendency to grow banal, Fanny discovered her true style in the genre she was entitled to: "salon pieces" for piano, with or without song. The *Songs Without Words* may well have been her idea: they were a means of communication for Felix and Fanny. It sometimes happened that Felix would playfully send the beginning of a piece to his sister for her to finish, and the reverse was equally possible. Gounod, whom Fanny met in Rome in 1840, claimed in his memoirs that Felix had published under his own name many songs without words actually composed by Fanny. There is no proof of this, and Felix Mendelssohn certainly did not need his sister to help him compose, but there is nothing to disprove it either.

The Overture to *A Midsummer Night's Dream* had been a great moment for Felix, bringing him recognition and success. He traveled to Stettin, where it received its first concert performance. The same success did not, however, await *Camacho's Wedding*,[39] which was his first and only attempt at public theatrical performance. While he was pleasantly diverted by the first rehearsals, he was soon disgusted by the petty behavior, scheming, and lack of professionalism he encountered in the theater. The first performance, on 27 April

1827 at the Königliches Schauspielhaus, was what is known as a *succès d'estime*, which did not satisfy the young man's pride.[40] There were no further performances and no other completed operas by Felix Mendelssohn Bartholdy, who had suffered a setback he would never quite get over. On 25 December 1827 Fanny wrote to Klingemann: "In any case, he's turned toward sacred music lately."[41] Felix and Fanny's training clearly placed them in the Lutheran tradition of religious music, where they were morally and musically more at ease than in opera.

This did not soften the blow for Felix. There followed what Sebastian Hensel's veiled words nonetheless oblige us to term a depression. The word "pressure" applies so aptly to Felix's education that the term "depression" seems natural. Thanks to another journey, Felix recovered. This time it was a pleasure trip with friends, involving long manly hikes across the Harz. They visited the part of Germany that lies between Bavaria and the Rhine, making stops at Baden, Heidelberg, and Cologne. The journey ended at Horchheim, near Koblenz, at his uncle Joseph Mendelssohn's house.

Women, unfortunately, did not have access to the same remedies against depression.

CHAPTER ELEVEN

The Mendelssohn Coterie

Felix entered Friedrich Wilhelm University in October 1827. This date marked the end of the instruction hitherto given in the Mendelssohn household, for Dr. Heyse had just been made Professor of Philology at this same university. Though very young, Felix had no difficulty in adapting; the education he had received enabled him to grasp points of great intellectual subtlety. He took Hegel's courses on aesthetics and studied history with Gans and geography with Ridder. Yet he was so accustomed to learning and sharing everything with Fanny that he couldn't bear to leave her at home. Thus he took her with him to the supplementary course in physical geography that Alexander von Humboldt was giving in the hall of the Singakademie.[1]

The name of Alexander von Humboldt recurs so often in the course of Mendelssohn studies that he seems almost a member of the family. During their youth the two Humboldt brothers, Wilhelm and Alexander, had known and admired Moses Mendelssohn. According to Sebastian Hensel, they took part in the *Morgenstunden*, the "morning lessons" that Moses gave his sons.[2]

Wilhelm von Humboldt (1767–1835) and his brother Alexander (1769–1859) belonged to a principal family of the Prussian aristocracy. They did their studies at Frankfurt-an-der-Oder and at Göttingen. While it is not absolutely certain that their friendship with Moses Mendelssohn's children dated from the *Morgenstunden*, it could very well have developed during the late 1780s in the salon of Henriette

Herz, for the Humboldts belonged to the *Tugendbund* (Confederation of Virtue), an association with no precise goal founded by Henriette Herz, Dorothea Veit, and Rahel Levin.[3] Here Wilhelm von Humboldt met another member of the confederation, Caroline von Dacheroden, whom he married in 1791.[4] Both brothers were scientists, but Wilhelm was more clearly committed to serving the state. He was among the men Hardenberg's government recruited to reform and modernize the Prussian state between 1810 and 1820. He had a marked effect on the cultural politics of that decade, partly through having founded Friedrich Wilhelm University, partly through his humanist idea of education and his interest in the humanities and comparative literature. A champion of a liberal constitution for Prussia, he saw his ideas collapse before the conservative, Metternichian reaction of 1819 and had to retire to his castle at Tegel.

Alexander, who was as much a geographer as a biologist, did not remain in Prussia. His accounts of his voyages are among the most important in that genre. In 1799 he organized a South American expedition during which he climbed Chimborazo and visited Cuba and the United States, returning to Europe in 1804. Henceforth he lived mainly in Paris. Between 1827 and 1828 he lectured at the University of Berlin, and although in 1829 he set off on another expedition through Russia to the Chinese frontier, the following year he returned to politics in Paris.

Alexander von Humboldt was rich but did not deal with much actual money: his fortune was in real estate and did not bring in a large income. The Mendelssohn Bank financed his expeditions and research, from the American voyage of 1799 to the work he did during the 1840s when Prussian King Friedrich Wilhelm IV was shocked that a great Prussian scientist should constantly rely on a Jewish banker to support him in his projects. But the ties linking Alexander von Humboldt and the Mendelssohn Bank were solid and profound, deriving from the humanist morality they shared and a love for science engendered by the ideals of Moses Mendelssohn and the eighteenth-century enlightenment. Joseph Mendelssohn and Alexander von Humboldt were friends, with all the trust and faithfulness that this implies, whereas the Prussian king never deserved anybody's trust. One morning in 1844 Humboldt arrived at Joseph Mendelssohn's home in great anxiety: the house he was renting was being sold by its owner, and all his botanical experiments were threatened.

That very afternoon, Humboldt received a letter from Joseph Mendelssohn informing him that he, Joseph, was the new proprietor and that he authorized him to remain on the premises indefinitely.[5]

The lectures Humboldt gave in Berlin in the hall of the Singakademie aroused immense interest. He was the ideal scientist, equally interested in people and in things; his knowledge and research were based on humanism and generosity. Young people were bound to listen passionately—especially the young Mendelssohns. As Fanny told her friend Klingemann:

You may perhaps know that Alexander von Humboldt is giving a course at the university (in physical geography), but did you also know that after an entreaty from the highest quarters he has begun a second course in the hall of the Singakademie, attended by everyone who claims to be educated and fashionable—everyone, from the king and all his court down through the ministers, generals, officers, artists, scholars, writers, wits and dullards, *arrivistes*, students, and women, even including your present unworthy correspondent? A frighteningly large crowd throngs to them, the audience is imposing, and the course is infinitely interesting. Gentlemen may laugh at us as much as they will; it is wonderful in this day and age for us to have an opportunity to hear something sensible, for once; we are enjoying this good fortune and trying to recover from the mockery. To give your mockery its full worth, I must further inform you that we are attending a second lecture series, given by a foreigner on experimental physics. This course, too, is being attended mainly by women. Holtey's lectures are also particularly well received this year.[6]

Life continued most agreeably at 3 Leipziger Strasse for the four young Mendelssohns and the circle of friends Felix brought with him from the university. All of them were funny, intelligent, cultured, favorably indulged by nature and by life. Felix was the center of everybody's interest, the apple of his parents' and his sisters' eye.

Into this erudite circle came the historian Johann Gustav Droysen (1808–1894), who attended the lectures by Boeckh and Hegel. He entered the Mendelssohn home as Felix's coach and easily blended into the family circle. Fanny described him as "A philologist of nineteen, in whom freshness, energy, and youthful enterprise combine with an erudition beyond his years, with a pure sense of poetry and a wholesome, pleasant, attractive mind."[7]

Droysen made his mark as a major historian in 1833 when he published his *History of Alexander the Great,* which marked an epoch in the study of Greek antiquity.[8] Both Fanny and Felix composed a number of lieder to his poems.

Other visitors to the Mendelssohn house included the legal scholar Ludwig Heydemann (1805–1874) and his brother Albert, a historian (1808–1877), both of whom joined in the "games" of these hyper-talented young people. Albert had taken part in Felix's long excursion through southern Germany in the summer of 1827.

The poet Ludwig Robert (1778–1832) and his wife Friederike, who was also a poet (1795–1832), lived in Berlin from 1822 to 1831; they were frequent visitors of the Mendelssohns and provided the two resident composers with texts,[9] Born Ludwig Levin, Ludwig Robert had converted out of conviction in 1819; he was the brother of Rahel Varnhagen (1771–1833) to whom he was much attached. Rahel Levin became famous, we may recall, thanks to her first salon, the one she held in her mansard attic during the 1790s. After two un-happy engagements she found a third, adoring suitor in the diplomat and man of letters Karl August Varnhagen von Ense (1785–1858), whose admiration for her knew no bounds. She married him in 1814, which enabled her to have what was termed her "second salon." Here she established a cult of Goethe with herself as high priestess, while her adoring husband drank in her every word. In fact Felix detested this type of game as much as he detested famous women of any kind, be they Bettina von Arnim or Henriette Herz. The latter did, how-ever, find some favor in his eyes on account of her charitable works—charity being consistent with the role of a respectable woman. Rahel took a more sympathetic view of Felix than he did of her: he danced, she opined, like a "civilized hurricane." When visiting the Mendels-sohns, Varnhagen behaved like an idolater—something the young people rather derided: he actually took a notebook from his pocket to write down Rahel's every word! One day Rebecka had the impu-dence to remark: "If we talked as much, without bothering to restrain whatever was passing through our heads, somebody could write down a few intelligent remarks of ours too."[10]

In this circle we encounter no less a personage than the poet Hein-rich Heine (1797–1856), himself a member of this same milieu of scholars and converted Jews. Born in Düsseldorf into a family of Jew-ish merchants, he had studied in Berlin from 1821 to 1823 and taken courses by Boeckh, Zeune, Raumer, Hegel, and Savigny. He converted in 1826, without a trace of conviction: "The baptismal certificate is the entrance ticket to European culture," he wrote at that time, though he would quickly be sorry for his deed. That same year he wrote to his friend Moses Moser: "Now I'm hated by Christians and Jews alike. I greatly regret having been baptized."[11] After the book *Germanomanie* was publicly burned in 1817—its author, Saul Ascher, had been protesting against the racist utterances of the German-Christian Assembly—Heine penned these alarmingly prophetic lines in 1820:

> Dies war ein Vorspiel nur: dort wo man Bücher
> verbrennt, verbrennt man auch am Ende Menschen.

> (This was but a prelude: wherever books are burned,
> They eventually burn people too.)[12]

The part of Cassandra is a thankless role. Heine was therefore received with very mixed emotions by the Mendelssohns, who admired his talent but disliked his blasé manners. In the face of general enthusiasm for Jean Paul, Heine retorted: "What's Jean Paul! He hasn't even seen the sea." To which Fanny replied: "Of course he hasn't, he didn't have an Uncle Salomo to pay for his trip." Heinrich Heine lived on subsidies provided by his uncle, the banker Salomon Heine, who supported him during his "years of wandering" between 1826 and 1830. Like Rahel, however, Heine viewed the entire question of Jewish assimilation with a bitterness the Mendelssohns were either unaware of or refused to recognize. Heine's recollections of his visits, nevertheless, were positive, and in 1829 he wrote to Droysen, their common friend:

Please remember me respectfully to the City Councilor's wife,[13] and slightly less respectfully to Fräulein Fanny's lovely eyes, which are among the most beautiful I know. As for chubby Rebecka, yes, please greet her for me too, the dear child she is, so charming and kind, and every pound of her an angel.[14]

To think Heine was one of Rebecka's admirers! The Mendelssohn ladies were not in any case particularly slender. But Heine irritated Fanny. She wrote to Klingemann, still in 1829:

Heine is here and I don't like him at all. He's too affected. If he let himself go, he'd be the most amiable lout who ever took advantage of a situation; if he made an effort to be serious that would suit him well too, for he has seriousness in him, but he exaggerates his sentimentality, and emphasizes what is already exaggerated, speaks endlessly about himself and continually looks at people to make sure they're looking at him. But didn't you ever come across Heine's *Travels in Italy*? It contains some magnificent passages. Even if one has felt contempt for him ten times in a row, the eleventh time he forces one to recognize that he's a poet, a true poet! Words sing for him, and nature speaks to him as she only speaks to poets.[15]

Heine predicted the longterm results of Prussian policy far too clearly not to make the Mendelssohns concerned about their German identity. He claimed that he visited only for Rebecka, who professed the most radical opinions of the entire family, and to whom he must have felt quite close.

Rebecka had some difficulty in asserting herself beside her elder brother and sister, and yet Sebastian later wrote that her "keen intelligence, her perceptiveness, and her sparkling wit caught everyone's attention."[16] Johanna Kinkel declares in her memoirs that Rebecka was an excellent musician,[17] but according to Rebecka herself: "My older brother and sister stole my reputation as an artist. In any other family I would have been highly regarded as a musician and perhaps been leader of a group. Next to Felix and Fanny, I could not aspire to any recognition." When Felix was preparing to leave for Italy in 1830, Droysen, who was among Rebecka's numerous admirers, wrote to Albert Heydemann: "Rebecka is to be pitied most; she will be twice as unhappy when Felix leaves for Italy. Hensel doesn't understand her at all, Fanny doesn't depend on her, and her parents don't like her very much."[18] Fanny and Rebecka were nonetheless extremely close to one another throughout their lives; Fanny wrote her lieder mainly for her little sister, who had a pretty voice and sang very well until she decided to stop practicing. There were differences in talent, and even after she was married, Fanny could not stop working. But Rebecka was still her most intimate friend. Both of them competed for Felix's affection. If Rebecka received less attention from her parents than her elder brother and sister, she found some compensation in these same siblings' love. On the other hand, not much remained for Paul, who receives only cautious mention from Sebastian Hensel, ever anxious to depict his family through rose-colored glasses. Intelligent and musical, Paul had his part to play in this band of four, but he never occupied center stage. This did not suit the temperamental, irritable adolescent, who ended up by becoming a mere banker.

If one considers that the great singer Anna Milder-Hauptmann, the philosopher Hegel, and the legal scholar Eduard Gans were also frequent visitors—not to mention the naturalist Alexander von Humboldt and the virtuoso violinist Paganini who also passed through the house—one has some idea of the cultural atmosphere in which the Mendelssohns immersed themselves. Fanny did not really have cause to wonder if her talent was unjustly treated, because she inhabited a world in which approval was worth as much as the highest artistic recompense.

It was during this period that Wilhelm Hensel returned from Italy, in October 1828, after an absence of five years. He was now thirty-four, while Fanny was almost twenty-three, and it is hard to estimate which of the two had changed the most. Fanny was as her mother had wished, developing happily and freely among exceptional friends. Wilhelm found himself entering a liberal, intellectual milieu that was quite foreign to him. He had not forgotten the promises made by Lea, Abraham, and Fanny, and had worked very hard toward this goal. The relationship did not pick up where the two young people had left off; Fanny belonged first and foremost to her family, her music, and her circle of friends, who did not look favorably upon this stranger taking over Fanny—Felix least of all. Wilhelm was not slow to react, displaying jealousy toward anyone or anything dear to Fanny—brothers, sister, friends, intellectual interest, and even music. He did not understand the household's mentality, and the house returned his exasperation. He became obdurate and rebellious. Fanny did not recognize in him the man she thought she loved; she became temperamental and would not accept that someone had come to wrench her from her happy, carefree life.

Abraham reminded her that she had no other destiny but matrimony, and that at twenty-three it was time to consider it seriously. For Fanny's birthday, 14 November 1828, he wrote:

We are both growing older 365 days a year; who knows how much longer I shall still be able to congratulate you on your birthday, or how much longer you will want or be able to listen to me.

That is why I would like to tell you today, my dear Fanny, that I am so satisfied with you on all the essential points, on all that is truly important, that I have nothing more to wish for. You are good, both in your mind and in your soul. The word is devilishly short, but it has guts, and I do not apply it to just anyone.

But you can still improve! You must take yourself in hand and concentrate harder; you must school yourself more seriously and eagerly for your true profession, a young woman's only profession: being mistress of the house. True economy is true generosity; he who throws money away must needs become either a miser or an imposter. A woman's profession is the hardest of all: she must constantly attend to the smallest detail; collect each drop of rain water so that instead of drying up in the sand it is conveyed to the river to spread blessings and well-being. She must notice every incident, without fail; do good every instant and use every instant to do good; this, and everything else you can think of on the subject, constitutes a woman's duty, a woman's difficult duty.

You certainly do not lack the soul, still less the intelligence necessary to carry out these duties faithfully; even so, you will find further matter on which to exercise your strength, harden your will, concentrate your energy, and judiciously choose and honor your obligations. Do this of your own free will, as much as you can! before being obliged to do so. While you still have the good fortune to live with your parents, practice doing many things better than they do. Give the building a solid foundation; there will be no scarcity of decorations.

I do not, however, wish to preach at you, and I'm not yet old enough to be talking drivel. Accept in your heart my fatherly wishes for your well-being, and my well-intentioned advice.

Your father[19]

Abraham had not changed with the passing of the years. In writing a letter of this sort at this time, he knew he was driving Fanny toward Wilhelm. Wouldn't it have been more sensible for Fanny to have married someone from their own intimate circle, or at least from their milieu? This would have meant running the risk of her marrying a Jew or a converted Jew, someone who had kept a name that Abraham wanted to forget.

A painter who was a pastor's son and had remained a Protestant corresponded perfectly to Abraham's scheme of social integration. Wilhelm knew, when he wrote to Luise in 1823, that Abraham would be on his side "when it came to a fight."

Fanny had to marry. Wilhelm no longer resembled the young man she had known, any more than she resembled the girl she had been, but she knew she could count on his constancy, his kindness, and his boundless admiration. If Wilhelm's jealousy did not make things easier, her own character was not particularly supple either; as the years went by her way of greeting people grew ever more abrupt and less amiable. She was utterly unlike the gracious, sweet young girls so often depicted in the nineteenth century, but Wilhelm loved her and wanted her just as she was. She would have what had been promised her, when a professional musical career had been denied: power in her own home, and the power to make a man extremely happy. The only man she knew whose strength could be compared to hers was Felix. The idea of embarking on life with a feeble copy of her brother held scant appeal, and we can understand Fanny for entering into Abraham's stratagem and seeking the antithesis of her brother and herself.

No one tells of the courage she nonetheless required. Out of discretion, Sebastian Hensel refused to publish the letters Fanny sent to Wilhelm at this time: a fiancée's letters are in the private domain. Every morning, Wilhelm's valet came to collect a letter in which Fanny defended herself, defended her world and her circle, and tried to make a few compromises. Wilhelm had reason to be jealous: Fanny's world was hostile to him, his puns were not well received, and the coterie spoke in a way that tended to exclude a stranger like him. He thus began by rejecting it entirely. Accordingly, Fanny showed herself willing to give up everything for him—her friends, even her music—but never her brother. Then she gently managed to win him over and win everything back.

One can well imagine how difficult it must have been to reconcile with reality the image each had of the other. Sebastian, who was able to consult his mother's letters as he wrote, admits that she was

often ill at ease in [Wilhelm's] presence, but as soon as night came and she was alone in silence with the ideal image of her beloved, such as she had grown used to thinking of him during all their years apart, she regained her determination and slowly succeeded in uniting image and reality within a single countenance. She kept her father's letter vividly in mind, for he had dictated to her that being mistress of a house was a young woman's true profession, and she tried eagerly to conform to it for the man of her choice.[20]

Work always contains a degree of interest as well as profit. And insofar as marriage entails obligation and compromise, both parties necessarily gain in self-knowledge. In 1828—just as it had in 1821 and again in 1823—the distance between two opposite poles formed part of the attraction and love felt by Fanny and Wilhelm. Perhaps, too, it was easier and less painful to remain faithful to an image that had lasted five years, and to compromise so that the image corresponded with reality, than it was to break a habit that had become a part of them.

Wilhelm's answers to Fanny's letters have not been preserved, but he did have another means of approach at his disposal: his talent as a portraitist. Just as he managed to win over Lea during his absence in Rome, he managed to win favor in Fanny's circle. He began with the most pressing case: Felix. On 10 January Fanny wrote in the diary she had just begun: "Hensel dined with us on Wednesday, he brought the sketches for Felix's portrait. The concept is magnificent, brilliant, and beautiful; even Felix is delighted, and I have found him altogether different toward Hensel since this portrait." Further on, she adds: "I was infinitely happy to hear that the two of them got on extremely well." This was by no means apparent at the start: like Rebecka, Felix tended to be liberal to the point of republicanism, as their father, the "citizen," had been in his youth; the extremely conservative Wilhelm, on the other hand, took loyalism to the point of an unconditional admiration for royalty, thus remaining in the tradition of the first wave of Romanticism. Moreover, Wilhelm earned his living thanks to the Prussian king, and being an honorable man would have considered himself guilty of disgraceful ingratitude had he shown any lack of respect toward the court. One day Felix even exclaimed "with unaccustomed vehemence," according to Devrient: "But Hensel, show a little more consideration for your brother-in-law's radicalism!"[21] The differences in their political positions were only reconciled harmoniously many years later, when age and circumstances had made Felix more attached to tradition. In the meantime, controversy remained the spice of life. Fanny seems to have been relatively indifferent to it: liberalism, conservatism, political opinions generally did not appear to affect private life or a woman's situation. Her conservative husband left her more artistic freedom than did her supposedly liberal father and brother. Although very interested in the state of the world, Fanny never held fanatical views concerning religious or political dogma. All she wanted was for her husband and brother to get along well as human beings—had they failed to do so, her marriage would have been impossible.

Lea's resistance still had to be overcome, and she behaved as disagreeably toward Hensel as her good breeding permitted. On Thursday 22 January 1829, however, Humboldt arrived with the glad news that Wilhelm had been appointed to the Academy of Fine Arts. Next day at noon Wilhelm asked Fanny's parents for her hand in marriage. Fanny recorded the event in her diary:

After a little over half an hour, Hensel returned and we came to an agreement within a few minutes. We went in and found mother very surprised, alarmed by the rapidity of the decision and incapable of pronouncing her consent. Father was immediately satisfied and happy, and *tant bien que mal*[22] we helped mother regain her composure; my brothers and sister were happy; Felix came home after two o'clock, astonished too at first, but when Hensel left after the meal, I had a conversation with him which made me extremely happy. What an angel he is! I cannot begin to describe his attitude toward Hensel.

That Abraham was pleased and satisfied will come as no surprise to those who remember his letter of 27 November 1828. For her part, Lea was probably still hoping for an entirely different destiny for her daughter. But Fanny had made her choice, in complete lucidity, and Lea would later understand that it was not so stupid after all.

That year Fanny had begun a diary she kept until the end of her life—that is, for another eighteen years. Strong pressures were at work around her: not only had she to marry, but it had been decided that Felix would go on an educational tour, first through England, then to Paris, then to Rome. Her father had decided thus: his son must prepare for the roving life that would be his—and that corresponded, moreover, to his restless disposition. He must also choose a city in which to reside. Paul, though not yet seventeen, had to start work behind a counter: it seems he had not been judged worthy of a university education. The world the four children had inhabited in their youth was at an end. Only Rebecka continued living as she had before. As soon as Fanny's engagement was announced, however, Rebecka's suitors came in droves: she was as rich as her sister, but far prettier and more amusing. Heine claimed he only went there when he knew Rebecka was at home. Even though Fanny knew she was beloved, even though she was very intelligent and had beautiful eyes, it must have been hard for her to feel so ugly when her sister was so engaging. Her exasperation appears in this letter to Klingemann, in which the female condition seems harder than she had foreseen:

I almost forgot to thank you for having waited until the announcement of my engagement before noticing that I was simply a woman like all the rest; for my part I had long been certain that a fiancé is just a man like all the rest. Besides, the fact that one is reminded of one's wretched woman's nature every day, at every step of one's life, by the lords of creation would be enough to put one in a rage and lose all femininity, if the problem didn't only worsen thereby.

Hensel has begun a life-sized portrait of Gans, shown almost at full height. Gans, who is actually half man and half child or wild animal, is thrilled to see himself on canvas. He comes frequently to our house and takes much pleasure in being with Rebecka, imposing Greek lessons on her during which these two highly educated persons read Plato together. I can think of nothing more grotesque! It goes without saying that people have deduced a more tangible relationship from this Platonic one, and that it is the talk of the town, although there are actually no grounds for speculation.[23]

Everyone knew that Fanny expressed herself directly and even with brutal frankness, and was accustomed to it. But here Fanny's speech is more than slightly bitter; it was the habit in middle-class families to wait for the elder daughter to be "settled" before "bringing out" the younger ones. This was yet another reason impelling Fanny to be married, but not her kindest moment in regard to her young sister!

CHAPTER TWELVE

The *Saint Matthew Passion*

Felix's departure, Paul's apprenticeship, and Fanny's marriage disrupted the band of four and upset the entire life of the family. Felix's departure alone would have been enough to crush Fanny: what was to become of her music? She had agreed to leave the stage entirely to Felix, vicariously experiencing the career her own talent merited—happy, while her brother was still with her, to see all their years of study coming to fruition in Felix's success. But how was she to bear his absence? His trip to England was only supposed to last a few months; yet it was only the prelude to other journeys, all designed to assist his self-discovery and find an ideal place for his artistic life. By 1829 Berlin had lost all the brilliance of the *Aufklärung* and had turned into a provincial, conservative town where not much went on. A musician of Felix Mendelssohn's caliber needed a capital city, decided Abraham, with theaters and professional orchestras. Fanny, however, had to resign herself to the mediocrity surrounding her, perhaps even to the thought of giving up her music. She became jealous of her brother, going as far as to look through his papers. Felix scolded her: "You'll get a rap across the fingers. . . . You went into my room? You looked through my things? Watch out, my pretty flower, watch out!"[1]

All these worries occurred at a bad time, for brother and sister still had a fascinating task to accomplish before Felix left. This task alone could have guaranteed the name of Mendelssohn a place in musical history: the revival of Bach's *Saint Matthew Passion*, whose first known performance had taken place at the church of Saint Thomas in Leipzig one hundred years before and was now being commemorated. The full glory of the undertaking redounded to Felix—and deservedly, for he poured all his knowledge, skill, and emotions into it. Nonetheless, it is odd that Fanny's contribution to the project has never been pointed out or even recognized, for her letters prove that she knew every note of the work (and one does not learn the *Saint Matthew Passion* accidentally), besides being acquainted with Felix's intentions as if they were her own. If one could possibly imagine a musical personality more steeped in Bach than Felix Mendelssohn it would have to be Fanny, whom her brother called the "Cantor with black eyebrows." Alexander von Humboldt, who in company with Professor Encke paid daily visits to a "magnetic hut"[2]—that is, a shed constructed of nonferrous materials, apart from some copper, which Abraham had had erected in the garden to allow him to take measurements of magnetic fields[3]—heard Felix and Fanny practicing the *Saint Matthew Passion*. They had, of course, much experience with arrangements for four hands; as early as 1823 Lea had asked Amalie Beer to send her children some works by her son, Giacomo Meyerbeer, saying: "Overtures to his operas in orchestral score would be welcome. Felix and Fanny are used to scaling them down to four hands without having previously transcribed them, and are very skillful at it."[4] Similarly, Felix and Fanny must have studied the *Saint Matthew Passion*, which they learned together, as if sharing the same pair of ears and the same heart. Felix took up the more glamorous position, between the chorus and the orchestra,[5] while Fanny remained as usual in the shadows, hidden among the altos in the chorus, behind her brother's gestures. Both were serving the same music and it mattered little to them who did what, as long as everything was properly executed. For Felix, however, this was merely the prelude to a brilliant career, whereas for Fanny it was the end of a youthful collaboration with her brother, sanctioned by a public apotheosis. Hence her anguish and depression.

This centennial performance did indeed constitute the crowning achievement of their musical education. It was also the most famous and important of the Singakademie's manifestations, symbolizing the outcome of the work begun by Fasch in 1791 and zealously continued by Zelter. It was, in effect, Felix's farewell concert to his homeland and youth; and many things contributed to its success, from the *Passion*'s score—which had been copied by Felix's friend and violin teacher, Eduard Rietz, then given to him by his grandmother Salomon for Christmas 1823—to the Sunday matinées, not forgetting, of course, Professor Zelter's rigorous instruction.

Fanny gave an account of the event to their friend Klingemann, dated 22 March:

For a long time Felix and Devrient had discussed the possibility of a performance, but the plan had neither shape nor outline until one evening at our house; next day they presented themselves in newly purchased yellow gloves (to which they attached great importance) to the Akademie administration. They went discreetly in and modestly inquired if the administration would kindly lend them the hall for a concert to be given for a charitable purpose? Certain that the music would please, they then proposed giving a second performance to benefit the Akademie.

These gentlemen, however, thanked them politely and preferred to accept an honorarium fixed at fifty thalers, leaving the disposition of the receipts to the organizers of the concert. Let me say in passing, they're still chewing over their answer. Zelter made no objection and rehearsals began the following Friday. Felix went through the entire orchestral score, made a few useful cuts, and instrumented only the recitative, *Der Vorhang im Tempel zerriss in zwei Stücke* (The Veil in the Temple Was Rent in Two). Otherwise everything was left as it was. People were speechless with admiration, and when a few weeks later the rehearsals moved to the Akademie itself, faces grew long with astonishment at the idea that such a work could have existed unbeknownst to them—members of the Berlin Akademie. Once they grasped that fact, they began studying the work with warm and veritable interest. Its new and surprising form aroused curiosity, and its subject was accessible and easily understood. Devrient performed the recitatives admirably. The enthusiasm of the singers, from the first rehearsal on; how they poured their heart and soul into the work; how everyone's love of this music and pleasure in performing it grew with each rehearsal; how each new element—first the vocal solos, then the orchestra—kept renewing the general wonder and astonishment; how Felix made everybody work so wonderfully well and accompanied the piano rehearsals from memory from start to finish—all that produced many unforgettable moments. Zelter, who had taken part in the first rehearsals, gradually withdrew from the proceedings, sitting behind the audience during the later rehearsals and during the performances, with exemplary resignation. So extremely favorable an opinion of the music then spread through the Akademie, and so lively and detailed an interest was aroused in every milieu, that all the tickets were sold the day after the announcement of the concert, and during the last few days they had to refuse entrance to more than a thousand people. On Wednesday 10 March the first reading took place that can really be termed successful, apart from a few unimportant errors committed by the soloists. We were just above the orchestra; no sooner had the doors been opened than people—who had already been waiting a long time—rushed in, filling the room in less than a quarter of an hour. I was sitting in the corner so as to see Felix well, and I had arranged the strongest alto voices near me. The choruses were impassioned with extraordinary strength tempered with a touching tenderness, as I had never heard them before, except for the second performance, in which they surpassed themselves. Assuming you remember the dramatic form, I am enclosing a libretto and will add that Strümer sang the Evangelist's narration, Devrient the words of Jesus, Bader the role of Peter, Busolt the High Priest and Pilate, and Weppler sang Judas. Schätzel, Milder, and Türrschmidt sang the soprano and alto solos quite remarkably. The hall, which was full to bursting, began to resemble a church, for profound silence and a spirit of contemplation reigned in the assembly, silent but for a few involuntary expressions of deep feeling and emotion; in this case one could justifiably say—as is often wrongly said of such undertakings—that an exceptional mood, a general and lofty interest, guided this performance, with everyone carrying out his duty according to his powers and a few even going beyond their powers. One of these was Rietz who, with the help of his brother and his brother-in-law, had assumed the burden of copying all the orchestral parts: none of the three would accept the slightest recompense once the work was finished. Most of the singers either returned their complimentary tickets or paid for them; thus there were only six free tickets for the first concert (Spontini had two of them) and none for the second.

Even before the performance loud cries were heard from the numerous persons who, unable to attend, were calling for a second concert. The business schools had joined the ranks of suppliants, but this time Spontini was on the lookout and applied all his friendly efforts to preventing a second performance.

Felix and Devrient defended themselves by adopting the most direct approach: they asked the crown prince, who had been interested in the work from the outset, to order a repeat performance. Thanks to him, the work was replayed on Sunday 21 March, the anniversary of Bach's birthday. Once again, people came in throngs; there were even more in attendance because the antechamber had been filled with chairs and every seat sold; the same was true of the small rehearsal room behind the orchestra. The choruses were even more remarkable than the first time, and the instruments magnificent; only a bad mistake by Milder and a few other smaller ones by the soloists spoiled Felix's mood. But on the whole one can say that no worthy undertaking could hope for a more felicitous result.[6]

The reaction of audience and participants alike indicates the significance everyone attached to this resurrection of the *Saint Matthew Passion*. The Mendelssohns financed it at a loss, but who would have thought to profit financially from a work that was sacred, not only in its primary religious sense but also in its social significance to the German people? Typically for the Mendelssohns, money was not supposed to enter into the matter, which is why Fanny was angry at the venal instincts of the Singakademie directors: after all, the concert involved the Akademie's very reason for existing. The first concert was given to benefit the Association for the Education of Morally Abandoned Children, and the second, to benefit the business schools.[7] In moving to the large hall named after it,[8] the Singakademie became an institution and forgot its unifying, moral role within the bourgeoisie; Felix, however, had remained entirely conscious of this role. Devrient records that, wearing their famous yellow gloves on their way to invite the singers to take part in the concert, Felix suddenly halted in the Opera Square and exclaimed: "To think it takes an actor and a Jew's son to give the best Christian music back to the public!"[9] Felix was perfectly aware that their social status was relatively marginal, just as he knew that this musical event was to mark—or should have marked—the final stage of integration in the history of Germany:[10] all the social classes represented here (with the middle class leading the way) were taking part in the unifying activity of choral singing, which here reached its apogee.

Fanny speaks of "several useful cuts": the Singakademie choir was playing the principal role in this performance, and twenty-two numbers were omitted, including eleven arias with four recitatives (among them *Buss und Reu* and *Ich will dir mein Herze schenken*) and four chorales.[11] This gave prominence to *Erbarme dich*, sung by soprano Pauline Schätzel, and emphasized the importance of the choruses. Unlike Zelter, Mendelssohn did not permit himself crude red pencil marks across a score he revered, and all his cuts were made very lightly by covering portions of the text, or with comments that could be easily removed. But the recitatives were still stylistically unperformable in their original form, and so Mendelssohn put the Evangelist's "cries"—especially the phrase *Und alsbald krähete der Hahn* (and at once the cock crew)—into a lower octave. The soloists came mainly from the Royal Theater; Anna Milder-Hauptmann (1785–1838) had created the role of Leonore in *Fidelio* in Vienna, and of Agathe in *Der Freischütz* in Berlin. Pauline Schätzel (1812–1882) also used to sing Agathe. Busolt sang bass roles at the opera between 1822 and 1831, while Bader (1789–1870) and Stümer (1789–1857) sang tenor roles. Auguste Türrschmiedt, contralto (born 1800, died sometime after 1860), specialized in singing oratorio. The soloists sang with the choirs, especially in the introductory chorus. The chorus comprised 158 singers,[12] while the orchestra was composed of amateur musicians from the Philharmonic Society Eduard Rietz[13] had founded in 1826, and reinforced by instrumentalists who, like the singers, came from the Hofoper. There were even some clarinets, which would sound surprising to our ears.

Fanny nonetheless emphasizes that everything in the score had been "left intact." Zelter's project would doubtless have involved modifying the vocal lines, as was his habit, according to "contemporary tastes" and the fashion of the Berlin school of lieder. Less timid in his approach, Felix Mendelssohn left Bach's music as it was in the orchestral parts, changing only the recitatives so as not to destroy the work's solemn and religious effect. In her own music, Fanny was never afraid to tackle dissonances and intervals that were not particularly "vocal."

After Felix had left for England, Zelter conducted a third performance for his benefit on Good Friday, 17 April. Fanny's reactions show that she had an inner understanding of the score, as evidenced by this letter to Felix of 18 April:

I didn't want to tell you anything at all about Monday's and Tuesday's rehearsals, so as not to cause you any of the pain that was filling my soul. Zelter himself played, and what emerged from these two fingers and his *total ignorance* of the score, you can well imagine. Gloom and anxiety spread through the choir, and your name was frequently mentioned. Thursday's rehearsal was not destined to allay these concerns. Z. did not beat time during the accompanied recitatives and only beat time in the choruses when he remembered to do so. Stümer performed miracles and stayed in tune while Z. played a constantly erroneous accompaniment. To give you some examples, Devrient was so disturbed he only inserted half the Last Supper, among other things, and immediately launched into *Trinket alle daraus* (Drink, everyone) in F major.[14] As usual Milder wrecked the duet, Schätzel struggled hard during her aria, and the small choruses *Der rufet dem Elias* (He is calling Elias) and *Halt lass sehen* (Halt, and let us see) got steadily worse. Z. kept interrupting furiously and was continually confused after the reversal of pieces in the Golgotha scene. This resulted in long pauses while Stümer, with more discretion and composure than I would have thought him capable of, quietly corrected him and Devrient remained seated like an perfect Ecce homo. At quarter past four the rehearsal was over; beside ourselves with weariness, strain, and anxiety, we returned home. This was after I had held a little council of war with Devrient, Ritz, and David[15] and we agreed that Ritz should beat time throughout while David should count rests as if his life depended on it, for the second choir was left to its own devices for all the succeeding entrances. After these clarifications, things went amazingly well. During the rehearsal Ritz had tried out your suggestion about the four clarinets and I had heard the chorus, but we found the result ineffective, for it sounded too shrill and the character of the organ was lost; and so it remained as in the original for the performance.[16] . . . The first chorus actually went very well. Ritz beat time and the instruments almost always came in precisely during Jesus's words, which was astonishing. Milder sang her aria very well, swallowed for an entire eighth-note, but the flutes waited for her. The Last Supper, very good. *O Schmerz* (O pain) was too fast and the pianissimo of the chorus got lost. Devrient sang *Siehe er ist da, der mich verräth* (See, he is there, the one who betrayed me) according to your instructions.[17] The duet remarkable, contrary to all expectations; the chorus weak. You can understand that Z. eventually atoned for his pleasures and conducted during the fermatas, but they weren't very precise either. Final chorus without piano, flutes remarkable. The alto aria good, amid the choral entrances; the tenors consistently the weakest. The small choruses good. In *Wahrlich du bist auch einer* (In truth, you are one too) the flutes bungled the beginning. Schätzel made the same mistake in *Erbarme dich* (Have pity) as during the rehearsal, but covered up so well that hardly anyone noticed. *Was gehet uns das an* (What does that matter to us) was the only chorus with a really hesitant beginning; *Der du den Tempel Gottes* (You who enter the Temple of God) much too fast, Ritz held back but it was already too late. Then followed the inevitable great scandal: *Ach Golgotha* began not on the fourth but on the eighth eighth-note, and with her customary logic Milder sang the *entire narration* half a bar too late, even though Zelter played her line correctly and with all his might on the piano. Ritz went over to the basset-horns and put her back in the right place, but not until the final bars. Rarely has anything so calamitous been heard. With admirable symmetry she spoiled the first piece the first time, the second piece the second time, and the third piece yesterday. When it was over, many people came up to me and lamented your absence. Bader and Stümer in the forefront. Stümer was most affectionate and said, You must have felt very strange today. In reply I paid him very great compliments. He was truly admirable, for Z. made so many mistakes in accompanying him, and played such different harmonies, that I still don't understand how he held up. Ritz also performed wonders, for Z. beat time only when he felt like it; if he couldn't grab his baton fast enough he used his hand, and when he forgot that too the choirs came in all by themselves. On the whole, it was a good performance for the public, but everyone in the orchestra felt where it was weak. I spent the entire evening thinking about the steamship. It was, incidentally, very crowded, the king stayed from start to finish. . . . I must add that Devrient took the score after the rehearsal and stuck the missing pieces back in very carefully with his saliva.[18] He's taking it away again and apart from that your score wasn't sullied in any way. Ritz played divinely. And now I think I'm finished.[19]

This long letter, which from beginning to end resembles the notes an assistant hands the conductor, gives some idea of Fanny's careful and attentive work throughout Felix's rehearsals: from where he stands, a conductor does not necessarily hear every aspect of an orchestra's balance and sound, and needs a trusted listener. Fanny's remarks about Zelter border on lèse-majesté: the musicologist Schünemann thinks it impossible that Zelter withdrew, "resignedly," from rehearsals for the *Saint Matthew*, or that his own score was not used for all the performances[20]—and emits squawks at the mere idea that Zelter did not practice the work! But the *Saint Matthew Passion* is a difficult work and even a great Bach specialist could not conduct it on sight. If the old gentleman had not taken the time to learn it, then he could not know it well. Fanny's frankness implies total agreement on Felix's part; from the point of view of his former students, it was Zelter who was committing a sacrilege with his cuts and pencil marks.

There is a question that has never been asked until now: if Zelter was not capable of conducting the work properly, who else could better have replaced Felix than Fanny herself, given her thorough knowledge of the score? It is an anachronistic question with no historical foundation, but not without interest from a musical standpoint. Fanny was not simply a pianist, as she was subsequently to prove in her Sunday matinées. She knew how to listen to orchestral textures, she had a sense of timbre, a perfect ear, sufficient authority to conduct, and a talent for organization stemming from her practical side.

CHAPTER THIRTEEN

Felix in England: The First Separation

Felix's departure came at a crucial time, for it coincided with the performance of this work on which brother and sister had expended so much effort. It was not surprising Fanny felt depressed, as one always does after a major accomplishment. And if the task one has just completed does not result in further projects, the problem becomes severe. It was, however, high time for Felix to escape from the parental tutelage. Everybody said so; as Zelter wrote to Goethe, "This boy is my consolation in life and it's a good thing he's leaving his parents' house."[1] Concerning the famous yellow gloves, Devrient had been amazed at the amount of parental control and pressure exerted on this young man of twenty. On the other hand, it was Fanny's destiny to put up with this tutelage, and even after her marriage she would have to deal with her parents' moods.

The months preceding Felix's departure were like a final bouquet for the Mendelssohn household. Musical evenings and receptions followed each other in rapid succession. Paganini had made his first appearances in Berlin that March and was invited to dinner at 3 Leipziger Strasse. On 9 March Fanny made this entry in her diary about him:

On Wednesday, Paganini's first concert. I shall take the time to write more about this wonderful, baffling talent, about this man who looks like a demented murderer and gesticulates like a monkey. A supernatural, wild genius. He is extremely exciting and provocative.[2]

Hensel took advantage of Paganini's presence to paint his portrait, and the Mendelssohns, to argue about him until midnight—minus Felix, however, who had gone to bed. Fanny mentions this in her diary on 19 March, but feeling obliged to give a reason for the argument. The Mendelssohn circle lived on its passion for debate and the verbal clashes engendered by debate. Ideas reigned supreme and everyone spoke plainly, in defiance of polite behavior. Although Fanny does not say so, the opinions expressed by Wilhelm—an almost constant guest in the Mendelssohn salon—were constantly out of keeping with the ambiance of the circle. Paganini, who called on them often during his stay in Berlin, had a most unusual character, one that could only provoke extremely diverse reactions, from the most conservative to the most Romantic. What exactly was a genius, and just how eccentric could his behavior be allowed to become? Should signs of bad breeding be tolerated? The discussion continued for a long time, and these questions were among those Felix and Fanny asked each other in the letters they exchanged, but when the debate become too personal, Felix preferred to withdraw into his room.

As a ceremonious way of saying goodbye to his family, Felix gave several organ recitals between 1 and 8 April in various Berlin churches: the Dreifaltigkeit Kirche, the Garnison Kirche, and the Parochial Kirche. Felix knew as well as Fanny that his departure marked the end of an era in his life, and of a certain carefree phase. Where else would he be wrapped in the cocoon of so closed and privileged a world? His anguish was transferred into his playing. "I have never heard anything more terrifying than the first chorus of the *Passion*, the way Felix played it," wrote Fanny on 1 April. The third concert, given in the Parochial Kirche, ended in the gathering dusk, and after a few organ pieces and choruses from the *Saint Matthew*, Felix ended with the *Tu es Petrus*. "It was very poetic," wrote his older sister on 8 April.[3]

The departure was set for Friday 10 April. Felix's friends came to say goodbye. Heine lunched with them on Wednesday, then Devrient and one of their women friends, Ulrike. They spent a musical afternoon together. Gans came to join them that evening. Next day it was Zelter and Gans who came to lunch at 3 Leipziger Strasse, and that afternoon the whole circle of young people met one last time. Berger came to hear his studies played and also his Fantasy in E

Minor, as if in final salute to his youth. "It was very silent, worrying, and unpleasant," wrote Fanny on 13 April. They rose at four o'clock on Friday morning and Fanny stayed with her brother until the last possible moment, helping him to dress and buckle up his suitcases. The travelers left at half-past five,[4] with Abraham and Rebecka accompanying Felix as far as Hamburg.

To console Fanny, her friend Droysen was quick to find her some work to do. "Droysen brought me a delightful poem about Felix which put me in a very good mood because the melody came immediately to my mind. I played my Easter Sonata."[5]

This Easter Sonata poses a musicological problem. Fanny mentions it in her diary, and Klingemann in a letter of 19 August 1829: "Among other piquant items I can tell you how we found ourselves on board an American ship arriving from New York, the *Napoleon*, which, along with every imaginable comfort in the 'Mahagoni' style, had a Broadwood piano, to distract people from too long a contemplation of things maritime. Felix then played me some of the first movement of your Easter Sonata, Fräulein fiancée, of which I had heard only talk until now."[6]

The manuscript of this sonata is currently untraceable. In 1973, however, the French pianist Eric Heidsieck recorded an Easter Sonata ascribed to Felix Mendelssohn Bartholdy,[7] the manuscript of which bears no signature. The owner of this manuscript will not allow anyone to consult the original, and even if one could recognize the hand of Felix or Fanny, there would be nothing to prove that one of them had not recopied the other's work. It should nonetheless be noted that the sonata, which is not recorded in any catalogue, was automatically attributed to Felix. No doubt the future will provide an answer to the questions raised by this piece. Fanny had certainly composed another piano sonata, in 1824, during another of Felix's absences—when he was visiting Dobberan with his father. The manuscript of this sonata in C minor, in three movements, is extant in the Mendelssohn Archives in Berlin, but it is not entitled *Ostersonate* and was written in the summer.[8]

Fanny was at least as upset by the thoughts occasioned by her brother's departure as by the departure itself. It is true that she was habitually surrounded by numerous friends, by her brothers, sister, and cousins, and thus mentions the meal taken alone with her mother on 13 April as an exceptional event. Given this impression of solitude—in fact entirely relative—Hensel's tender concern assumed full importance.

If Wilhelm had felt jealous of Felix, of music, and of everything surrounding Fanny as long as he himself had not yet found his place within the family circle, no one proved better at understanding Fanny's feelings once he saw he was accepted. He, too, was the brother of a sister who expressed her feelings so passionately to him that Fanny must actually have seemed rather reserved with regard to Felix:

> And when I sang the pains of love,
> And of the distant loved one,
> My heart thought of no one
> Other than my brother.
> I think of you as young brides do,
> Cruelly deprived of their beloved.[9]

No wonder Wilhelm took such rhetorical precautions in telling his sister of his love for Fanny and the influence she had acquired over him! Rather than marrying, Luise Hensel preferred to content herself with a "celestial fiancé" who was clearly less liable to change his mind. Her friend Hedwig von Olfers, whose salon she frequented, nonetheless described her as a very pretty girl, in whom "gentle piety was linked with grace"; although serious, she was "sensitive to humor and to wit."[10] She refused proposals of marriage from Clemens Brentano, Wilhelm Müller, Ludwig von Gerlach, and Ludwig Berger, and led a nun's life, though without actually taking the veil (she had, we recall, converted to Catholicism in 1818).

This was an intelligent woman, ultrasensitive and thus inclined toward a jealousy her dignity required her to control; Fanny could only write to her with sincerity and generosity, speaking of her own brother in such a way that Luise would understand she had not lost Wilhelm:

Berlin, 30 March 1829
Allow me to take advantage of the last moments of the day to send you my most cordial wishes, my dear sister. Wilhelm told me it was your birthday today: had I known earlier, you would have received this letter during the day, whereas it was almost midnight when I began it.
What can I tell you, dearest Luise? I know Wilhelm will read these lines,

yet I am telling you I love him very much, that I am entirely moved by the desire to make him truly happy, that I am truly sorry when the small but frequent frustrations imposed on us by social life seem distressing to him; that I hope to satisfy him deeply in our marriage. I have told him and can also tell you that even when I became engaged I did not hope to be as happy as I really am. And since my happiness has grown steadily up to this point, I may justifiably hope that it will always continue to grow; and since I shall be happier with each passing day, I shall watch Wilhelm's happiness grow too. I should thank heaven twice, since it gave me Wilhelm just as we are facing a long separation from the elder of my brothers. This separation is harder than I can tell you or anyone else, because it cannot be expressed, and because nothing is harder to communicate or make another person feel than pain. I am not afraid, however, that simply because I love Wilhelm, I will ever love Felix less: I absolutely cannot imagine possessing a heart so narrow that a brother or a woman friend must cede first place to the beloved, as if it were a house whose rooms were all partitioned.

Forgive me if I stop here now; in truth I am too upset and distracted by the thought of being separated from my brother for so long—and more briefly from my sister—to be able to write to you in peace; I shall be more expansive after he has left. For today, I leave it to Wilhelm to continue.

Your sister Fanny[11]

Wilhelm could only proceed in the same vein:

Dear Luise, what can I add to Fanny's words? She has in fact spoken for me too, since everything she says about her brother and herself can be applied to us. I can understand her pain at being separated from Felix, for I have to bear being separated from you and she is quite right in saying that fraternal love does not need to make room for another; this proves that true love already contains something divine, unlimited, and infinite while still on earth. That is why we consider it a preparation for the hereafter.

Love as a foretaste of the hereafter: Fanny and Wilhelm's religion was certainly rather less austere than Luise's. This sister—whom Wilhelm had not seen since a brief meeting at Bamberg in 1828—subsequently came to live at 3 Leipziger Strasse from 1833 to 1838, to be near her mother.

Despite the adoration the Mendelssohn children felt for their parents, there were times when they had to fight to survive. When they married or started their professional activities, each of them had occasion to react against the parental wish for total assimilation. They all remained Protestants—from conviction, of course, but also out of social necessity: a Prussian who worked in Prussia had to keep the same religion as his prince. The same did not hold true for names: belonging to the Mendelssohn clan could not be disavowed. One might forget one's name was Itzig or Salomon, but in no way could one deny the great ancestor Moses Mendelssohn.

Abraham had therefore adopted the name Mendelssohn Bartholdy, but without a hyphen, as we have seen; this way, the "Mendelssohn" could be dropped. On official documents, he appeared as City Councilor Bartholdy, and after their visit to Paris in 1819 he had visiting cards printed for his son in the name of Felix M. Bartholdy. It was clear to him that the name Mendelssohn must disappear with the next generation. The crisis and conflict between generations was triggered by Felix's trip to England, where for the first time the young man was able to introduce himself as he wished. Fanny's letter of 7 July 1829 informs us that, here again, the children thought as one:

I have just finished writing you a long family letter, dear Felix, and must now add this short, private dispatch, as follows: Father suddenly noticed that in several English newspapers you are mentioned simply as Felix Mendelssohn; he thinks this is premeditated on your part, and wants to write to you today about it. Mother, who tried to dissuade him, told us yesterday. I don't know if he's going to or not, but yesterday evening Hensel and I decided to write you this letter in any case. If it's unnecessary, then it won't do you any harm and may even be of value. If you find it unpleasant, then simply forgive me. I know and approve of your intent to give up this name which none of us likes, but you cannot do so immediately because you're still a minor and I don't need to remind you of the disagreeable consequences it could have for you; suffice it to say that Father is aggrieved. If questioned, you can easily pretend it was a mistake, and carry out your plan at a more opportune time. The real purpose of my letter is to dispel much of the anxiety, heightened by time and distance, which Father's letter might give you. As you yourself said recently, letters of the alphabet are very cold and dead, and thus it's easy to cause a misunderstanding, especially as Father always writes less agreeably than he really thinks; that is why we wanted to send you a few friendly words on the matter. Perhaps you will be deeply annoyed to read a third version of what Father has expressed one way, and Mother in another way, but as I said, you will forgive us an ill-expressed good intention; we know each other well, I think, and everything is as it was between us. It gives me little pleasure that you, who send us only welcome news, should so often be subjected to unpleasantness from here, and that this should be the way your family life continues while you are abroad. I wish strongly that things could be different, but for now this is how it is, and if it please God, will lead to much that is good.[12]

Wilhelm added:

Remember that to renounce one's name in public implies a criticism of its having been adopted, and even if this criticism is not intended to be wounding, coming from the son, it will offend the father.

In other words, an appalling punishment awaited the twenty-year-old son if he did not submit to his father's wishes—a punishment all the more dreadful for not being precisely stated. Would he be disinherited? Disowned? That seems excessive. But Fanny did say: "Suffice it to say that Father is aggrieved." We may apply this utterance to every deed in Fanny's life, and Felix's life too. Despite her musical talent, Fanny did not violate her father's wishes in that domain until he was dead, and even then very timidly, especially as Felix had assumed his father's role in discouraging her from publishing. The meaning of Abraham's life was yoked to his children's obedience. This is an extract from the letter he wrote Felix:

I must suppose that you have either deliberately omitted the family name of Bartholdy I had adopted, or else neglected to include it, or allowed other people to omit it. In any case I only see you mentioned as Mendelssohn, both on the concert poster you sent us and in all the newspaper articles, and can only explain this unanimity by assuming that you caused it.

I am extremely displeased by the matter, and if you were the cause of it, you were very much in the wrong.

A name, after all, is only a name, no more no less—except that, until freed of paternal authority, your first, simple, incontrovertible duty is to be known by your father's name. Second, you have the rational, everlasting duty to suppose that what your father does, he never does without serious reflection and without good reasons.

After enumerating these reasons, which we already know, Abraham concluded with this remarkable sentence:

I repeat, there are as few Christian Mendelssohns as there are Jewish Confucii. If you are called Mendelssohn you are *eo ipso* a Jew and that does not suit you, if only because it is not true.[13]

Felix solved the problem by keeping the name Mendelssohn Bartholdy, without a hyphen; doubtless he considered himself subject to "paternal authority" until his father died—that is, until 1835, by which date his career was too far advanced to permit a change of identity. And how, after the death of somebody one loves, is one to execute a plan that displeased that person when he was alive, especially if it's only a matter of a few syllables?

Paul, who was the least loved and least known of the children, though proud and very attached to his family circle, followed his brother's example; perhaps more practical in character, however, he added a hyphen between Mendelssohn and Bartholdy. The different branches of the family could thus be distinguished when necessary!

Once the two sisters were married, they obviously did not have this problem. Yet they had absolutely no intention of repudiating Felix. When Fanny gave someone a manuscript of her own she signed it Fanny Hensel, née Mendelssohn Bartholdy. None of the children had the courage to wound their father by completely renouncing the name he hoped to see them all adopt.

The breathing space allowed the youngest brother seems very thin indeed. On 1 May 1829 Fanny wrote to Felix on the subject of Paul's confirmation—Paul was only sixteen and a half at the time:

I'm happy to be able to tell you we're all extremely pleased with Paul; hard work, and the fact of having to be away from us, are doing him much good, and when he comes home at night he is certainly very tired, but at the same time so sweet and nice that we rejoice with all our hearts. His employer is very satisfied with him and the sudden departure of a clerk has given him the opportunity to advance rapidly. Since we were so recently in church dispatching our last little brother into the adult world, the major changes of this past year came vividly into my mind: changes that have pushed us apart and yet together again![14]

Paul's character is indicated only through veiled allusions, suggesting that it must have been extremely hard, in the Mendelssohn household, not to be entirely up to standard—or even to be different.

The impression of unanimity conveyed by the four children comes not so much from their characters as from their need to remain united when confronting the power of their parents, which did not diminish with age. Lea had been speechless with amazement when her eldest daughter announced her engagement, but subsequently made her pay for the independence of the decision. Fanny noted in her diary that she and Wilhelm were alone together for the first time on 3 February 1829,[15] and then on 19 March made this brief entry: "On Sunday afternoon there was a very unpleasant scene with Mother on the subject of our marriage and I was unable to calm Hensel down afterward."[16] Not until 19 March did she write: "Only now am I truly engaged."[17] Had Lea finally withdrawn her opposition? Fanny missed the presence of Felix in her relationship with her mother. Lea must certainly have suffered as much as Fanny from the young man's absence, for he also served as a link between Lea and the outside world, and she had projected all her aspirations onto him. Paul never entered into the equation and was dismissed even before Felix had left Berlin. Fanny and Rebecka inherited the task of supporting their parents emotionally and providing outlets for their moods, since their rationale for living apparently needed some support.

That Felix was extremely important both to his mother and his sister is evident in this letter of 27 May, in which Fanny speaks of her problems with all the humor she could muster:

It's the same with little things as it has always been. I'm not very annoyed for myself, but just as it used to afflict me on your account, I now feel badly for Hensel, who is nearly as affected by it as you were. Mother has never learned to say yes to anything, and that still gives rise to some highly disagreeable moments. I recently had a most distressing scene with her on the subject of my marriage. If one takes a broad view of the situation, she is kind and good, although incorrigible, and the trifling problems disappear. But none of us is as good and intelligent as you are, which is why no one can obtain anything at all from Mother. You are our Alpha and Omega and everything that lies between. You are our heart and soul, and also our head; the rest can go hang itself. We're all very fine when you're not there, but we no longer amount to much. You are a kind of ruler of the roost who has something the rest of us possess to a far less degree. . . . In fact, for me there are two kinds of people: you and everybody else. Beckchen is going to read this, but I'm not embarrassed because she knows very well that she's here, and Hensel, and three or four other people, and that she could write the same thing too.[18]

Rebecka and Fanny competed for pride of place in Felix's heart. They would steal pens from each other's hand, and when two or three pens were available, would write over what the other one had said, which made the results particularly indecipherable—except perhaps to Felix. Beckchen was so amusing that Fanny couldn't stand it any longer and wrote in the same letter:[19] "The child is so funny, the old black-browed Cantor can't keep pace." This Bachian joke gives some idea of the role still played by the elder sister, both morally and musically, in regard to her younger siblings.

Fanny and Wilhelm always did everything they could to bridge the gap between them and to make each other happy. Wilhelm resorted successfully to his old stratagem for softening up the Mendelssohns: his drawing. Fanny delightedly described the portrait he did of Felix before he left:

We shall keep a fine memento of him here, Hensel's life-sized portrait of him, from the knees up; a complete likeness, as good as one could wish for—a pleasing and delightful picture. He is seated on a bench in the garden (a lilac bush is in the background), with his right arm resting on its back, his left arm against his body, fingers raised; the expression on his face and the movement of his hands suggest he is composing.[20]

If any whiff of distrust still remained with regard to the intruder, issuing from so different a milieu to seize Fanny, Wilhelm was able to dispel it with a final pictorial feat known as *The Wheel* (see Figure 11). Fanny explained it at length to Felix—for whom the drawing was intended—in a letter dated 15 August,[21] and which reached him while he was visiting Scotland.

The Wheel.
What is this wheel? It is self-explanatory and self-evident, and is a moral person. The accompanying dossier was written for you during a joyful reunion in Charlottenburg on Saint John's day, but it was not sent earlier because the following message, a visual representation, had been roughly sketched that day in big freehand drawings, and subsequently finished piece by piece.
Does that need explaining? Don't you recognize the young man in the middle, the wheel's axis, dressed in an English tailcoat with Scottish accessories? Doesn't he look like a regimental oboist? But the entire fine company revolves around him and is dancing to his little flute. Fish separate him from the Continent and a curious dolphin is nibbling at the freshly written music

in his pocket. The woman walking on his head is unmistakably Authority in a blue coat, which she wore that day despite the heat, with mittens to protect her hands from the mosquitoes. The C above her head—the moon containing the man in the moon—will reveal everything you don't yet know. The delicate silhouette beside her is dancing a galop with your shadow, since you're not within reach. The A represents a small fruit tree up which a little man is climbing on a ladder. The F is a signpost, inscribed "Berlin." The friendly man leaning forward, holding his neighbor's ball of wool in one hand and a silver tray (how poetic!) in the other, is bringing you your favorite dish, a Moor's head. As you see, the unities of time and place have not been respected, for according to the plot this scene should take place at Leipziger Strasse on Sunday night, whereas someone in the D is retelling a wheel story, in which it's known that actually no Jew, but rather a headmaster, fell into the water. He stands with hands outstretched and one can see him screaming while a water sprite tries to seize his feet. The ball of wool leads us by the shortest possible route to the knitted stocking and its mistress. I don't think you'll fail to recognize the sister of the Nose. Her M is striding about as solemnly as a respectable minuet. The one rolling toward the wheel, full of daring impetus and who has unjustly depicted himself as a brake shoe—for he is really no hindrance to this wheel—needs neither praise from me nor any introduction, for what does he have to do with me? It's true that in my hands I'm holding a chain to which he is attached, but what does that signify? (I too once was asked.) I shall not say another word on the subject of the two stupid interlaced otters, because it cannot escape you that the B consists of two little goats, curiously grouped, and that the F is looking toward London through a telescope. This was true when it was drawn, and will still be true when you open this letter. The handsome man who follows was cutting silhouettes out of lime-tree leaves when he was sketched, and has poked his nose eagerly into his work. The front side of the paper has turned into a silver moon, otherwise it's all been copied *tale quale*. Its H is showing you two modern ballet dancers. I'll say nothing of the other, but the entire world knows about it. Besides, the inscription above is not unrelated, for the handsome fellow was wearing black stockings on that day, and shoes with long laces, which made a particularly striking effect against the white unmentionables [trousers]. The small person who comes next is wearing large mameluke sleeves buttoned at the wrists: you will probably know why (but I don't know why two people are reaching up over their heads toward a friendly A). She is holding a flower that is growing right up to the nose of our gentleman brother who is gratefully pouring a dewdrop into the calyx. I always claimed it was a silver groschen. The little boy above is blowing into his alphorn and calling out: "Ho ho, little goose, come back home."[22]

The Wheel is the name of the circle of which Felix was the central figure; that is why Wilhelm wanted to send him a friendly memento of it, while at the same time indicating his desire to belong too. Felix, of course, is the wheel's hub, and his two sisters, whom he called his otters, are its central figures. Fanny holds the chain in her hand, while Wilhelm swings about at the end of it, still uncertain of his future in this little group but henceforth capable of dealing humorously with the situation. The way Fanny expresses herself in the letter is completely obscure, likely to be understood only by a few initiates, and one can well understand Wilhelm's irritation: for months he had faced enigmas and jokes, the key to which escaped him entirely. And by the time that Fanny, making great efforts to translate, showed him the key, the joke had altogether lost its flavor—if indeed he managed to find the joke amusing. In a letter to Felix dated 17 June,[23] Rebecka maliciously observed: "Yesterday evening, while engaged in delightful conversation in the magic moonlight with her extremely ardent fiancé, Fanny fell asleep. . . . Why? Because you are not there." Hence Wilhelm's feeling of not belonging to the wheel. Clearly Rebecka, with her radical opinions, was in no hurry to accept him. After all, Fanny did not necessarily fall asleep because she was bored; she may simply have felt comfortable. But the Mendelssohns let nothing go by, and Wilhelm was still at the stage of having to prove his social aptitude. In an age when photographic mementos did not exist, Wilhelm's talent as a portraitist performed a valuable service for the scattered family members. When Felix received *The Wheel* and a portrait of Fanny he thanked Wilhelm properly, but—typical of the obligatory, exacting Mendelssohn behavior—not without including a few homespun truths. Felix also sketched, although he did not do portraits and confined himself to landscapes:

Your drawing is quite sublime and makes me truly happy when it looks at me, for that is what it does; it is so inspired and beautiful, and so like its subjects, and funny, and so forth; where the devil did you dig up such ideas? The large portrait of Fanny is very fine, but I don't like it. I can see it's magnificently drawn, and that the resemblance is striking, but as for her posture, clothing, gaze, or all her sibylline prophetic side or rapturous enthusiasm, you haven't caught my Cantor! Such enthusiasm doesn't flow upward or heavenward, through grandiose gestures or into crowns of wildflowers, for all that would be apparent at the first glance!—and that is not how it should be; on the contrary, it must be discovered gradually. Don't take this badly, court painter, but I've known my sister longer than you have, I carried her in my arms as a child (exaggeration!), and I am truly an ill-bred, ungrateful lout, incapable of thanking you properly for the rays of sunlight you periodically send me. If you could see how often I sit quietly opposite your drawings, alone in their company and nowhere more so than in London, then you would receive the thanks you deserve, but as for saying it!? Down with words. Accept my joy as thanks.[24]

Fanny had said of this portrait, or another like it: "He's painted me with a floral crown again. People will think I was born with this accessory upon my head."

While *The Wheel* was still in the works, Fanny was composing her *Nachtreigen* (Nocturnal Round). This time no cryptic language of the circle was involved: Wilhelm wrote the text himself. Dated June 1829, it might correspond to the Saint John's (or Midsummer) day that had witnessed the birth of *The Wheel*. This was possibly the first time Wilhelm and Fanny worked together, a habit that would subsequently become an essential element of their conjugal life. Wilhelm presented her with a poem glorifying the Supreme Being and love. Fanny turned it into a mixed chorus for eight unaccompanied voices. In the beginning the female voices (two pairs of sopranos, two pairs of altos) sing softly of the wonder of nature and the divine mystery; then the men (two pairs of tenors, two of basses) sing about the joy of living, as experienced by "the man who has been freed of his limits." The women ask them not to disturb the divine order with their cries and to join silently with their circle. The men comply, "won over by the holy power of their appeal. Remain thus in peace and joined together just as God brought you here." All conclude together in a fugue for eight voices, to the words "Let us receive and think together of the Unique." In spirit, the poem is reminiscent of Schiller's *Ode to Joy*: pleasure and joy linking people regardless of social or human barriers, while love, like friendship, gives intimations of divinity. The reference to Beethoven is even more direct in the second entrance of the women, then of the men, for the musical line recalls Beethoven's theme, but in inverted form. This manner of treating a melody, and the subsequent fugue, are entirely baroque in inspiration and have nothing classical or Romantic about them. On the other hand, the cult of the Supreme Being and the references to Schiller and Beethoven situate Wilhelm and Fanny in their own era: the right to conjugal love was the great achievement of the age, and Fidelio the model for all wives. In Wagner's *Der fliegende Holländer*, Senta sacrifices herself out of faithful love, thus redeeming the Dutchman; in *Die Frau ohne Schatten* (The Woman without a Shadow), Hofmannsthal transforms the married couple into guardians of divinity. But Fanny and Wilhelm are not at that stage yet. They have simply succeeded in "joining what fashion had arbitrarily separated."[25] To be sure, Fanny did not take herself for Fidelio, but her attitude toward Wilhelm was deliberately protective, like Leonore's attitude to Florestan.

The collaboration between painter and musician began with a cycle of six lieder on poems by Droysen, commenced on the day Felix left; Fanny sent him the manuscript with an ornamental miniature painted by Wilhelm. The cycle comprises five stirring lieder for voice and piano and ends with an unaccompanied vocal trio, *Wiedersehen* (Reunion)—an unexpected effect. Fanny entitled the cycle *Liederkreis*, inscribing it "For Felix during his absence in England in 1829," and sent it to him with these words:

I beg you not to consider these lieder as if they came from afar, which would give them only relative value, but as if I had composed them with one or two mistakes and was asking you to criticize them. There is one that I count among my best lieder, I want to see if you agree with me, you'll sing it very well. You'll also see that Hensel, although the laziest of correspondents, is busying himself on your account.[26]

The cycle Fanny sent Felix is preserved in the Bodleian Library.[27] The idea of bringing music and drawing together on the page transforms a normally utilitarian manuscript into a work of art, decorated with a graceful miniature and elegantly transcribed in Fanny's hand. Of course, the idea was hardly new, and once again the Mendelssohns evince a certain archaism! Gothic style was all the rage in architecture, but the work Fanny and Wilhelm did together possesses an exceptional charm that goes beyond mere fashion. Felix was delighted with it—indeed, the music made so strong an impression on him that as late as 30 January 1836 he would write: "I don't know a better song of yours than the English one in G Minor, or the end of the *Liederkreis*."[28] Clearly, their roles were now definitively reversed; Felix's trip to England proved extremely successful. Both the *Mid-*

summer Night's Dream Overture and the Symphony in C Minor, Opus 11, were successfully performed in orchestral concerts, and Felix also had a reputation as a pianist. England suited him: there, too, the tradition of Handel oratorios had been maintained. He studied all the scores of ancient music he could find in libraries—as he did wherever he went—and recognized how greatly he had benefited from Zelter's solid instruction.[29] He also demonstrated that he could earn a lot of money: the concert he gave to benefit the poor people of Silesia brought in 300 guineas,[30] and several English editors proposed publishing his works. Felix was thus no longer an amateur. Yet he particularly wanted to avoid becoming a traveling virtuoso, preferring to be taken seriously as a composer and conductor.[31]

His family henceforth endowed Felix with the aura of a master. Fanny in any case recognized him as something she could never be, because he had what she had never had: access to the outer world. Thus she was all the more touched by his compliments. He combines them humorously with the description of his trip to Wales, where he had got on very well with a companion he had met along the way—who certainly could not have expected a scolding from Felix:

If only he hadn't tugged at my sleeve on the stage coach while I was singing Fanny's first lied, *Stören möcht ich* (I would like to disturb), in order to show me a snare designed to catch enormous salmon, I would never have quarreled with him or scolded him. But these lieder are more beautiful than one can say. I swear, I'm speaking as a cool critic, and I find them very pretty. They prove that true music exists, which is as if the quintessence of music had been grasped, as if the soul were made of music. These lieder are like that. Heavens! I know of none better.[32]

One could scarcely be more laudatory. Felix sent an English musician friend named John Thomson to see his family, asking them to treat him kindly:

Show him what's likely to please and interest him; let Fanny play the piano for him, often; he should hear her lieder, sung by Beckchen; give him a good idea of music *abroad*; Father once reproached me in Paris for not being sufficiently nice to foreigners and I think he was right. But I've given up that fault since I've been away from you; . . . now it's up to you to continue![33]

An article subsequently appeared in the *Harmonicon* on 30 March 1830, signed by a J. T. and entitled "Notes of a Musical Tourist":

I possess twelve published songs under Mr. Mendelssohn's name, which he wrote when a boy of fifteen. . . . But the whole of the twelve are not by him: three of the best are by his sister, a young lady of great talent and accomplishment. I cannot refrain from mentioning Miss Mendelssohn's name in connexion with these songs, more particularly when I see so many ladies without one atom of genius, coming forward to the public with their musical crudities, and, because these are printed, holding up their heads as if they were finished musicians. Miss Mendelssohn is a first-rate piano-forte player, of which you may form some idea when I mention that she can express the varied beauties of Beethoven's extraordinary trio in B-flat.[34] She has not the wild energy of her brother, but possesses sufficient power and nerve for the accurate performance of Beethoven's music. She is no superficial musician; she has studied the science deeply, and writes with the freedom of a master. Her songs are distinguished by tenderness, warmth, and originality: some that I heard were exquisite. Miss Mendelssohn writes, too, for a full orchestra by way of practice. When I was in Berlin she had, for this purpose, begun to *score*, for a modern orchestra, one of Handel's oratorios, and shewed me how far she had advanced![35]

How fortunate the John Thomsons had called and left this information about persons who were themselves too modest to do so! This shows that everyone close to them knew Fanny had published under her brother's name, and John Thomson was no more shocked than anybody else. On the contrary, what emerges from his article is that a woman did not "come forward to the public" without attracting disagreeable reviews. Praised for her talent, Fanny is further praised for her discretion, and John Thomson is not about to suggest that she emerge from anonymity. We may also wonder what became of the orchestration of the Handel oratorio. Clearly, Fanny was as interested as Zelter in Felix's research, but as always, she remained in the shadows.

The letters exchanged by the Mendelssohns during this first prolonged absence (about eight months) would in themselves fill an entire book: they wrote to each other almost every day, usually at length. The hours spent at the writing desk fully justified that piece of furniture's existence. Felix missed his sisters badly; he had met an English family, the Taylors, whose two extremely charming daughters reminded him of his two "otters." He was able to chat and laugh with them as he did with Fanny and Beckchen, and also talk to them about his sisters. Felix had many plans involving them: first of all, Fanny's wedding was approaching fast, and she had asked him for a "Prelude and Chorale," without however specifying the date of the ceremony. Felix reproached her for this vagueness on 11 August, but the date of 3 October was not fixed until 2 September.[36] After that came his parents' silver wedding anniversary, which would have to be celebrated properly, on December 26; and finally, Felix planned to take his entire family with him to Italy the following year. Though greeted enthusiastically by the younger generation, the project was countered by the absolute veto of Lea, who would not leave her garden on any pretext at all.

CHAPTER FOURTEEN

The Wedding

It was clear that Fanny would have to await Felix's return before marrying. Without his presence, no celebration could be planned. Fanny had asked him to compose the music for it, although she had several ideas of her own: "I already have my organ exit quite clearly in my head. G major, the beginning with pedal," she wrote to him on 25 August. "In any case I am extremely happy at having managed to convince myself that being engaged has not hurt my music. Once I've produced a good piece after I am married, I shall feel relieved and believe I can make progress in the future. But isn't it true that I've never done anything as good as the lieder I wrote for you, and the piece written by and for Hensel isn't bad either."[1] Felix was supposed to meet his father in Hamburg and travel through Holland with him before returning to Berlin. But on 16 September he fell from a carriage and hurt his knee; the wound was sufficiently deep and painful for him to have to spend two extra months in England, looked after by the faithful Klingemann.

Instead of attending his sister's wedding, all Felix could do was to write her a letter conveying his good wishes:

London, 25 September 1829
This is thus the last letter that will have time to reach you before the wedding. For the last time I am addressing Miss Fanny Mendelssohn Bartholdy, and there is so much I would like to say. . . . Whether I say it well or badly or do not say it at all, you both know I'm still the same, but I have the feel-

ing I've completely lost control over something I previously felt master of; and thoughts concerning everything that's about to change and reestablish itself—thoughts which should have merged into a single one expressed at the beginning of my letter—come to me one by one, vague, half-wild, and impossible to put in order. . . . Go with the ebb and flow; marry and be happy, fashion yourselves a life that I shall find beautiful and that I can share when I visit you (which will be soon); stay as you are and let the outside world bump along as it will; besides, I know both of you, and so all is well. Whether I call my sister Fräulein or Frau doesn't greatly matter. A name doesn't alter much.[2]

Extremely emotional, Felix was in fact afraid to go home and face all these changes. Is it coincidence that he admits to losing control of his life at a moment when he had just lost control of his horse and fallen from the carriage? Despite repeated requests from his sister, he proved incapable of composing the organ piece he had nonetheless promised her. In his anguish he expressed himself all the more tenderly to Beckchen, who was still "unchanged": "You cannot imagine how I love you and how I need you near me in order to feel happy, how many hours of happiness you've brought me, and how I shall never think or feel otherwise as long as I live. Never!"[3]

As for Fanny, she noted Felix's absence as dryly as possible in her diary, probably to mask her sadness: "This week, two letters from Father. One came from Rotterdam accompanied by a magnificent letter from Felix, from which it unfortunately emerged that they would not meet each other, and in which Felix confirmed irrevocably that he would not be coming to the wedding; yesterday another letter from Amsterdam, announcing that Father would leave yesterday. He sent me a wonderful bridal gown."[4]

The preparations were by now too far advanced to think of postponing the ceremony, and the engaged couple had no wish to do so. Fanny had already received other presents from her father, for which she thanked him in a letter of 19 September:

The famous chest arrived and its contents naturally surpassed any previous description of them: once again you have brilliantly proved your good taste and munificence. Each item is the finest I have seen in its domain: embroidery, fabrics, patterns—everything is perfect, Nathan the Wise certainly never brought anything more beautiful back from his travels! The splendid veil caused much emotion among the female hearts here; in fact it is not the fashion here for brides to wear a veil, but I find it so beautiful, and so appropriate, and it would show me to such good advantage—especially on account of my red neck—that I have a great desire to be the first to wear one, and certainly I shall not be the last. Everyone else in the house advises me to do so, Hensel and many others, and yet we are afraid it may cause too much of a sensation; in short, the outcome of the debate is still uncertain. Ribbons, shawls, everything is of the best; and so again, best thanks for everything.

We are very busy these days and spend most of our mornings in shops—and here I cannot adequately express my admiration for Mother, for she is tireless. It's as if she never felt so well, or so much in her element, as when she's too busy to have time to breathe. It's almost impossible to thank her directly, [especially][5] as one would have to be thanking her all day, and so I want to do so here because she's going to read it, and because I owe you as much gratitude as I do her; this gratitude, although it has always been felt, has never been as concentrated as it is now, when I am indebted to you not only for your present attentions, but for not having to leave the paternal roof.[6]

The fiscal side of things seems to have posed several problems, and the Mendelssohn parents made the couple very aware of the differences in their financial situations. Wilhelm's appointment to the Academy of Fine Arts on 21 February 1829 was viewed as an indispensable condition of the marriage. He could not, however, guarantee his wife the standard of living to which she was accustomed, and this meant that both Fanny and Wilhelm were indebted to her parents. It was decided that the Hensels would live in the garden house, that is, in the wing of the princely family dwelling that faced the garden.

The marriage contract[7] established Fanny's fortune at 18,613 reichsthalers and ten silver groschen. "Herr City Councilor Mendelssohn Bartholdy," who remained the trustee of this fortune, agreed to pay Fanny five percent interest per quarter and to add the sum of 1500 reichsthalers per year, for as long as this money remained in his keeping—a promise that would become null and void should Fanny decide to retrieve her fortune. The engaged couple married in accordance with the law of separate possessions. Fanny's fortune and any acquisitions she might make or have made remained under her control, with the stipulation that she would have to provide for the house if it became necessary.

It seems rather contradictory to be simultaneously so much under the paternal thumb and so independent of one's husband. Abraham had received control of Lea's fortune, even if Lea never let him forget where the money came from. But Wilhelm was not a banker. Given her considerable wealth, Fanny's methods of keeping house demonstrated how successfully Lea had brought her up. Fanny had not married for money and she behaved like a painter's wife, content with the means he possessed. The Hensels did not live off Fanny's money, which was put aside, comprising a fortune that was used by the next generation.

For his part, Wilhelm had no thought of making a good business deal either. He married into a milieu superior to his own, but it was not in his character to behave like a kept husband. Naturally he was on the lookout for a studio, and hoped to find one in Prince Albrecht's palace, on the other side of the Mendelssohns' garden.[8]

Meanwhile, the two organ pieces had still not been composed, and since one is never so well served as by oneself, Fanny herself composed an organ prelude on 28 September.[9] Tension was mounting rapidly, and Fanny suffered repeatedly from raging toothaches. On 23 September she noted that she had had a third tooth extracted, that she had quarreled with Hensel, and that Rebecka had an abscess on her nose.[10]

The wedding day finally arrived, but that very morning Fanny took the time to send a long letter to her beloved brother, telling him she thought of him so much that her first pleasure of the day had been in finding a quiet moment in which to write to him and weep over his portrait. She assured him once again of all her love, saying she knew he would never bear a grudge against Hensel and was happy to think that in six weeks he would be able to see her house and be pleased with it. Only then would she know if all was well.

Just as my room came to life yesterday when the paintings were brought in (the sketch for your portrait is hanging above my writing table), so will the paintings come to life when you come in and frolic on the blue sofa,[11] and feel savagely at ease.

You can picture the scene: me at my writing desk which looks extremely colorful, with ink and eau de Cologne living harmoniously together; Beckchen at the window, finishing the bouquets for my bridesmaids—for you know I have to give away flowers, and that in three of the bouquets there's some myrtle, and that the girls who have myrtle in their bouquets will be the next to be married. The weather is fine and all the minor incidents have turned out well thus far.[12]

Next she told him about the previous day, which she had spent listening to her organ piece—it "sounded well" when Grell played it[13]—before busying herself with errands, visits, presents, Hensel's sister's dress,[14] and putting various things in order. At eight o'clock the family gathered for a "peaceful" wedding's eve celebration,[15] and since they could not find the *Pastorella* which was to be played while everyone was leaving the church, Hensel suggested that Fanny herself compose another piece.

I had the effrontery to begin in the presence of all witnesses; I finished it at half past midnight and I don't think it's bad. . . . It's in G major, I already knew the theme because I'd thought of it before you promised to send us one, but the actual composition dates entirely from yesterday.

People are beginning to bustle about round me, it will soon be eleven o'clock, the wreath ceremony begins at one and the nuptial blessing is at three. I think of you constantly, as calmly as usual; Hensel, who was here a moment ago, says to send you his best wishes, and I'm especially calm because I know he likes you. . . . May you feel fresh, happy, and contented today—I am certain of it; or I would not be able to be those things myself. Goodbye for now, stay as you are, you'll find everything here just as it used to be, even the novelty. For the last time,

Fanny Mendelssohn Bartholdy

Beckchen sends you lots of love, she has something wrong with her nose and is suffering grotesquely from it. My wreath has just arrived, it's magnificent—very thick, fresh and green with many, many buds. It was a present from Beckchen.

More than a week later on 14 October, Fanny confirms in her diary that this was how she spent her day, and further adds:

Around one o'clock, I received additional splendid presents. I looked nice. . . . The ceremony took place at four o'clock. Wilmsen's[16] sermon of no interest, the church full. I talked to the whole family and many friends. We spent a few moments visiting Aunt Meyer,[17] then had the wedding dinner at home at six o'clock; some very anxious hours followed and we separated from the others at nine o'clock; our sisters brought us over here and I shall say nothing of the rest.

Several visits on Sunday morning, then at noon and in the evening we went over there alone. On Monday and Tuesday we ate over there again, on Wednesday at Marianne's after receiving a letter from Felix that still brings tears to my eyes when I think of it. On Thursday we set up house, but we always go over there in the evening. There were many people there on Sunday. Today we hoped in vain for a letter.[18]

"Over there" is of course the wing where Fanny's parents lived. The affair does not seem to have been exactly a picnic from start to finish. There was nothing unusual about all the commotion and work involved, but then again, not all brides write their own organ music. It is interesting to note the conditions in which a woman had the right to express herself: although it took place in public, marriage was essentially a private event, and consequently Abraham made no objection to one and even two of Fanny's works being played. It is distressing to see the words "some very anxious hours" penned by Fanny. How unfortunate that a young woman of twenty-three had to experience this wait, in a strangely public fashion, before confronting the unknown, with embarrassment and fear as her dominant emotions. Once again, this was entirely "normal," but in Fanny's case the anxiety expected in a young bride was complicated by the fear of losing her music, inspiration, and identity. Rather archaically, she seems to have endowed virginity with a power that a "woman" (if indeed she was not already such a thing when still a virgin) might lose through carnal knowledge of men. The words "I looked nice," *Ich sah gut aus*, are touching when one knows what grief her ugliness caused her.

The young couple thus moved into the garden house, a dwelling full of charm, especially in summer. The Hensels occupied the apartment on the right, and the apartment on the left was rented between 1829 and 1830 to the Devrients. It was highly chic to live at the Mendelssohns' and very convenient for the Sunday matinée rehearsals, but in winter the temperature in the *Gartenhaus*, even when it was heated, never rose above 14 degrees Celsius. Therese Devrient wrote in her memoirs: "The apartment was too unhealthy and uncomfortable for a family of four children. It was all on one level, had no cellar, and the windows, surrounded by thick creeper, did not allow the sunlight to pass through and we often seemed to be breathing musty air. The Mendelssohns were sufficiently understanding to accept our reasons. Thereupon Hensel admitted that nothing could be more agreeable to him, for he had looked vainly for a studio; this confession further facilitated the idea of our move."[19]

Abraham then ordered major remodeling in the house and had

two walls on the left side knocked down so that Hensel's studio would face north, as is best for painters.[20] Far from sulking over such ideal conditions, Wilhelm began painting from morning till night, and in 1831 he opened an atelier for students.[21] This contributed to the regularity of his income, which otherwise depended on the sale of his paintings and on royal commissions. But in both the garden house and the main building there were always lodgers who lived in attics on that side of the courtyard.

The idea of a banker's daughter spending every winter of her life in an underheated corner of a palace seems extraordinary but does tally with the image the Mendelssohns wanted to give of themselves: material comfort had no meaning and ostentatious luxury mattered even less, for only art and moral values were sufficiently important for one to devote one's life to them. Fanny's character was now formed, and henceforth she remained as her son described her:

She was a petite woman, and had inherited a crooked shoulder from Moses Mendelssohn, although this hardly showed. Her finest features were her eyes, which were large, somber, and very expressive, with a short-sightedness people did not notice. Her nose and mouth were quite pronounced and she had beautiful white teeth. That she often practiced the piano showed in her hands. She was lively and decided in her movements, her face was very animated and truthfully reflected all her mental impressions; dissembling was impossible for her. Everyone she met noticed at once what she was thinking, and what she was thinking of them; for just as surely as her joy was manifest at the sight of somebody she liked and was happy to be with, heavy, menacing frowns appeared on her forehead and around her mouth whenever some antagonistic apparition put her in a bad mood. I have never seen anyone who so intensely enjoyed anything beautiful: a fine day, handsome people, a wonderful talent, a beautiful landscape. She would gulp in fresh air to the bottom of her lungs, and claim that this was one of life's greatest pleasures. Her irritation at anything ugly was manifest with equal intensity, as was her anger at anything evil. She was very intolerant of boring, dull, pretentious, shallow people and had several *bêtes noires*[22] who caused antagonistic feelings she could not control. Her expression then took on an air of such deep unhappiness that she often plunged us into wild hilarity, when the cause proved utterly disproportionate to her bad mood. Once that was dispelled, she would laugh about it herself, only to prove equally incapable of mastering her feelings the next time it occurred. She was quite indifferent to material wealth: good food and drink, comfort, clothes, luxury of any kind— none of this was necessary to her life; on the other hand, she could not live without the company of a small circle of cultivated, intelligent people, or without the pleasures of art. A taste for freedom was profoundly rooted in her nature: she showed great reserve toward the aristocracy, and toward the pretensions accompanying birth and money. Social calls and what are known as "social duties" were extremely vexing to her, and she avoided them whenever possible. But she was a faithful, constant friend to all those she judged worthy of being close to her, and was capable of making any sacrifice for them.[23]

An appealing character, therefore, but far from easy to live with. The stern Cantor evoked by her brother is readily recognizable in this description. Although extremely restless, Felix was always a charming, amusing companion, closer to Beckchen in drollness. Paul was serious-minded, like Fanny, but showed more interest in money and birth than did his siblings. That Sebastian speaks of Fanny's "taste for freedom" indicates how unusual the concept of individual freedom was at that time, for men and women alike.

Moses Mendelsfohns Examen am Berliner Thor zu Potzdam

1   Moses Mendelssohn was invited to Potsdam by Friedrich II at the request of a foreigner who was a guest of the king. In the illustration, Mendelssohn is passing through the Berlin gate in Potsdam; the king, however, did not take the trouble to meet him. (Geheimes Staatsarchiv)

2   Portrait of Moses Mendelssohn. Oil on wood, by Johann Christoph Frisch,
1786. (Mendelssohn Archive)

3 Abraham Mendelssohn Bartholdy. Drawing by Wilhelm Hensel, 1823. (Kupferstichkabinett)

4 Lea Mendelssohn Bartholdy. Drawing by Wilhelm Hensel, also probably done in 1823. (Kupferstichkabinett)

5   Fanny Mendelssohn
Bartholdy. Drawing by
Wilhelm Hensel, 1821.
(Kupferstichkabinett)

6   Felix Mendelssohn
Bartholdy. Drawing by
Wilhelm Hensel, also
probably dating from
1821. (Kupferstich-
kabinett)

7 Rebecka
Mendelssohn Bartholdy.
Drawing by Wilhelm
Hensel, 1823. (Kupfer-
stichkabinett)

8 Paul Mendelssohn-
Bartholdy. Drawing by
Wilhelm Hensel, 1828.
(Kupferstichkabinett)

9 3 Leipziger Strasse; after 1882, but its appearance had not altered.
(Märkisches Museum)

10   The *Gartenhaus* (garden wing) of 3 Leipziger Strasse, where the Hensels
lived. Watercolor by Sebastian Hensel, 1851. (Mendelssohn Archive)

11 *Das Rad, The Wheel.* Drawing by Wilhelm Hensel, 1829.
The young man in the middle: Felix. The two stupid otters: Fanny and Rebecka.
The handsome man cutting out silhouettes: Albert Heydemann. The short
woman: Auguste Wilmsen, possibly the daughter of the minister who officiated
at Fanny and Wilhelm's wedding. "Our gentleman brother": obviously Paul
Mendelssohn-Bartholdy, whose slightly pompous character Fanny hints at in
this phrase. The "Higher Authority": Caroline Heine (1811–1888). The dainty
silhouette dancing with Felix's shadow: her sister Albertine Heine (1814-1879),
future wife of Paul Mendelssohn-Bartholdy. The friendly man leaning forward:
Droysen. The "mistress of the knitting," sister of the "nose": Heydemann's
sister, Minna. The man unjustly treated as a brake shoe: Wilhelm Hensel. The
letters drawn above each head also have a meaning, as Fanny explains.

12   Fanny Mendelssohn Bartholdy. Drawing by Wilhelm Hensel, 1829.
(Kupferstichkabinett)

13   Felix Mendelssohn Bartholdy. Portrait for Goethe by Johann Joseph Schmellers, 1830. Reproduced in Arnd Richter, *Mendelssohn*. Mainz: Schott, 1994.

14   Rebecka Dirichlet. Drawing by Wilhelm Hensel, undated, after 1840.
(Kupferstichkabinett)

a Polterspass 2. Oktober 1829: final evening as a bachelor, 2 October 1829.

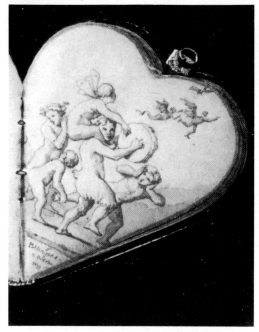

b 6. März 1830: Sebastian moves inside his mother's womb, 6 March 1830.

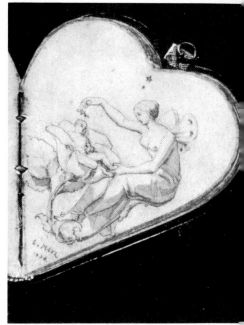

c 16. Juni 1830: birth of Sebastian, 16 June 1830.

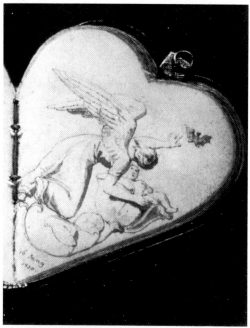

d 1. November 32: Fanny miscarries, 1 November 1832.

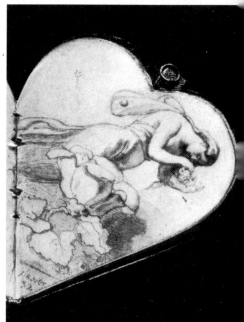

15 Pages from the heart-shaped notebook Wilhelm gave to Fanny, which they filled with music and drawings. Private collection. Reproduced in *Mendelssohn-Studien*, vol. 7. Berlin: Duncker und Humblot, 1990.

16   Wilhelm and Fanny Hensel. Engraving by August Weber, Leipzig 1854.
(Mendelssohn Archive)

17   *An die Ruh* (To Peace), autograph manuscript by Fanny Hensel, undated;
illustration by Wilhelm Hensel; poem by Ludwig Heinrich Christoph Hölty
(1748–1776). (Mendelssohn Archive)

18   Sebastian Hensel and Walter Lejeune Dirichlet. Drawing by Wilhelm
Hensel, 1834. (Kupferstichkabinett)

19 Fanny Hensel playing the piano in Rome in 1845. Drawing by August Kaselowsky, a student of Wilhelm Hensel. Reproduced in *Klavierwerke* by Fanny Hensel, edited by Fanny Kistner-Hensel, Munich: Henle.

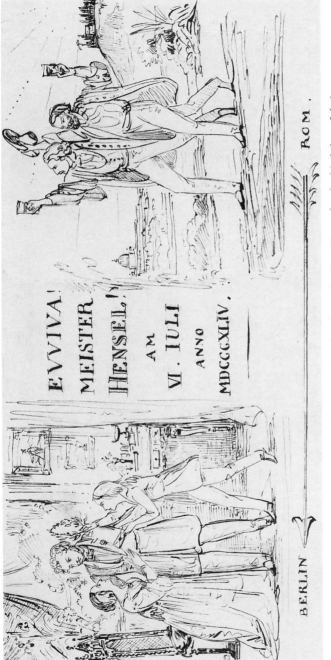

20 Letter from Rome, sent by August Kaselowsky and Julius Moser for the birthday of their teacher, Wilhelm Hensel, 6 July 1844. Drawing by Julius Moser. (Mende.ssohn Archive)

21 Gounod, Bousquet, and Dugasseau. Drawing by Wilhelm Hensel, Rome 1840. (Kupferstichkabinett)

22   *Der Maiabend* (May Evening), autograph manuscript by Fanny Hensel, undated; illustration by Wilhelm Hensel; poem by J. H. Voss. (Mendelssohn Archive)

CHAPTER FIFTEEN

The Silver Wedding

For some months Felix had been bubbling over with ideas for his parents' silver wedding celebration. The injury to his knee had prevented him from attending his sister's wedding, but his family was still very much in his mind. Upon his return from his trip through Scotland and Wales with his friend Klingemann, he wrote to Wilhelm Hensel from London on 10 September 1829:

This is how things stand: a young lady we both esteem highly, my dear brother, happily begins her letters to this effect, but nothing ensues; the difference between us is that I am her brother, and something important ensues. This, then, is how it stands: we must create a committee to arrange the silver wedding festivities. I had previously thought Fanny should preside, but in her first proposals she gave so much consideration to a certain family (for example, this evening we're alone at the Hensels' house, we're lunching at noon at the Hensels', and so on) that I declare her guilty of bias, *perhorrescire*, I reject her and Beckchen is the one who should be *chairman*. You, Fanny, and I shall be ordinary members, Droysen an honorary member and Klingemann an external member. The session has begun. I ask liberty to speak and I have a proposal to make: how would it be if we celebrated the event this way: three light comedies, each of one act,[1] performed with costumes, song etc. and accompanied by a full orchestra (I'll assume the costs of this, and of the festivities in general; to this end I'm engaging in a little musical peddling), in the following order: no. 1, *Soldatenliebschaft* (The Loves of a Soldier),[2] that is, the famous work by me which bears this name, and which our parents still like, without changing a note of it and with the original cast. What do you think? Isn't that a brilliant idea? Then a new light comic musical by Fanny, for which Hensel will have to write the text—pleasant, light, full of nice twists, very tender and beautiful. Then an idyll by me, for which my head is full of ideas; it must be very pretty, with roles for a sedate couple, to be played by the two Hensels, then later there'll be the neighbors' daughter, a lunatic rural policeman, a disguised sailor or soldier, or who knows what else? A village march, with lots of A major everywhere. From time to time there can quite properly be ice creams, cakes, allegories, pro- and epilogues—I think this will amuse our parents far more than a simple orchestral concert. . . . You'll make a splendid debut, Hensel; don't be afraid to sing, we'll take care of you.[3]

Felix did not return to Berlin until 8 December. In his pocket was his new light musical, with a libretto by Klingemann: *Die Heimkehr aus der Fremde* (The Return from Abroad).[4] The following day he read it to his delighted sisters, and to Devrient who was to play the country policeman.[5] For Hensel, who was tone deaf, Felix had written a part all on the same note. As yet, however, Fanny had done nothing but await Felix's return; she admitted to Klingemann[6] that the outline of her *Festspiel* had been waiting since the summer and that she had not expected to produce more than a piano accompaniment to complete it. Felix's arrival stirred things up; Hensel wrote the text in a single day and Fanny composed and orchestrated the music in the space of a week. The plot was familiar: three sisters, representing the recent wedding, the silver wedding, and a future golden wedding, sang the praises of conjugal love; they were preceded by three heralds.

Therese Devrient gives a slightly different version:[7] according to her, Fanny wrote her *Festspiel* before Felix returned, and "naturally" assigned the soprano part to her, since Therese was her friend and an habituée of the Mendelssohns' private concerts. But, taken aback first by the "complicated" nature of the piece, then alarmed by a sustained high B, the young woman refused to sing this note on stage—adding in her memoirs that her husband preferred to know she would be sitting in the audience. She clung to her decision despite Fanny's despair and Rebecka and Wilhelm's anger, until Felix took advantage of his charm to convince her—just as his talents as a conductor were soon to sustain her in this theatrical ordeal, so difficult for a proper young lady to endure. Whether the childhood friendship linking her to Fanny endured this trial with similar success is debatable.

The dates Therese gives for the composition of the *Festspiel* do not agree with those in the letters the Mendelssohns sent Klingemann, but Therese was certainly truthful about her refusal to sing Fanny's work. Fanny must have felt not only hurt but panic-stricken to see that performance of her present or future compositions would depend on the moods of a petty little bourgeoise who had been too nicely brought up to perform in public. Still confined to the private sphere, Fanny could only ask "friends" to perform her works. She cannot have greatly regretted seeing the Devrients leave the neighboring apartment several months later.

In spite of this incident—so tedious for Fanny—the festivities were moving along well. Lea told Klingemann[8] that on the morning of 24 December they distributed warm clothing among twenty-five people—men, women, and children—before giving each other the customary presents in the evening. The next day Lea's family paid her a surprise visit: her brother-in-law Joseph, her sisters-in-law, "even proud Aunt Jette," Betty and Heinrich Beer, her nephew Alexander, his wife Marianne, their children, the Heyses, Marianne Saaling, Dr. Becker, Gans, the Heydemanns, Droysen, Marx, the Varnhagens, the Roberts—all came to congratulate her, as did the Redens (Count Reden was the Hanoverian ambassador; from 1825 to 1831 this embassy was situated on the second floor of 3 Leipziger Strasse). The celebration began immediately with some scenes prepared by Gans: Robert read a poem, the "children" sang a chorus from Cherubini's *Les Deux Journées*[9] and brought a wreath; everybody wept, and the "children" played a movement from the *Children's Symphony* which Felix had composed the previous year. This was followed by Gans's play, in which Betty Beer acted the part of a French dancer, Marianne Mendelssohn played a student, Marianne Saaling was a soubrette from Berlin, and Friedericke Robert finally appeared as a muse, holding Marianne Mendelssohn's daughters—Marie and Margarete—by the hand. The two little girls then presented Lea with a silver wreath and cup.

The next morning at breakfast, Lea and Abraham received a present from their children—a sofa—and a "magnificent vase given to Mendelssohn by a man who owed him many thanks,"[10] as Lea told Klingemann. "It is as precious as those which monarchs own or give each other, for Hensel designed the tiny decorations with incredible care, and supervised the making of it at the porcelain factory. . . .

That there be no lack of serpents, stars, shells, dolphins, and symbols of every kind is guaranteed by Hensel's creative imagination."[11]

The long-awaited evening finally arrived. The festivities took place in Lea's bedroom, the garden house concert hall being impracticable in winter. Lea continued her enthusiastic description:

Felix had a real theater built with an elevated platform for spectators; there were more than 120 of us, most of whom were seated. His orchestra was very select: first violins, Ritz and Ganz; cellos, the other Ganz and Paul, to whom Felix had given a solo. Fanny's *Festspiel*[12] was sung by Busolt, Landsberg, and Paul! and by my daughters and Therese Devrient. Paul sang in the trio, played well and cut a very good figure. The three heralds had magnificent costumes which came from the Royal Tournament of Potsdam. Therese, crowned with roses, symbolized the first wedding; Rebecka— whose dress and veil were richly embroidered with diamonds and who wore myrtle in her hair—the silver wedding; and Fanny, who was adorned in the same manner, but entirely in gold, represented the golden wedding; all three were pleasing to look at and made a truly touching impression.

They wore quite different costumes for your light musical, in particular bonnets of black velvet decorated with gold. Fanny and Rebecka were more spontaneous and confident than I would ever have thought them capable of being; the former was distinguished by her tranquil, pomaded, matronly side and the latter by her gaiety. The youthful tenor has a most agreeable voice and artistic way of singing, and everybody liked him; it was a great pity that Devrient spoiled his serenade with inopportune witticisms. What a delightful Klingemannism this serenade is, with its "obbligato" night watchman! Oh, if only you were Felix's scribe! The result would be entirely different from what the Parisian factory produces. I mustn't forget Hensel, who played Schulz rather as a caricature, but most amusingly: Professor Gans declared it was worthy of the school of Schröder.[13]

What a lot of care and work—and what an audience—for this essentially private entertainment! Obviously, Lea Mendelssohn Bartholdy was happy and proud beyond description. Fanny herself said so, a few lines further on in this same family chronicle addressed to Klingemann: "You remember how joy suits her, and rarely has she looked as happy as she did that day—in other words, she's never been more beautiful." Considering the children she had, Lea could certainly tell herself that she had led a successful life, completely fulfilling her role as a professorial mother.

So sound an artistic education had she given her offspring that they could join in with professionals, with no discernible difference. In Felix's case, this had been apparent for some time. Henceforth he was not only the conductor, the moving spirit, and the principal composer in the family; he could also, thanks to his earnings, cover the festivity's expenses. Even the child she appreciated least, Paul, could nonetheless play in an orchestra, along with the best professional instrumentalists in Berlin—violinists Eduard Rietz and Leopold Ganz and cellist Moritz Ganz![14] Much to his mother's amazement, he was also capable of singing and acting on stage—though this surprised her less than the sight of her confident daughters. At the very beginning of the letter she expressed her astonishment and admiration: "And what do you say to Fanny, composing a *Festspiel* with orchestral accompaniment, and acting in it herself, with the greatest of ease?" The habit of performing in the narrow confines of a supremely elitist and critical family circle had made her daughters capable of putting on an entertainment after only five rehearsals, of behaving like experienced actresses, and of completely forgetting that a woman should not make an exhibition of herself—something the supposedly more "feminine" (and from our viewpoint, more stupid) Therese Devrient would prove incapable of forgetting. Naturally, Felix had assigned the leading role to Eduard Devrient who, despite vocal problems that had forced him to give up singing, remained an accomplished actor and peerless man of the theater. Poor Hensel was reproached for taking caricature too far, but what is a man to do when he has only a single note to sing and is none too sure which one it is, even with all his "colleagues" prompting him on stage?

The case of the "young and tender" tenor deserves further mention. The Mendelssohns had desperately been searching for somebody to play the part of Hermann, for Felix was still hampered by his injured knee and could not undertake the role.[15] They had heard about a "young student named Mantius, who was all the rage in Berlin salons," as Rebecka put it,[16] and although suspicious of anyone outside their circle, they had bowed to necessity. Eduard Mantius (1806–1874) was a law student who, according to Therese Devrient,[17] sought her husband's opinion of his talent before deciding to become a singer. These light musical comedies given at the Mendelssohns' proved to be the first step in his career: he was subsequently engaged by the Berlin Opera between 1831 and 1857. He also sang oratorio.

The gap separating amateurs from professionals seemed short indeed: Felix Mendelssohn and Eduard Mantius crossed it with no concern, except in regard to practical matters. But for women, especially married women, the distance was unbridgeable. Marriage designated women the guardians of home and hearth and private realms. Such was the case of soprano Pauline Schätzel (1811–1882), who had taken part in the *Saint Matthew Passion* and sang major roles at the opera: Agathe in *Der Freischütz*, among others. She retired from the stage in 1832 when she married publisher Rudolf Decker (1804–1877), and thereafter gave only a few concerts—a circumstance that proved advantageous to Fanny, who recruited her for the *Sonntagsmusik*.

Thus the year 1829 ended successfully. Even so, the future was still uncertain for Felix, who would continue his distinguished wanderings across the whole of Europe; as for Fanny, whose social future was already mapped out, there should have been no further cause to mention her. Henceforth Fanny Hensel found herself subject to the threefold imprisonment of her private life: trapped first, inside the provincial town Berlin had become; second, in her marriage and maternity; and third, inside her home, which was simultaneously a protective microcosm and a prison, and from which not even matrimony had extricated her.

Fanny did not, however, allow the private world in which she was confined to smother all possibility of manifesting her talent. She managed to forge herself a musical destiny which, like the silver wedding festivities, unfolded in the space where public and private spheres met.

CHAPTER SIXTEEN

The Young Couple

As early as 1823, Lea had complained to Amalie Beer that musical life in Berlin encouraged neither artistic work nor creativity: "Alas! There's a terrible dearth of outstanding models here, and Felix and Fanny have to find all that within themselves."[1] Lea was perhaps exaggerating slightly, but for some time Berlin had certainly been a depressing city with no significant history. To be sure, the Napoleonic invasion had caused all traces of the *Aufklärung* to disappear, but that was already in the past, and from 1810 on the liberal reforms of Stein and Hardenberg might well have been expected to lend new impetus to cultural life. This was not the case, and the Karlsbad decrees only confirmed the most conservative aspects of the Metternich reaction in central Europe. The result was a lasting restraint imposed upon the press and the circulation of ideas. Hence Felix's joy at being able to travel through England, a country in which individual freedoms were traditionally respected—if one avoided visiting the Bethnal Green slums, whose wretched inhabitants were crammed together, after being driven there by the agricultural crisis of 1815. Hence Heinrich Heine's joy at being able to live in Paris, amidst a flourishing literary milieu; welcomed with open arms by Gérard de Nerval, Théophile Gautier, Dumas, and Balzac, Heine could justifiably write to Hiller in 1832: "If anyone asks you how I feel here, tell them 'like a fish in water'; or rather, tell people that when a fish in the ocean asks about another fish, the second fish replies, 'I feel like Heine in Paris.'"[2]

Enlightened men, indeed, were generally inclined to flee. But the women, enlightened or not, stayed where they had been put. Fanny was reduced to observing the world from Berlin. On 4 January 1829, her diary begins thus:

This year will bring about a major break in our family life: Felix, our very soul, is going away; the second half of my own life awaits me. Paul is going into the world: everything is in a state of movement and change at home, just as it is among most of our acquaintances and in the world. Greece is free, that is, at the mercy of the European powers assigned to pronounce judgments on its position; Turkey is up in arms, and Russia, after an important military campaign, is back in its winter quarters.[3] England is on the one hand overshadowing Ireland, which is desperately demanding its civil and political rights,[4] and on the other hand maintaining an ambiguous policy toward Portugal as protector of the Donna Maria Gloria;[5] France is a mediator of Greek freedom in Morea (her scholars in Egypt, Champollion) while engaged in constant inner struggle with the Jesuits and the Ultras (Béranger); Spain is ruined by factions and devastated by yellow fever; Portugal is in a lamentable state of anarchy, Don Miguel ill, perhaps dead, with his mother opposed to him, Don Pedro lukewarm and indecisive.
I'm going back to 3 Leipziger Strasse.[6]

This is an astonishing bulletin. Fanny's sympathies for the freedom of nations and for civil rights are clearly expressed, as are the political stances toward Greece and Ireland common to all Romantics of her generation. The most significant element in this state-of-the-world bulletin is her utter lack of interest in Germany, Prussia, and even Berlin; the reader is swept from distant Portugal to the Mendelssohns' garden, without the slightest transition. Prussia had, however, regained considerable political importance: swayed by fears of revolution, Austria had agreed to let Prussia dominate the Germanic Confederation in exchange for an alliance. Between 1828 and 1834, Prussia also succeeded in negotiating a German Customs Union of which it assumed the leadership. There was thus ample reason for a Berliner to think something was taking place in her country.

But public opinion seemed to have disappeared, or at least lost the ability to express itself. Perhaps the condition the city had fallen into was partly to blame. Sand had eroded the monuments of Friedrich II's city, and no lasting answer had been found to the problem of which governmental body, state or municipality, would assume the costs of running the town.

In 1830 Berlin was a relatively small city of 240,000 inhabitants which had retained its fortifications. Most of the houses consisted of two or three unadorned stories. The countryside began right outside the city gates, and sometimes even inside the city walls: Luisenstadt, for example, had remained a vast zone of gardens and fields. This was the region formerly known as Köpenicker Feld, situated south of the historic center and east of Friedrichstadt (the eighteenth-century section of the city, where the Mendelssohns lived), and renamed in 1802 in honor of Queen Luise. Opinions vary on the subject of Luisenstadt as it was then: an idyllic, dreamlike place for some people, with walks and countryside a few steps from civilization, but for more practical minds, inaccessible in summer on account of the dust, and in winter on account of the mud. Nonetheless the city was growing in size and was destined to grow even larger. Chancellor Hardenberg's agrarian reforms had proved profitable for the *Junker* —the landed German gentry—and an impoverished peasantry had taken refuge in Berlin. These bankrupt peasants had nothing in common with the French, Czechs, and Jews who had been drawn there in preceding periods to populate a city with scrupulously controlled rents. There was no dearth of plans for urbanizing Luisenstadt.[7] The architects Mandel and Schmidt had submitted plans in 1821 and 1825 respectively, but nothing much resulted from them as the city and the state could not agree how to share the expenses. It was only in 1842 that King Friedrich Wilhelm IV decided to start work on Lenné's plans; in 1845 he had the Landwehrcanal built at the site of the fortifications, and in 1848 the Luisencanal. But these measures came very late, and speculators had already begun—wildly and with no state control, quite the reverse—to take over many sites.

The channeling of water was still rare, and this posed serious problems to the growing city. Sidewalks barely existed, and the pavement consisted of ill-cut blocks of granite. The dust and smells became intolerable in summer, as did the dirty grass and thick masses of mud in winter. Filth certainly bore its share of responsibility for the cholera epidemic that broke out in the winter of 1831, killing numerous Berliners, including the philosopher Hegel. In 1841 water mains were built which lacked proper drainage and spilled over into the street, making matters even worse.

In 1830, however, the streets were still deserted. One day Felix bet he could walk from west to east all the way down Leipziger

Strasse, from his house to the Dönhoffsplatz (that is, the length of Friedrichstadt to the limits of the old city and the Luisenstadt) with a crown of roses on his head; he won his bet, because he encountered no one. A few rare hackney cabs somehow made a living; there were streets where only one cab per day passed, on average, and very few foreigners came to Berlin where there were only two postal deliveries per week. Gas light was very slowly being adopted in the houses. People were thrifty, and life was simple and quiet, as befitted the bleakness of the Brandenburg region. That was how Sebastian Hensel described his childhood town.[8]

The local council did not seem particularly concerned about either its town or its district, as Fanny's diary implies. Why would the middle classes of a country that had no constitution feel concerned about the public welfare?

Everyone in his own home, everyone for himself: "There's no better place to be than the bosom of one's family." The political role models were the royal couple, who owed it to themselves to display an impeccable conjugal morality.[9] It was good form to be thrifty, and even rich people did not allow revellers to disturb the nocturnal peace: at ten o'clock at night, the city was deserted.

Felix's grand project of a family trip to Italy fell flat. Fanny wrote to him on the subject on 21 September 1829:

The one thing that would hold us, Hensels, back, would be financial considerations. . . . I live with a fear I cannot overcome, first of all that we would not be able to save enough for the journey, and second, that our parents might not[10] be right to disapprove of our giving ourselves a treat as divine as it would be expensive, and which would absorb at the very least a whole year's income, instead of limiting our expenditure at the start of our marriage and living quietly and fulfilling our duties here. If we wanted to arrange it differently—you know that Hensel had some idea of seeking a position there—this would mean a very long stay indeed, which also gives us much cause for reflection. In short, dear Clown, tell me something sensible about the matter. . . . If we decide to live like students now (and Hensel is certainly more eager to), spending everything and starting all over again later on, I'm afraid our parents would hardly be pleased with such a plan and neither of us wishes to decide on anything without their consent (of course, we have yours.)[11]

The old Italian dream was still alive in Fanny's mind. The Hensels would have liked to see a Prussian equivalent of the Villa Medici founded in Rome. Jacob Bartholdy had worked toward this goal, but without much tangible success. And it was stipulated in Fanny's marriage contract that she could not dispose of her money without forfeiting her pension and Abraham's management of the fortune. The Hensels thus found themselves subject to the parental veto—or rather, bound by the approval of parents "so generous" that Fanny cannot express her gratitude without adding an extra negative which makes her say the opposite of what she intends. Thus she admits her desire to go and breathe in the pure air of Italy and enjoy its blue skies; to enjoy, too, that feeling of freedom one acquires as soon as one leaves home. But prudence was in order, and to simplify matters further, the Mendelssohn parents were offering Wilhelm a studio in his very own home, a lure no painter could resist.

The *Gartenhaus* that Abraham and Lea offered them was such a model of discomfort that the Devrients themselves had not managed to live there for very long. It was a house without a cellar, therefore humid; a house without double glazing, therefore icy cold in winter—never above 14 degrees Celsius, as we have seen—and the inhabitants had constantly to wipe the window panes, which were covered with drops of water.[12] On the other hand, the drawing Sebastian did in 1851 of its façade framed with ivy shows how idyllic it looked in summer. But what a Spartan existence! Once again, simplicity held sway in Berlin, even among the rich, and Fanny didn't even have a carpet in her bedroom.

Like sensible children therefore, the Hensels set up house quietly on Leipziger Strasse. It so happened that in March 1830 Felix's fabulous plans were jeopardized by an attack of measles which a sickly Rebecka caught the day before her brother was due to depart for Italy. He was supposed to set off again, still unaccompanied, on a journey lasting two years through southern Germany, Italy, France, and England. With "a fiancé's tender concern"[13] Felix complained to Devrient that he could not say goodbye to his contagious little sister. But as luck would have it, he caught the measles too, and his departure had to be postponed for several weeks; he did not leave Berlin until May. Paul fell ill as well.

By this time it was out of the question for the Hensels to think of going with him, for in March Fanny had felt the baby stirring inside her. Fortunately, she was the only one of the four siblings not to contract measles, but even so, she had to remain in bed after 24 May because there was some threat of a miscarriage. This did not prevent the child from arriving on 16 June 1832, two months before it was due. Fanny named him Sebastian Ludwig Felix, in honor of her favorite composers: Bach, Beethoven, and her own younger brother. Sebastian would later describe the problems he experienced in school, having a name so uncommon at that time;[14] since he was also most unusually dressed and small of build, he had to project a fair amount of authority and self-confidence in order to assert himself. His godparents were Zelter and the sculptor Rauch.[15] As the baby was extremely weak and his chances of surviving very slender, he required a lot of care, thereby causing the Italian project to be put off for the indeterminate future. Not only did the child bear the name of his mother's favorite composer, but after the events of July, Fanny—fired with enthusiasm for the July revolution in Paris—also made him wear tricolored rosettes sewn into his swaddling clothes.[16] Wilhelm saw no need for this; he was now more conservative than ever, detesting the French and the middle-class opinions held by Abraham and Lea.

Fanny, Felix, and Rebecka comprised the liberal wing of the family. It was not customary at the time for women to express their political opinions—although this had not been the case during the *Aufklärung*; women only regained freedom of expression in the salons during the years that preceded the revolution of 1848. Their intellectual independence was among the things that distinguished Fanny and Rebecka from bourgeois women whose education and family situations were more ordinary. They were only really understood in their own home, a fact that excluded them further from a certain social milieu. They maintained their role as "women" by tempering the violent arguments between Abraham, Felix, and Wilhelm.[17] Without Rebecka's cheerful presence, the atmosphere tended to be rather tense; Fanny could not bear quarrels either and did all she could to preserve harmony in the family. In this way the children of Abraham Mendelssohn Bartholdy always remained very close to Joseph Mendelssohn's two sons, Benny and Alexander. Fanny and Alexander's wife Marianne had an intimate friendship lasting from childhood until Fanny's death. On the other hand, tensions still existed between Joseph and Abraham. Joseph's wife, Aunt Hinni, did not feel particularly at ease at 3 Leipziger Strasse, where she was alarmed both by the intellectual jokes and the drafts.[18] In fact, Hinni judged this latter inconvenience to be a contributing cause of Fanny's brutally sudden death.[19]

Aunt Hinni was, however, delighted to ascertain the conjugal happiness of the two Hensels, who got along marvelously well. The studio Abraham had built for Wilhelm was extremely helpful to his work. Wilhelm did an enormous amount of painting, going to his studio immediately after breakfast and staying there until night. After the main meal, which the Hensels took at half-past four, Wilhelm would return to the studio, if it was still light, or else take advantage of the garden, or he might begin drawing again, an occupation he loved passionately. He left a thousand or so portraits in pencil, which constitute a most useful documentation of his contemporaries. The abundance of these sketches proves how truly good-natured he was. It took a real affection for one's neighbor to spend time with so many different people and feel at ease with them all, whatever their social background. Although his portraits were good likenesses, they were also very idealized; the numerous portraits he left amount to little more than a collection of lovely eyes. Fanny, who was never taken in by anything, observed that "Wilhelm would draw a grandmother in swaddling clothes."[20] He was nonetheless quite capable of doing portraits of the dead, and drew not only Schinkel, Varnhagen von Ense, and Friedrich Wilhelm IV in that state but also his own wife and his brother-in-law Felix.[21]

Wilhelm's studio opened onto the music room, so that he was hardly ever separated from his family. That Fanny play the piano or compose was an indispensable condition of his painting. She thus settled into a happy and complete existence. On 9 April 1830 Felix wrote to his friend Rosen: "Hensel is incredibly diligent and works all day long, in the strictest sense of the word. Fanny has acquired a comfortable, maternal side while retaining all her warmth and inner strength: I can never be too glad about her."[22]

Wilhelm assisted Fanny during all the difficult and dangerous moments of Sebastian's birth. Born into such favorable conditions, the baby grew, quickly attained his normal weight, and by August was as fat and healthy as his mother could wish. Fanny fed the child herself for a while, then entrusted him to a wet nurse. She was so busy she had no time to open her diary, and there is a gap between 16 August 1830 and 4 March 1831, on which date she records both her family problems and her happiness with Wilhelm:

In regard to our own activities and life, everything has recently undergone some modifications: all summer, since Sebastian was born, Wilhelm has slept in the yellow room while I've stayed in the bedroom with the child and a nurse. Even though I would often go to join him in the evening and then spend the entire night with him, it was still a great hardship for us not to be together all the time; we were deeply happy when Wilhelm moved into his new studio, giving up his bedroom to the child, and taking his place. Since then we have only used one bed. Wilhelm has grown used to having my head resting in the hollow of his arm, and now we prefer night to daytime. It seems impossible to us that our love and happiness can still increase, and yet that is the case: every day we fall more in love and every evening we tell each other how happy we are. Our unity and peace are all the more apparent in that we are always happy and satisfied when we are alone or simply in our own home, but alas, always in a bad mood when we come back from over there, and we need some time to become ourselves again. And yet, they could be very happy too. But a few faults suffice to cast shadow over many virtues, and certain people can embitter the lives of those around them.[23]

All is well at the Hensels': Wilhelm reads this passage in the diary and finds it amusing.[24] Clearly, Fanny's parents' tempers had not improved, and now Rebecka was the one to suffer the consequences. The Mendelssohn children had to run a veritable gauntlet in order to marry, and now it was the younger sister's turn to be tested.

Rebecka did not lack admirers: there was the poet Heinrich Heine, that preeminent lover, and other, more serious ones, even if they did behave like little boys. Thus Professor Eduard Gans—who used to read Plato with Rebecka—and the mathematician Dirichlet came to blows over her. Fanny mentioned this to Klingemann in one of her letters: "Gans is happy to scuffle with Dirichlet, the very handsome, very pleasant, and very learned mathematics professor, who looks like a student full of the joys of living—or to put it in good German, they fight like schoolboys."[25]

The battle over Rebecka's lovely eyes was won by the mathematician, Gustav Peter Lejeune Dirichlet. Rebecka then had to put up with abundant teasing from her brothers and sister. Alexander von Humboldt had brought the young scientist with him to help measure the magnetic fields in his "observatory" in the Mendelssohns' garden.[26] Born in 1805 at Düren, Dirichlet had been totally absorbed since childhood by his passion for mathematics. At the age of twelve, he spent all his pocket money on mathematics books that were too difficult for him, saying he would read them until he understood them.[27] Though not rich—his father had only a postmaster's salary on which to raise eleven children—his parents gave him the best education they could. With a gift like his, there was no choice but to go and study in Paris; this he did in 1822, becoming tutor to General Foy's children. Dirichlet caught Fourier's attention in a lecture he gave at the Paris Academy on Fermat's theorem. The Foys' salon was a meeting place for people opposed to the current regime, and Dirichlet subsequently met Alexander von Humboldt there. In 1828 Humboldt secured a position for him at Breslau, and the following year had him brought to Berlin, first as a professor at the war college, then at the Architectural Academy and the university.[28] The young man had become one of the greatest mathematicians of his day; his research focused on the theory of numbers. Dirichlet's Cut, as it is known, states than one can always surround an irrational number (that is, a number that cannot be represented by a fraction) by a rational one (that is, fractions), as closely as desired; for example, rational numbers above or below a root of two are those whose square is higher or lower than two. This seems relatively obvious, but in fact it settled the notion of irrational numbers and clarified the mystery that had shrouded them since Pythagoras's time.

One day many years later, Sebastian Hensel told him it must be a heady sensation to be foremost in one's field. Dirichlet said he had not yet reached that stage, but that he was among the top ten or twelve. "And who are the others?" inquired Sebastian, to which Dirichlet could only reply: "The other one is Gauss."[29]

Like Fanny, Rebecka was not prepared to marry for money. Marrying a mathematician of genius seemed an obvious destiny for a woman of her intelligence and culture. Why then did the Mendelssohn parents oppose this match? Admittedly, Dirichlet was a Catholic, but since this was neither whim nor conviction on his part, simply the religion of his parents, his conversion posed no problems. We do not know to what extent he was a free thinker, but it is certain that the Dirichlets constituted the political left wing of the Mendelssohn family. In February 1831, when Rebecka announced her decision to marry Dirichlet,[30] Lea did not remain stupefied and speechless as she had in January 1829, but instead exploded in a fury and painted her daughter's future in such somber colors that Rebecka, "beside herself," took refuge at the Hensels'. Fanny and Wilhelm intervened and tried to restore calm, but the engagement was not concluded until November. The wedding took place in May 1832, and like the Hensels, the Dirichlets began their married life in an apartment at 3 Leipziger Strasse.[31]

Lea's reaction to her daughters' marriages remains a mystery. Of course, Dirichlet was only a rather impecunious professor of mathematics, but nonetheless he had regular, even honorable employment and the Academy of Sciences in Paris was asking for his services. We can suppose that Lea was more concerned with money and social position than she wanted to admit, but this would contradict the entire logic of her life, not to mention her moral standards. Another hypothesis can be advanced: unlike her husband, she did not want her daughters to marry. She herself had given everything to her children, but did she really want Fanny and Rebecka to do the same? The support she provided Fanny later on, in her moments of self-doubt, indicates that she did not approve of her elder daughter's talent being suppressed. Far more perceptive than her husband, she was capable of seeing even her own marriage in perspective and asking herself questions, even if she couldn't find an answer to them. Yet Lea's reaction to her daughters' weddings was anything but intellectual. Her main argument was based on doubts about the reciprocal love of the "intended" pair. Perhaps Lea did not believe in love generally, and particularly not in love as destiny. She had not wanted Fanny to turn into a lovesick dreamer as a girl—a state for which Fanny in any case showed no inclination—and did not willingly allow love to invade her children's lives. Perhaps this aspect of Lea's character influenced Fanny in her determination to continue with her music and not to invest so much of herself in her marriage as to destroy her own identity.

The period following her lying-in nonetheless filled her with anxiety: she was bereft of ideas and could no longer compose. She spoke of this with humor and with her customary detachment where personal matters were concerned: "Meanwhile, I've gone back to being someone who devours new potatoes and takes walks in the evening air, someone capable of enjoying herself and who is enjoying herself, and every day my little one grows bigger. I haven't done any composing yet; I had many ideas when I was not supposed to, but now the well-known drought is setting in, which I've picked up from the weather."[32] The letter probably dates from the end of July 1830, but the lack of inspiration lasted until autumn and Fanny began to worry.

She found little encouragement in Felix. He had pledged his sister to the profession of motherhood and watched delightedly as she grew larger during pregnancy. From Rome, he intimated very clearly that she had fulfilled the duty imposed by their father ("You can still improve!"), that she was henceforth going to be perfect and confined by her perfection:

Stay happy, radiant, and contented, with no real changes from now on, for you scarcely need to improve much henceforth; may your good luck continue: such, in the main, are my birthday wishes. For you cannot expect a man of my caliber to wish you musical ideas; you are insatiable to complain of their absence; *per bacco*, if you really wanted to, you'd be able to compose (cf. "The Life of a Wandering Musician" or "Felix in Rome"); and if you don't want to, then why are you complaining so dreadfully? If I had my child to coddle, I wouldn't want to be writing scores, but because I composed "Non nobis,"[33] I cannot, alas, be holding my nephew in my arms. But seriously, the child is not yet six months old, and you'd already like to be thinking about something other than Sebastian? (not Bach). Be glad you have him; music is only absent when it's not in its right place and it doesn't surprise me that you're not an unnatural mother. I nonetheless wish you everything your heart desires for your birthday, and so I'm going to wish you half a dozen melodies—but that won't help you.[34]

No one could express his lack of sympathy with more affection. Everything that Felix wrote was doubtless true but not terribly encouraging, and could only have made Fanny feel something between annoyance and suffocation. Yet Felix had enormous admiration for his sister, as he himself generally realized when he met other female musicians. While passing through Munich he flirted with the pianist Delphine von Schauroth;[35] the two performed a sonata for four hands by Hummel, with great success. He spoke of her in these terms to his sister:

I simply wanted to tell you that the young girl played extremely well and that she greatly impressed me the first time we played together (for we have already played that piece), and as I was listening to her playing alone yesterday morning, still in the greatest admiration, it suddenly crossed my mind that we have a young lady in the house behind us who has an idea of music entirely different from most ladies, and I thought I would write and send her greetings from the bottom of my heart. You are of course this lady, but I tell you Fanny, I only need think of certain of your pieces to feel tender and sincere, even though one has to tell a lot of lies in southern Germany. You really know what the good Lord had in mind when he created music; it's no wonder people enjoy it. You also know how to play the piano and if you ever need a greater admirer than me, you can paint him or be painted by him.[36]

Further on there is another reference to *Italien*, Queen Victoria's future favorite:

Yesterday, a noble countess was praising my lieder and said, in the form of a question, Isn't the Grillparzer one delightful? Yes, I replied, and she immediately thought me immodest, until I explained everything, and said who the composer was and promised to let the company benefit from the compositions you would soon be sending me. If I do so, then I'm a workhorse or a peppercorn: but you won't be sending any.

Enlightened though he was, Felix may vaguely have supposed—as Fanny had, a few months earlier—that young virgins possessed creative powers that disappeared with matrimony. Fanny had feared as much, and various backward notions may well have lingered in her brother's mind as well. Fortunately, Wilhelm came of different stock and though exceedingly conservative was not afraid of his wife. The abundance of portraits and miniatures by Wilhelm indicates he preferred painting or drawing on a domestic scale. Of course, he was a court painter by profession, and earned his living through commissions of more or less monumental size, or else through making copies of Raphael. But Wilhelm did not spend his life traveling, as did Felix; he spent it in his private world, sharing everything with his wife and quite unafraid of being dominated by her. He needed to feel she was working, in the same way and at the same time that he worked. As Fanny wrote to Felix, at the very beginning of their marriage: "My husband makes a point of having me sit down at the piano every morning, immediately after breakfast, for afterward I'm constantly disturbed; this morning he came and without saying anything put a piece of paper on the piano; five minutes later I called him back and sang him the music, which was set down on the paper in another quarter of an hour."[37]

The intention was not to produce major works but rather to establish a constant exchange between painting and music. For the birthday of one of their women friends, Wilhelm had the idea of painting a small box on which Fanny would write a song. Fanny found the idea far too splendid for the occasion, but Wilhelm generously declared it out of the question to keep their ideas to themselves. The box has unfortunately been lost, but one private collection still contains a heart-shaped notebook, covered with pictorial and musical comments by the Hensels (see Figure 15). Wilhelm had brought a similar notebook from Italy for each of the brothers and sisters, which he gave them for Christmas in 1828. These were extremely fine presents, considering how expensive and precious paper goods were. Rebecka's notebook was shaped like a star but has vanished without trace. There is no mention of such a notebook having belonged to Paul, even though it seems unlikely he did not receive one. Felix used his to keep a record of his appointments in London. The heart-shaped notebook which Fanny received was a small gilt-edged album measuring six by seven centimeters, containing forty-one pages of high-quality paper.[38] Between Christmas 1828 and August 1833, Wilhelm and Fanny filled the notebook with alternate pages of music and drawings: it forms a kind of diary. Fanny wrote down fragments of musical phrases, either themes of lieder which were scarcely altered in the final version, or else transitional passages one or two bars long. At the beginning of the notebook, Wilhelm wrote a little poem:

> Wohl diesem Büchlein gleicht das Herz
> Du schreibst hinein Lust oder Schmerz.
>
> (This little book is like one's heart:
> What you write in it brings joy or pain.)

Then his sketches alternate with Fanny's jottings. Initially abstract, they become more personal after the birth of Sebastian. On 6 March 1830 a fairy waves a butterfly over a child asleep inside a flower, indicating Sebastian's first motions inside his mother's womb: the butterfly symbolized the baby's soul. Then on 16 June 1830 a bat, representing an evil spirit, is chased away from the baby—still inside a flower—by an angel. Husband and wife made no further entry in the notebook until Christmas 1831, when a poem for Sebastian appears, with three drawings by Wilhelm and six outlines by Fanny. A sad episode follows: there is a theme for a cradle song by Fanny, completed in October 1832; then on 1 November Wilhelm drew the same fairy of 6 March 1830, but this time its wings are drooping sadly and the child is upside-down inside his flower. This is the sole extant indication that Fanny suffered a miscarriage at that time. Wilhelm was able to paint even when he was unhappy. Fanny, on the other hand, confided nothing in her diary between June 1832 and May 1833 and made no further jottings in the heart-shaped notebook; Wilhelm did six more sketches in it, but the final pages remained empty.

These were not easy years for anyone. Although the Hensels were happily married, life in Berlin was made generally gloomy after 1831 by an outbreak of cholera which effected drastic cuts in the population. Fanny caught the disease but recovered; when she started keeping her diary again on 26 May 1833, it resembled an obituary column: "Summary of people we have lost during the past two years." The names of thirteen people follow, including Aunt Jette and Hegel in 1831; the violinist Rietz—Felix's friend, who had taken part in the *Saint Matthew Passion*—in January 1832; a very close friend of Fanny's, Ulrike Peters, who died of a "nervous disorder" in February; Goethe, in March; Zelter, in May; Ludwig and Friederike Robert, in June; and Rahel Varnhagen, in March 1833.[39]

Given the circumstances it was no wonder Fanny fell ill during the summer of 1832, or that she lost a child. Felix was at home again that summer, and Fanny was all the more unhappy in that her illness prevented her from taking full advantage of his presence: "Felix was there for the whole of the previous summer, and had I not been constantly unwell, we could have spent some wonderful moments together."[40] Doubtless, these would have been the last such moments for some time, for Felix knew by then that there was no future for him in Berlin. Despite her poor health, Fanny mustered enough energy to overcome the effects of the numerous bereavements and her difficult pregnancies. The musical life she organized around her was soon to remind her that she was not simply a mother and a domesticated woman.

CHAPTER SEVENTEEN

Sunday Musicales: The *Sonntagsmusik*

To help herself recover from the usual postpartum depression, Fanny decided to reinstate the *Sonntagsmusik*, which Abraham had started in 1823 to benefit his elder children, particularly Felix.

In thus deciding to create a musical circle for herself, Fanny was not starting from scratch, nor was she inventing a new Berlin phenomenon. From 1820 on, the Biedermeier salon in Berlin had been essentially a musical salon, from taste and necessity. These were no longer conversational salons, since speech was no longer entirely free and women did not discuss politics. Bucolic poetry replaced conversation as a form of entertainment, and music opportunely lent meaning to words that would otherwise have seemed rather vapid. The whole of Berlin society tended to accord an almost religious importance to cultural models and waxed enthusiastic over music, theater, and the visual arts, which were capable of uniting opposing factions in a world full of tension. Thanks to the abstract and irrational nature of music—an art the government wanted to make accessible to every social class—the German people saw themselves reflected therein.[1]

Accordingly, much music-making took place in Berlin salons between 1815 and 1848, whether in the homes of Elisabeth von Staegemann, Princess Luise Radziwill, Amalia Beer, or Lea Mendelssohn Bartholdy. The two latter salons were the most brilliant.[2] Mother of both composer Giacomo Meyerbeer and poet Michael Beer, Amalia Beer compelled recognition by virtue of her personality and the tartness of her remarks; she was known as the Queen Mother. In the

Staegemann and Radziwill salons the entertainment was more varied, alternating between music, poetry, and minor games, whereas the Beer salon was almost exclusively musical—which did not prevent theatrical people and political or scientific celebrities from frequenting it. Lea Mendelssohn Bartholdy, however, did not occupy a throne in her salon, which was distinguished from the Beer salon by its familial character: it was hosted by an entire family, and especially by the mother and two daughters. As Devrient had perceived, Lea put the guests at ease and let Felix and Fanny shine, while Rebecka radiated good humor. Thus Fanny had only to pick up and continue with work already begun—except that in Berlin the conditions for listening to music were changing from year to year.

At the time when Abraham had launched the *Sonntagsmusik*, instrumental concert life in Berlin was very impoverished. There were two orchestras, the Berlin Opera orchestra and the Royal Chapel orchestra, but the actual organization of concerts remained hazy and was left to private initiative.[3] For the Beers and Mendelssohns, inviting musicians into their salon was more than a rich man's fancy—it was a musical and sociological necessity. Musicians needed private performances in order to exist, and Berliners needed them in order to hear instrumental music. This nonetheless contributed to the citizens' impression of living in an unimportant city: as with city management, the government refused to intervene decisively, and the local council did not feel able to assume responsibility for an orchestra or for organizing a series of concerts.

Fanny was quite aware of this state of affairs, and of the role she might have played had she worn "unmentionables," or trousers. As early as 1825 she wrote up a plan for organizing concerts, which in her view should be attached to the Singakademie:

Berlin, 17 March 1825

Proposal to establish an
instrumental music lovers' association.

The present state of instrumental music in Berlin requires the efforts of capable, expert men;[4] this declining art needs a strong hand to raise it, otherwise it will disappear in the bad taste of the time, the egotism of the organizer, and the pandering to the public.

The sole classical instrumental institution in Berlin, the Möser quartets,[5] benefit from a faithful audience even though the organizer is little concerned with captivating listeners with novel and unusual features, and even though the performances often lack perfection—whereas this genre, which can only count upon its own intrinsic value and dispenses with additional support, demands perfect execution.

Berlin possesses many gifted amateurs who are lovers of this art; the lack of a rallying point for so many scattered talents is tangible. People do what they can by inviting into their homes, when their means permit, quartets or other smaller or larger groups. There are innumerable such private gatherings here, but, being isolated events, they have no effect and propagate an amateurism more harmful than favorable to art. If all these individual rays, feeble in themselves, could unite in a single bright beam, they could then diffuse their light in the world, just as the Singakademie concept has spread out from its birthplace and taken root throughout Germany.

Symphonies constitute the major form in this vast domain of instrumental music. Our association must therefore set its sights in this direction. Fasch's Singakademie could serve as a model for our institute, as far as structures are concerned, but its aims must and will remain essentially different. The Singakademie, which is only interested in sacred music and whose members are for the most part women and young girls, must for this reason distance itself as much as possible from all publicity: serious music is indeed appropriate for churches and not for concert halls, and women of private backgrounds shy away from appearing before an audience.

Our association is quite a different case. Here we find only men who have gathered for the same purpose, namely, to perform great instrumental compositions in a worthy manner. Here everything lends itself to publicity. Vibrant and exciting music demands an enthusiastic audience and loud applause; a large orchestra requires a full hall, otherwise it becomes deafened by its own noise, and an audience gathering for a festivity is as suited to symphonies that are universally joyful, lively, and noisy, as is a small, quiet, devoted circle meeting for a religious chorale or a strict fugue.

Let us now seek a means of obtaining our objective.

A man who is capable, expert, and enthusiastic about the project will undertake to found the society and manage its founding members. There will be a public subscription,* each member will pay eight reichsthalers yearly, in addition to an entry fee of three reichsthalers. The costs to be calculated and considered will be as follows:

1. Rent, heating, and lighting of a hall.
2. Service.
3. Music desks and other necessities.
4. Pay for those wind instrument players who cannot be found among amateurs but can most appropriately be selected from regiments.[6]

To save money on scores after the society is first established, we shall have to subscribe to a lending library, until the society is rich enough to think of having its own library.

In the event that these unavoidable expenses are covered by the first subscription, the society could be organized in this way: two meetings per week, from 7 to 9.** We shall study symphonies and other instrumental movements under the direction of a conductor. He will stand next to the first violin, and be the sole judge of works chosen: symphonies and, to introduce variety, other large instrumental compositions. If the conductor sees fit, compositions and concert pieces by members of the society could also be performed. After the society has assembled regularly for a certain time and has studied the necessary number of pieces, we shall announce twelve subscription concerts for the winter at a subscription cost of six reichsthalers. There will be one every two weeks, while the three meetings between concerts shall be used for studying and preparing the concert. An annual salary will be paid the conductor from the revenue of these concerts, and if a surplus exists, a fund shall be established with which the society can subsequently buy music and instruments. Among the active subscribers will be men who want to take charge of the administration and management of receipts. Nothing must be undertaken unless the costs are covered.

As for the organization of the association, the choice of a conductor—in case the founder wants to resign—or the examination of prospective members, etc. etc.,*** it will be time to consider all that when the project nears maturity.

It is probable that the establishment of such a foundation, or any other one like it, would be appropriate here and now. One may suppose that a town as musical as Berlin would encourage and support such an undertaking in every possible way. And what splendid fruits may we expect when our institution shall some day be linked to the Singakademie with a view to great musical performances; when both forces strive toward the same end, performing the works of Bach, Handel, Haydn, Mozart, Cherubini, and Beethoven with appropriate perfection! May it soon be granted us to move toward this fine goal, and that the Berlin public will help us in this task, as long as we work with all our strength to sustain it with ardor, in word and in deed!

---

*Each amateur skilled in any instrument at all will be accepted, with a preference for good violinists. At first we shall accept everyone, without the slightest reservation, so that the institution can begin as soon as possible. It is rare to find wind players among amateurs, but we cannot doubt that they will apply themselves to winds, as soon as they see this opportunity to practice them.

**The number of meetings, like the contributions to be paid, must be organized according to the needs and wishes expressed by the majority of members.

***Examinations must not be held before the number of members needed to begin has been attained. Until then everyone who presents himself must be accepted without examination.[7]

When did Fanny take the trouble to write down this project? And for whom? No one knows. She wrote it carefully, taking care not to repeat certain phrases. Was this designed solely to be read in the Mendelssohn home? Lea, who disliked inaccurate, hasty work, had passed on to Fanny—among other domestic qualities—her managerial sense, along with an extremely practical and active mind. In any event, the project description proves Fanny's passion for instrumental music. Berlin did not have the orchestral tradition of other European towns; rather, it had a tradition of choral singing combined with a particular fondness for lieder. Instrumental music had figured so prominently in the education of Felix and Fanny Mendelssohn that they were bound to suffer from its absence. It must be noted that Fanny makes no essential distinction between the nature of chamber music and symphonic music, only a quantitative one. When Abraham invited an orchestra to play with his children, it was, according to Devrient, to play "concertos and trios." For a pianist, the style and difficulty are the same.

Fanny insists on not imposing auditions on the amateurs applying for membership in the group. This shows that they were on the whole very capable—or that she had great faith in the efficacy of work. But her bursts of lyricism indicate she had another purpose: her enthusiasm, and the enthusiasm she ascribes to the amateur players of Berlin and which she had already noticed in their homes, endows this great plan with a religious, unifying dimension. It is reminiscent of the heroic exaltation of Schiller or Beethoven: "All men are brothers. . . ." The concert hall supersedes a place of worship, where particular religious dogmas and political opinions are equally inopportune.

Not for one moment does Fanny think of joining the association, simply of "supporting it ardently." Unlike Felix, she did not learn to play the violin. Was it considered less private than the piano? She does not even comment, observing drily that women exclude themselves, according to their own standard of privacy. Perhaps the plan was written with her brother in mind: Felix, whose women were all working for his future. But the very next year, in 1826, Felix's close friend Eduard Rietz—the violinist whom the Mendelssohns adored—founded a philharmonic society consisting of amateurs. Did Fanny draw up her plan for him? She certainly cannot have been a stranger to it.

In April 1827 the Singakademie was to inaugurate its new hall, in the midst of Berlin's monuments, with the Mass for sixteen voices by Fasch.[8] Beginning in 1828 there followed several performances of major oratorios by Handel and Graun, and Rietz's new philharmonic society played *Judas Maccabeus* with the Singakademie on 17 January 1828. It was this same orchestra, enlarged by instrumentalists from the Royal Chapel, that Felix conducted in the revival of the *Saint Matthew Passion*. Whatever the quality, or lack of quality, of an ensemble of amateurs, the motivation that drove people to undertake such arduous work was truly astonishing. Without a doubt, this enthusiasm had to do with the religious atmosphere surrounding performances of the *Passion*, and this group sense was a foretaste of the national unity that would coalesce by 1871.

Unfortunately, Rietz died in January 1832. Felix left home for good shortly afterward, and as she cuddled her baby Fanny must have wondered how to satisfy this passion—and, more or less consciously, how to participate in this great movement without a man to serve as an intermediary between herself and the public world. She therefore decided to revive the *Sonntagsmusik*. Indeed, no matter how difficult they were to live with, the Mendelssohn parents were still exceptional human beings: what other woman at that time would have been allowed to organize her own concert series? One can see why their children never ceased to idolize them.

Felix proved delighted with his sister's idea, and wrote to her from Rome: "I cannot tell you, my dear Fanny, how pleased I am by your plan for the new *Sonntagsmusik*. It's a brilliant idea and I implore you in God's name not to let it slip into oblivion; instead, you must ask your nomadic brother to compose something new for you. He'll be happy to do so, and is only too delighted with you and your idea."[9]

Fanny wanted to form her own chorus, a most important element of the plan. The concerts were to present vocal and instrumental music alternately, with Fanny playing solo piano in between. "I don't think this will do any harm, either to you or the audience," added Felix. The mere fact of hearing about the concerts inspired him to compose music for Goethe's *Die erste Walpurgisnacht* (The First Walpurgis Night). "The thing has taken shape, it's turned into a big cantata with full orchestra and could be made very jolly." All these projects radiate *joie de vivre*, as does the famous *Italian Symphony* which "will be the gayest piece I've ever written, especially the finale." But the *Walpurgisnacht* would always remain one of Fanny's favorite pieces, one she included often in her concerts throughout her life. In fact she was probably conducting a rehearsal of it on 14 May 1847 when she died.

Felix was not the only one to be composing cantatas. Fanny wrote four between June 1831 and January 1832: *Lobgesang* (Hymn) was completed on 14 June 1831 for Sebastian's first birthday. The work has the form of a cantata by Bach: a pastoral introduction, a chorus, an alto recitative, a soprano aria *O dass ich tausend Zungen hätte* (O that I had a thousand tongues), and a final chorus. Its subject concerns some sort of action of the graces in regard to the child's birth. The biblical quotation in the alto recitative makes this clear: "A woman when she is in travail hath sorrow, because her hour is come: but as soon as she is delivered of the child, she remembereth no more the anguish, for joy that a man is born into the world."[10] The infant Sebastian was placed under the great musician's sponsorship—which did not prevent Felix from sharply criticizing the work's instrumentation. He did so in a letter written six months later, when he was visiting Paris for the last time and Fanny had already gone on to her next piece:

I felt pangs of conscience reading your most recent score, which you so skillfully conducted for Father's birthday, and reproached myself for not having said anything about the previous one—because with me, colleague, you can't get away with it so easily! How the devil could you think of having the horns in G play so high? Have you ever heard a G-horn attack a high G without playing a false note? I ask you! At the end of the introduction, just when the wind instruments come in, isn't this obviously a low E that these same horns have to play? Well, doesn't this low snoring of the oboes entirely destroy the pastoral and flowery character of the piece? Don't you know that you have to obtain a special license to write a low B in the oboe part, and that this is only permitted in very particular circumstances, such as a scene with sorceresses, or when you want to express great sorrow? In the A major aria, hasn't the composer covered the song with far too many other voices, so that the delicate intention and pleasant melody of this piece—so successful in other respects and containing so many fine things—is eclipsed or at least impoverished by them? But seriously, this aria is splendid and particularly charming. I have, however, some reproaches for the two choruses, bearing on the texts rather than on you.[11]

Felix had many problems with texts, which were frequently too "concrete" for his taste. In regard to the choruses of *Lobgesang*, he complained that "the words involve no music in a necessary manner." He did, however, remain quite aware that this problem was really his own problem, and that his own lieder could be criticized for not rendering the words but rather the emotion of the text and, consequently, for being able to dispense with words. Hence, his partial recomposition of the recitatives in the *Saint Matthew Passion*. But he had unreserved admiration for all the purely musical aspects of his sister's work: "As for your music and its composition, it is very much to my taste: there is no female pedantry hidden in it anywhere and if I knew a Kapellmeister who had produced such music, I would set this man up in my court." At the end of his letter Felix mentions his meeting with Kalkbrenner,[12] saying he did not much approve of the latter's desire to become a "Romantic" in order to appeal to contemporary taste, but that Kalkbrenner had spoken to him of "his lovable little sister, whom he liked so much, with her fine talent for composition and piano."

Brother and sister had the same problems and the same ideals; they were two Lutheran musicians who as Romantics and Berliners entertained the same ambiguous relationship with texts. A text, such as the one just quoted from the Bible, is not necessarily emotional. But music, according to Felix, is always inspired by temperament, by emotion. In his view it follows that not all texts can be put to music. This assertion nonetheless contradicts the education in counterpoint inherited from Bach and Kirnberger, in which music is not emotional but abstract and symbolic, with the function of communicating the divine utterances to the community. Between these two opposing poles lurked a further necessity: a melody must be fluid and easily remembered. This was the principle uttered by their father Abraham, in his fidelity to the late eighteenth-century concept of nature. The *tafellieder* and other Berlin lieder would have no other rules. Felix never found an opera libretto to his liking, for his demands were con tradictory. The idea of composing an opera never even occurred to Fanny: not only was this quintessentially public world not permitted her, but it was not her world at all! Felix and Fanny only felt at home in a concert atmosphere of religious intensity. In England Felix had been shocked by the casual behavior of the audience during a performance of the *Messiah*; the Berlin audience had behaved very differently while listening to the *Saint Matthew Passion*. The two oratorios that Felix wrote, *Saint Paul* and *Elijah*, were his great masterpieces—to say nothing of his psalms. Here he managed to turn his contradictions into a virtue, reconciling Romanticism and abstraction.

Immediately after writing the first cantata—thus before she received Felix's criticism—Fanny composed another biblical cantata. Completed on 31 October 1831, it was based on the story of Job (*Hiob*). This time she used a large orchestra, adding trumpets and timpani: every windowpane in the garden room must have reverberated! Instead of a central aria, she introduced a trio for soprano, tenor, and bass. After *Hiob*, between 9 October and 20 November 1831, Fanny wrote another biblical composition, entitled *Oratorio*. This was not a particular narrative, but a series of extracts from the Bible, with religious feeling as its guiding theme. As in *Nachtreigen*, Fanny employed a mixed chorus with eight voices, and added three trombones to the orchestra. It is not known whether Abraham's birthday, mentioned in Felix's letter of 28 December, was celebrated with *Hiob* or with the *Oratorio*.

The choice of texts shows that Fanny, who had received the same education as Felix, was probably far more comfortable with abstract thought than he was. Felix was right in calling her his Cantor, for she came closer than he did to the symbolism of Johann Sebastian Bach. Unfortunately her confidence in Felix was utterly blind, and it is impossible to tell what her music might have been like had she persisted in choosing her own texts, without requiring his emotional support.

The final work in this period cannot really be considered a cantata, unless it were a highly secular one: it comprises a dramatic scene from the Greek legend of Hero and Leander, and was written during the illness of Fanny's friend Ulrike. Wilhelm wrote the text for it and the work was completed in three weeks, between 4 and 21 January 1832. This was Fanny's final attempt at composing for voice and orchestra.

All this work demonstrates that if Fanny's conjugal life had any effect upon her inspiration, it was actually rather a positive one. These works were performed in the *Sonntagsmusik* with great success. It is not certain, but is highly probable, that the usual orchestra was invited to perform them. Fanny had by this time formed her little chorus. As Felix's letter of 28 December 1831 confirms, Fanny conducted chorus and orchestra skillfully—that is, her conducting was precise and effective, like her brother's, with no showy effects.

In Felix's absence, Fanny had made a happy and fulfilling life for herself. Every event, such as Christmas or a birthday, was marked by a celebration, with Fanny and Wilhelm offering their talents as a present. Wilhelm's studio was full of lively students. Eva Weissweiler points out that Fanny's manner of spending Christmas would not offend anyone's convictions: it was a particularly convivial event, in which everyone subscribed to the custom of reciprocal present-giving.[13] The Mendelssohn circle was still composed of Jews or converted Jews, and it did not present a problem if Wilhelm's family or students held to "other forms of religion," for tolerance, friendship, and peace formed the basis of Fanny Hensel's creed. As her choice of texts for the cantatas proves, religion and morality were important to her. After Christmas 1831 she made this entry in her diary, about the students: "I was delighted to see these young people and to draw them into our circle. I think this is the best way to make them care about each other, and to exert a moral influence over them."[14] Religion is here understood in its strictest sense of bond or relationship. The Hensels' guests that Christmas were their parents, their brothers and sisters, Wilhelm's students, Ulrike, Gans, and Marx. Marx had just made peace with Abraham after the concert Fanny had conducted for her father's birthday; Fanny could not tolerate quarrels and was always the first to attempt to reconcile people she loved. Abraham's character did not leave her much respite! Nevertheless, just as it seemed that unity, peace, and happiness were about to settle on the family for a long time to come, Felix's return brought about some highly unpleasant events.

CHAPTER EIGHTEEN

Felix and the Singakademie: The End of a Dream

Felix returned from his European journey at the end of June 1832. He had become a new man, certain of his likes and dislikes.[1] He loved the Swiss countryside, liked Italy but not Papism, and had been completely disappointed in Paris, where he never set foot again. Thanks to the *concerts spirituels* given under the Ancien régime, the French capital nonetheless had a tradition of symphonic music: under Habeneck's direction[2] the Paris Conservatory Orchestra assembled the best instrumentalists in the city, forming an unrivaled group. Felix gave a successful performance of Beethoven's G Major Concerto with this orchestra, but his *Midsummer Night's Dream* Overture met with only modest approval from the audience. To make matters worse, the orchestra refused to play his *Reformation Symphony*, judging it "too academic . . . , with too many fugatos and not enough melodies"[3]—a crushing setback which the young composer had difficulty accepting. In Paris Felix divided his time between museums, the Chambre des Députés, and chamber music concerts, rather avoiding the more up-to-date artistic activity that had been fermenting in the city since the 1830 revolution. Eric Werner criticizes his "petty bourgeois puritanism,"[4] while being equally astonished that so young an artist, intent on making his mark, simultaneously rejected the classicism of Cherubini, Hummel, and Moscheles, and the Romanticism of Chopin, Liszt, and Berlioz. Werner also points out that if Felix refused to grapple with Parisian musical life and made no real effort to assert himself, it was because he hated competition. Kalkbrenner, for one, was capable of all manner of petty deeds against him,[5] and Felix could not tolerate it. A model of generosity when it came to helping his colleagues, he quickly lost his composure when he felt himself subject to comparison. His visit to Paris, of which he gave few details, left him with bad memories on more than one account: an attack of cholera, which was also breaking out in Paris; the news of Rietz's death, followed by that of Goethe; the knowledge that Zelter would not survive Goethe by long[6]—all this was enough to distance a rather spoiled young man from a place which, in any case, had not exactly welcomed him as the Messiah.

There followed a comforting visit to England, where Felix consistently experienced his greatest successes. Here he met his friend Klingemann again, and the English visit restored his self-confidence and good humor. This long journey of two years, in which he roamed through Europe looking for a place where he could work, had convinced him that such a place existed only in Germany. He had even decided, quite unpretentiously, that he had a mission, which was to help endow German orchestras with the same dynamism and solid structure as the Paris Conservatory Orchestra. Between Fanny and Felix there was truly a communion of minds on this subject.

When Zelter died on 15 May 1832, the post of director of the Singakademie became vacant. Felix's entire family pressed him to return promptly and seize this opportunity to obtain a stable position in Berlin. Felix had no desire to: all the publishers he met were at his feet, asking to buy his works as soon as he had written them. He knew, therefore, that he could support himself by composing: besides, the "citizen" he had become was no longer willing to abide by the constraints of a small city. Revolution had swept over Europe and Berlin had not budged an inch. Felix returned more of a radical than ever; he knew he would receive political sympathy and understanding from his sisters and a few friends like Dirichlet, but this was scarcely enough.

His family nonetheless managed to convince him to apply for the post. There was nothing else for him in Berlin—no orchestra, and the Berlin Opera, which was still dominated by Spontini,[7] did nothing to attract him; quite the reverse. The Singakademie administration seemed likely to welcome the appointment of so talented an artist: a musician as studious as he was learned, a member of the academy since childhood, Zelter's favorite pupil, and above all, a brilliant conductor who had successfully rehearsed and performed the extremely difficult *Saint Matthew Passion*—that most sacred of German liturgical works, the core of evangelism, and the masterpiece of the great Johann Sebastian Bach. Everything augured well for his appointment, but the Singakademie was no oligarchy, and on 22 January 1833 it proceeded to vote as follows for Zelter's successor: 148 votes for Rungenhagen; eighty-eight votes for Mendelssohn Bartholdy; four votes for Grell, the organist at Fanny's wedding.

Has anyone heard of Rungenhagen, in this day and age? Carl Friedrich Rungenhagen was born in Berlin in 1778 and died there in 1851. He became a teacher at the age of eighteen, and as a member of the Singakademie had been Zelter's assistant until he succeeded him. He wrote operas, oratorios, church music, and, being a good Berliner, numerous lieder.[8] The members of the Singakademie chose a risk-free leader, Felix's senior by thirty years, a musician who did not have a mania for traveling and had no desire to find out what was happening in the world outside Berlin. They chose maturity rather than youth, reason and habit rather than genius. And why not, if those were indeed the only reasons? But rumor had it otherwise: a Christian organization, it was said, could not appoint the son of a Jew as its director.[9]

Felix felt as if he had been publicly slapped in the face. The Singakademie offered him the post of assistant director, to which he replied, "in polite terms, that they could go hang themselves."[10] The Mendelssohn Bartholdy family abandoned the Singakademie, causing losses and stirring up commotion. Felix's increasing renown as a composer and Rungenhagen's evident mediocrity subsequently endowed the Singakademie's decision with the dimensions of an historic blunder, which it tried to repair by performing the young composer's works, but Felix, of course, was lost to them forever.

Fanny did not enjoy her subsequent encounters with members of the Singakademie. Some years later, she would write to her brother: "Yesterday they sang *Don Giovanni* at the Deckers' house and I was the accompanist. Grell the music director and Schneider the organist stood beside me supervising my contribution, but I didn't give

Grell the satisfaction of making a mistake. Good God, what an ugly man he is! And what a blockhead! He only opened his sagacious mouth after Elvira's aria, when he said to his neighbor: the aria has a fine orschestra."[11] [*Sic*, indicating a fault in Grell's pronunciation.]

Abraham was to be pitied most: this man who had spent his entire life cultivating reason must have felt helpless in the face of such stupidity. Perhaps he could dismiss various unpleasant remarks, which we would now term antisemitic, as merely anecdotal: insults shouted at his children came from street urchins; the nobleman who had yelled *Hep, hep Jude* at Felix was a cretin; the rumors circulating during the cholera epidemic, claiming that the Jews had poisoned the well-water, were the last remnants of a superstition of illiterate people.[12] But the Singakademie represented the most cultivated elements in Berlin. The golden age of reason now receded into an uncertain future which Abraham would certainly not live to see. According to Devrient, Abraham's irritability increased as he grew older. Not only was he having to cope with this setback, but he was also going steadily blind—a sad ending to his life.

His children were actually far better equipped to deal with antisemitism than he was: they were learning to distinguish between anti-Judaism (that is, a rejection of Jewish customs) and antisemitism. Years later, in 1855, Rebecka wrote to her nephew Sebastian concerning a book she found "too Jewish for a Jew": "I think it senseless to devote a large book to the life of a mediocre mathematician . . . who was not made more intelligent by the fact that he knew Moses Mendelssohn and Lessing. But I did find it interesting personally, for I remember the stories Father and Mother used to tell, and even Father's deep hatred of Judaism, which I often found unpleasant, became more explicable and understandable as a result."[13] Rebecka had come a long way since the day she wrote to her brother describing the visit of a cousin of Moses Mendelssohn, an uneducated man named Dessauer: "I don't hate Jews, but this was really too much."[14] Felix replied curtly from London: "What do you mean, you 'don't hate Jews'? It's really too nice of you not to despise your own family. I demand a complete explanation of the Dessauer business in your next letter." The younger Mendelssohn children had thus absorbed some of their parents' anti-Judaism, which in the parents' case stemmed from their assumptions that Judaism was at odds with the rationalism of the *Aufklärung* and at odds with science, which they loved; perhaps above all was their desire for cultural assimilation which they expected would open all the doors of the civilized world to them.

The ultrasensitive Felix had probably never quite recovered from the unpleasant incident at Dobberan, while Fanny left no written trace of what she thought. Anyone studying her life learns to interpret this silence; Fanny would not write about a disagreeable or vile event. But novelist Fanny Lewald has left no doubt as to the opinions of Frau Hensel, whom she met during the 1840s:

I received a most pleasant welcome from the composer's two sisters, whom we met for the first time at a reception given by Fräulein Solmar. They, too, were Jewish, even though they had married Christians, and had retained a marked affection for their race, which is always a sign of education and independence of character among Jews. . . . It was a very healthy aspect of Felix Mendelssohn and his sisters,[15] to have maintained this affection for the race they belonged to, and I recollect with pleasure the value they attached to the memories of their family's past.[16]

As adults, the Mendelssohn children had obviously nothing to prove to anyone as far as culture was concerned. What worthier representatives could there have been of the Germanic world? Though capable of reacting disdainfully to all forms of antisemitism that resulted from ignorance or other people's wretchedness, they did not, for all that, deny that they had converted or repudiate their own origins. As direct descendants of Moses Mendelssohn, this was the last thing they were worried about.

The part played by Doris Zelter—their old professor's daughter—in the failure of Felix's candidacy at the Singakademie is not entirely clear. Doris, whom the Mendelssohns had always welcomed like one of their own children, indulged in backstage intrigue, vulgarly bartering both her influence and the collection of scores she had inherited.[17] She was certainly a disappointment to the Mendelssohns. But this was nothing compared to their consternation when, in 1833, the correspondence between Goethe and Zelter was published.[18]

To publish letters that were by definition private was in itself improper and unseemly. In Jane Austen's final novel, *Persuasion*, the heroine, Anne Elliot, is ashamed when she discovers something unpleasant about her father in a letter not addressed to her: "Anne could not immediately get over the shock and mortification of finding such words applied to her father. She was obliged to recollect that her seeing the letter was a violation of the laws of honor, that no one ought to be judged or to be known by such testimonies, that no private correspondence could bear the eye of others, before she could recover calmness enough to return the letter."[19]

Not eavesdropping and not reading other people's letters was part of the code of honorable behavior; it had to do with respect for the individual and the protection of privacy. An author may produce a work intended for publication, but how can one justify the posthumous publication of something that is not a work at all—something that is in effect a conversation between two people and which possibly concerns other persons who may be very upset by revelations they neither authorized nor desired? Besides, is a full-length correspondence all that interesting to read? It presumes an unwholesome curiosity on the part of the reader, or else the specialized knowledge of researchers. Admittedly, the letters of the Mendelssohn family are particularly appealing. In a "literary" correspondence, however, it is acceptable for letters to be handed round—the example of Madame de Sévigné comes to mind—and in those circumstances they lose their strictly personal character and move into a narrow zone between public and private domains, like Fanny's concerts. In this respect the correspondence between Zelter and Goethe proved very disappointing.

Since Abraham was now almost blind, books of general interest were henceforth read aloud in the Mendelssohn household. Wilhelm's sister Luise had joined the Mendelssohn, Dirichlet, and Hensel families, and would live at 3 Leipziger Strasse until 1836. Despite the listeners' vastly different backgrounds and beliefs, opinions on this correspondence were unanimous. Goethe and Zelter did not refer to the Mendelssohns as equals, but with a condescension that implied that their Jewish origins made them second-class Christians. Thus Zelter said of Abraham: "He treats me very favorably and I can dip into his cash, for he's become rich during the general wretchedness without, however, damaging his soul."[20] Felix's first visit to Goethe is announced in these terms: "Of course, he's the son of a Jew, but not Jewish himself. The father made a great sacrifice in not having his sons circumcised[21] and in having them properly brought up; it would really be unusual[22] if a Jewish boy became an artist." As for Lea, Fanny, and Rebecka, they were described in 1823 as "the Old Testament's youngest grandmothers."

Fanny confessed her consternation to her brother:

I'm writing to you today to relieve my feelings in regard to Zelter's correspondence, which has put me in a constant, silent rage. It is, of course, administered to us in small doses: since Father cannot read in the evening, we read it aloud to him over there, and the book receives a more than mediocre appraisal. Father, too, is extremely angry about it and for once we are all unanimous on the subject, and have not yet argued over a single word. I am deeply grieved for Zelter, who has left so unfavorable an image of himself to posterity. Goethe's reputation is more capable of withstanding a slap, and at the same time his letters are infinitely better than Zelter's; however, both can only stand to lose by this publication. On Zelter's side predominates a baleful and disagreeable attitude which we always sensed in him but which we always rationalized: here it bursts forth undisguised. Personal interest, selfishness, a disgusting and completely unintelligent way of idolizing Goethe, an indiscreet disclosure of other people's business—excusable in intimate letters, but which should have made publication impossible; all this and many other things[23] really make me despise this book. It contains this example, among others, of incredible ignorance: Zelter asks Goethe what Byzantium is and receives the desired information. Is that what one writes to Goethe for! The vacuousness of the entire collection is beyond all anticipation. Its sole content is theatrical tittle-tattle and gossip, and it becomes obvious that Goethe can't think of much that's intelligent in reply. Ugh! In addition, we have the joy here of listening to all those who justifiably feel offended at seeing themselves trounced in it, without anybody asking what they thought; there are people who are described as veritable jailbirds. But enough of this unwholesome topic; the memory of a man I was fond of, and would gladly have continued to admire, has been ruined forever by this book.[24]

Zelter was, in fact, Sebastian's godfather. Henriette Mendelssohn, Aunt Hinni, was not pleased with the book either. She wrote to her son Benny and daughter-in-law Rosamunde about it:

Have you read Goethe's correspondence with Zelter yet? You'll be astounded to see to what extent the turnips from Teltow are destined to be immortalized. You will also read some magnificent words by Goethe, however, and Zelter has some fine lines too. But what I cannot forgive Zelter are his vulgar and frequently treacherous remarks about people who thought he felt esteem for them. One can at a pinch forgive this or that remark when one realizes he didn't intend them to be published when he wrote them, but certain things are really too gross.

How the editor of these letters, Dr. Riemer, can assume responsibility for publishing such coarse remarks about August von Schlegel,[25] I cannot conceive; there is also a passage about Abraham Mendelssohn which I find very spiteful. Here we certainly have reason to say, May God protect us from our friends. Anyone acquainted with Mendelssohn knows that his wife was rich before the war began, and none of the Mendelssohns needed to take advantage of the general poverty to cut a good deal, but the insinuation is perfidious. . . . I wonder just how far the publication of intimate letters will be taken. In short, dear Rosa, you'll be able to collect all my letters, full of blobs of ink, and then posterity will know what heroines we were. Don't do it.[26]

Rosa did later publish Hinni's letters. Like Brendel Mendelssohn, Henriette Meyer had been engaged while very young and was already promised to Joseph Mendelssohn at the age of thirteen. But she was among the winners in life's lottery, spending an entirely happy and carefree existence with a man who was kind, intelligent, and generous. She was a charming woman, extremely tolerant and sensitive, deeply affected by insults to herself and those dear to her. She did not get along perfectly with Abraham, but this in no way altered her support for him. To read that Zelter claimed to have flirted with her in his youth made her as indignant as it did to see Goethe's lengthily expressed concern over an order of turnips.[27]

It is hard to tell whether the Mendelssohns were more indignant at Zelter's malice or at having been mentioned in public without their consent. Zelter wrote many complimentary things about Fanny—about her work, her compositions, and her interpretation of Bach—but Fanny showed no sign of being grateful. She again wrote to Felix on the subject:

You'll soon be receiving the sixth volume of the Goethe–Zelter letters, the last in the series. The editor took the trouble of adding an index, thanks to which anyone who knows the alphabet can without difficulty check to see who has been praised or insulted (which comes to the same), and how often (58 times, in your case). Figaro! you'd say if you were there, but I can't do anything about it;[28] it annoys me intensely that in a country where there's no freedom of the press, and where public officials must thus be left untouched, harmless private people are attacked as if by thieves issuing from a wood: these gentlemen discuss and slander them as their pens dictate, and then divide up the right to hand out honors. It's said of me that I play like a man, and I have to thank either God or Zelter that this remark is not followed by any of the unseemly observations with which the book is blessed. You'll see that Father is criticized several times for not having let you visit Sicily. No one would read a book like this in England, because they're used to personalities there, and that is its only interest, but I think that publishing things about private persons cannot in any circumstance be a good thing and is in any case indelicate.[29]

After seeing two different problems converge—antisemitism, on the one hand, and the publication of private letters, on the other—one begins to wonder if the distinction between public and private was not a snare and a delusion. The private opinions of public figures such as Goethe and Zelter had repercussions for private persons, who found themselves dragged willy-nilly into public view. Fanny and Hinni had been brought up to believe that a woman must not make people talk about her; at once protective of and protected by the family circle, they lived at the very heart of private life. To expose them threatened the very direction of their lives. Fanny was intensely aware of this and incessantly enraged: having given up the possibility of a career, she should at least have had the right to be left in peace.

There is also the question of whether religion is a private or a public matter. In a secular state, it remains strictly a question of conscience. But in nineteenth-century Prussia, it had a foot in both camps. Abraham and Lea Mendelssohn converted and made their children convert for essentially public reasons, so as to belong to the predominant religion and take their places in the social chain. Nevertheless, these conversions took place in utmost secrecy, like truly personal events. Give someone like Zelter the opportunity and right to express an opinion on the subject, and a universally known opinion could contradict any idea of freedom of choice. A private individual should have the right to present himself in public as he wished, with names and labels of his choice. But this was not what happened: no matter how often the Mendelssohns converted, in vain did they privately consider themselves Christians; they would not be recognized as such in public, and whether or not they accepted it, they would remain Jewish. It was enough to drive a rational man crazy, and infuriate his children.

Religion changes over time: the cult of the family and unconditional respect for the all-powerful decisions of its representative, the father, yield to the power of money and the prospect of a good business deal. Fanny was conscious of this and hoped for a financial failure that would discourage the publishers. "I trust Duncker will suffer serious losses that will open the booksellers' eyes," she wrote again to Felix, "and that we shall be spared other presents of this kind now in preparation. Among other things—cheer up now!—Goethe's correspondence with Bettina von Arnim.[30] I can see you making faces from here. Hegel's diary, and so forth."[31]

The Singakademie had been untrue to its founders and betrayed the *Aufklärung*: no longer was it an ensemble of voices all united in a single exhalation and by the same moral sense. The Mendelssohns—descendants of the Itzigs, of Sara Levy, of Moses Mendelssohn, and themselves an integral part of the life and meaning of the Singakademie—left the institution. This rift implied a social failure in regard to the ideas of unity and integration. Felix left Berlin to become music director of Düsseldorf on 20 May 1833. Fanny remained, of course, a private person in the full sense of the word, with yet another reason to enclose herself in the microcosm of Leipziger Strasse. In rejecting Felix, Berlin also deprived itself of the very man who could have diversified the town's musical activities, created a great orchestra, and transformed it into a musical capital.

CHAPTER NINETEEN

Frau Hensel's Music

Fortunately Fanny did not need the Singakademie in order to assert her musical personality; rather, this noble institution was more likely to have needed her. Fanny's *Sonntagsmusik* continued more brilliantly than ever. On 28 October 1833 she noted in her diary the programs of the most recent matinées:

First concert:
Quartet by Mozart
Beethoven's G major concerto
Second duet from Fidelio. Devrient and Decker
Concerto in D minor by Bach

Second concert:
Triple concerto by Beethoven, with Kins and Ganz
Hero by Decker
Felix plays his concerto and Bach's D minor concerto.

Third concert:
Variations by Felix, with Ganz
Quartet by Weber
Finale from Oberon, Decker
Quintet by Spohr
Song of the Sea from Oberon

Fourth concert:
Beethoven's trio in E major
String quartet by Felix in A minor
Beethoven's D major trio

Fifth concert:
Mozart trio G major
Scene from Der Freischütz, Decker
Trio by Moscheles
Aria from Iphigénie[1]

To the right of this list, she indicates how often the various composers were played in her concerts:

Beethoven, six times
Bach, twice
Mozart, twice
Weber, four times
Felix, three times
Gluck, once
Spohr, once
Moscheles, once
Me, once

Pauline Decker had become a close friend and valued collaborator who did not haggle over the repertoire and was not afraid of theatrical performances. That same year Fanny composed a work for Saint Cecilia's day—Cecilia was the patron saint of music and also Fanny's middle name—the score of which unfortunately belongs to a private collection.[2] Once again she confided in Felix:

In two days I composed a verset for the *Saint Cecilia Mass*, of which Mother has probably sent you the text; I was in such a hurry that the parts for the accompaniment have not yet been copied. The whole thing was arranged as a double surprise: first of all Decker appeared without singing, then she sang a few notes without being seen, and then she sang in a veritable tableau vivant, from memory of course, which created a magical effect. It's certain she was much more beautiful than usual. . . . She had had her costume and hair done in the style of Raphael's Cecilia, and this suited her wonderfully well. The angels were in white, and Röschen Behrend wore a headdress of her own light blond hair, which was untied and came down to her knees; she has the most beautiful regular features and deep, dark eyes. Wings, some glitter on the forehead and shoulders, excellent lighting which didn't spoil a thing—in short, I wish you could have been there, you would have fallen in love and given us a fine quartet which would have been most welcome.

Clärchen Jacques, a pretty child of eight with black curly hair, was by no means an ugly angel either, and little Therese Türrschmidt,[3] though far less pretty than the others, played her part extremely well. The two older girls held their scores in their hands, like angels in old paintings, and that was particularly charming too. Incidentally, the scenery was completed without the help of a single craftsman; Wilhelm and his students did it all, and the beautiful organ was manufactured in the studio. I'll just add that there is one movement in the music which I find quite good.[4]

Decker learned her music by heart in less time than it took to say so and had her own costume made, as was the custom in the theater, but without asking any fee. The artistic team of Wilhelm and Fanny was as effective as ever: Wilhelm could do everything except sing. Fanny went to endless pains to create a performance that met her ideal standards, and she never stinted on enthusiasm if she found something beautiful. In any case, she felt encouraged to continue, noting in her diary the high and low points of her matinées:

One day, one of my matinées practically fell flat: no one came, apart from Kubelius, who was kind enough to leave me to myself. But once, Decker sang the Queen of the Night's first aria, and I don't remember what I played. Another time I played Hummel's quintet and Mozart's D Minor concerto, and Decker sang *Fidelio*. The previous time I had played the Sonata in A Major and Trio in D Major by Beethoven. . . . As for Decker, she's performed the following works, up to this point: *Oberon, Semele, Zauberflöte, Opferfest*,[5] *Don Giovanni, Die Schöpfung, Iphigénie*. This last performance took place yesterday, 7 January, and went very well. On the whole, I find it very entertaining to hear and accompany these performances. She has a very free and pleasant voice, she sings wonderfully well, and I'm completely enthusiastic about her.[6]

Fanny would have been wrong not to be excited over a soprano capable of singing both *Fidelio* and the Queen of the Night. Even in an era less inclined to specialization than ours, this was still a vocal feat. Fanny again expressed her pleasure to Felix—"It's splendid to make music with Decker, she's so talented!"—while at the same time telling him how overwhelmingly busy she was; there was hardly time to write because "there are so many cows with tails that need untying."[7] Preparing for performances at her level, or at Pauline Decker's level, required considerable energy, and Fanny did not spare herself:

I have had to perform and rehearse a lot lately; if only I could, just once, have as many rehearsals as I would like! I really think I have enough talent—for example, I have the gift of making things clear to people—but these amateurs! If I were Jean Paul, I would add a page here devoted simply to them, there certainly would be no lack of material!

What she was rehearsing with them was nothing less than *Fidelio*. She wrote to Felix about the performance:

My *Fidelio* has just ended. Given the circumstances, it went very well and the people in the audience, who are starting to be as numerous as before, were delighted. Decker sang marvelously, and all the amateurs tolerably well. You ask who the tenor is: Herr von Dachröden, who takes great pains and has a handsome voice, which he uses for singing, and a handsome face, which he uses for posing—in the studio. Then there's a very short student, Jörg, with a fine voice that sounds like a parody of Mantius: he sings Jaquino. In addition, Antonie Nölinchen, Busolt, and Riese. The poor fellow is incredibly awkward musically, but thanks to a most touching perseverance, he managed to make only half as many mistakes as I expected, and sometimes he even sang very well.

It would take more than that to discourage Fanny. Some months later, she sent Felix a letter that almost burst the bounds of modesty:

Although I'm very busy with festive events, I must sit down and make some comments on the letter Mother is writing to you at this very moment: you mustn't think I've become a complete idiot or gone mad in your absence. Besides, it's been a week full of music. And so Mother must certainly have told you about the Königstadt orchestra[8] on Sunday, and how I stood before them like a *Jupiter tonans* wielding the baton. This is how it came about: Lecerf[9] had his student play and hurt his fingers in the process, until I went and fetched your little white baton and handed it to him. Afterward I had my overture played and sat down at the piano;[10] whereupon the devil, in the form of Lecerf, whispered to me to take the baton in my hand. Had I not been so horribly shy and embarrassed at every stroke, I might have conducted fairly well. I found it very entertaining to hear the piece for the first time in two years, and to find it almost exactly as I had imagined it. People seemed to like it very much: they were very kind, praised me, criticized a few impractical passages—and are coming back next Saturday. It was an unexpected event which brought me sudden happiness. Tomorrow Iphigénie will be launched, it's very well cast too.[11]

Two days later, she added:

My letter got no further, the day before yesterday, and I can give you a direct report on Iphigénie, which went very well. I wish you had been there: the way the three voices sounded and supported each other will not be heard again for some time; it was really wonderful.[12] I've never heard a torrent of sound like the duet between Bader and Mantius. Decker was in fantastic voice and sang steadily better all the way through, but Bader was sublime. He had never sung the part and arrived at yesterday's rehearsal in a rather *maussade* mood,[13] saying the role was too low for him. But after the first act he became a different person, and he thanked me very warmly yesterday for enabling him to sing the role. To my great joy I've managed to win him over so thoroughly that he offered once and for all to sing whatever I want, whenever I want—chorus, solo, anything. And he is going to sing, I swear! . . . Incidentally, there were a hundred people here yesterday, our parents took part in the festivities; they had invited several of their acquaintances, and so I had the honor of seeing the mayor in my home, Herr von Bärensprung, the Ölrich family of Bremen, etc. On our side there were several English people, including Lady Davy, a charming woman who had lots to tell me about you. . . .

By the way, my chorus was magnificent: eight sopranos, four altos including Türrschmidt and Blano, with Bader and Mantius as tenors; it was splendid and I was really surprised by a few passages. Devrient, who had taken on the role of Thoas, canceled at the last moment as usual, and Busolt was kind enough to sing in his place.[14] As for everything else, the garden was wonderful, the rose bushes were in bloom, and the hall decorations unsurpassed.

In the meantime every trace of yesterday has disappeared and nothing remains but a few scattered notes still ringing in my ears. Addio, Mother wants to write to you too and I have to correct my instrumental parts because my Königstadters will be here again tomorrow.

Eight months later, on 8 March 1835, Fanny informed her brother that she was leading "a very nice chorus of ten sopranos, two altos, a tenor, and five basses."[15]

The standard of the concerts improved steadily during the following months, attracting both listeners and musicians until even Abraham was filled with admiration and surprise: "The undertaking is now so grand, and of such a high level, it cannot stay like that for long."[16]

Felix and Fanny discussed music a great deal in the letters they exchanged during those years. Both were preoccupied by problems of musical programming, even though one was a professional and the other an amateur. The question of pitch arose as soon as the Königstadt theater orchestra arrived at Fanny's house. Felix asked her for a tuning fork for Düsseldorf and his sister informed him that thanks to Spontini the pitch kept rising in Berlin, whereas she had heard that in Paris the pitch had just dropped by a halftone.[17]

Their exchanges were not limited to pitch. Scores came and went between Berlin and Düsseldorf: Felix constantly needed copies and pieces he had left "at home"; he would send her his new scores, receive Fanny's new ones, and then they would exchange criticism. In December 1833 Felix conducted an opera for the first time—*Don Giovanni*—and was working on his oratorio, *Saint Paul*. He met Chopin at Aix-la-Chapelle during Pentecost 1834, and Fanny also expressed a keen interest in meeting the composer.[18] Felix was unhappy in Düsseldorf, however, frustrated by the poor quality of the orchestra and by its mediocre musical goals. He resigned from his position in November 1834 and gave his farewell concert in July 1835; in January 1835, the town of Leipzig had already invited him to be conductor of the Gewandhaus Orchestra. This was an ideal position for Felix, who now found himself at the head of the finest orchestra in Germany, in a city of libraries and scholars, and with plenty of time to compose. He conducted his first concert there on 1 October 1835.

In Düsseldorf, Felix did not live very far from his cousin Benny, who was a professor in Bonn, and from his Uncle Joseph and Aunt Hinni who had their summer home at Horchheim. Once again he found himself in the familial ambiance so dear to him, with very close relatives at hand; yet he still needed to maintain his epistolary relationship with his family in order to preserve his emotional equilibrium. The letters he exchanged with his sister show to what point the two had remained "twins" in their behavior, and even in their arguments. They almost had an altercation over Paganini and the notion of "progress" in art. Fanny claimed that after Paganini, no one could listen to or play the violin in quite the same way, whereas Felix railed against the French newspapers that spoke of *une révolution du goût*.[19] For Felix, what was good was always good, and what was bad was bad. People could progress, but not art. Fanny, whom he still called his Cantor even though the designation had long since lost its meaning, replied:

"*Je demande la parole*,"[20] and you're certainly not going to deny me that from Düsseldorf.

That times change, and with them, tastes; and that we change with the tastes of the time—this cannot be denied. To be sure, there is also a positive Good in art and I hope you don't deem me so abandoned by God as to think that everything we recognized and will always recognize as being pinnacles of art is subject merely to fashion. Hännchen in the *Seasons* will age as little as Alceste or Matthew the Evangelist. But even in the Good one finds an incredible quantity of nuances, and since art, or taste, or beauty cannot be demonstrated by the principle of 2 plus 2 equals 4, there comes a moment (and I think this mainly concerns performance) when the outer world, or the inconstancy of the time, or fashion (express it as you will) exerts an influence. You remember as well as I do that at one time we were thrilled to bits over Spohr's music. Now it doesn't thrill us to the same extent; and yet his music is the same, and we are still the same people, but our relationship to Spohr has changed. Let's go back to the previous example, the one concerning violinists. There's certainly a great deal of positive Good in Spohr's playing, and this won't disappear, but there's also a sugary side, and in its day this tendency may have contributed greatly to his fame. Then came Paganini with his wild, powerful, imaginative playing and all the young violinists tried to imitate him and scratched horribly on the G string. Consequently, in listening to Spohr again several years later I'm unintentionally more aware of his sugary side, because my ears are now accustomed to the opposing tendency. Taken as a whole, the audience is naturally the first to feel this influence; individuals are more or less subject to it, but I think no one can claim to be totally free of it. I could easily furnish numerous examples of another kind, in which things we previously liked now strike us as boring and dull, or even strange and intolerable. Such changes naturally never involve what is the highest or best of its kind, but I'm convinced that the Good could seem more or less acceptable, depending on how it relates to its own era. Answer that, clown! Must I enter this entire correspondence in my book of arguments?[21]

Felix realized he was bogged down in this debate and powerless to answer, but it was a debate he enjoyed all the same.[22] It is curious to see what effect a religious education may have on a person's attitude to art. For the Mendelssohns, music was religion; and if Fanny's words were transposed into a religious context, one would obtain a letter similar to the one Abraham wrote for Fanny's confirmation. Fanny reasoned, in the spirit of Plato, that art is always a form of art, just as religion is a form of religion, and even if "positive" or absolute Good exists, in this world it assumes a particular form, in both art and religion. Wisdom consists in submitting to the absolute and to the variety of forms. For both Fanny Hensel and Felix Mendelssohn Bartholdy, music lived and was experienced through a feeling of general enthusiasm. This recalls the Schilleresque aspect of *Nachtreigen*: "Let us receive and think together of the Unique." Nothing is true unless it is experienced by everyone. Neither Fanny nor Felix was of the opinion that only a select few had access to absolute Good or to supreme Beauty; according to them, those values lost their meaning unless they were shared. Although their privileged education could have made them exceedingly elitist, Fanny and Felix, on the contrary, lived only for and through others, at least where their ideas were concerned. Thus Felix was in for a terrible shock when he came into contact with the outer world, which could only disappoint him—as was the case in Berlin, Paris, and Düsseldorf. Only infrequently did he encounter the exalted working atmosphere and moral generosity of Leipziger Strasse, and the contrast between his ideals and reality was so painful for him that he could not bear for his sister, too, to side with "fashion."

But was there any other way for a musician to show her work to the public? After writing a quartet between 26 August and 23 October 1834, Fanny began to grow depressed. She took two months to finish it, which was a long time compared to the gestation period of her cantatas, but then, don't composers consider quartets to be the preeminent form? Few people were available to judge her work. Whatever the reason—whether because of an inner or outer lack of inspiration—Fanny wrote no work of stature for almost ten years. Four months after completing the quartet, she wrote to her brother in a murderous mood, criticizing herself and unceremoniously cutting him down to size while she was about it:

The aria *Wer nur den lieben Gott* leads me to tell you that in several of the solos in your smaller sacred works I discern a kind of habit I wouldn't really call mannerism, in fact I don't really know what to call it: something exaggeratedly simple which doesn't seem entirely natural, coming from you; a kind of short rhythm, for example, which has a childlike quality—but also a childish quality that doesn't seem to me appropriate to the genre as a whole, nor to the serious treatment you give the choruses.[23] . . .

Thanks for your thorough critique of my quartet. Will you have it played? You know, I find our correspondence very proper now: perhaps it's not as funny as when Beckchen and I used to sit next to each other fighting over the pen, but our letters are quite sensible now and concerned with serious matters. It suits me very well if it stays like that.

I wasn't able to write to you last week, because I was deep in study of your *Rondo brillant*.[24] It was launched yesterday, Sunday morning, accompanied by a double quartet and a double-bass; it met with general approbation and I was crazy enough to play it twice, even though I was ill with a bad cough and utterly worn out. But I wanted to so badly! I've written a soprano aria that you'd prefer to my quartet regarding form and modulations; it holds together well, and yet I had completed it before you wrote to me on this subject.[25] Considering I'm neither eccentric nor overly sentimental, I've been wondering how I came to compose in this tender style? I think it comes from the fact that we were young during Beethoven's last period and, of course, we had assimilated his art and style. But that style is very emotional and wrenching. You have gone through and beyond that, while I've remained stuck in it, but without the strength through which that sensitivity can and must endure. That's why I think you didn't hit the right mark in me or address the right issue. It is not so much the compositional skill that is lacking as a certain approach to life, and because of this deficiency my longer pieces are already dying of old age in their infancy: I lack sufficient strength to sustain my ideas and give them the necessary consistency. That's why I'm best at writing lieder, where an appealing idea may suffice, without much strength to develop it.[26]

That Fanny lacked energy is rather hard to believe. On the other hand, she had certainly never concentrated simply on composing. Her letters indicate that she was constantly interrupted by visits, by domestic tasks, by her husband, or by her child. She took two months to write her quartet while seeing to numerous other matters. Fanny never had six months or a year to devote to herself, with no outside interference. In comparing herself to Felix, did she consider that for years the young man had been concerned entirely with himself? Nobody in the world possesses from birth the strength to complete a difficult project requiring great perseverance. Or more exactly, everybody has this potential strength, but to develop it requires not only willpower but time, besides having a "room of one's own," as Virginia Woolf puts it.[27] Although Fanny's situation was more favorable than that of other women, she felt she had not developed her creative energy, either because she had not had the time, or because it had not been given her. She could have blamed this on her situation, but that is difficult to express credibly when those around one are extremely understanding; furthermore, it can lead to bitterness. Fanny preferred to take the blame herself and assume responsibility for her shortcomings. To surmount them, she would have needed the support, reassurance, and encouragement of someone in whom she had complete confidence musically—Felix, in this case. This period marked the beginning of a depression that lasted several years and prevented Fanny from composing anything but short piano pieces and lieder; Felix did encourage these and thought she excelled in the genre. He was certainly correct in that, and in deprecating her own talent Fanny shows how depressed she was: a short story is not a novel and does not require less energy, simply another form of energy. An "appealing idea" is not enough: one has to be able to express it rapidly and economically. Fanny remained frustrated, not having had the chance to cultivate her talent through contact with the outer world, or through her own development. Although not really aware of the injustice that had been done her, she was nonetheless its victim.

CHAPTER TWENTY

Frau Hensel's Family

Fanny certainly led an active, spirited family life. She devoted much attention to her child, but not at all in the same way her own mother had: Sebastian did not receive a minutely supervised education but spent his childhood in relative freedom between his father's studio and his mother's music room. Until his cousin Walter was born, he was constantly with adults.[1] In July 1833 Rebecka gave birth to a little boy, and despite the three years' difference in their ages, Walter was a good playmate for Sebastian—almost a brother (see Figure 18).

Naturally, Fanny had brought into the world an utterly outstanding child whose teeth and hair grew normally, events she did not fail to enter in her diary: "I've never seen a child so intelligent, pretty, and nice."[2] She told Felix of her adventures as a mother: she had organized a children's party, attended by the Heyse children, around a small table with miniature napkins and cutlery. Little Paul Heyse—the future Nobel prize winner—had eaten too much, and Sebastian and Paul, aged three, had proposed toasts in the manner of slightly tipsy adults.[3] Fanny also mentions that she took Sebastian for a walk every day and was amazed at his linguistic progress.[4] Her two sisters-in-law, first Luise and then Minna, assisted her with domestic tasks and with Sebastian's education. Minna did not come to live with her brother until 1835, following the death of their mother whom she never left, and helped with the housework without a murmur of complaint. Luise, however, had a harder time putting up with Fanny's authority, and resented anything that distracted her from religion. Consequently, concerts and cuddling were equally unwelcome. In order to bring her various undertakings to fruition, Fanny presumably had to order her little world about rather briskly, causing Luise's strong personality to bristle. Religious tolerance prevailed in the household, but the fear of Hell that dominated Luise must have had a dismaying effect upon her family.[5]

Luise thus introduced a different tone into the small boy's education, and did not hesitate to put him in his place whenever his mother gave him too much praise. One day when the child had learned Mozart's lied to a text by Goethe, *Ein Veilchen auf der Wiese stand* (A violet was growing in the meadow), his mother congratulated him on his sensitive reaction to the violent death of the flower, crushed by the shepherdess's heel. Sebastian went to boast about it to his aunt, who tartly replied: "Yes, children do sometimes cry over the silliest things." "Old witch," retorted the little prodigy, his feelings hurt.[6] The anecdote is told not by his mother, but by Sebastian himself. Fanny has only pleasant stories about him: "Would you like a book about Sebastian, and another one about Walter?" she asked Felix in a letter of January 1834:

Beckchen will write you one about Walter, beginning with the tooth: it's appeared! I could write you a very long book about Sebastian, he's the sweetest little boy. Yesterday he ate at Beckchen's and came back down while we were still at table, having duck with turnips. After several fruitless attempts to obtain another meal, he began to flatter us most tenderly, saying, "Dear Mother, please make me happy and give me a little bone with nothing on it, and I'll pretend there is something on it." And when he saw we couldn't keep from laughing, he went on more boldly, "And then give me a turnip." . . . This morning he said to me: "I love you most of all, there's no stranger I love as much as you." . . . Yesterday he said to his father, "Father, you always have the same colors, and yet you paint such different pictures: Aunt Beckchen, and the Moor, and the Jews; how can this be?" (That's his expression.) Recently he overturned a glass of water into my slippers, and since I was preaching moral behavior to him, he said: "Mother, don't you still love me? I was only being clumsy, not naughty."[7]

Sebastian's Aunt Rebecka gave him a lamb for his fourth birthday, but it was so wild that Fanny pretended the animal was a "horse in disguise."[8] On the subject of meals, which his parents had at an unusual time—lunch at five in the afternoon probably so that Wilhelm could take full advantage of daylight—Sebastian relates that his mother "limited his food, because at the time this was thought beneficial for children." He thus stole off to see Clement the gardener, who lived in the basement of 3 Leipziger Strasse, and stuffed himself with all the richest food. Of Huguenot extraction, Clement taught him some imaginative French and an equally whimsical way of playing chess.[9] These visits also enabled Sebastian to play with children of his own age!

Fanny's thoughts continued to center on Felix, who was still the Phoenix of the women of the house—the subject of a family joke. In 1833 he embarked on another visit to England, this time with his father. Abraham was supposed to return to Berlin at the end of the summer with his son, but that was not what transpired: instead, Abraham announced that Felix's place would be taken by a certain Alphonse Lovie, a painter whose musical abilities Abraham praised warmly. Fanny was disappointed not to see her brother come back, and the whole family wondered about the mysterious Alphonse Lovie. He turned out to be none other than Felix himself[10]—to the great surprise and joy of the entire household! Felix stayed only a few days, but during this visit he performed his own G Minor Concerto and Bach's D Minor Concerto in a *Sonntagsmusik*.[11]

For his part, Wilhelm Hensel had been named professor of historical painting by the Prussian king in June 1831.[12] In July 1833 he began work on what would prove to be his most important painting, his *Christ before Pilate*, which was exhibited the following year at the Berlin Academy. Wilhelm had devoted much time to this painting, sketching a considerable number of faces; according to the memoirs of Adolf Bernard Marx, these drawings included "Polish Jews and women with expressive faces selected from the Jewish community."[13] Hensel also had his wife and son pose: this study is still preserved in the Mendelssohn Archives. The painting depicts the moment when the people tell Pilate: "May his blood be on our heads and on our children's heads," whence the presence of the infant Sebastian. Despite Friedrich Wilhelm III's desire for thriftiness, the painting was purchased in 1835 and installed above the altar in the Garnisonkirche. It was burned in a fire that destroyed the church in 1908.

Naturally, Fanny had to support her husband in his work: owing to the canvas's imposing size, the actual painting was difficult and tiring to complete.[14] Moreover, Wilhelm suffered badly from toothaches and stomach pains. As for the doctor treating him, Fanny concluded in the letter she wrote Felix about Paganini that when all was said and done she did not much believe in revolutions, and found it intolerable that "neophytes of homeopathy behaved as if the kingdom of heaven had just received them, and as if no one had ever been cured before they arrived."[15]

Caring for the sick was an important part of a woman's life, especially in the Mendelssohn household where everyone seems to have had a very fragile constitution. Fanny herself suffered constantly from headaches. Lea caused everyone considerable alarm in April 1834, when she experienced a fit of weakness that developed into tachycardia. She had Fanny write to Felix, advising him to take precautions, since he too was subject to attacks, and to alert his doctor so that the problem might be prevented. The remedy proposed by Lea's doctor, Stosch, was rather impractical for an active man: applying ice-packs to the chest! Fanny gave two reasons for her mother's illness: first, they had just discovered that Paul was secretly engaged to Albertine Heine; and second, Varnhagen von Ense had proposed marriage to Marianne Saaling. That Paul, too, should have to battle for the right to marry is even harder to understand than the struggles of his sisters. Paul had left for London in 1831 to perfect his education as a banker in the house of B. A. Goldschmidt, where Abraham had invested some money. To everyone's astonishment, Goldschmidt went bankrupt and Paul went to Paris where he joined Leo, who had formerly represented the Mendelssohn brothers and had now opened his own business. Paul's wish at that time was to return to Berlin and work in the family bank run by his cousin Alexander; he would thus be near the young woman he had secretly become engaged to before his departure. His omnipotent father Abraham, however, was against this— even though Albertine Heine was utterly without fault, and from the same background as the Mendelssohns. She was the daughter of the Berlin banker Heinrich Carl Heine (1776–1835), who had no connection either with Friedrich II's banker Veitel Ephraim Heine, or with the poet Heinrich Heine and his Hamburg family. But she had been part of the Mendelssohn coterie since before 1829, and appeared in Wilhelm's drawing of the *Wheel*, which dated from the year of his marriage. Like her friends, she had converted during childhood, in 1825. But Abraham had quarreled with her father. Extremely unhappy, Paul wrote to Fanny from Paris, begging for her help.[16] For the Mendelssohn children, mutual support was both a duty and a habit. Fanny could not tolerate quarrels: Paul returned to Berlin in May 1833, although his marriage to Albertine was not decided on for quite some time. He went to work in the Mendelssohn Bank, becoming a partner in it four years later. He also directed his own banking house named Paul Mendelssohn-Bartholdy, in Hamburg. Paul had obviously decided to adopt the hyphen between Mendelssohn and Bartholdy. He married Albertine on 27 May 1835, and their union proved extremely happy. It would be hard to imagine a more rational love affair, and yet the Mendelssohn parents were anything but rational in their objections to this perfect daughter-in-law!

The adventures of Varnhagen and the beautiful Marianne seemed far less reasonable to their friends and acquaintances in Berlin. Rahel had died on 7 March 1833 and Varnhagen was scarcely out of mourning when he chose a replacement for her, one year later:[17] so much for having treated Rahel like a reincarnated goddess! Berlin society was all agog; no other event caused so many tongues to wag, be it the rebellion of the silk-workers in Lyon or the fact that Wilhelmine Schroeder-Devrient was singing at the Berlin Opera. Marianne and Varnhagen were both forty-nine.[18] Lea was badly shaken because Marianne was her niece and she was very fond of her. Fanny wrote to Felix: "Marianne Saaling came and sighed throughout the entire lunch, and we're taking turns with Albertine so that she doesn't drive Mother completely mad; never has there been such a scandal. But hold your tongue about it."[19] Fanny could not abide scandal-mongering: "I'd put my hand in the fire and swear it's all lies and slander, because I'm sure of it." In the end Marianne gave up the idea of marriage, being unable, as she put it, to accept conjugal intimacy.[20] The broken engagement caused as much scandal as had the engagement itself. Fanny again wrote to her brother: "Marianne and Varnhagen are officially no longer engaged; she is in Freienwalde, he is very merry. Both are behaving *on ne peut pas plus mal.*[21] The whole business is so disgusting that not much sense can be made of it, don't you agree?"[22]

So constipated with virtue was the society of 1834 that nobody could say exactly what was shocking in Marianne's comportment, but it certainly did not help that she acted openly and got herself talked about—as did Varnhagen. But was it simply a difference in generations? One person in the family came vigorously to Marianne's defense. This was Dorothea Schlegel, who took up her pen in Frankfurt and strongly reproached her niece Rebecka for adversely judging a woman who was trying to find her own way: "How is it that you're attacking poor Marianne so mercilessly? . . . Whether or not she's culpable doesn't much matter; she's depriving herself of everything that makes life happy! . . . I find it unpleasant to think that you and possibly your entire circle are being so pitiless toward her."[23] Dorothea had remembered the scandal of her own divorce and was feeling sympathy for Marianne. Seen from a distance, it is hard to understand how, barely thirty years after the *Aufklärung*, Prussian society had become so puritanical as to cry shame over a broken engagement. Dorothea and many of her female contemporaries had managed to divorce and lead a far freer life than was conceivable in 1830. Fanny was as shocked as everybody else; the only difference was that she hated to speak ill of anyone, just as she detested any thought of scandal.

Lea subsequently recovered from her tachycardia, and Marianne devoted herself to charitable works.

Meanwhile, Wilhelm's career required him to do a certain amount of traveling. He had to make a name for himself and his painting, and try to obtain commissions in order to support his family. His studio was flourishing, for he was a good professor, much loved by his students. The Hensels planned to go to England in the spring of 1835 and informed Mary Alexander, a friend of Felix and Abraham's, of their visit while at the same time asking her not to tell Abraham. The life and letters of the Mendelssohn children—who were no longer really children—testify to the awe in which they held their father, whom they simultaneously idolized and feared. Mary Alexander had translated some poems by Heine, of which Fanny had set three to music. In the letter advising her friend of her intentions, Fanny included the three lieder decorated with drawings by Wilhelm.[24] The announcement of Fanny's impending arrival was enough to frighten Miss Fanny Horsley, one of Felix's charming English lady admirers: "Mr. Hensel and his wife, who is Mendelssohn's sister, are coming to spend several months in England this autumn. I'm sure she'll terrify me with her piercing gaze and strict manner, which everyone who's seen her speaks of so mysteriously."[25]

An energetic woman cannot hope to have the reputation of being easy to get along with. The Hensels, however, did not go to England: their plans for the year 1835 involved going to Paris first, and their domestic family arrangements made a prolonged absence impracticable. Abraham's cataracts were getting worse, and Rebecka and Fanny had to take turns reading to him and writing his letters. "He puts up with his pain so patiently and sweetly, and with such kindness, it's impossible to describe; all his remarkable qualities are becoming evident this year, and his character is mellowing and improving," wrote Fanny to Felix on 8 March.[26] It is equally hard to describe the adoring attitude of Abraham's children. But if Fanny went away, then Rebecka had to stay behind. It was not simply because they were oppressed that women stayed at home; it was also out of necessity. Rebecka's cheerful character seemed to undergo a transformation around this time, and she took a dim view of the Hensels' plans. Her own projects were thwarted by them, and someone had to sacrifice herself to the family obligation of never leaving their parents alone.[27]

There was another obligation to consider, and that was Wilhelm's career. It was also decided that on the way to France the Hensels would stop off in Cologne, where Felix was conducting the Lower Rhine Festival. They would return from Paris via Boulogne and Belgium. This entailed a long journey, and so the family solved the problem of separation by accompanying them *en masse* to Cologne, where they would have the pleasure of seeing and hearing Felix conduct Handel's *Solomon*. "Even at the gates of Hell, put me among the altos," wrote Fanny to her brother; "and let me tell you this: if you make an unseemly fuss over me so that people are eager to hear me play, I won't come at all. In any case, I'm so unreasonably afraid of you (and apart from you, I'm not afraid of anyone, except perhaps of Father) that I never actually play well in your presence; for example, I would never try to accompany anyone when you are there, even though I know I do it very well. I can see you from here, torturing me in Düsseldorf; I'll be nervous and confused, I'll bungle the notes and fly into a temper. Especially as they're used to hearing you play everything I know."[28]

The concert in Cologne was a success, but Lea had a slight attack while returning to Düsseldorf and the Hensels did not leave for Paris until they felt reassured about her health. Felix accompanied his parents back to Berlin, and the Dirichlets left for Ostende.[29]

Everywhere he went, Felix lauded his sister's playing. He told

Marie Bigot's mother, Madame Kiéné, that Fanny was coming, praising her in these terms:

You will be delighted to renew acquaintance with my sister, for she's an excellent woman; her entire character is so sweet and calm, and yet so full of life and fire, that you are certain to like her. Moreover, she is so remarkably gifted musically that, if you feel like hearing music at all now, you will be pleased to let her play for you often. I am extremely sorry that since her marriage she can no longer compose as diligently as before, for she has written several pieces—in particular, some German lieder—that are among the best we have in that genre, but on the other hand it's good that she finds much joy in her home, for women who neglect it, whether in favor of oil painting, poetry, or double counterpoint, invariably remind me of the Greek from *Les Femmes savantes*, and I'm afraid of them. This is not, praise God, the case with my sister; and yet, as I told you, she has continued to practice the piano ardently and has even lately made great progress.[30]

Madame Kiéné had not seen Fanny since she had visited Paris as a little girl in 1816. We may well wonder why Felix thought Fanny composed less since her marriage, considering that she had sent him at least three cantatas, a dramatic scene, and a string quartet. She had only grown discouraged since the previous winter, and Felix was largely responsible. "I'm afraid of them," he writes, of women who might want to compose rather than do housework. Could he perhaps have needed Fanny, symbolically, to sacrifice her talent even more for him? It would only have been a symbolic sacrifice, of course, because Felix had plenty of talent of his own. So why was he afraid of women who asserted their competence? And why did he lie, or lie to himself, about Fanny's composing? Only he could have provided a reply.[31]

The Parisian world discouraged Wilhelm in whatever intention he might have had of living there, just as it had Felix. According to Fanny, the amount of intrigues and petty behavior that went on outweighed any advantage the French artists gained from being widely exhibited.[32]

Wilhelm was received by the Société libre des beaux-arts (Free Fine Arts Society), where he gave a lecture on the making of Majolica ware, a lecture subsequently published in the society's annals.[33] While in Paris the Hensels met Delaroche, Horace Vernet, and Gérard; Fanny was wildly enthusiastic about Gérard's portraits of Talma,

Mademoiselle Mars, the young Napoleon, Humboldt, and Canova.[34] They only spent a month in Paris, which was really not enough to see everything, especially as Wilhelm's health forced him to spend a lot of time resting. They also received a seemingly unpleasant visit from Giacomo Meyerbeer, who had moved to Paris and who described their encounter in one of his letters:

Today I paid a visit to Frau Professor Hensel who is here with her fool of a husband. He was sufficiently ill-bred not to call on me, which is why I went to see them. They were very penitent about it, but so frostily polite that I felt chilled despite the July heat. Fanny's ugliness is indescribable. Although she is perpetually plain, it seems to me that two years ago she looked like Venus in comparison.[35]

Felix Mendelssohn and Meyerbeer could not have been on worse terms. Tension and rivalry was building up between the two, with Meyerbeer, supported by Heine, in Paris; and Felix, supported by that discerning critic, Robert Schumann, in Leipzig. The two fronts represented opera, money, and petty intrigue on the one hand, and concerts, oratorios, and puritanism on the other. Felix may well have told Fanny something about Meyerbeer that made her dislike him, and since she would have been incapable of concealing her thoughts, Meyerbeer probably noticed!

These were turbulent times. While a popular uprising was being brutally repressed in Berlin, the month of July witnessed Fieschi's attempted assassination of Louis-Philippe in Paris. On the point of taking their leave, the Hensels had occasion to experience the fear caused by this event: the bomb that exploded on the king's path killed several national guardsmen, some spectators, and several people in the royal party.[36]

Accompanied by Sebastian and Minna, the Hensels continued on their journey toward Boulogne, a maritime health resort. But they had great difficulty in finding lodgings because the town was full of English people. The lodging they did find turned out to be rather insubstantial: after a violent rainfall, the roof fell in and the room was flooded with water. Fanny suffered from an eye infection, the cost of living was extremely high, the weather was appalling, and the postal service abysmal. They did not leave Boulogne with happy memories. Even so, they met Heine while they were there; an English writer named Sarah Austin, who was a friend of Felix; and their dear friend Klingemann, who had not yet made Wilhelm's acquaintance. One of Heine's witticisms made them laugh: disturbed by an English-woman's inopportune chatter in the reading room, he observed, "Madam, if my reading disturbs your conversation, I can go else-where."[37] The Hensels traveled home through Belgium, where they visited Bruges, Ghent, and Antwerp; Fanny termed them fifteenth-, sixteenth-, and seventeenth-century cities. In Ghent she was sorry that the nineteenth century was beginning to leave its mark rather too distinctly; nevertheless, even here she felt there were enough fine things to fill ten cities like Berlin![38] They admired all the early masters they managed to see—Memling and the Van Eycks, then Rubens in Antwerp—and also old churches. The Hensels made their first railway journey between Brussels and Malines, thanks to the line which had just opened between those towns.[39] Then they went to visit the town hall at Louvain, before rejoining the Dirichlets in Bonn. Unfortu-nately they were unable to take their time on the return journey as they had wished: Wilhelm's mother fell ill and they arrived in Berlin on 27 September just a few days before her death, which occurred on 4 October. "Today we buried my mother-in-law," wrote Fanny. "For the first time in my life I have watched someone die, and seen what steps are taken following a death. There is something extraordinarily solemn about a life nearing its end, and the moment when the thread breaks in favor of the hereafter; there was nothing revolting or fright-ening about it, she was fully conscious when she died, at peace, and hoping for redemption. How glad I am that we returned in time."[40]

After her mother's death, Minna moved in with the Hensels.[41] The Dirichlets returned to Berlin on 14 October, passing through Leipzig on the way and bringing Felix and Moscheles with them. Several festive days followed, which were, according to Sebastian, among the happiest his mother ever spent.[42] The grand piano was moved into the front wing of the house, news of the event spread through Berlin, and friends and acquaintances came in droves to hear the two star pianists. This was the last time that Abraham and Lea had all four children gathered round them, and that the entire family would assemble. Felix promised to return at Christmas and then went back to Leipzig, where he had just become director of the Leipzig Gewandhaus Orchestra, having conducted his first concert there on 1 October 1835.

The music did not cease with Felix's departure. Fanny's afternoon concerts had a new recruit: the baritone Franz Hauser, who had come to spend a season in Berlin, and whom Felix had introduced to his family. Hauser's passion for Johann Sebastian Bach, whose scores he was collecting, naturally endeared him to Fanny.[43] Her extremely brilliant "musical Sundays"—which Abraham had thought it impossible to improve upon—were still thriving. Fanny had two Bach cantatas performed, partly to honor Hauser, partly to take advantage of his presence.[44]

There was a further family celebration for Fanny's birthday. On 18 November, Abraham had a slight cough and spent an uncomfortable night; the doctors who were summoned reassured his family. At ten o'clock the next morning he wanted to rest, and died in his sleep half an hour later. In Fanny's words: "His face was so handsome, tranquil, and unchanged that we were able to stay near his dear body, not only without fear, but with a feeling of being truly uplifted. His expression was so peaceful, his forehead so pure and noble, his hands so soft: it was the death of a just man, a fine, enviable death. I pray God to give me one like it and all my life I shall try to deserve it as he deserved his. It was a most reassuring and beautiful image of death."[45]

Wilhelm left immediately to fetch Felix from Leipzig. Of the four children, Felix had been the most attached to his father: "almost fanatically attached," as Sebastian would later say.[46] Abraham had strongly encouraged him to write his oratorio, *Saint Paul*, and thereafter Felix felt it his filial duty to complete the work. The entire family was crushed by this loss, disoriented as if the driving force, the reason for existing, the meaning and explanation of their lives had suddenly disappeared. Lea went to live with the Dirichlets, while Paul took charge of the family affairs. The Mendelssohn Bartholdys had lost their center of gravity. Now that their omnipotent paterfamilias had gone, they had to redistribute all the roles, and Felix took over Abraham's role in regard to Fanny.

CHAPTER TWENTY-ONE

Rebuffs

Hensel continued to work on his new painting depicting Miriam and the exodus of the Jewish people from Egypt, for which Fanny, Rebecka, and Albertine all posed. Fanny was becoming steadily more depressed and less self-confident. Felix's criticisms discouraged her; she thought he did not appreciate her music and took no interest in it. On 5 January 1836 she wrote and asked him, almost timidly: "I'm also very sad, and it's truly not out of vanity, that I haven't been able to thank you in such a long time for liking something musically acceptable of mine. Did I really do it better before, or were you simply easier to please?"[1]

Felix nevertheless wrote back to protest, on 30 January:

I deny it all and I assure you I have every reason to be thankful for everything you create. If I don't like two or three successive pieces quite as much as other things you have written, this has no more serious cause than that you now compose less than you did before. It used to be that if one or two lieder, and then a third one, were too rapidly conceived and hastily composed, I may not have liked them; we didn't think too much about the reasons for our disapproval, but we had a good laugh about it. . . . Then the good pieces would start to come back, just as they are doing now. Even so, they cannot follow in such swift succession now, for you will henceforth have to think of many other things besides composing beautiful lieder. And it is surely better this way. But if you think your recent pieces are in any way inferior to the older ones, you're completely mistaken. I know of no better song of yours than the English one in G minor, or the end of the *Liederkreis*, and so many more recent ones. You know full well that there are entire notebooks of yours that I liked less than others because, faithful to my sign, I'm a nitpicking Schuhu and I belong to the savage race of Brothers. But as you know I like all your pieces and especially those which are close to my heart. You must write back quickly and admit how unjust you're being in implying I'm a person with no taste, and promise not to do it again.[2]

Felix went on to demand criticism from both Fanny and Rebecka, not only of his *Saint Paul* but also of his Opus 32 Overture, *Fair Melusine*. Fanny was supposed to confine her participation in professional musical life to this contribution to Felix's career, thus maintaining a modest and "feminine" character.

The question that should be asked here is: did Fanny need a sugar-coated pill—people telling her that what she composed was beautiful and she herself perfect—or did she need more pertinent encouragement? Whereas Felix was freely developing his ideas by composing the oratorio *Saint Paul*, she must have felt that her own talents and desires craved a more complete commitment. Felix had begun work on *Saint Paul* in July 1834 and finished it in the spring of 1836[3]—an unceasingly persistent creative effort that Fanny could only envy. Her husband and brother were planning monumental works, while she herself did not feel empowered to do likewise. Wilhelm, of course, desired nothing more than to see her compose, but only Felix's approval could have endowed her with sufficient self-confidence to begin a major work, and perhaps to think of sacrificing some of her role as model wife and mother. In any case, Fanny thought it was already too late; had it been forthcoming, Felix's encouragement would have been like some final glimpse of happiness, a last-minute chance that should be grabbed at, though without real hope. A work like *Saint Paul* is not written on the spur of the moment; Felix had previously done a great deal of composing, had traveled and matured, and had nothing else to do but think of himself and his music.

Felix gave a lot of work to copyists, and in a letter of 1 January 1836 he asked his sister to have a copy made of the piano score of *Saint Paul* which was in her possession, and to send it to him.[4] As it happened, Fanny's small family was then in good health, and she decided on a little jaunt to Leipzig at the end of the month. Presumably this was to take the score to him herself, or else to ask her brother for the encouraging word he never wrote, but she did not succeed in obtaining such a word. Back in Berlin, she addressed a further supplication to him:

Finally, I'm going to discuss myself again, for even though it's very unpleasant to act as one's own advocate, we are accustomed to speaking plainly to each other. You told me in Leipzig I would do better not to write sacred music any more, since my talent does not lie in that direction. Since I've been back home, or more exactly, this past week, I've played through many of my previous sacred compositions. I feel I must first tell you that in my opinion an honest person is the harshest possible judge of her own previous works. Many, in fact most, of them bored me so much I scarcely had the patience to finish playing them, but some—for example the aria *O dass ich tausend Zungen hätte* and a few choruses and recitatives of the so-called "cholera music"[5]—pleased me so much that I frankly rejoiced, foolish as that may sound. I think it a good test when one is pleased with one's things after a long time has passed in which one has completely forgotten them. Yet what you told me fell on stony ground and I have grown mistrustful—even though I think on the whole I can do better now than I did then, and would already have begun to rework a few pieces had not your interdiction deterred me.[6]

The reactions of both brother and sister are totally irrational. An interdiction! How could they allow such a word, and what game were they playing? It would seem that while Felix was investing all his efforts into a piece of sacred music, he was unwilling to see his sister do the same. Even his choice of subject, the apostle Paul, is significant: was it not Paul who forbade women to raise their voices in religious meetings?[7] In the months following his father's death, months that witnessed the birth of his oratorio, Felix was certainly more nervous and irritable than ever. Realizing this, he wrote Fanny these few consolatory words to thank her for her visit: "If only I had not quarreled with you so, the final evening and next day! It's odd, I scarcely thought of it while we were together, but as soon as I was alone in the carriage it came flooding over me and I could have thrashed myself. I know you forgive me, but I have still not managed to forgive myself."[8]

Although extremely attached to his family and to his sister, Felix would have preferred them to weigh less heavily upon him at that time. This explains his ill humor and negative attitude toward Fanny, whose upbringing had forced her to abandon part of herself, so as not to overshadow her brother. Did Felix blame her for having made only an incomplete sacrifice? According to general opinion—for everybody found him hard to live with at this point—it was time for Felix to settle down and start his own family.

In June of that year, Fanny went with Paul and Albertine to hear Felix conduct *Saint Paul* at the Lower Rhine Festival. On the way she stopped in Frankfurt to visit her Aunt Dorothea, who was now an old lady of seventy-two.[9] Once in Cologne, she bewailed her solitary state—like any respectable woman, she was not used to being alone. At that time, being alone meant without one's husband or one's son. In Düsseldorf she nonetheless went to stay with her friends the Woringens, and learned that one could feel at home without being in one's home. She took part in the rehearsals for *Saint Paul* as a member of the altos, and did not scrimp on admiration for the work:[10] "I cannot recall having experienced such strong emotions, composed of both sadness and joy."[11] Fanny knew the work well: during the concert, one of the "false witnesses" lost her place in the score. Pale as death, Fanny sang her the notes so unerringly that the chorus soloist was able to recover. After the performance Felix told her he was glad it had been a "false" witness! Fanny also heard one of the *Leonore* overtures, which was seldom played because Beethoven did not like it. "That man had no taste!" she concluded.[12] In addition, she heard Felix conduct Beethoven's Ninth Symphony—the first time she had heard the orchestral version. "This colossal Ninth Symphony, so vast and, in places, so terrifying, was performed as if by one person. The subtlest nuances and most hidden meanings came to light; textures were differentiated and made comprehensible; and then it became on the whole sublimely beautiful. A gigantic tragedy, whose finale is intended to be exalted but capsizes at its climax and slides into the opposite extreme, into burlesque." Until then, Fanny's only knowledge of the work had come from reading the score or playing it on the piano. How frustrating it must have been for her to live in a town with no symphony orchestra, amateur or professional!

Although Fanny was very happy to see her brother and talk to him during rehearsal intermissions, he was no longer her sole source of happiness—in fact, this obviously depended more on Wilhelm and Sebastian now. She expressed this clearly in her diary: "I feel sure that where a woman is concerned, there can be no pleasurable excursions without her husband and child and I shall never part from one or both of them again unless it is absolutely necessary."[13] On the other hand, she always looked to Felix for musical recognition, and the dejection this caused her remained quite apparent. As she wrote to Klingemann:

I'm including with this letter two piano pieces I've written since Düsseldorf; you can judge whether they're suitable for the hands of my unknown young friend. I leave it up to you, but must not fail to tell you how pleased I am that there's an audience in London for my little pieces—something totally lacking here. Less than once a year does someone copy something, or even ask to hear it. And in recent months, ever since Rebecka stopped singing, my lieder have been lying there completely unheard and unknown. When one never encounters either objective criticism or goodwill, one eventually loses the critical sense needed to judge one's work, while at the same time losing the wish to create it. Felix, who could easily take the place of an audience for me, can only reassure me sparingly for we are seldom together. I am thus more or less alone with my music. The pleasure it gives me—and gives Hensel—stops me from going to sleep entirely, and given the total absence of external encouragement, I construe my persistence as a proof of talent.[14]

Fanny felt alone with her music because Rebecka was now thoroughly absorbed in family life. Although she had an attractive voice, she had never been a great singer and her health was becoming increasingly fragile. In addition, Fanny's friend Pauline Decker had experienced some difficult pregnancies and was unable to resume her musical activities until October. Although less idle than this letter suggests, Fanny was cruelly affected by her absence. The amateur musicians among whom she found herself confined were so inferior to her that it was understandable if she was often bored, particularly as she had no hope of ever seeing her situation alter.

Some days after this letter to Klingemann, Fanny wrote to Felix, asking first for additional information about the beautiful young girl he had met in Frankfurt, then lamenting Decker's absence, which made it impossible to rehearse *Saint Paul*. She also railed against musical life in Berlin:

Since Hensel wished it, I have begun playing again on Sundays. Unfortunately the Ganzes are not there, and I am really too spoiled to enjoy being accompanied by beginners. As the strict master ordered, I've continued to compose piano pieces, and for the first time managed to complete one that sounds brilliant. I don't quite know what Goethe meant by demonic influence, of which he spoke so often toward the end, but this much is clear: if something of the sort exists, then you exert it over me. I think if you seriously proposed that I become a good mathematician I would have no particular difficulty in doing so, just as I might stop being able to make music tomorrow, if you thought I couldn't do it any more. Therefore be very careful with me.[15]

Fanny was imprisoned in her private sphere and wanted Felix to pronounce the words that would deliver her: audience and publish. But clearly, these were just the words he did not wish to utter, even when she prompted him, as in her letter of 28 October that same year:

You ask what I've composed and here is the reply: half a dozen piano pieces, as you instructed. I'll send them to you with Paul. Play them through if you have time, or have one of your students play them, and let me know what you think. It is so natural for me to be your student that I'm always able to do best when you tell me, do this or that. In the recent past I have been asked many times to publish something; should I do so?[16]

For the Cantor to have become her student's student, and use the word "natural" in this connection, indicates Fanny's psychological condition during this whole crisis. Felix responded in the negative. Fortunately Hensel, though tone deaf himself, did not see it in this light, and Fanny returned to the attack on 22 November—Saint Cecilia's day. Cecilia was the name of the girl from Frankfurt to whom Felix had become engaged on 9 September; curiously enough, it was also one of Fanny's names, for she had been baptized Fanny Caecilia.

With regard to my publishing, I'm like a donkey between two bales of hay. To tell the truth, I have rather neutral feelings on the subject, but Hensel desires it, and you are opposed. In any other matter I would of course comply unconditionally with my husband's wishes, but in this particular case your consent is too important to me, for without it I should undertake nothing of the kind.[17]

One should never say never. Early in 1837, the music publishing house of Schlesinger came out with an album comprising lieder by various composers, as was customary at the time. It included a lied by Fanny, *Die Schiffende* (Sailing by).

Felix wrote Fanny an extremely nice letter about this publication, on 24 January 1837:

Do you know, Fenchel, that your lied in A major from Schlesinger's album is all the rage here? Or that the *Neue musikalische Zeitung* (I should say, its editor, who dines at the same hotel as I do) is crazy about you? That everyone says it's the best piece in the album—which isn't much of a compliment, because what else is good in it? And that everyone really likes it very much? Are you a real composer now, and are you enjoying it?[18]

Fanny replied on 27 January 1837:

My composership, consisting of one lied, has not brought me any enjoyment, dear Felix. On the contrary, I find all the shouts and trombone blasts the Schlesingers have emitted over this wretched album quite repulsive.[19]

Fanny always sought to diminish her own part in things, but the publication of one lonely song by a musician who had already composed extensively certainly had something ridiculous about it. Nevertheless, it is worth noting that the editor of the *Neue musikalische Zeitung* was none other than its founder, Robert Schumann. Fanny's lied was sung in Leipzig in early March 1837 during one of Felix's concerts, of which he gave the following account:

I want to write very seriously to you about your lied yesterday, for it was very beautiful. You already know what I think, but I was curious to see if my old favorite—which I had only heard in our green room with the engravings or in the garden room, with Rebecka singing and you playing the piano—would still have the same effect on me in a crowded concert hall, by lamplight and following loud orchestral music. Thus concerned, I began to play your pretty wavelike motions, alone in the silence while everybody listened as quietly as mice. Yesterday evening I liked it better than ever before, and it was very well received by the audience, who murmured each time they heard the theme with the long E, and applauded loudly at the end. Although Grabow sang it far less well than Beckchen used to, it was nonetheless a good clean performance, and the last lines were very pretty. Bennett, who was in the orchestra, sends you his best and says to tell you what you already know, about the lied. As for me, I'm expressing thanks on behalf of the public in Leipzig and other places for your having published it against my wishes.[20]

Once again, as in her childhood, those close to Fanny fully recognized her worth and talent. Yet she was supposed to keep them to herself, like children who could not be born. Was this, indeed, the deep-seated reason for the "accidents" mentioned by Felix in a letter to Klingemann: "My elder sister has met with another sad accident"?[21] Fanny spoke of these mishaps herself: "I was not to blame at all for the most recent accident, in fact I'd been feeling so well right up to the moment it occurred, that I'd been very hopeful."[22] On 2 June she was still happy at not having gone to Leipzig, since this would have made her feel responsible for the "accident."[23] Sebastian remained Fanny's only child. So deeply dejected did she become that Lea, who was as worried as Wilhelm, took up her pen and begged Felix to encourage his sister. This initiative shows that Lea, intelligent and demanding woman that she was, understood perfectly what a miscarriage implied, and that she had not raised her daughters to imprison them in marriage; she still recalled the salons of the *Aufklärung* and the freedom of thought manifested there. By 1837, however, nineteenth-century ideology and the cult of the family were firmly entrenched, and Fanny was completely at their mercy. Just as Lea had tried to protect the adolescent Fanny from a sentimental passion that would have harmed her intellectual development, she now wished to help Fanny's talents blossom in the outside world. Wilhelm was entirely in agreement with her. Since this first lied had been so encouragingly received, why not keep on publishing? Fanny's inability to give birth to other children could only strengthen their arguments, and increase their urgent desire to help her emerge from depression. But Felix disappointed their expectations.

The family had a further reason for being annoyed with Felix: he was married in Frankfurt on 26 March 1837, without any close relative having met his fiancée. Perhaps he wished to avoid the problems experienced by his brother and two sisters, but his siblings were nonetheless offended. The one member of the family to attend his wedding was Dorothea Schlegel, who lived in Frankfurt. The young lady was entirely suitable: her name was Cécile Jeanrenaud (1817–1853) and she was the daughter of a pastor in the French Calvinist community in Frankfurt. Born near Lyons in France, she was pretty, well-mannered, charming, sweet, and a talented painter. Fanny noted that her brother's marriage symmetrically matched her own. Cécile did not sing as drastically out of tune as Wilhelm, but she was certainly no more of a musical threat to Fanny than Wilhelm was to Felix. On several occasions Fanny expressed a wish to meet her brother's fiancée before the wedding—again the archaic notion that a woman changes when she is no longer a virgin. For Christmas 1836, she sent Cécile a lied she had just composed on a text by Goethe: *Ach, um Deine feuchten Schwingen* (Oh, for your damp wings), together with the copy of a duet between Suleika and Hatem that Felix had published in his youth (Opus 8, no. 12); both were decorated by Wilhelm.[24] Cécile appeared delighted. But Felix did not bring her to Berlin to meet his family, and this eventually created strains between him and his relatives, particularly Fanny. Witness the letters pregnant with tension exchanged between Leipzig and Berlin on 2 June 1837, when Fanny wrote:

If you think of the time when we were always together, when I immediately guessed what thoughts were passing through your mind and knew your latest compositions by heart before you had even written them; if you remember how exceptional our relationship was, even for a brother and sister, because of our common musical pursuits, then I think you'll agree that it's been a strange deprivation for me to know that all this time you are happy as I have always fervently hoped you would be, and yet not even to have met your beloved, your wife. . . . For the past three years we have only seen each other for a few days, and hastily at that. Unfortunately my husband has as little to do in Leipzig as you have in Berlin.

. . . To tell you everything, it seems to me that distance, which will certainly leave no effect on me, has not left you completely unchanged—not, perhaps, in regard to me, but in regard to my family. I can't recall the last time you asked me for news of Hensel's work or Sebastian's progress. . . . Tell me I'm mistaken, and I shall be happy to believe you. . . .

The musical spleen you derided stems naturally from the fact that I have scarcely played or listened to any music this winter, and then suddenly three virtuosos came, one after another—Döhler, Clara Wieck, and Henselt. You know how easily downcast I become, my nerves were frayed at the time, and I felt I had aged incredibly. But since then I have recovered again, and obtained a copy of Chopin's études, several of which I'm diligently practicing.[25]

In the same vein, but much more nicely, she wrote to Cécile:

I must tell you that when someone describes your beauty to me, I start to shout at him! I've heard quite enough about it, and lovely eyes were not made to be heard.[26]

The reply Felix sent his mother did not satisfy his family's expectations:

You write to me of Fanny's latest pieces, telling me I should persuade her to publish them. And yet you really don't need to praise her new compositions for me to be extremely happy about them, or for me to find them beautiful and remarkable, because I know very well who wrote them. Nor do I need to say that should she decide to publish them, I shall help her in every way I can, and spare her unnecessary trouble. But as for persuading her to publish them, that's something I cannot do, for it's against my ideas and convictions. We have already discussed it a good deal and my opinion has not altered. Publication is a serious matter (or at least, it ought to be) and I think it should only be done if one intends to present oneself as a composer throughout one's life, and to remain one. This nonetheless implies a succession of works, one following another; if only a few isolated works are published, then only vexation can result—or else it becomes what they call a manuscript for friends, and I don't like that much either. And if I know Fanny, she has neither the wish nor the vocation to become a composer. She is far too self-respecting a woman for that; she sees to her house and thinks not of the public, nor of the musical world—nor even of music, except when her primary activity's been carried out. Publishing could only disturb her in that, and this is an idea to which I cannot reconcile myself. Forgive me, but that is why I shall not persuade her. If she decided in her own right, or to please Hensel, I am ready, as I said, to help her as much as I can, but encourage her to do something I do not find proper—this I cannot do.[27]

Felix Mendelssohn Bartholdy must have been a trifle deaf in regard to his sister. Fanny did not publish at this time. She waited another nine years before committing herself to the deed. She could not, like her brother, prove an uninterrupted "succession of works" from childhood on. At thirty-two, she was a woman exhausted and depressed by miscarriages and by the forcible abortion of her talent.

The Woringen family, whose father Otto (1760–1838) represented the Prussian government in the Rhineland, had grown close to the entire Mendelssohn clan in Düsseldorf, and could not abide the thought of their being divided by a quarrel. After spending several weeks at 3 Leipziger Strasse—a happy, musical visit, despite another epidemic of cholera—they took Fanny to Leipzig in November 1837, and she was finally able to meet Cécile. She wrote to Klingemann about her:

Finally knowing my sister-in-law has removed a stone from my heart, for I cannot deny that I was filled with unease and ill-humor on this point. But she is such a lovable person, so unaffectedly simple and refreshing, with such an even, happy disposition that I can only pronounce Felix fortunate to have found her. She loves him more than one can say, but does not allow him everything and greets his sudden whims with a serenity that may perhaps break him of them. So light, clear, and natural is she that her presence makes one think of fresh air.[28]

Considering how Fanny loved to breathe in gulps of fresh air, this was quite a compliment she paid her sister-in-law. Her bitterness toward Felix is apparent: he was not easy to live with, and it was better not to depend on him.[29] All was forgotten and everybody loved each other as they had before; yet if one looks objectively at the quantity of letters exchanged, one notices that their correspondence declined after 1837. While for the single year of 1829 Fanny wrote forty-six letters to her brother, an average of twenty-five per year during the years 1834 to 1836 and twenty in 1837, one reaches a figure of ten after 1838; that is, almost one letter per month (not counting, of course, the years when Felix lived in Berlin). Even if brother and sister were still close, life had broken their privileged relationship—or at least, Fanny had learned not to count on her brother. As for Felix, consciously or unconsciously, he had truly adopted Abraham's role in regard to his sister.

CHAPTER TWENTY-TWO

Life in Berlin

Felix still required his sister's active participation in his own composing: he sought her advice and opinions and wished to benefit from her experience, but the arrangement was not reciprocal. Fanny, on the other hand, set about introducing her circle of Berliners to *Saint Paul*. On numerous occasions she had extracts of it performed in the Sunday musicales—which, contrary to Abraham's expectations, had continued to develop, turning into events that encompassed far more than simply family and friends. They were now attended by people whom neither Fanny nor Wilhelm knew, and the Hensels' apartment was so crowded that there was scarcely room for the singers.[1] Despite her depression, Fanny continued to make music at a high level—perhaps spurred on by her distress, as sometimes occurs. Her salon certainly had few rivals in a Berlin so deprived of concerts.

The Singakademie performed little that was original, whether ancient or contemporary. In February 1836, Fanny had come home saddened and annoyed by an extremely mediocre performance of Handel's *Israel in Egypt*.[2] Not until February 1838 did the august officials of that body, impelled by feelings of guilt concerning Felix, decide to have his *Saint Paul* played and sung, whereupon they approached Fanny and asked her to come and advise them. Felix was sympathetic: "You, meanwhile, are condemned to listen to the rehearsals of the Singakademie, which must be hard for you: I know from experience what an unspeakable feeling it is to sit there with one's fingers itching, unable to help because the most expressive words are useless, only the stick can help (I mean, the conductor's stick)."[3] Once again Fanny attended a performance that would have gone far better had she herself been able to take the baton.

Naturally, she had no such intention. She was content to miss her brother, feel her fingers itch, and put Rungenhagen to work. This was Fanny's first visit to the Singakademie since Zelter had died, and thus she encountered a host of "living and deceased ghosts."[4] During the rehearsals Rungenhagen respectfully asked her opinion after every chorus—which she gave, with her customary frankness; he also came to see her the following Saturday so that she could play him the soloists' arias. The leader of the orchestra, Pieter Hubert Ries,[5] also asked her innumerable questions, particularly about the tuba that had sometimes been added to the organ part in churches. As she declared to Felix:

Now, the said tuba is a monstrosity which transforms all the passages wherein it is used into besotted brewers. And so I fell on my knees and begged them to take pity on themselves and leave the tuba at home. Rungenhagen helped me to my feet and granted my plea. Yesterday was the first full rehearsal, and it far surpassed my expectations. To my great joy, I can tell you that I was quite delighted with many things. The choruses, now taken at the correct tempo (a few slightly too fast), were sung with fire and power, with all the nuances that one could ask for. The good old ram's head really took a lot of honest pains, and everybody was astonished at his liveliness. Many people realized which way the wind was blowing. But I kept very calm, and didn't take myself for the Don Quixote of *Saint Paul*, so I hope I haven't made any enemies—except, perhaps, for the tuba player. Ries came to see me again today. These past few days I've dispensed all the good advice I'd stored up in the larder, and now I feel quite stupid.[6]

At that time the German middle classes never drank beer, which was considered a vulgar and contemptible beverage. Sebastian Hensel maintained this opinion throughout his life,[7] but he would live to see his children and their generation transformed into beer drinkers. The tuba was as incongruous in Mendelssohn's music as beer was at his table, and all this helped fuel his rage against the Singakademie. Felix did not realize that his own bitterness—which was in any case amply justified—deprived Fanny of a possible outlet for her talent; she might have exercised it at the Singakademie, if only from the wings. Of course, she might also have ended up quarreling with Rungenhagen, who caused her deep irritation most of the time. But the fact remains that it was only on Felix's behalf and with his permission that she went out at all. Since Felix had become the director of the Leipzig Gewandhaus after being rejected as director of the Singakademie, Fanny was really the one to suffer punishment.

She was still afraid of her brother, as is apparent in letters where her fear shows through her jokes: "I'm a very poor Minister of Foreign Affairs," she says apologetically on one occasion.[8] Fanny was Felix's musical representative in Berlin, just as Paul was his business representative. She had become a kind of hostage. Many people approached her asking for permission which only Felix could grant: for example, the right to publish his works or send him texts. Fanny would point out that Felix lived in Leipzig[9] and that a letter "duly stamped and mailed would reach him two days later in good health"; to protect her brother, she would however add that he was "a very busy man, uncertain of his spelling, and his secretary was ill." Such precautions are customary in protecting famous men who are often in demand, but they also show how afraid Fanny was of displeasing him and incurring his wrath.

Through Felix, Fanny had occasion to meet many performing artists whom the composer recommended to his family. This was how she came to know the singer Clara Novello (1818–1908), famed in musical history for having inspired Robert Schumann's eight piano pieces entitled *Novelletten*. Felix found her rather cold, though highly musical, and thought she should give only concert performances. He was astonished at her successes in Berlin that season. Novello was welcomed warmly by the Mendelssohns and gladly took part in Fanny's Sunday musicales; in January Fanny put on *La clemenza di Tito* with Decker, Novello, and a soprano from the Royal Opera, Auguste von Fassmann, who had unconditionally offered her services.[10] In February Fanny mentioned another "gathering," "composed of Jews and actors," where she heard the "masked trio" from *Don Giovanni* sung by her friends Fassmann, Novello, and Mantius—the best performance she had ever heard of that piece.[11] Fanny nonetheless agreed with Felix about Clara Novello's lack of acting skills. Seeing her awkward, timid stance, the Mendelssohns took pity on her and did what they could: Rebecka offered her a fan, Paul a bouquet, and Fanny a wreath. Thus adorned, Novello was able to concentrate on her vocal line.[12]

Another important event took place during that same month of February 1838. For the one and only time in her life, Fanny took part in a public concert. She described it in a letter to her friend Klingemann:

Last week there was a concert which caused a sensation in elegant society here. It was of a kind often given elsewhere: amateurs playing to benefit the poor, with tickets twice the normal price. The chorus was almost exclusively composed of countesses, ambassadors' wives, and officers. As a lady of acceptable rank I too was earnestly invited to play, and so for the first time in my life I played in public, choosing Felix's concerto in G minor. I was not at all afraid—my acquaintances were kind enough to be nervous for me, and despite a rather wretched program the concert as a whole aroused so much curiosity and interest it raised 2500 thalers.[13]

For once, Fanny had occasion to assess her market value! To be considered an amateur did not please her at all, for the sugary repertoire typical of salons was certainly not her style—as the programs of her Sunday matinées attest. Fortunately, Clara Novello also took part in the concert, and Fanny considered it "poetic license indeed to count her among the dilettantes."[14]

Fanny herself was surprised she had not been nervous on that occasion. As we know, one of Fanny's most pronounced characteristics was a lack of self-confidence. She was unanimously considered a great pianist who constantly practiced her instrument. Drawing-room concerts, which she had given all her life, are far more frightening than official ones because the audience is nearer, but Fanny did not yet know that it is much easier to perform on a real stage and that her salon experience enabled her to face all manner of musical situations.

"You're playing in concerts!" wrote Felix appreciatively.[15] "Bravischischisimo. That's splendid and wonderful. If only I could hear you!" Never for one instant did Felix cease to admire Fanny's playing. There were others who expressed regret that Fanny did not stuff her middle-class attitudes into her pocket and embark on a career as a concert artist. One of these admirers was Dr. Reiter, who had a conversation with Felix on this subject, one November evening in 1835: "He tells me you should become an itinerant artist, and that you'd make the others appear insignificant. I asked him 'Pourquoi?'[16] because I was freezing; it was yesterday evening in the stairways of the concert hall, and he went on and on telling me how amiable you both were."[17] Wilhelm Hensel, of course, might have been a little unhappy, had his wife become a permanent traveler like her brother; he was ready to do almost anything to ensure her happiness, but not give up his family life!

A critic of the English musical review *The Athenaeum* was of the same opinion:

Had Frau Hensel been a poor man's daughter, she would have been known throughout the world, alongside Frau Schumann and Madame Pleyel, as a female pianist of the highest order. Like her brother, she had in her compositions a touch of that southern vivacity so rare among the Germans. More feminine than his, her playing bore a strong family resemblance to her brother's in its fire, neatness, and solidity. Like him, too, she was as generally accomplished as she was specially gifted.[18]

Had Frau Hensel been a poor man's daughter, would she indeed have been able to play the piano? Would she really have been "generally accomplished," and would she have had the opportunity to cultivate her talent? Women were subject to this contradictory principle: either they had not sufficient money to study, or else the money they had not actually needed to earn themselves prevented them from ever leaving their homes. Frau Schumann and Madame Pleyel belonged to families of musicians—traveling players, as it were—a species beginning to be elevated by Romanticism. But they did not have easy lives. It is still conceivable that Fanny, with her privileged background, might have gone further and performed in public, since other women were doing so. Did she lack courage, and was she too conventional?

Quite possibly, but there is also the chance that her Judaic origins would quickly have been held against her. She did not have the right to contravene the general morality, which stipulated that a woman's duty consisted of looking after her home. Then again, Clara Schumann's life may have been rather too difficult; perhaps she would have preferred to lead an easier one, had she been able. Moreover, Fanny may not really have wanted to be a "pianist," in the sense the word was beginning to acquire. At that time, piano technique was making what is known as "progress." Since the phenomenon of Paganini, instrumentalists and public alike were fascinated by the "demonic" power a single individual could exercise over a crowd of people, aided by the sparks drawn from his instrument. Intrigued,

Fanny went to hear the new performers and returned feeling distinctly out of phase. In November 1835 she mentioned her intention of going to hear Madame Pleyel: "She interests me very much, both as a beautiful woman and a fine pianist. One would not go to her to learn proper behavior."[19] (Camille Pleyel had just obtained a divorce.) Her style of playing must still have been among those Fanny admired, whereas she felt increasingly alienated from the Thalberg school.[20] In December 1836 she went to hear a young virtuoso named Döhler, hoping to learn "the latest progress in technique";[21] all she heard, however, was an unending series of variations that added nothing to the music. The musical world plunged Fanny into a dolorous ordeal: the gap between technique and taste. There were virtuosos giving public performances she could not possibly admire from a musical standpoint, performances that strove for pianistic effect at the expense of artistic quality. Klingemann was made privy to her thoughts on 3 April 1837:

I shall probably spend my entire life intending to buy an English grand piano, or some kind of grand, although I need one less than ever. In the light of all these demonic sparks and fashionable affectations I find my playing incredibly antiquated, and I'm withdrawing ever more into my shell and my own insignificance.[22]

This was too much for Felix to accept. He wrote to Lea on 13 July of that year:

I'm very vexed that Fanny should say the new school of piano playing is completely over her head. That's utterly untrue. Her playing far outstrips that of all these boys. They can bring off a variation or two and a few artful tricks, but even the public is no longer blinded so easily by all this speed and affectation of speed. We need a soul to transport us. For that reason I might prefer to listen to D for an hour, rather than hear Fanny for an hour, but after a week I'd be too bored to listen, and would immerse myself in the other style again, which is the right one. They're all the same, those virtuosi; they're like Kalkbrenner in his day, and will live to see themselves go out of style unless they have something more than their fingers. Fanny has something more, and so she has nothing to fear from any of them.[23]

At that time Fanny had not yet heard the grand magician, the most esteemed virtuoso of all: Sigismond Thalberg. He came to Berlin in

January 1839. "Your big shot," as she described him to Felix, dined with Lea, "who kept him to herself."[24] The Hensels met him at Alexander Mendelssohn's house, but Thalberg did not play at private social events. "One really must go and watch these wizards as they play—I'm going to obtain in advance the pieces he'll play, and get the most out of them. These gentlemen make things incredibly easy for themselves, despite all the difficulties, and don't need a single rehearsal because they perform everything unaccompanied, reckoning it all in terms of the most money earned in the shortest time." She found Thalberg, whom she saw again taking tea at her mother's, guilty of "behaving like a virtuoso, showing off, and being very pleased with himself." When he announced first one and then another farewell concert, she felt he "disdained none of the virtuoso's tricks." To be sure, he was a great pianist. But she was not a pianist who would enjoy "performing unaccompanied" for a long time; performing "with accompaniment" would be what we call playing chamber music. Fanny was surprised at pianists who became virtuosos rather than musicians. Apart from the fact that middle-class women were not supposed to make exhibitions of themselves, she had no desire to become a "circus animal." She was glad that Felix had never turned into this uninteresting species of musician: shallow, ignorant, self-sufficient, and vulgar. Fanny was justified in feeling out of step with the times, since she herself played, or had other people play, nothing but Bach, Mozart, Haydn, and Mendelssohn, with an occasional incursion into Weber, Spohr, and Cherubini. Her taste was simultaneously out of date and impervious to fashion; moreover, in Berlin she was alone in representing her point of view. The Singakademie belonged to a sterile conservatism, and in striving for effect the traveling virtuosos showed they belonged to an equally sterile modernism. Fanny realized that her place in the musical world was situated in a steadily shrinking zone—not simply at the borderline between public and private domains, but also at the frontier between a living tradition and reverence for a past that had run its course.

During the same period, in March 1839, Felix was conducting Schubert's Symphony in C Major, "The Great," which had been introduced to him by Robert Schumann. Felix was in a position to fight for his ideas and to give life to them. For this reason he refused to confine himself to the role of virtuoso pianist. This was not Fanny's intention either: had some desire impelled her to emerge from her condition as a housewife, it would more likely have been a wish to conduct, like her brother. There again, their talents were alike: they had a desire to experience music with other people, to share and organize it. The *Sonntagsmusik* proves as much, as does the small choir which she continually rehearsed. Fanny spoke with some disdain of the technical "pirouettes" performed by pianists who refused the musical difficulty of rehearsing with unknown musicians.

Artists visiting Berlin had to sustain the costs of a concert themselves, including that of renting the hall. To attract an audience and bring variety to the performance, they naturally invited colleagues to take part in the evening, returning the favor by going to play in other people's concerts. Franz Liszt nonetheless saw fit to give eleven concerts on his own in the hall of the Singakademie, between late December 1841 and February 1842, "without orchestral accompaniment" as the *Allgemeine musikalische Zeitung* noted.[25] Yet he also took part in a concert given by the tenor Pantaleoni—thus enabling the singer to fill the hall—and in two of the concerts given by the pianist Döhler. Liszt's personal magnetism justified his solo appearances on stage, and the fascination he exerted on the public established the image of the lone pianist, solitary as a long-distance runner. This unvarying habit shocked no one, in Liszt's case. But in 1837 the *Allgemeine musikalische Zeitung* criticized Clara Wieck, who had been performing regularly in Berlin since 1832, for having given a solo recital at the Russian Hotel, resulting in a "rather monotonous musical evening."[26] On the other hand, she was praised in 1839 for taking part in a concert Zimmerman had organized,[27] in which, "discreetly accompanied by Herr Zimmerman and Herr Lotze," she played "Beethoven's great D major trio in masterly fashion, both in regard to speed and interpretation." Then in March 1847 she performed her husband's piano quintet. Like Felix Mendelssohn, Robert Schumann was a champion of tradition and urged his wife to concentrate on the great composers and to play Bach and Beethoven rather than fashionable composers such as Herz and Henselt. In this sense Clara Schumann, like Fanny, might well have felt out of step with the times, but she had moved in the opposite direction. From having been a virtuoso she had become a musician, thanks to Robert's influence. Even if there were still musicians like violinist Charles de Bériot[28]—who shared concerts with his sister-in-law, singer Pauline Garcia, in Berlin in May 1838—concert programs were tending to become standardized, enabling a single star performer to shine. This was how the nineteenth century fostered the advent of individualism in music.

This unexpected development made it even harder for Fanny to gain access to the professional world as a pianist. Felix tried to reassure her, but in fact he, too, found himself left behind by the evolution of modern life, albeit in an entirely different way. Even though he had a firm footing in the active world and was in a position to express his ideas, the social changes introduced by industrialization and a growing tendency to worship money, speed, and individuality were undermining the moral sense that had been instilled into him—even calling into question the meaning of his life.

In 1838, Felix was finally able to utter his encouragements in person because in April the "Felicians"—Felix, his wife Cécile, and their new baby Carl, who was born on 7 February—came to Berlin to spend the summer at 3 Leipziger Strasse. Fanny was, of course, delighted, and Rebecka too. Felix was to bring her copies of the Bach cantatas in Hauser's collection, thus giving added inspiration to the Sunday musicales. Fanny complained of not having composed that winter, but she had played a great deal: "I no longer know how it feels when one wants to write a lied. Will the feeling return, or was Abraham simply old? The cocks are not crowing over it, and no one dances to my little flute."[29]

Felix returned to Berlin just as Wilhelm was leaving for England: Wilhelm departed on 27 May 1838, without his wife. He had just completed a vast painting, *Christ in the Desert*, which, along with his *Miriam*, was intended to gain the favor of the English court. He arrived just in time to attend Queen Victoria's coronation. The sight of his paintings hanging in the gallery at Buckingham Palace next to the Van Dycks, Rembrandts, and Rubens caused him much anxiety, but the queen purchased *Miriam* nevertheless. The Duchess of Sutherland wanted a copy, but Hensel declined to make one, and so she commissioned another on the same theme, *The Shepherdess in the Land of Goshen*. Lord Egerton also commissioned a painting on the life of the Duke of Brunswick, and Wilhelm completed that painting the following year.[30] Filled with enthusiasm, the queen wrote in her diary: "I have been to see two very fine paintings by a German painter named Hansel [sic]: they are really very beautiful. I saw the painter himself."[31] Wilhelm had thought of copying the Raphael cartoons owned by the English crown, but this suggestion was rejected by the Prussian Minister of Culture.[32]

Meanwhile, Fanny stayed in Berlin and spent a happy summer with her brother. She took a liking to Cécile, calling her a *Sonntagskind*—which could mean both "Sunday child" and "child of a sunny day." Unfortunately, the Felicians' visit was interrupted by an outbreak of measles. Seized with alarm Wilhelm returned hastily from London on 17 September, but Felix and his family had already gone back to Leipzig. Cécile and Felix had both caught the measles, as had Sebastian and Rebecka.

So successful was Wilhelm's trip to England that instead of the Italian journey they had talked of for so long, and finally planned to make the next year, the Hensels decided to spend the season of 1839–1840 in London. Once again, Fanny confided in Klingemann, expressing a certain anxiety: "I am quite aware that I shall be in a difficult position, for in many respects people have expectations of me which I cannot fulfill. I'm not good at showing off, and my natural awkwardness is greatly increased by the fact that I'm aware my husband's friends are expecting a prophetess or a heroine, whereas it's a dwarf that will arrive."[33] The journey did not take place, however, for it took Wilhelm longer than he expected to paint the commissioned works.

Family duties continued to eat up Fanny's time. Luise Hensel moved out of their house, where she had lived since 1833. There was no real disagreement between her and Fanny, for they got on like two intelligent women quite capable of making the compromises necessary for cohabitation. But life with the Hensels did not really suit Luise, who complained several times in her letters to Clemens Brentano about the amount of work that Fanny left her to do. Whether or not her share of domestic tasks was justly apportioned, Luise certainly hated the disruptive effect that housework, music, visits, and Sebastian had on her contemplative existence. Everything except religious meditation disturbed her. She went to live near Heidelberg with some friends by the name of Schlosser, Roman Catholics like herself.[34]

As the years went by, the number of cows whose tails Fanny had to untie had increased to twenty-seven—as she told Cécile.[35]

The joke lost its humor. That winter Rebecka was terribly ill. First she caught the measles; then she had recurrent toothaches. In November, she lost a little son of thirteen months, who fell ill and died in the space of thirty-six hours. Rebecka was then confined to bed with "nervous pains in the face."[36] Was this a case of shingles, or a continuation of her dental problems? According to Fanny, the pain of losing her child took the edge off her physical pain. Wilhelm made two sketches of the child on its deathbed and made an oil painting from them, so lifelike that it brought some consolation to the grieving parents. On hearing of the child's death Felix came to spend a few days in Berlin, but Rebecka scarcely noticed his presence in the delirium of grief. Fanny remained at her side, and since she had once again given up the idea of going to England, she promised to accompany her sister on a cure and spend the summer with her at Heringsdorf on the Baltic sea. As the moment of departure grew steadily nearer, Fanny became increasingly irritated at the thought of having to leave her husband—who had also had to forego his visit to England—for the sake of being bored in a resort. But Rebecka's health remained so fragile, bordering on nervous collapse, that Fanny could not go back on her promise and had to resign herself to visiting the "herring village."

That year, the concerts had been particularly difficult to organize, but just as the situation was becoming desperate Felix sent his family an English contralto, Mary Shaw (1814–1876), with a letter of introduction. He had met her in England and invited her to Leipzig to take part in the Gewandhaus season of 1838.[37] She was reasonably successful in Berlin, though not as popular as Clara Novello had been. Her interpretations of Handel oratorios were remarkable, and the soprano Fassmann enthusiastically visited her to study the *Messiah*.[38] She performed in two of Fanny's Sunday matinées, singing in *Saint Paul*, which she had taken part in when it was first performed in England. Felix considered Shaw and Novello to be the best concert artists then available in Germany, thereby creating a rivalry between them and causing the other singers a degree of annoyance. Mary Shaw made her debut at La Scala, Milan, in 1839, but the depressive state of her husband, the painter Albert Shaw, prevented her from pursuing her career. She subsequently gave lessons and, still later, married someone in the legal profession with whom she lived at Hadleigh Hall.

Mary Shaw's presence in Berlin in 1839 was very helpful to Fanny because Decker was not there, which always tended to complicate things. The demands of her career also caused Fassmann—another favorite of the Mendelssohns—to move from place to place a lot. Fanny tried to send her brother another young singer, Hedwig Schulz (1815–1845), for the Gewandhaus concerts, but Schulz preferred an engagement with the Berlin Opera.[39] It was most generous of Fanny to think of parting from a singer she had need of herself, in Decker's absence! The young singer passed up the opportunity of working with Mendelssohn. Then as now, opera proved more attractive to singers than did concerts.

That summer, then, Rebecka and Fanny set off with their respective sons, Walter and Sebastian, and Wilhelm's sister Minna.[40] Heringsdorf had not yet become a fashionable spa but did have the advantage of being close to Berlin. It was a fishing village with rather uncomfortable lodgings, and Fanny hastened to the nearest town, Swinemünde,[41] to rent certain indispensable items: a commode, plates and dishes, and a piano, of which she broke a string as soon as she laid hands on it. The piano tuner was urgently summoned, but his visit proved disastrous: he broke two other strings and tuned the instrument two tones lower instead of one. The two sisters appealed to another craftsman and were finally able to make music and sing a number of duets: Rebecka, who had given up singing after her marriage, rediscovered an old habit. Fanny could not exist without organizing little musical festivities; to avoid frightening her guests, however, she reattributed many of the compositions she had brought along, in fact by Felix and herself, ascribing them instead to the more fashionable "Thalberg, Herz, Liszt, and Bellini"—or so she told Felix.[42] Impressed as they were by the rigor and serious nature of post-baroque aesthetics, the Heringsdorf audiences might well have been dismayed had they known that the music was really by the Mendelssohns!

Fanny was very worried when Rebecka went for her first swim, although Rebecka bore the experience very well;[43] Fanny naturally took part in the cure too. Today we may well wonder what there was to bear, but at that time it was unusual for women to engage in open-air activity. Great care had been paid to the Mendelssohn boys' physical education, *mens sana in corpore sano*, but obviously this was not true of the two girls, who were scarcely allowed to go for a walk unless suitably escorted. According to Yvonne Knibiehler, "The vogue for bathing in the sea was probably what accelerated the emancipation of the female body."[44] This would explain Fanny's reticence when confronted with an unknown phenomenon from which she expected nothing but boredom—and also her joy at experiencing a new pleasure. Given her love of fresh air, she was bound to enjoy being in the sea. It was also great fun for the children. Fanny's letters give indications of the general good humor, while the two sisters grew even closer through having shared this liberating experience. It is hardly necessary to mention the solidarity resulting from hardships common to all women at the time: childbirth, miscarriages, and infant deaths.

A Russian frigate lay at anchor in Swinemünde, and in describing it Fanny found occasion to express a resolutely pacifistic creed—even in a letter to her husband, whom she knew to be an admirer of Russia and things military. Once again, and in the nicest way, she underlined this difference in their opinions, knowing full well that tolerance had always been a part of their love and way of life:

On reaching the bridge, the first view is truly imposing, and anyone who gazes unreflectingly—as most people do—can only be delighted and agreeably diverted. But if one considers the amount of skill, knowledge, time, and trouble here applied, and then the additional pains needed to keep this veritable work of art in such clean working order that the armory looks like a jewel box and every cannon a luxurious piece of furniture; if one further considers that the noblest human powers are here employed to a murderous and cannibalistic end, then one might well learn what fear is, if one did not know already. When the evening meal finally began, with a dozen sailors surrounding a stewpot hanging from the ceiling, their Slavonic faces gazing dumbly at the grey porridge that was to feed them, I assure you I was closer to tears than to laughter! And these are not the vilest of men! A naval battle has always seemed to me the height of barbarity, and seeing this warship has only strengthened my opinion. A highly civilized barbarity! How will we be judged by some future race of men, wiser than we are, who will abolish war and the principle that right equals might, and institute a tribunal of all countries? There will still be a few wars and duels, but they'll become increasingly rare and humanity will finally be able to start discussing Christianity. That's why Louis-Philippe is the man I admire, for he's the *Napoléon de la paix*,[45] and he means to try and put the world in order through a European congress, which is a grand idea. Now you'll be laughing at me and my politics of peace, but I'm right nevertheless, like all women are.[46]

It's evident from this letter that the "noble ideals" of the twentieth century were handed down to us by people of the nineteenth century who were themselves heirs to the Enlightenment. In 1839 Fanny was still faithful to the idealist revolution of 1830, and to the dream of unity between monarchy and nations. In politics, as in her own family life, Fanny valued peace above all else, and for her peace also implied justice and liberty.

Immediately after Fanny's return from Heringsdorf, the Hensels decided it was finally time to realize Fanny's cherished dream, and left for Italy on 27 August 1839. They spent a week in Leipzig with Felix and Cécile. Felix was comfortably settled in life, happy in his work and extremely creative.[47] Between 1838 and 1839, he completed two string quartets (in E-flat major and D major, Opus 44 nos. 3 and 1); the *Ruy Blas* Overture, Opus 95; the Cello Sonata in B-flat Major, Opus 45; the Serenade and Allegro giocoso for Piano and Orchestra, Opus 43; numerous lieder; and Psalms 95 and 114, which form a bridge in his sacred music between *Saint Paul* and the beginning of his work on *Elijah*. Cécile was pregnant with another child, Marie, who was born on 2 October of that year. Fanny felt so at home in her brother's family that she did not realize until they left Leipzig on 4 September that the voyage of her dreams was beginning: that she was setting off for the long-desired unknown.

The Italian Idyll

CHAPTER TWENTY-THREE

Italy

The journey lasted a year. It was no small affair, in terms of either time or money, and Wilhelm's success in England had certainly helped the Hensels realize this cherished dream. Sebastian went too, and would later complain of the vexing destiny that had taken him on all the major journeys of his life when aged only five, nine, and then fourteen.[1] The poor child nonetheless derived some benefit in terms of education and amusement, and later lamented that "Italy's pearls had been cast before such a piglet." The number of servants they took with them is unclear, but at the very least there was their cook, Jette.

After leaving Leipzig, the Hensels traveled through Bamberg, Nuremberg, and Augsburg before reaching Munich.

In Regensburg, Wilhelm met with a comic misfortune. Convinced that an archeological site of the Roman city Castra Regina must still be in existence nearby, he set off with his family in the heat and dust, searching for a Roman aqueduct; this turned out to be a modern edifice containing a steam-driven machine that pumped the water for the town's inhabitants! At the sight of Wilhelm's horribly disappointed face, Fanny and Sebastian had to run and hide their uncontrollable laughter, and Fanny forbade the child all mention of the "sad remains of the Roman colony of Castra Regina."[2] They went to contemplate the "Valhalla" then under construction near Regensburg but did not admire it much, unable to feel very enthusiastic about this pompous example of neoclassical architecture built in honor of German genius.[3] "Bavaria is one vast construction site," exclaimed Fanny, charmed by the creative will of the Bavarian King Ludwig I, even if she reserved the right to be critical of the result.

Fanny had a favorable experience in Munich: "I didn't know a soul here, and so my head is stuffed full of new things and new people, but it's always pleasant to find one is welcome abroad and hospitably treated."[4] In other words, the self-proclaimed "dwarf" knew how to make people like her, after all. The Hensels went to all the museums and met numerous artists. Fanny made the acquaintance of Delphine Handley, *née* Delphine von Schauroth—a pianist whom Felix had met before her marriage. The two women got on very well: Fanny liked hearing her play Felix's first piano concerto and was delighted at her intelligent improvisations: "A rare talent in a woman," she declared. She was happy to take advantage of the good impression Felix had left behind him but saw, too, that she was welcomed on her own account and treated as an equal by a woman who had far more self-confidence.

The Hensels left Munich on 24 September, continued on their way through the Austrian Tyrol, and had the good fortune to see its wonderful landscapes on a fine sunny day. They visited the castle of Hohenschwangau; as befitted the taste of the Bavarian Crown Prince Maximilian, the castle constituted a model example of neo-Gothic architecture. "You cannot imagine what they do in Gothic here," wrote Fanny to her family[5]—reacting as a good Berliner accustomed to the classical architecture of her town, which was proud to be known as the Athens of the Spree. The fashion for Gothic was then at its height. Fanny subsequently declared:

Their own era has such an extraordinary influence on even the greatest minds that Goethe had no access to the wonders of Gothic architecture, and that can only be the result of a strong prejudice. I wonder what our prejudices are, which we do not even recognize, since we are their prisoners?[6]

Later, when he came to describe his childhood, her son Sebastian went on to say that the Hensels, the Mendelssohns, and all their contemporaries generally disdained rococo, whether in architecture, painting, porcelain, or furniture. Charlottenburg was considered ugly and Sansouci dull, preserved only out of "historical piety." Romanticism was in full swing. In Italy as in Ghent, Bruges, and Antwerp, the Hensels did not seek out anything dating from after the seventeenth century. The word "Gothic" covered rather broad aesthetic and historical ideas.

Crossing the Alps reminded Fanny of the journey to Switzerland when she was young. In the Finstermunz pass, she remembered the Gotthard:

A quick climb up a magnificent road, between two rock walls; on one side, the Inn, which is roaring ever more deeply below; then, just where the romantic beauty of the place is at its height, the road suddenly turns inward, as in the Uri pass; for want of a Devil's Bridge one arrives at a fortification the Austrians have built on and in the rock in the narrowest part of the valley; suddenly one finds oneself on a peaceful green plateau, as at Urseren, and the wildness of the river, which descends in cascades just before the fortification, suddenly grows calm and it runs softly—as softly as a Tyrolean river can, for they all seem made of champagne rather than water. After advancing for some time across this plateau we saw a formidable mass of mountains silhouetted in front of us, and in response to our queries, were told that the new road passed through the Stelvio pass. I must admit that my heart was gripped by inexpressible emotions.[7]

Italy, at last! Fanny could barely speak, while Wilhelm was delirious with enthusiasm. Once they were past the frontier, every pebble took on a different air. Only Sebastian was mystified: he had read that Hannibal, when crossing the Alps, had shown the whole of Italy to his exhausted troops. The child thus expected to see the entire boot of Italy stretching before him, as far as Sicily and the Mediterranean Sea. Instead, he saw nothing but successive ranges of mountains—an enormous disappointment.[8]

The Stelvio pass is on the road to Milan. On their way there, the Hensels stopped at Lake Como, and it was here that Fanny first discovered Italy. Even though she had probably already seen olive trees, "real" chestnut trees, and mulberry trees, it was only beside the lake that Fanny succumbed to the charm of the Italian landscape. In her enthusiasm she found the place "compelling" and strongly recommended it to Beckchen: "This place was made for you."[9] Finally she saw the long-anticipated lemon, orange, and fig trees, roses, and aloes: "An almost demented vegetation," forgetting the beauty of the terraces sloping down toward the water. But after this enchanting stage the Hensels arrived in Milan, and their stay in that city suggested that the journey might ultimately prove disappointing. "It was *écrit là-haut*, decreed from above that we should not meet anybody in Milan."[10] Fanny did not find dirt picturesque, and she was plunged "up to the ears" in it; monuments were not enough to satisfy her, for "such a hunger for traveling is a veritable chasm." The wretched state of northern Italy distressed her. Milan was still fairly clean in appearance, but in Verona she was scandalized by the dilapidated condition of the works of art. She found the Amphitheater amazing: "Truly Roman, grandiose, proud, and cold. . . . Human beings fought there against wild beasts and we, posterity, stand admiring every stone. Aren't we mad, with our antiquity?"[11] Padua gave her "a revolting impression of decay." A Saint Anthony by Titian elicited a more sympathetic response: "As soon as I become a Catholic, I'll make him my patron saint. He wakes up glasses and dead plates, it's most useful around the house."[12]

Venice, where they arrived on 12 October, at last proved capable of making her forget the squalor.[13] She had been expecting, as in Padua, nothing more than "dead magnificence." Her journey continued in the footsteps of her brother and of Goethe, whose *Journey to Italy* she quotes abundantly in her letters. She saw and admired everything, like a well-prepared tourist led by an experienced guide, but did not forget to hold her nose. In Venice, apart from the beauties of the place, she was charmed by the animated alleys: "The crowd, as in Paris; the mass of cafés and boutiques." The Hensels did the obligatory trip by gondola toward San Giorgio, then on the Grand Canal; they were dazzled by the Titians and Tintorettos of Santa Maria della Salute and by the Veroneses and Bellinis in the Accademia. After ten days in a hotel, however, Fanny had been bitten so badly by mosquitoes she could hardly open her eyes. And not just by mosquitoes; as she wrote to Rebecka: "I assure you, I am going to write a monograph about the flea. I know its favorite haunts, the way it moves, its favorite walks when sated, and what is worse! all this collectively."[14] The Hensels then decided to lodge with the brother of the painter Leopold Robert (1794–1835) who lent them an apartment. Among their first visits when they arrived in Venice was one to the atelier of this Swiss painter, a student of David; his paintings depicting scenes from Italian life had been very successful, and the Hensels recognized their authenticity at many points along their way.

Robert's suicide and the published account of it were very much present in Fanny's mind, and a kind of Romantic pilgrimage drew her to the places where the painter had lived and died. The Hensels accepted his brother's offer all the more readily since it allowed them to sleep without mosquitoes and fleas for the first time since reaching Venice.

At the same time as Fanny was getting to know the throng of Latins, she was tasting the local food. Thus, for the first time in Italy, she began to appreciate the bread and butter, the *stufati* and *umidi* (stews), the cheese grated in soup—a dish that seldom varied—rice soup, noodle soup, vegetable soup; she also liked the pears, strawberries, and wine. If the coffee was too thick, she "changed into a shepherdess, and drank milk." She decided, with Sebastian, to add wine to her water, for they had contracted colic and a mixture of water and wine was considered a remedy for this malady of traveling.

Drinking water was then a rarity in Venice and a privilege of the rich. Some *Forlani*—thus called because they came from Friuli—carried water on their heads in copper buckets and sold it from house to house. Most townspeople drew water from the canals. One day, the gold cross a Friulian woman wore around her neck fell down a well. Wilhelm promised to reward a fisherman if he went down inside the well to look for the jewel, holding onto the man while he did so. Thanks to this deed the *Forlana* retrieved her treasured cross and Wilhelm made himself very popular among the people, besides acquiring a model, for she willingly agreed to sit for him.[15] This episode shows yet again that in Wilhelm's dealings with people, he did not recognize social barriers and was as comfortable with a Prussian officer as he was with a peasant woman from the Italian mountains.

During the evening, the Hensels went to cafés and read newspapers. The news that reached them from Germany told of an unchanging political situation: "The princes' plot against the people is continuing, and nobody dares say where this might lead. The lesser princes are the worst," wrote Fanny.[16] The Customs Union, or Zollverein, had been in force since 1 January 1834. Prussia had been cunning enough to convince the provincial customs unions gathered around Saxony and Bavaria to regroup around her. By 1848, only Hanover and Mecklenburg did not belong to the Zollverein. The conservative policies of Metternich had allowed Prussia to direct the German confederation in exchange for an alliance against all revolutionary movements. As a good German liberal, Fanny was therefore disgusted that her country's fate could be decided—and, contingent upon this, its unity—without any kind of popular participation. The liberal dream of a constitution linked to a federal state was vanishing before the autocratic power of princes.

The Hensels left Venice on 4 November in driving rain, making it impossible for them to cross the river Po. In fact, the water had not risen very high, but the Cardinal of Ferrara's legate forbade them to cross. They were only authorized to do so two days later, when the water level was even higher—though not as high as the crossing fee. The Hensels paid 26 paoli instead of 3, with the Cardinal's legate taking two thirds of that: such were the hazards of traveling in a corrupt state![17]

The travelers naturally stopped in Florence, visiting the Palazzo Pitti at some length. Fanny would have preferred to change the arrangement of the paintings, replacing them with Titians and other masterpieces that had been left in the shadows or else badly hung. She was completely baffled by the negligent treatment accorded objets d'art: painters copying canvases left their palettes lying on mosaic tables, and the muddy clothes they wore against the rain were left to dry on velvet-covered sofas that had no protective covers. To a sensible Prussian housewife, brought up to be prudent and thrifty, this seemed simultaneously negligent and madly prodigal.[18] On their way to Rome the Hensels admired the town of Orvieto, but spent an appalling night at Ricorsi, where their inn looked so much like a den of thieves that Fanny suggested staying up all night. There were, however, no further misadventures, and they reached their destination, Rome, on 26 November at ten o'clock in the evening. They rented a four-room apartment near the Monte Pincio for 30 scudi per month, a sum that Fanny deemed quite reasonable. There was no view from the apartment, which was on the third floor, but after unpacking their belongings the Hensels soon felt at home.

Wilhelm was thrilled about being reunited with his old friends and acquaintances and about revisiting scenes from his youth. Fanny was delighted by this, as she was by hearing people talk of Felix: "The names of Wilhelm and Felix are like two sweet pillows for me here. I am thus at greater pains and must be devilishly nice to be a credit to my family."[19] At first, the bad weather prevented her from taking full advantage of Rome, and local society seemed very dull. She took part in a dilettante concert in the house of Ludwig Landsberg (1807–1858), a former violinist from the Königstadt theater orchestra in Berlin. Landsberg had moved to Rome, where he held musical evenings and rented pianos for 10 scudi a month. He offered to rent one to Fanny at a friendly discount of 9 scudi, but the piano was so poor that she refused. These musicales did not match the level of the *Sonntagsmusik*, and Fanny derived little enjoyment from them. Rome seemed empty to her, and the ambassadors were not giving any balls that winter; as good musicians, the Mendelssohns loved dancing. She was astonished, moreover, to meet nothing but bachelors: why, she inquired, had Saint Ursula's eleven thousand virgins not disembarked at Rome? "Children are among the rarities here; ancient monuments are far more numerous." She did nonetheless unearth a little boy of eight as a companion for Sebastian, hoping her son would pick up French and Italian from the child. In his memoirs Sebastian mentions another companion, the grandson of the sculptor Thorvaldsen;[20] apparently the boy's tutor, an Italian priest, tried so hard to convert him that in the end Sebastian took flight. He was obviously not going to learn the local tongue from Jette, their cook, to whom he often turned for comfort; instead, he was taught by another Italian tutor who could only translate into English. Much to Fanny's admiration, Sebastian was able to pass from one language to another—something his mother could not do.[21]

Curiosity about ancient music led Fanny to the Sistine Chapel, just as it had Felix; being a woman, however, she could only attend the ceremony from a distance and from behind a grill. Since her short-sightedness prevented her from seeing much, all she could do was strain her ears to catch the "mediocre, out-of-tune singing of the Papal Chapel."[22] She nevertheless decided to go there again in order to become more familiar with this style of music, which was an unusual one for her.

When Felix went to Italy in 1830, he met with better luck in his approach to old Italian music. A Prussian diplomat and historian named Christian Josias von Bunsen (1791–1860) had been in Rome between 1823 and 1838; a great friend of the Mendelssohns, he had welcomed and encouraged Wilhelm during his Italian years. Bunsen, who was a great fan of Palestrina, organized concerts in his home with singers from the Sistine Chapel, and planned to publish a new edition of Palestrina's works. Thanks to him, Felix made the acquaintance of the "black-robed priests" of the papal choir. He impressed them with his improvisations, thereby facilitating his contact with this type of music.[23] But in 1839 Bunsen was no longer in Rome, and Fanny had to stay behind the chapel grill to listen and get an idea of it. She then wrote to her brother expressing her astonishment, as a German musician, at having heard so weak a choir from such a distance—quite unlike the Singakademie. Papal music seemed to her to consist of a succession of badly sung parallel fifths.[24] And even if she had been able to get to know them, would the papal choristers have been willing to communicate their knowledge to a woman? Especially an impudent woman, who took a malicious delight in appearing in all the places that were forbidden her, just for the fun of being thrown out at the door?[25]

On 7 December, Fanny entered the Villa Medici for the first time, for the Hensels had been invited there for dinner:

Yesterday evening we had our first meal with Ingres[26] (director of the Académie de France) who welcomed us most cordially and has fond memories of Paul; to distinguish him from Felix, he always refers to him as "your brother who plays the bass so well." You know Ingres is a great violinist in the sight of God; after dinner we played trios, and this happens on Sundays too. The whole Academy of France gathers then, genuine "*jeune France*" in style, with beards and hair trimmed *à la* Raphael; almost all are handsome young fellows I can't blame . . . for pining after the balls given by Horace Vernet, for there's absolutely no dancing to Ingres's little flute—only the most highly classical music is played. And so on Sunday evenings you can occasionally think of us as being at his house. You can imagine how much I thought of Felix in this house. What a grandiose institution this Academy is, and how lucky the French artists are! One of the most talented engravers, Calamatta, works constantly for Ingres and engraves his portraits himself— which really means having a good life. And how beautiful the Villa Medici is, and how enviable it is to be its director in the world's premier city for fine arts, with every possible means at one's disposal, influencing the cream of the youth of one's own country. There can be nothing finer for an artist, but unfortunately they are all quite blasé about it. They don't know how lucky they are, and need shaking up a bit to jolt them out of their complacency.[27]

How Fanny must have wished that Wilhelm could obtain such a position! "There can be nothing finer for an artist": in Fanny's view, art, whether pictorial or musical, was a matter of ethics and of communion through thought. Wilhelm was a good teacher, much loved by students such as Kaselowski and Moser. For Fanny—as for her epoch—the quality of Wilhelm's paintings, good or bad, could not be held distinct from their contents, any more than Wilhelm's artistic quality could be held distinct from the manner in which he conducted his life. In other words, an artist owed it to himself to be good and an exemplar in the eyes of the community. Ingres, on the other hand, gave priority to his art, and his directorial duties weighed on him. He was thus quite unlike Fanny and Felix Mendelssohn, who were brought up with the idea that art has a very strong moral and religious foundation, and that one's first duty is to communicate this. Should art be seen as a function or a game? This is the question raised by the relative positions of the Mendelssohns and Ingres.

Fanny was far from forgetting to visit the Vatican and paying the tribute of respect due the rooms reserved for Raphael. When Christmas was approaching, she realized that for the first time in her life she would not be celebrating it at home. Even so, she prepared a tree for Sebastian with the help of branches of cypress, myrtle, and orange trees, and loaded it with fruit. The grapes, she declared, were delicious, but neither the apples nor the pears nor the pastries were as good as those in Venice.[28] Yet the cook from Berlin, Jette, had learned to make German cakes in the heart of Italy. Thus the Hensels spent a happy Christmas; Wilhelm gave Fanny an ivory-encrusted chest and Fanny gave Wilhelm a sketch by Veronese.[29]

Wilhelm also showed her the Casa Bartholdy, then inhabited and furnished by some English people; Fanny could only imagine what it must have been like. Although she never tired of enjoying the mildness of the air, she could not understand how so rich a soil yielded so little and so poorly, compared to the Brandenburg region where northern tenacity worked wonders: asparagus, despite a frigid minus-20 degrees Celsius. "Oh, if only Napoleon had subjugated Italy instead of France, been content with that, and organized it from top to toe! I think France would have managed very well without him and Italy would now be, as it used to be, Paradise on earth!"[30]—an enormous political speculation on her part.

Wilhelm fell ill, and for six weeks the Hensels did not leave home. When he recovered, the carnival was in full swing, and Fanny, much to her surprise, was swept along in the festivities. Never would she have imagined that she could have so much fun amid the noise and general madness. People in the crowd threw plaster, sweetmeats, and flour at each other—this was rather crude—and also flowers. Far from withdrawing, Fanny flung herself wholeheartedly into the battle. Everything was a diversion for her: costumes, coachmen disguised as women, farces, fantasies. As she wrote to her mother:

You can't imagine everything there is to do and see during a drive along the Corso. You have to look all around, observe all the silly things being prepared, notice where the next missile will leave from so as to take cover as best you can, respond in the same manner, assemble and sort out the munitions thrown into the coach, chat with the elegant masks climbing onto the running board, be friendly while awaiting the best moment to throw something in their faces—all these important matters require so much attention and dexterity that at first one scarcely knows where to begin. Yes, it's incredible, but so rapidly does one progress in madness that one is quite offended when a coach goes by without throwing something, for that is incorrect. Do you recognize me, dear Mother, having fun for hours amid a hum and noise that cannot be compared either to the roar of the sea, or to the roaring of wild beasts, but only to the Corso in Rome?[31]

If Felix Mendelssohn has generally been paid the compliment of not being too German, Fanny demonstrates here that she, too, could let herself go in an Italian crowd.

Fanny waxed far more enthusiastic about her contact with street life than about Roman society, which she still found very boring. She complained to Felix of not having seen anyone significant that winter: Liszt had spent four months in Rome the previous year—what a pity she had missed him![32] She did, however, go for walks in Rome and the surrounding countryside with Wilhelm and his painter friends, and was enraptured by the clearness of the air. She continued to deplore the ravages inflicted by the modern world on ancient and medieval architecture: how beautiful it must have looked, in the fifteenth and sixteenth centuries!

An unexpected event was deemed worthy of being reported to 3 Leipziger Strasse:[33] after a winter of splendid sunshine, when no overcoats were necessary, it snowed in Rome on 25 March. When the fine weather returned, Wilhelm and Fanny took the trouble to scramble through the mud to the heights of Trinità del Monte, for the exceptional pleasure of looking down on Rome as it lay beneath the snow.

The journey to Italy had already been magnificent, but Rome was soon to bring Fanny even happier memories.

CHAPTER TWENTY-FOUR

The Roman Festival and the Académie de France

When they were invited to Ingres's residence on Sunday 5 April, the Hensels met the painter Horace Vernet, whose whole appearance reflected his exotic tastes. "With his oriental garb, his long beard, striking features, brilliant eyes, and brown skin, he looked truly like an Arab," recounted Fanny.[1] But oriental exoticism was more than a matter of appearance for Vernet, and the Hensels were charmed by what he had to say about Africa.

What he described touched strongly on a subject we had often broached, so much so that we spent half the night in serious discussions—only to conclude, in true German style: "Duty first, then wait and see." A Frenchman cannot understand that, and when Wilhelm told him his greatest longing was for that country, he looked at us in astonishment and said Wilhelm could be there in two weeks. The blissful breezy way in which Frenchmen take hold of situations as they crop up and know how to deal with life has something so contagious about it that at the time I really saw no obstacle or difficulty; I immediately suggested to Wilhelm—quite sincerely and with the best will in the world—to go with us as far as Trieste and take a boat from there. But then I had to give in to his serious, respectable arguments. What an impression this made on me, to think my very existence requires him to make such sacrifices! For with a single daring deed and a few clear words, Vernet brings to life something we had discussed at great length together, something we had imagined, felt, and known about, and in a short time it will become common property. The future of art is to be found there. And this deed could have been accomplished by Wilhelm, had he let himself be carried away by the idea. We Germans always have to wait! And miss the right moment, every time! And always arrive too late! Why does it have to be so difficult to rise above one's epoch, one's family, one's own self! I am deeply stirred and troubled by this question, to the bottom of my soul.

Wilhelm's paintings were not to be bathed in African light. He had made Fanny queen of his interior world and shut himself inside it with her. In countering her proposal, he must certainly have argued that a husband is responsible for his wife and is duty bound not to leave her alone. Admittedly, the journey between Trieste and Berlin would have posed problems for a woman and child, even with a servant, but nothing really insurmountable. Fanny possessed more than enough energy and character and could easily have coped. But the kind of work Vernet was suggesting to Wilhelm would have threatened his entire persona—the solid, Prussian, good little boy side of him, and the family-oriented mentality he used in this case as a rationalization. These reasons were not pleasing to Fanny, who was also protected by marriage but who had had little choice.

While Vernet was there, the Hensels let him pose in a manner most pleasing for the model: Wilhelm drew while Fanny played. Horace Vernet had arrived at their house adorned in all his exoticism and had only an hour to spend with them. They had lunch, Vernet spoke of his plans, Fanny played when he fell silent, and Wilhelm sketched portraits. It was a most civilized way of bringing the arts together and of spending a pleasant afternoon.[2] Wilhelm refused to venture from his shell and set forth to discover the unknown, but this refusal to develop enabled him to remain in a very poetic world where he was happy and could do idealized portraits of his numerous friends.

On Good Friday Fanny was finally able to obtain a more accurate idea of music in the Sistine Chapel:

I found a place right in front and since the Swiss guard later allowed a few women to draw near the grill, this time I had a remarkably good view of all the ceremonies, and the adoration of the cross is certainly one of the finest. The Passion was sung first, and this time I managed to keep the thread and follow perfectly until the end. The divisions are essentially those kept by Bach; Jesus was sung by a fine bass voice, the Evangelist by a rather shrill baritone. The people's choruses were by Vittoria. The words are sung once in very short, four-voiced movements, without any development, and yet these short musical movements provide important relief from the incredibly monotonous narration of the Passion. . . . Naturally, there is no question of expression. The words are sung with some pathos but also with a curious rapidity. This interested me greatly and my attention did not waver for a second. At the same time I thought constantly of Sebastian Bach. This rigid form of song reminded me vividly of ancient mosaics, except that I find it even stiffer and more funereal. The resemblance is nonetheless very credible, for they are children of the same era; I think this type of singing would be appropriate in a Byzantine church too. Here in the Sistine Chapel, however, where the visual arts are abundantly represented and are almost overripe in their maturity, the poverty and petrified style of this type of singing is in sharp contradiction. On the other hand, the songs proper to the Sistine Chapel (though I have yet to hear a piece of music constructed the way our great masters intended) are far more recent in character, more sugary, almost rococo. I am intentionally expressing myself strongly, so as to remain clear for my own purposes later. Music does not reach its artistic summit here and would be better represented if they rendered Allegri's song with more simplicity; I shall return to this point.

The Pope appeared after the Passion. There followed a speech in Latin with much pathos and exaggerated shouts; then came prayers. They pray according to rubrics for God and the entire world, omitting nothing, and at each rubric the Pope and cardinals genuflect. The Catholic Church has even degraded this very ancient, simple, and beautiful manner of worshipping the cross; they have turned it into a ridiculous formality, as with so many other ceremonies, curtsying like women dropping in for coffee. They only remain standing during prayers for the Jews. *Tout dégénère entre les mains des hommes.*[3]

As far as she can, Fanny avoids referring to Judaism, just as she avoids all potentially polemical topics. Even if he had read something she had written on the subject, Sebastian would probably not have published it in 1879 and would not have thought himself unfaithful to his mother's memory if he destroyed it. The mere mention of a prayer delivered standing for the Jews is most valuable, coming from her pen. Next day, Easter Saturday, she wrote that the baptism of a child symbolically representing pagans and Jews would take place without them and that they would stay at home and rest while waiting for the Easter bells to ring; the bells were to ring throughout Rome, beginning in Saint Peter's and then in all the other churches, until the ordinary people joined in, beating on their pots and pans while the cannon thundered.[4] Perhaps, as the daughter of Jewish parents, Fanny felt offended by the Roman clergymen's disrespectful behavior; it is even more probable that as an expert at a religion of tolerance and humanity she turned aside from this demonstration of obscurantism.

The visit she paid the painter Overbeck on 3 May did nothing further to convince her of the benefits of Catholic art: "We went to Overbeck's house to see his piously boring, dully poetic, and flatly presumptuous painting. One could say many things about it, but I haven't sufficient patience. I must, however, mention the sainted man's incommensurate pride in depicting himself in a corner of the painting along with Veit and Cornelius, as if they were the sole elect of the present time. *Je trouve cela colossal!*"[5] Years before, Lea had observed that Catholicism led to fanaticism and bigotry. This was not, of course, an absolute truth, but as far as the Nazarenes were concerned, the statement was unfortunately quite accurate. Such tendencies could not suit Fanny: the conviction that any one sect possessed an absolute, immutable religious truth was utterly opposed to the Mendelssohns' way of thinking.

Fanny did not, however, take to her heels that Friday. She listened with equal attention to the continuation of the Passion ceremony, admired the pieces by Palestrina, and thought that the Pope emerging from beneath a dais looked like a Chinese Mandarin beneath a parasol. In the meantime, Wilhelm had made drawings of half a dozen cardinals. They returned to the Sistine Chapel that afternoon, for Fanny had "decided to listen to this kind of music as precisely as possible." She found Allegri's *Lamentations* beautiful but astonishingly monotonous. And they went on for three hours, during which time darkness fell; one by one the lights went out, and while everyone was dropping with exhaustion, a quartet of singers softly intoned Allegri's *Miserere*. "It was," Fanny remarked, "a striking effect, which for two hundred years had never once failed to make its annual impression on the audience. One could see from the way it was done that everything here is efficiently and intelligently calculated to impress the senses. How anyone can say his soul is taken in by such cunning calculations will always be a mystery to me."[6] Allegri's *Miserere*, she went on, was a very simple piece in which the same phrase was repeated ten times. The chorus only consisted of nineteen members, who "sang traditional, slightly rococo ornamentation." They sang a third of a tone lower with each entrance, which was not unappealing in the context but would have caused a scandal at the Singakademie.

The disparity between painting that verged upon decadence and music that was primitive, seen in relation to the history of harmonic evolution, did not strike the composer Charles Gounod (1818–1897) as it did Fanny. On the contrary, he remarked in his *Memoirs*: "Palestrinian music seems to be a sung translation of the vast poem of Michelangelo, and I should be inclined to think the two masters illuminated each other, intellectually, in mutual light: the spectator develops the listener, and vice versa, to such an extent that after a while one is tempted to wonder whether the Sistine Chapel is not the product of a single, shared inspiration."[7] Fanny's thoughts on the subject were of quite another order. Gounod's admiration is purely romantic: he associates works of art that are essentially different, whereas Fanny once again displays her culture and her analytical turn of mind. In the Sistine Chapel, Fanny was struck by the importance placed upon pictorial technique, an importance that contrasted strongly with what she perceived as a dearth of musical technique. But Fanny was familiar with Hegel, whereas Gounod perhaps was not.

Fanny spent the latter part of that Good Friday at the home of Countess Kaiseroff, who had the idea of having Pergolesi's *Stabat Mater* performed as a chamber work, with a tenor and a bass accompanied by an instrumental quartet. The piano part was entrusted to Fanny, who was so bored she almost fell asleep at the keyboard: "Good heavens, we had sufficient senile music in our body."[8]

The Hensels' stay in Rome was nearing its end: visitors generally waited until the Easter holidays were over before leaving the city. In theory, Fanny and Wilhelm had seen and heard everything, and yet their best days in Rome were still ahead of them. A small circle of artistic friends had formed around the Hensels. It included three students from the Villa Medici—two musicians, Bousquet and Gounod, and a landscape painter, Dugasseau, who was "pleasant rather than talented," as Sebastian would later say.[9] There was also Charlotte Thygeson, a relative of the sculptor Thorvaldsen and an excellent pianist who, like Fanny, belonged to the world of amateurs. Completing the circle were three Prussian painters: August Kaselowsky (1810–1891), Eduard Magnus (1799–1872), and Friedrich August Elsasser (1810–1845). Fanny and Wilhelm organized their days around their friends. Wilhelm painted in the morning, they had lunch at one o'clock, everyone went for a walk in the afternoon, and in the evening the Hensels either went out or invited friends in and made music. "We haven't spent three evenings alone this winter, it seems to me," wrote Fanny to Beckchen.[10]

She was immeasurably happy. The young Frenchmen's admiration for her knew no bounds: to receive such approbation was an entirely new experience for her and brought her an equally new self-confidence. "Bosquet and Dugasseau make things difficult for me," she wrote during April.

They never forget what I've played for them several months before, even if it was only once; one really could not have a better audience. I'm also doing a lot of composing at the moment; nothing stimulates me more than being appreciated, just as disapproval disheartens and depresses me. Gounod is, in a certain way, passionately moved by music—something I did not immediately notice. He's extraordinarily fond of my little Venetian piece and of the one in B minor I wrote here; he also likes Felix's duet, his Capriccio in A Minor, and above all, the Bach concerto[11] I must have played for him at least ten times.[12]

At this point in their travels, the Hensels would have liked to spend another winter in Rome, but reason told them not to extend their visit beyond the end of May.

It's costing both of us a great sacrifice to leave Rome; I would never have thought that it could make so deep an impression on me. I won't deny that finding myself surrounded by such admiration and respect is partly responsible. I was never courted like this when I was young, and who can deny that it's very pleasant and encouraging? Everything here is conspiring to keep me in Rome—and how wonderful that would be for my Wilhelm and his work! But it isn't possible, and our decision is firm.

Both Berlioz and Massenet praised the joyful conviviality that reigned among the residents of the Villa Medici. Away from their Parisian studies they behaved like frolicking colts—rather erudite ones, at that; endless laughter accompanied their picnics in the country, and Fanny lived amid a carefree gaiety that she had never known before. In her own youth, all the Mendelssohn children's games had taken place in front of Lea, and the scholarly tone appropriate to the entertainment of child prodigies had had to be maintained. In Rome, surrounded by Frenchmen, Fanny finally realized the meaning of the word liberty.

On 2 May, Fanny heard mass in the Greek church where she enjoyed both the music, which seemed relatively recent, and the performance. Afterward she "gave a concert" at her home:

That evening I played several pieces and again concluded with the Bach concerto, which made people so enthusiastic—although they've often heard it before—that they kissed my hands and pressed them warmly, unable to contain themselves. Gounod especially, who is in any case terribly lively and can never find the words to tell me the influence I have on him and how happy he is at our house. The two men are very different: Bousquet is quieter and more inclined toward French classicism, whereas Gounod is extremely romantic and passionate. The discovery of German music is falling on him like a bomb landing on his house, and it may well cause some damage.[13]

On 8 May, there was a further reunion:

In the evening, Magnus and our Frenchmen—or rather, the three Caprices, as they now call themselves: Bousquet is the "Caprice in A"; Gounod, the "Caprice in E"; and Dugasseau the "Caprice in B-flat." We played much music, as is our wont, chatted and laughed a lot and stayed together until very late. Bousquet showed me the cantata he has begun—it contains some very fine passages. In his case, I think that knowledge of German music can only prove beneficial, whereas Gounod is dazzled and half crazed by it. He seems far less mature to me, but I know nothing of his music; I won't count a scherzo he recently played me, asking if he might give it to me, for it was very bad; it seems to me that the influence of German music is already discernible.[14]

The partying went on, but Fanny did not forget the diary she was keeping of her travels—happily for us:

On 13 May I went with Sebastian to Santa Maria sopra Minerva, where Michelangelo's statue of Christ is, together with many tombs, some of them popes; on one side there was a calvary with frescoes, which I managed to get myself chased out of by monks, as is my favorite habit. The Frenchmen came in the evening, and Wilhelm began doing their portraits. Naturally there were a lot of jokes while this was going on. Whoever was posing had the right to choose what I should play, and so I played almost all of Fidelio, many other things, and Beethoven's C major sonata last of all. Gounod behaved as if drunk and said a lot of silly things, and when finally he exclaimed with great enthusiasm: *Beethoven est un polisson* [Beethoven's a rascal], the others said it was time he went to bed and took him home. It was half past midnight once again.[15]

Years later Gounod also remembered these evenings in his *Memoirs*, although he makes no mention of his impassioned state:

That same winter, I had the pleasure of meeting Fanny Henzel [sic], Mendelssohn's sister. She was spending the winter in Rome with her husband, painter to the King of Prussia, and her son, who was still a child. Madame Henzel was an incomparable musician, a remarkable pianist, a woman of superior intelligence, small and slender, but endowed with an energy revealed in her deep eyes and fiery gaze. She had rare gifts as a composer. . . . Madame Henzel sat down at the piano with that good grace and simplicity possessed by people who make music because they love it, and thanks to her prodigious memory I was introduced to a host of masterpieces from German music which, at that time, were completely unknown to me. These included numerous pieces by Sebastian Bach, sonatas, fugues and preludes, concertos, and numerous compositions by Mendelssohn which for me were like revelations from an unknown world.[16]

Gounod does not recount the mad Roman nights when he had to be put to bed. Throughout his life, Charles Gounod's character was exceedingly unbalanced. There was something excessive about his attachment to his mother, and Fanny, who was thirteen years older than the young Frenchman, may well have furnished him an image of this mother he missed so badly, and from whom he was parted for three years. He may well have sought a maternal figure in the strange and scandalous affair he embarked on with Mrs. Weldon, who took him with her to England for several years.[17] Certainly he surprised Fanny on several occasions with inappropriate bursts of enthusiasm she took for immaturity, but sometimes the company of irrational persons can be most enjoyable.

With some emotion, Fanny told Felix that she was to play Bach's triple concerto at Landsberg's house—the same concerto Felix had performed in Leipzig in March with Franz Liszt and Ferdinand Hiller. Fanny was to play with her friend Charlotte Thygeson and another excellent "dilettante." Embarrassed, she went on: "But there will be quite a difference between the performances, of course. I tell you, the French admire nothing but *Bacque* now—it's too funny!

I've had to play the D minor concerto at least a dozen times and they're head over heels with delight. They're also an excellent audience for your work."[18] To her family in Berlin, she expressed her pleasure in "playing this piece in Rome and winning new friends and disciples for our 'Old Man of the Mountain.'"[19] Amateur evenings, whether the Berlin *Sonntagsmusik* or the Landsberg concerts in Rome, certainly played an important role in nineteenth-century musical life.

In making Bach known in Rome, Fanny was continuing the work that Felix had already begun in 1830. He had made the acquaintance of an elderly priest, Fortunato Santini (1778–1862), who played and collected music, and generously made his magnificent library accessible to Felix. For his part, Felix sent and introduced him to scores by Bach and Handel.[20] Ten years later, Santini was a diligent host to Fanny, and the two music-lovers exchanged scores continually.

Out of all the excursions and evenings that Fanny describes in her diary, two dates stand out with particular clarity—two exceptionally perfect days she would not forget at any price: 20 and 31 May. On the morning of 20 May the little band of friends assembled (without Gounod) for an unusual picnic.[21] Scattered through the gardens of the Villa Wolchonsky, a most heavenly spot, they all had to produce something in their respective arts. At lunchtime, Elsasser produced a watercolor, Wilhelm a study in oils, and Kaselowsky and Dugasseau arrived with drawings. As for the musicians, they had set each other tasks: Fanny had brought Bousquet an Italian poem which he turned into a pleasing duet, and Bousquet gave Fanny a collection of poems by Lamartine, of which she set a few verses to music. After a cheerful meal, the artists all returned to their diverse occupations—or lazed about—and the musicians went to rehearse two, three, and four-voiced lieder by Felix and Fanny. "You'll laugh when I tell you how these lieder were allotted, but a rogue never knows his limitations," wrote Fanny to her family. "I sang the soprano part! and Bousquet, whose voice is no stronger than mine, sang the bass; he should, if anything, be a tenor, and he speaks no German at all." In spite of these obstacles the rehearsal went extremely well. Around four o'clock a splendid thunderstorm broke out, followed by a no less remarkable rainbow which they admired from the windows of the Villa Wolchonsky, while sampling Jette's cooking. The early evening was spent in the garden, until the fireflies came out; the musicians then gave a performance, in front of an illuminated bed of roses, of the songs they had been rehearsing. The evening concluded with a lottery, the prizes consisting of an engraving by Raphael, a purse that Fanny had crocheted, and several of her compositions which her friends particularly liked. Naturally, the latter items fell to the least musical members of the group, and Fanny had to promise to recopy them. The party ended around midnight. This was truly an ideal day for Fanny; admired and appreciated by all, she was in a position to make everyone happy. Art was happily allied with the beauty of landscape, and the world seemed absolutely perfect.

Wilhelm expressed the general opinion of this outing: "The day ended as happily as it had begun. Fanny, the queen of the party, who dominated it all from the heights of her spiritual throne, can describe it, she who received the fruits of our labors as a tribute. May she transform this pleasure into other joys!"

As a little girl, Fanny had renounced the pursuit of her talent to make way for her brother. This provincial woman who had been placed in his shadow received in the artistic capital of Rome a kind of consecration that made her forget the cost of her sacrifice. She lived the equivalent of many lives in several months:

What have I not experienced and felt here in Rome! During these clear nights lit with the southern moon and filled with pleasure, I have thought many times of the first night when Wilhelm was ill, when I sat at his bedside in mortal anxiety! Yet after all these changes and experiences, I don't feel I have aged; on the contrary, I feel rejuvenated. Such journeys bring one everlasting riches.[22]

During their last days in Rome, the Hensels no longer wished even to sleep and would spend part of the night walking. Fanny could no longer bear a roof over her head, avoided going to the Vatican, where she felt shut in, and stayed on her doorstep taking advantage of the mild air. Nor could she bear to be without a bunch of flowers in her room; this was considered unhealthy, but Fanny took no notice and was none the worse for it.[23]

These final days were simultaneously sad and splendid. Everyone was aware that an episode in their lives was coming to an end, that a parenthesis was closing on a moment of exceptional happiness. On the evening of 30 May, after going for a walk to make sure the fireflies were still there, the Hensels went home to receive more farewell visits. First Father Santini took his leave:

Then came Dugasseau, and Bousquet, Gounod, and Charlotte immediately afterward. I was very tired and depressed, and to avoid bursting into tears again I went to the piano and played the two allegros from Beethoven's sonata in F minor. Meanwhile Wilhelm began lighting the lamps arranged round the portraits of the three, and I promised Bousquet that if he posed nicely I would play the allegro of the B-flat major sonata. In the meantime Charlotte played a few pieces, whereupon I kept my word and played the allegro in B-flat major and two lieder by Felix; then Gounod fell at my feet and begged me to play the adagio while the Bellays and Bruni were arriving. Elsasser and Kaselowsky were there too. Elsasser had the very nice idea of drawing a landscape underneath his portrait, and sat down at the piano to work. Wilhelm drew Signora Bruni. I played the sonata in C-sharp minor and two pieces by Felix, whereupon Elsasser begged me to play the A-flat major sonata with variations; I had played the first two movements when singing was heard in the street below, and we were most pleasantly serenaded. Landsberg, Magnus, Baron Bach, Quatrocchi, Schanzky, and Bruni stood with torches beneath the portal opposite and sang three four-voiced lieder, very prettily and well. Wilhelm went down and brought them up; I could not let them have the last word, and played the little Romance sans paroles in E major. Then Madame Bellay sang my Italian cavatina twice, Wilhelm drew Bruni wearing a mask, on his wife's portrait, *et pour finir* I played the Bach concerto. It was past one-thirty when the company broke up, all grateful, moved, happy, and excited. I wrote a little more in my diary and went to bed at three.[24]

Fanny needed to record all this happiness in order to be able to relive it once she returned to wintry Berlin. Of the pieces she played, her listeners were probably not able to distinguish clearly between those she had composed herself and those composed by Felix. She probably maintained this ambiguity, no doubt preferring to attribute her own works to Felix, so as not to draw immoderate attention to herself. Her friends in Rome made this difficult, however, refusing to let her disappear behind a modesty they found unacceptable.

The two triple portraits of painters and musicians mentioned in this extract from her diary are among Wilhelm's most interesting drawings. After posing for the painter, his models usually wrote a poem or a word of dedication next to the drawing. Elsasser's idea gave added depth to the triple portrait, with the painters shown in profile, in three-quarter view, and head on. The union of the arts was complete.

That night of 30 May the Hensels slept only a few hours before going to spend the next day at the Villa Medici.[25] For some time a party had been planned in this exceptional setting, but Ingres had one idea about it and Fanny had another, and this rather delayed the realization of the plan.

On Sunday 31 May, we were invited to spend the entire day, beginning with morning coffee, at the Académie de France to make music in the magnificent loggia there, as I had wished. The weather, which had been heavy and overcast for two days, was kind enough to prove infinitely favorable and the day was decidedly one of those so pleasant as to be unforgettable. The Academy garden, normally open to the public, was closed, and Ingres had invited only the residents, the regulars, and a few of my friends, such as Elsasser and Kaselowsky; when I expressed regret that Charlotte Thygeson was not there, they sent someone to fetch her and she spent the rest of the day with us. I assure you, it's wonderful to make music beside a gushing fountain; seldom have I been as happy as I was that day. Papa Ingres was in the seventh heaven of delight at hearing so much music and at accompanying Beethoven—although a small silent war had broken out between us, for I rushed ahead while he bumped along behind, and in a certain manner we bit each other musically. We played almost without stopping, until lunch. The bearded rascals stayed lounging on the steps and on the bases of pillars, and all through the day they were surprised that people could spend an entire day having fun like this. It took our arrival from Berlin to show them how to pass the time agreeably in the most divine accommodation in the world. The day slowly passed, and we ate a splendid lunch. After lunch we alternately made music and walked about the garden, sitting in my favorite grove to rehearse the four-voiced lieder. Ingres took us to his studio to view the long-overdue painting, which should have been finished two weeks after we arrived.[26] The composition is good and the concept noble, but it's singularly weak in regard to drawing and color, and far from complete. We saw the room that Vernet had had decorated in Turkish style, and went up the Villa's tower, where I had never been before; from there I contemplated the magnificent sunset for the last time, not without many tears. Then we came back down. The piano had been moved into the large room, dusk had fallen, and a strange feeling took hold of the assembled company. I improvised at length, very softly, for I would not have been capable of playing loudly; everything was hushed and everyone felt wounded by any noise. I played the adagio from the concerto in G major, the one from the C-sharp minor sonata, and the beginning of the great sonata in F-sharp minor. Charlotte, Bousquet, and Gounod were seated very close to me. It was an hour I shall never forget. Thereupon we went in to dinner, then onto the balcony, where it was quite delightful. Incredible stars, lights in the town, fireflies, a long shooting star, a church illuminated in the distance on a hill, warm air, and deep inner emotion felt by everyone.

We then moved to one end of the room and sang the lieder, which were very well received. At the very end, I was again asked to play by several people—I had to play the Fantasy by Mozart, and repeat the first and second Caprices. After that the lieder were sung again, it was midnight and our time was up: "They weep, and do not know the reason why?" This was the last music we played in Rome.

I would have received Ingres's tender embrace more gracefully had the young men not all been present; it must have seemed a huge joke to them. I can certainly say we gave them the best day of Ingres's entire directorship.

Fanny had finally met with the admiration and appreciation she deserved, and would thereafter know she need not be afraid to meet the gaze of foreigners—quite the contrary. Her nervousness before embarking on a journey indicates how greatly she desired recognition and how anguished she became at not being appreciated. The happiness she experienced in Rome opened a path to her: she would only find lasting fulfillment when she took the risk of confronting a new and wider audience, presenting her works to the public in full confidence of their power to charm.

CHAPTER TWENTY-FIVE

Journey's End

On 1 June 1840 the Hensels spent their last day in Rome and observed the last sunset of this sojourn that had been "painless, but for the passing of time." They left Rome the next day, their curiosity to see Naples getting the better of their henceforth prevalent wish to return to the calm of home. Rome represented both the culmination of their journey and the happiest, brightest period of Fanny's life. What followed next was simply part of a journey rather than being a crucial event.

Bousquet accompanied them as far as Genzano and told them some very interesting things about Gounod which must have reminded Wilhelm of his own mystical temptations.[1] Germans were not alone in submitting to the influence of Rome; the Eternal City could also produce a species of French Nazarene that was more radical and more socially oriented. In Fanny's words:

We had already spoken of Gounod several times, and Bousquet kept criticizing him and saying how sorry he was that Gounod failed to take part in that lovely day.[2] Then he told us how Gounod had let himself become involved in religious commitments, and how afraid he was for him on account of his weak character. Father Lacordaire, whom the Frenchmen had often mentioned in my presence, had gone through his novitiate that winter in Viterbo, received his ordination, and now wanted to spend some time in Rome, preparing to found a new house in France. Apparently Lacordaire is *une tête chaude* of great imagination, whose plans involve artists in particular, for he hopes to act upon the public through them rather than through the clergy. In the course of the winter, Lacordaire approached both Bousquet and Gounod; being very impassioned and easily influenced, Gounod completely adopted his views, to such an extent that Bousquet foresees a time when he'll renounce music in favor of the cloth. Bousquet himself stopped visiting Pater Lacordaire when he understood his intentions, for he said he did not feel strong enough and the man's eloquence was terrifying. The Association of John the Evangelist in Paris was composed only of young artists, united in the common goal of practicing a Christian art with which to convert worldly minds, though without resorting to other priestly polemics. It seems they asked Father Lacordaire to give them some rules, and Gounod apparently belongs to this brotherhood. In Rome this winter there was a whole group of young men from prominent families, several of whom had followed other professions and who now intended to enter the priesthood with a view to emancipating the world along religious paths. All this is very curious, especially in regard to the appalling materialism and insatiable greed that presently govern many Frenchmen. This is a reaction against such tendencies at their most extreme.[3]

Father Henri Lacordaire (1802–1861) had not in fact been ordained a priest that winter but in 1824, when he renounced his profession as a barrister in Paris—retaining, however, an impassioned eloquence from this first vocation. He was a leader of the Catholic liberal movement, and with Father Félicité de La Mennais (1782–1854) founded the newspaper *L'Avenir* which had as its motto "God and Liberty." Liberal Catholics were censured by Pope Gregory XVI in 1832 and La Mennais left the Church, but Lacordaire submitted and completed his novitiate between 1839 and 1841 among the Dominicans of Viterbo. On his return to France, he reestablished the Dominican order which had been abolished since 1792 (the concordat of 1801 made no reference to the regular orders). He was elected to the Constituent Assembly in 1848. His influence on Charles Gounod was powerful: when Gounod returned to France in 1846, he became organist at the Church of Foreign Missions on the rue du Bac, where he performed numerous works by Bach and Palestrina, and decided to study for the priesthood.[4] Known as Abbé Charles Gounod, he lived among the Carmelite Friars and took courses at the seminary of Saint-Sulpice. The revolution of 1848, however, changed his life completely: he gave up foreign missions, the Carmelites, Saint-Sulpice, and the cassock, turning instead toward musical theater. The European Catholics who belonged to the Romantic movement were all rebelling in their way against the rise of the middle class and the growing tendency to worship money. Looking either to the past or to the future, they sought a countering force to oppose the rising tide of liberal economics that the state was doing nothing to stem. Fanny and Wilhelm were well acquainted with the Catholicism of German Romanticism, with its antisemitism and the mysticism that had transformed its political ideas into a cult of the royal family. The Catholicism of French Romanticism had a social aspect and a political bias that were far more pronounced, and included an essential value: liberty. The act of allegiance to Rome may appear archaic and conservative, but it was part of a current of opposition to the bourgeoisie of Louis-Philippe and its "insatiable greed." Fanny had accurately perceived the critical cleavage between the generous idealism of the young and the materialism of the ruling class— a schism that led to the 1848 revolution.

As exhausted by the fermentation of ideas as she was by lack of sleep, Fanny derived little benefit from this part of the journey, but Sebastian forbade her to sleep.[5] In Naples, the Hensels stayed in a princely dwelling, unlike any they had encountered so far. Not only was it large and comfortable, but it had an enormous balcony with incomparable views over the bay of Naples, Capri, Vesuvius, and the coastline as far as Sorrento. Lending a touch of animation to this splendid scene was a British fleet composed of "three three-deckers, as peaceful and majestic as if they had come specially to beautify our view. But in fact they came to exert gentle pressure on the government of Naples in regard to the sulfurous Sicilian affair." The kingdom of Two Sicilies was indeed in a state of perpetual rebellion against the absolute monarchy and was demanding a constitution. But what mattered to the Hensels was having the sea virtually beneath their feet, and a fish vendor who brought them fresh sardines. The normally intolerable noise of the city scarcely reached them. At night the stars, along with lights coming from the British ships, the fishing boats, the town, and the nearby villages all formed a ring around the "column of fire" cast by the moon into the sea. The Hensels enjoyed the final days of their holiday. Even so, Fanny was slightly dismayed to read in the French newspapers that there was talk of bringing Napoleon's ashes from St. Helena[6]—but this did not prevent her from going back out onto the balcony to enjoy the fresh air and the splendid view.

One day, as she was about to enter the municipal museum, Fanny met the singer Pauline Viardot.[7] "I recognized her at once and we celebrated this affectionate reunion. Unfortunately she is only here for a short time—and even more unfortunately, we were both in Rome at the same time without knowing it, for the last few days." What a pity that the great French mezzo-soprano, who was also a composer, did not take part in that memorable 31 May at the Villa Medici![8]

The Hensels were quite familiar with the duties of "tourists" and fulfilled them assiduously, letting themselves be fascinated by the popular frenzy on Pentecostal Monday. "Near the church, the deafening noise and jostling reached colossal proportions. . . . I noticed many countenances that were completely African, and black negroid skins; a young girl was playing a tambourine and laughing in an untamed African way. Inside the church, a man was crawling along on his knees, licking the entire floor—what a vow! We left the carriage in the shade while Wilhelm went for a walk and drew. We both agreed that this festival would make a perfect frieze, it was truly a romantic bacchanalia!"[9]

Thus they dutifully went to the museum, saw the archeological collections of Pompei, and visited Ischia and Vesuvius. These excursions were far from comfortable—especially the one to Vesuvius, which they visited on 16 June for Sebastian's tenth birthday present.[10] The volcano was so difficult to approach that Fanny had to be carried to the top by porters. But this proved so alarming that she preferred to make the descent on foot, after visiting "Satan's headquarters."

The death of King Friedrich Wilhelm III did not perturb them, nor did it prevent them from going by boat to see the ruins of Pompei—an excursion lasting six days. On their return the weather was so hot that Fanny decided not to accompany Wilhelm to Sicily; she and Sebastian spent the time at their sumptuous abode in a room where, amazingly, it was cool. Wilhelm set off on 2 July and in his absence Fanny received a visit from Gounod, Bousquet, and another Frenchman named Normand. She was sufficiently puritanical to be delighted that a Madame D. was present, amid all these young men![11] The little group allowed itself the pleasure of going boating on the sea, and Fanny wrote to her husband: "I hope you don't disapprove of these boat outings, I can't really refuse without being suspected of a prudishness the young men would find ridiculous."[12] These young men managed to instill a certain taste for freedom into Fanny, and cannot be praised enough for that. Meanwhile the Neapolitan nights were becoming steadily lighter, and Fanny could even discern the coast of Ischia from her balcony. She also went swimming in the sea: "This morning I became an intimate acquaintance of that lady, the Mediterranean Sea, and my tongue is convinced she's ten times saltier than the Baltic Sea; it was heavenly."[13]

On 21 July, Wilhelm came back from Palermo, delighted with a town he found even more ostentatiously wealthy than London. His boat was late, plunging Fanny into a state of panic that Sebastian tried in vain to calm; she had at this point lost all taste for traveling and all adventurous spirit. Despite the Mediterranean beauty of Naples, the Hensels wished only to return to their own home: "When the mouse is full, it finds the flour tastes bitter. The worries and the cheating that go on—naturally often worse here than elsewhere—have never seemed so tedious and detestable to us, and I miss my honest homeland."[14] Fanny's eyes had been bothering her since Venice and now hurt so badly she could hardly open them. Sebastian had jaundice and looked like a lemon.

The Hensels departed for Genoa on 11 August.[15] Fanny was astonished at not having shed a single tear from her dream balcony, considering that when she left Rome she had wept four weeks in advance. The crossing lasted for four days, during which Fanny was seasick and Wilhelm very content, because there were people he could talk to and even draw. The sea was very rough for most of the voyage, and Fanny was afraid. Once in Genoa, where they arrived on 14 August, they sated themselves with Rubens, Titian, and Van Dyck; they also heard tell of Louis Napoleon Bonaparte's landing in Boulogne, his attempted rebellion, and subsequent imprisonment.[16] "A crazy, horrible man!" exclaimed Fanny, who was decidedly no Bonapartist.

In Milan, which they reached on 18 August, Fanny was happy to note the progress she had made in understanding painting during the course of the year. After all the Italian churches she had been visiting, she finally spoke of the Milan cathedral with "the inner conviction that this is the true style of church, the finest church in Italy—and it was built by a German. One has to admit there's something magnificent about the human mind, and God created nothing finer."[17] Fanny really only found what she sought in religion in Lutheran Protestantism, which had shaped both her moral and aesthetic sense.

Her final letter from south of the Alps was written on 24 August, in Airolo.[18] In Como they looked up their friend Ferdinand Hiller, went boating on the lake with him, and visited the Villa d'Este. Next day, in Bellinzona, they made the acquaintance of Count Gonfalonieri, with whom they spent one of the most interesting evenings of the entire journey. The count had spent fifteen years interned in the prison of Spielberg (abundantly mentioned in *The Charterhouse of Parma*), where after ten years of incarceration, the sole item of news to have reached him from the outer world was the death of his wife. After being in exile in the United States, France, and Belgium, he had just been authorized to see his father, then aged eighty-two, at which juncture the emperor realized it was probably a mistake that he had not yet been given amnesty. Gonfalonieri asked for news of Jacob Bartholdy, whom he had known well, and Eduard Gans, who had died in 1839 while lunching with Rebecka.[19] Perceiving the culture, gentleness, and open-mindedness of this man, Fanny grew indignant at the treatment he had received at Austrian hands: "No books during that entire time! One cannot imagine such cruelty, such moral torture."

The Hensels made the journey between Airolo and Zurich in the same carriage and with the same coachman, taking the Gotthard road which had not yet been finished in 1822. They reached the pass just as the sun was setting, and had to travel on to Hospental in darkness. The brake shoe broke, and as a precaution, they completed the descent of the Gotthard on foot. Fortunately, it was warm. Fanny noted in her diary that the innkeeper overcharged them more that night than had happened anywhere in Italy![20]

The next morning Fanny again saw the landscapes which had so impressed her during adolescence: Andermatt and its little church, the Devil's Bridge—unfortunately, in driving rain. Despite the foul weather, they went in one stretch to Flüelen, traveling via Lake Lucerne as far as Brunnen, undeterred by the storm. From Brunnen they continued as far as Arth on Lake Zug, arriving in a downpour of hail. There was no resemblance to the journey made in 1822: Fanny now thought only of returning home. Wilhelm was rather frustrated and decided, once the storm had passed, to set off at one o'clock in the morning to climb the Rigi. He came back at eight, crestfallen and sweaty, without having seen anything at all, for all the paths were unpassable. The failure of this epic climb was the subject of endless jokes among the Mendelssohns.[21]

Experiencing no further problems other than the awful roads, the Hensels crossed the German border on 28 August. At Offenburg they decided to make a small detour through Strasbourg, admiring the cathedral before continuing on toward Frankfurt which they reached somewhat exhausted on 30 August. They had traveled almost continuously since leaving Milan, so great was their haste to get back to Germany. They stayed three days in Frankfurt, resting and having their clothes cleaned, before leaving on 3 September for Leipzig, where they spent a week with Felix. He was on the point of setting off for his sixth visit to England, and they met rather by chance, for Felix had been ill and had to postpone his departure.[22] He, too, would have liked to spend a winter resting in Italy, and this would probably have altered his destiny, but he was turning out the work of at least two people, if not more, as though he were Lea, Fanny, and Rebecka. The burdens weighing on his shoulders did not permit such whims. He now had two children, Carl and a little daughter, Marie, born the previous year, whom the Hensels now saw for the first time.

They arrived in Berlin on the evening of 11 September, having been away for more than a year. Fanny waited a few days before completing the diary of her travels:

It is Wednesday today and we have been back for six days. Political events loom threateningly. The king has given a resolutely negative answer to the corporations' demand for a constitution. The French are openly rearming. Everything seems troubled, somber, and sad; in addition, it is stormy, rainy, and windy outside, and so cold that my fingers are numb. From a cultural point of view, it seems there is absolutely nothing to be expected from the king. Later on I shall give an account of the effect which all this, and our return, has had on me, when the present has become the past and the storm has dissipated or become still. Experience has taught me that one should not write these things under the influence of a fleeting impression.[23]

The journey was over, and with it the happiest months of Fanny's life. What could she do from now on to recreate the pleasant atmosphere of Rome?

End of the Entr'acte

CHAPTER TWENTY-SIX

Felix and the Temptation of Berlin

The Prussians had made a curious acquisition in the person of the new king, Friedrich Wilhelm IV (1795–1861). Known as the "Romantic on the throne," he had aroused great expectations in his youth, when he was simply the Kronprinz. Cultivated and consumed with good intentions, he wanted to be loved by all; lost in knightly dreams, however, he insisted on retaining absolute power, only to find he had no idea what to do with it.

Ironic as ever, Heinrich Heine lampooned him in a satirical poem, *Der neue Alexander* (The New Alexander), which parodied Goethe's famous *König in Thule* (The King of Thule):[1] in Heine's version, *Es war ein König in Thule* (There was a King of Thule) became *Es ist ein König in Thule, der trinkt Champagner* (There is a King of Thule, and he drinks champagne).

The better to obtain champagne and other pleasing wines, the King of Thule should conquer Alsace-Lorraine and Paris, too, while he's about it. Ah, but if only he could follow an idea through, and find the means to implement his policy! Nevertheless, "The New Alexander" continues:

> I am not bad, I am not good
> Nor stupid, nor intelligent;
> If I moved forward yesterday
> Then I move back today.

An enlightened obscurantist
Who is neither stallion nor mare,
Yes, I am equally enthusiastic
About Sophocles and the serf-owner's stick.

I put my trust in our lord Jesus
But also adopt Bacchus
As protector, always the mediator
Between the two divine extremes.

This character, who could have been even more dangerous, was widely caricatured, a practice to which his potbelly lent itself most admirably. In keeping with his ideal of enlightened absolutism, he sought to attract artists and scholars to Berlin and was prepared to spend any amount of money to that end. In fact, what he wanted was to buy himself a court in the style of Louis XIV. He had the philosopher Friedrich Schelling (1775–1854) appointed to the University of Berlin, to hold a chair previously occupied by Hegel. According to the king, it would have been a good thing if Schelling and his "philosophy of revelation" unifying faith and science had driven out the "dragon of Hegelian pantheism." Schelling failed to do so and left in 1841.[2] Friedrich Wilhelm IV then brought in "names" such as the poet and orientalist Friedrich Rückert (1788–1866), who disliked the urban noise and was delighted to leave Berlin in 1848.[3] The king managed to attract the writer Ludwig Tieck as well as the brothers Grimm and the painter Cornelius, lending weight to the literary movement known as *Junges Deutschland* (Young Germany), but this was not what the public of 1840 expected from a sovereign.[4] The generation of Romantics, so rich at the beginning of the century, had disappeared—they had either died or been forgotten by a public whose tastes had changed and who did not approve of an author's being made a vassal to those in power. Ill at ease as a writer at the service of the state, Eichendorff left his post in 1844. Bettina von Arnim, however, continued writing letters to the king, attempting to draw his attention to the wretched condition of the people. The cult of feudalism and aristocracy could scarcely be reconciled with the growing power of the middle class. Friedrich Wilhelm IV was completely unaware of these social divisions and hoped naively to reconcile the social classes at a time when the Ancien régime subsisted only on images and memories.

From the very beginning, Fanny seems to have perceived accurately the cultural and political situation in the reign of Friedrich Wilhelm IV. Her doubts proved to be well founded. As she wrote to Felix on 5 December 1840:

First we must see if there's any movement in the artistic sphere. If it's true, as everyone is saying, that Cornelius is going to come, this would prove that at least there are plans. For if it's a case, as was believed until now, of only carrying out the sketches of Schinkel's frescoes, then they've not turned to the right person in choosing Cornelius. Schinkel never emerges from his lamentable state; his intellectual possibilities have been completely destroyed. My husband is perhaps the sole artist from here who would sincerely applaud the arrival of Cornelius. The Grimms are arriving any day now, and it seems there are negotiations with Rückert. With all that our papers are as pitiful as ever, the pietists have the upper hand and the government of one person seems to be blooming. What do you think about French politics? How do you like the debates in the Chamber? Isn't it depressing! Depressing for us too, because philistine thinking spreads and tells people: you see what a constitutional state is like![5]

Menacing events loomed, and ideas were burgeoning. A kind of realistic Romanticism, henceforth opposing what it called philistinism, would claim the people's right to be granted a constitution. In all this, Friedrich Wilhelm IV cut a naively blind and pretentious figure.

The king had to have "court musicians." Accordingly, influenced by Alexander von Humboldt and the diplomat Bunsen, he invited Felix Mendelssohn Bartholdy to come to Berlin. The story of Felix's relationship with the Prussian crown covers almost four years, and the role seems to have been continual torture for him. In effect, the king wanted a musician of great renown to gild the artistic escutcheon of his court; he was prepared to pay the necessary price but, in return, would not give Felix anything to do. It was the king of Prussia's pleasure to offer a great artist the opportunity of wasting his talent in a glorious void.

Over the years, several possibilities were offered to Mendelssohn, who was always tempted by the thought of returning close to his family. The first idea involved founding a school of music, and Mendelssohn went as far as to draft a proposal. It was in vain: the project came to naught, although it was taken up again in 1869 when the Berlin Hochschule was founded. On 3 April 1843, however, Felix founded the famous Leipzig Conservatory, becoming its director and turning it into a model of its kind. The people of Leipzig had never really let him leave: during those court years he divided his time between Berlin and Leipzig—not forgetting visits to England (1842 and 1843), Düsseldorf, Zweibrücken, and Dresden. He had a back-breaking schedule—unusual for conductors at that time—and ruined his health. Berlin was an extremely bitter pill for him to swallow. Whereas he was welcomed like a god in England, and appreciated and admired in Leipzig where they gave him everything he needed for his work, in Berlin his plans and ideas encountered nothing but niggardly incomprehension.

Good intentions were not lacking. The king—who, as Heine ironically pointed out, admired Sophocles—ordered him to compose incidental music for *Antigone* in the new translation by Boeckh. The work received its first performance on 28 October 1841 at the Royal Theater in Potsdam; it went well, but it had taken all Mendelssohn's talent to make palatable the pedantic idea of resurrecting a Greek tragedy. The next attempt, however, was more than a mere success. On the initiative of Ludwig Tieck, who collaborated in the translation, *A Midsummer Night's Dream* was performed on 14 October in Potsdam, with Felix's celebrated music, which included the overture he had composed in 1826. The work was subsequently revived in Berlin at the Königliche Theater. He wrote two more examples of incidental music, one for Racine's *Athalie* and the other for *Oedipus at Colonus* by Sophocles. He declined to compose choruses for the *Oresteia* of Aeschylus.

Eventually, in September 1842, a final project was suggested, but by this time Felix could not bear it any longer and requested an audience with the king precisely in order to tender his resignation.[6] He was unable to find the necessary working conditions, orchestra, and discipline in Berlin. The day before his audience with the king, Felix informed Lea of his decision, and Lea, who was usually all sweetness and gentleness, erupted into one of the scenes normally reserved for the marriage of her children. If Felix left Berlin now, when she had grown used to the idea of his being close to her again, was this not a further, dreadful breach of faith in regard to her? Fanny and Wilhelm hastened to calm her. The next day, instead of dismissing Felix in a rage, the king was as pleasant as could be. So Felix needed an orchestra? Nothing could be more natural, and the king himself would see he was provided with a highly select one, with a chorus of thirty outstanding singers that the composer could conduct at all the religious festivals, just as he could write music for all manner of occasions—oratorios, or whatever he pleased.

Thinking of his mother, Felix could only accept. The orchestra was not created in a day, and Felix kept colliding with administrative problems and the monarch's indecision. Varnhagen von Ense wrote in his diary: "The King said to Count von Redern: 'Bunsen told me of an elderly organist, Nicolai; you must find him for me; we must make him organist of the cathedral.' 'But then Mendelssohn would resign at once.' 'Oh well, in that case, no.' On another occasion: 'I would like Meyerbeer to compose the choruses for *Athalie*.' 'But at Your Majesty's command, Mendelssohn has already composed them—it would give rise to terrible hostility.' 'Yes, yes, Meyerbeer must compose them too.'"[7]

As if to be sure of creating a real problem, the king had summoned both Meyerbeer and Mendelssohn, appointing one to the theater and the other to the church. It is difficult to give an accurate assessment of the relationship between the two families, but as we have seen, Giacomo Meyerbeer could be most insulting.

It might not have been so bad if the indecisiveness of Friedrich Wilhelm IV had only afflicted Felix, who had resources of his own. Unfortunately the dictum *Es ginge wohl, aber es geht nicht* (It could work, but it won't work) was not applied to the cathedral choir but to the imperial crown, which the Frankfurt Parliament offered the Prussian king in 1849 to bring about German unity. Friedrich Wilhelm refused, on the grounds that this crown was offered by the people. Such phenomenal, almost criminal, stupidity could only pass into history.

CHAPTER TWENTY-SEVEN

1840–1844

In the meantime, Fanny was becoming accustomed to life in Berlin again and distilling the inspiration she had found in Rome.

While reading the dramatist Raupach's adaptation of the *Niebelungen* legend,[1] she had the idea of setting the story to music. She confided her idea to Felix, who responded with enthusiasm, but neither brother nor sister did more than think about the proposal. Both Fanny and Felix were conscious of how difficult it would be to carry out a project of such scope.[2]

That autumn, Fanny composed a cycle of piano music, *Das Jahr*, (The Year), comprising twelve pieces each named after a month. This attractive idea allowed her to have quite different pieces following each other while maintaining a general unity. She composed *February* first, on 28 August, in memory of the Roman carnival, and completed her cycle around Christmas, with *December*. The work concluded with a *Nachspiel* (Postlude), based on the chorale *Das alte Jahr vergangen ist* (The old year is over). She also composed *Einleitung zu lebenden Bildern* (Introduction to Tableaux Vivants) for narrator and chorus, certainly intended for performance in her concerts.[3]

Toward the middle of December, she revived her Sunday musicales. On 28 September she had already told Felix she was working on his Trio in D Minor, Opus 49, and was finding it very difficult but hoped to include it in her next *Sonntagsmusik*.[4] She also had great difficulty in finding a piano she really liked. Felix had made her buy a Viennese piano that she found weak in the middle register. To her the ideal instrument appeared to be the Erard Felix had bought in England for her friend Pauline Decker—but it had cost 1000 guineas![5]

Felix's frequent presence in Berlin lent additional luster to the *Sonntagsmusik*, with the possible drawback—from a twentieth-century point of view—that it pushed Fanny further back into the wings. In her day, she was respected as a very great lady in the Berlin musical world. The writer Paul Heyse noted proudly in his memoirs that as a child he had been permitted to attend all Fanny's concerts:

An illustrious company filled the huge room, and very few among them could not have proved their right to be sitting there through an intimate knowledge of music. It was considered a great distinction by the musical celebrities passing through to be judged worthy of the honor of an invitation to these matinées. Boeckh was among those permanently invited, and near him old Steffens,[6] whose venerable countenance was transfigured as he listened to the intelligent playing of our hostess, or the singing of her friends as they interpreted Felix's charming quartets. The great glass doors were left open to the garden and sometimes the song of birds was mingled with the music. It was here that *Die letzte Walpurgisnacht* (The Last Walpurgis Night) was first performed when just completed by the composer. Numerous fine piano pieces and lieder were sung and played from manuscripts whose ink was scarcely dry. Sometimes the beloved brother and master came in person from Leipzig and honored one of these matinées with his wondrous playing. Then the room was transformed into a temple wherein an enthusiastic congregation imbibed each note as if it were a celestial revelation.

I myself would stand with my friend Sebastian on the threshold of the neighboring room, stretching my tall body on tiptoe so as not to miss a note and to observe the faces all around the piano. I also saw the blond mane of the young Franz Liszt, then in the midst of his first triumph in Berlin, and in the first row of the audience a beautiful blond countess who left the room on the arm of the happy young conqueror.[7]

By "Last Walpurgis Night" Heyse probably meant the completed version of *Die erste Walpurgisnacht* (The First Walpurgis Night), which Felix had started working on in 1831 at the very beginning of his sister's *Sonntagsmusik*, and which he did not finish until 1844.

Liszt had made an overwhelming impression in Berlin, as he did wherever he went. Describing a Liszt concert, a dazzled, almost frightened Varnhagen wrote that the composer "held heartbeats in his power."[8] His personal magnetism, along with the impact of his playing and stage presence, enabled him—without any form of accompaniment—to cast a spell over the audience filling the hall of the Singakademie. The newly established fashion of performing alone for an entire evening was justified by Franz Liszt—but only by him! He could not omit going to Fanny Hensel's house. It is hard to say who was the more honored in this case, the guest or the hostess, but that goes to show what an exclusive level Fanny's musicales had reached. Could the beautiful blond countess have been Marie d'Agoult? Sebastian Hensel further attests to the high quality of the *Sonntagsmusik*:

My mother's Sunday matinées flourished, and were frequented by an extremely glittering public; this, as much as the music, contributed to the interest they aroused. Sometimes Cornelius, who had just moved to Berlin, would be the focus of attention; sometimes Bunsen and Felix; sometimes Thorwaldsen. Around them gathered a numerous assembly comprised of Berlin's most notable, attractive, and distinguished residents. The seventeenth volume of portraits by my father bears witness to the select society which gathered in our house that year: the volume contains portraits of Thorwaldsen; the singer Pasta; the violinist Ernst, who often came to our house; and Unger-Sabatier and her husband. In addition, there was Liszt, who aroused delirious enthusiasm during his very first visit to Berlin; Lepsius, the celebrated Egyptologist; Böck [Boeckh], the great philologist, who lived in our house at the time;[9] Mrs. Austin, the well-known English writer. The intelligent, understanding face of Prince Radziwill, son of the composer of Faust, concludes this volume, which is among the more interesting of the entire collection.[10]

The great singer Giuditta Pasta (1797–1865), who had created numerous roles in operas by Rossini and Bellini, passed through Berlin during July 1841. Fanny went to hear her and was very impressed by her tragic stature and tasteful ornamentation—particularly in *Norma*—but horrified at her intonation: Signora Pasta sang between a quarter and an eighth of a tone flat! Felix had already been distressed by this during his visit to Paris, and matters had not improved with age.[11]

Fanny's activities did not allow her to give Sebastian the same upbringing she had received herself. In fact, none of Lea's grandchildren received such an education. Sebastian spent his childhood surrounded by adults, in the "ideal artistic atmosphere" created by his parents,[12] but learned nothing in a disciplined manner. While he knew many things, his solfeggio, to take one example, was not particularly solid. Most of the time he played with the gardener Clement's children, with "street urchins capable of any kind of silly behavior," or else with Walter Dirichlet, his junior by three years. Fanny gave him his "first instruction,"[13] he declared—meaning, doubtless, that she taught him to read. Then he was sent to a school, the Liebesche Schule, which seemed so lamentable to his family that they called it the Libysche Wüste, the "Libyan desert." Sebastian, however, was thrilled to be with children of his own age. In October 1840, after the Hensels' return from Italy, Sebastian and Walter were sent to the Schmidtsche Schule at 9 Leipziger Strasse—practically next door. Fanny hated the idea of corporal punishment, which was practiced there, but Sebastian was never subjected to it. On the contrary, he was disgusted by the privileged treatment accorded the rich children, an injustice he became aware of for the first time in his life. He was reminded later of his schooling when he read Dickens's novel *Nicholas Nickleby*. Until then, he had always considered the gardener's children as his equals, and their basement apartment at 3 Leipziger Strasse struck him as a dwelling to be envied.[14] At home he had always seen the servants being extremely well treated, and the cook Jette had of course become his great friend and confidant during the long Italian journey. Having been raised according to humanist ideals, Sebastian was astonished to discover social inequality and the power of money, and stood up for his less fortunate friends in school.[15] In bringing him up, Fanny followed Henriette Mendelssohn's advice rather than Lea's method: she encouraged Sebastian's talents but did not push him. He seems to have been gifted at everything and very aware, intellectually; he would complain later, however, that he knew many things but had no method. In fact, he had such facility that no one—especially his teachers—noticed his blank spots! Unlike Paul Heyse with his pompous style, Sebastian displayed modesty and talent in his writing. To his parents, it seemed logical that he would choose an artistic profession.

The family was increasing in size: in 1840 Rebecka had given birth to another son, Ernst (Abraham's Christian name), and in 1841 Cécile produced a third child, Paul. This made a pleasant little group to take for walks in the garden, and the neighboring farm animals were even more warmly regarded for awakening the children's curiosity and delight.

In the midst of this fascinating, animated life, happy in the thought that her eldest, favorite son was coming to see her at Christmas and that his problems with the Prussian king were settled, Lea had a fainting spell one Sunday in December 1842 while lunching merrily with her family and friends, the Woringens. It was 11 December; that evening she fell asleep "with warm hands," as Sebastian put it, and in her normal state; at nine-thirty the next morning, after a "brief, slight struggle," she died.[16] Was the final, passionate argument she had had with Felix over his resignation a contributing factor in so sudden a death? We may well wonder. The family was naturally plunged into mourning but experienced some consolation in the peaceful, painless manner of Lea's departure. Fanny wrote in her diary: "We could not have imagined a happier death for her; word for word, it was exactly what she said to Albertine last summer when she confided that, without medication and without losing consciousness, she would like to be taken from this life she loved, in full possession of the intellectual brilliance which had been her lot in life." The Mendelssohns did not celebrate Christmas that year. They seem to have lost their bearings but were perhaps less shaken than by Abraham's death.

The sudden deaths occurring in the Mendelssohn family took them in the midst of lives that were certainly active but not healthy. Good health was a blessing they did not possess. Fanny's lively letters were pitted with illnesses of every kind. In a letter of 5 December, Fanny wrote to Felix of "coughs, sore throats, toothaches, nosebleeds" affecting the whole family, adding, with a mixture of optimism and humor, that "nosebleeds have weakened me less than last year, but a severe chill is making up for that."[17] The family was affected by cardiovascular problems, and the Mendelssohns' vitality resulted more from their nervous energy than from robust health.

Dirichlet left for Leipzig with little Walter, thus enchanting and consoling Felix who adored children. The Hensels decided in their turn to visit the "Felicians," and set off on 21 February; they spent a week in Leipzig, which had been connected by rail to Berlin since September 1841. It took seven hours to travel the two hundred kilometers separating the two towns. As Fanny described the visit:

Much music was made: we heard Gade's C Minor Symphony, his first work, which justifies great expectations. Felix was utterly delighted by the work, too, and had it rehearsed most lovingly. Berlioz was in Leipzig at the same time as us, his strange habits often scandalized the inhabitants and Felix had his hands full smoothing things over. To mark the end, Berlioz proposed an exchange of batons, "as old warriors exchange weapons," and whereas Felix sent him his light, elegant baton in whalebone covered with white leather, Berlioz sent him an incredible limewood bludgeon still in its raw bark, with an open letter beginning with the words: "*Le mien est grossier, le tien est simple*" [Mine is crude, yours is simple]. A friend to whom Berlioz had confided the task of sending it had translated: "I am crude and you're a simpleton." He was mortally embarrassed and did not know how to cover up this implied insult to Felix. We also heard Clara Schumann, she plays ravishingly well.[18]

Felix had just discovered the young Danish composer Niels Gade (1817–1890), who had fired him with enthusiasm. Berlioz was an old acquaintance whom Felix had met during his first visit to Rome in 1830. The two men liked each other, although Felix did not quite grasp the Frenchman's cast of mind, for Berlioz derived his ideas from the world of literature and philosophy and was not at all interested in baroque music; for his part, Berlioz did not understand Mendelssohn's attachment to a highly structured musical tradition and found the German "too fond of dead composers." Fanny, too, was in some perplexity with regard to Berlioz. Inspired by the shrieks of Flora, her latest niece, she wrote on 4 March 1845: "When Berlioz has found a place for the fifty grand pianos he finds indispensable, I shall advise him to have a wet nurse sit at each, with a nursing child who has been hungry for several hours; I'm sure the public, especially the mothers of the children, would be very moved."[19]

Clara Wieck (1819–1896) had married Robert Schumann in 1840. She was then a very young woman who already had behind her an accomplished career as a child prodigy. Fanny also met Robert Schumann, who was so impressed by this meeting that six months later he noted in his diary: "Madame Hensel, Mendelssohn's sister, whose mind and depth of feeling speak through her eyes" (*Madame Hensel, Mendelssohn's Schwester, der Geist und Tiefe aus den Augen spricht*).[20]

Cécile was pregnant with a fourth child, a little boy who was born on 1 May and christened Felix. As for Sebastian, he was absorbed in a costly and devouring passion: collecting insects.

After having spent two years in Rome, Gounod made a year-long detour through Germany before returning to Paris. He stopped in Florence, then Vienna where he met the composer Nicolai.[21] After visiting Prague and Dresden, he arrived in Berlin at the end of April and stayed until 15 May, scarcely leaving Fanny's side. As she then wrote:

He stayed here for the entire time without going out, and was given a very friendly welcome by the whole family. He saw nothing of Berlin, except for our house and garden, and the family, and heard nothing except what I played for him, although we encouraged him to look around. . . . We found him much developed since Rome; he's extremely gifted, with a musical intelligence and an accuracy of judgment which could scarcely go further; at the same time, his feelings are delicate and tender. This lively intelligence is particular to him, even outside the domain of music; thus I could not hear him read German without feeling real pleasure, and was astonished at the talent with which he had mastered the essence of the language. Thus he read several scenes from Antigone, and to my great surprise he understood them. Another thing that sways me in his favor is the true affection, and respect, he feels for us, and which he demonstrated in coming to Berlin, for he only undertook the journey in order to visit us. His presence was a very lively musical stimulus for me, for I played and discussed music a great deal with him during the numerous afternoons I spent alone in his company, for he generally remained with us after twelve. We also discussed his future at length, and I don't think I was mistaken in depicting oratorio as the impending musical future in France; he was so impressed that he began seriously to be concerned about the choice of text; he is going to choose Judith. In short, he showed us perfect trust in everything; he completely deserved the friendly reception given him, by us and by my brothers and sisters, for which I am most grateful to them. Everybody liked him very much.[22]

What did Fanny mean by "us"? Had Gounod gone out of his way to see Wilhelm and Sebastian? It is difficult not to read between the lines—even read into the lines—and see that Gounod showed her great tenderness and that she was deeply touched. Before setting forth again for Paris he spent four days in Leipzig where Felix made him welcome and gave friendly encouragement. Gounod returned to France with musical knowledge of an unusual kind for a Frenchman: he had absorbed and understood Palestrina and Bach, and this exceptional learning experience was the basis for what became known as the "renewal of the French school." Fanny's influence has been completely underestimated: music history preferred to dwell on the influence of Mendelssohn, with whom Gounod spent only four days. It is true that the French composer only mentioned Fanny in his *Memoirs* when strictly necessary. Apart from the text quoted in connection with Fanny's stay in Rome, Gounod omitted to mention his visit to Naples and the boating excursions, and said little of his trip to Berlin—except to note that an illness obliged him to stay two weeks longer than intended, and that Fanny sent him her doctor. This would seem to indicate that "Madame Henzel" mattered more than he dared say. In any case, the time they spent together, first in Rome, then in Berlin, proves that Gounod owed his knowledge of German music to her and not to Felix. Gounod's *Ave Maria* may well owe something to Fanny's lieder and "songs for the piano," with a pianistic style itself indebted to Bach preludes with the additional accompaniment of a melody. Bach and Fanny deserved better, but it was an age of sentimental affectation, and Gounod acquired great renown thereby.

In thinking that the musical future of France lay in oratorio, Fanny overlooked one thing: the world, to which she would shortly cease to belong, thought ever increasingly of profit. And which earns more money, an opera or an oratorio? The paying public must be seduced, and where does it find more pleasure, in the theater or in church? Naturally, sacred music still existed in the nineteenth century, and Gounod composed some, but to term this the musical future of any country in the world was really going too far!

The time was soon to come when it would no longer be a matter of organizing concert series with practically no budget, with benevolent artists, and an invited audience. Amateur societies were going to have to make their efforts profitable. When that happened, women were dispatched into a private sphere that was absolutely insulated from the public world.

If Gounod learned a lot from Fanny, he repaid her in kind through his admiration, which gave her the stimulus and encouragement necessary to compose. That autumn she even ventured to write a piano sonata in G minor—one of her most interesting works, conceived in the Romantic style as an uninterrupted fantasy with no break between the first three movements, and an attacca before the fourth.[23] During that year she also wrote a piece inspired by *Faust*, which included choruses from part two; unfortunately, the work has either been lost or is buried in some private library.[24] Did she discuss it with Gounod? Their views of Goethe's masterpiece did not really coincide, for the Frenchman was more interested in part one, and in the passages involving Margarete.

Was Fanny still acting under Gounod's stimulus when she wrote to their friend Franz Hauser—a former baritone, now a singing teacher in Vienna—submitting one of her works to him? The results of Fanny's action are unknown, but at least it proves she was trying to emerge from the routine of life in Berlin:

Dear esteemed friend,

Enclosed please find the piece of music through which, on your amiable suggestion, I wish to make the daring attempt to attain the dignity of a member of your association. Please excuse and correct all the pedantic faults committed by a woman and a dilettante; a dilettante is already an alarming being, a female composer even more so, but when the two entities are united in a single person, she becomes the most alarming creature that can be imagined.[25]

There could be no better way of poking fun at omnipotent manhood. With all her modesty, Fanny is quite aware that she is no worse than the majority of composers, and that the prejudice against women had no justification in reality—whence this ironic exaggeration, describing the female composer as a virtual demon.

Fanny stayed quietly at home that summer, watching everybody else rush about. In July the Dirichlets left for Italy in their turn, and Wilhelm embarked on a second trip to England.

After their journey to Italy the Hensels became rather worried about their financial situation, especially as Wilhelm's paintings, *Christ in the Desert* and *Miriam*, had remained in England and had not yet been sold. Admittedly, Wilhelm had been commissioned by Lord Egerton to do a painting depicting the Duke of Brunswick before the battle of Quatrebas in 1815, and worked on this during the winter of 1840–1841. The painting was finished in 1842 and met with great acclaim when exhibited at the Akademie der Künste. It was also exhibited in Brunswick at the request of Duke Wilhelm August, who commissioned a further painting on the life of his father. The king of Prussia decided to have *Christ in the Desert* brought back from England—the equivalent of a commitment to buy.[26] Wilhelm worked hard! Wishing to return to England to obtain other commissions and keep himself and his paintings in the public eye, he obtained a commission from Friedrich Wilhelm IV to paint a portrait of the little Prince of Wales, the future Edward VII (1841–1910). He set off for London via the Potsdam–Hamburg railway, with a letter of recommendation from the Prussian king to Queen Victoria. Wilhelm duly worked on the portrait of the royal child, and later sent a copy for the Buckingham Palace collection. He also did portraits of Queen Victoria and Prince Albert. The queen purchased *Miriam* with a ring Wilhelm subsequently gave Fanny, who found it "madness to wear seven or eight thousand thalers on one's finger."[27] His return from England took far longer than expected, and as in Naples when awaiting his return from Sicily, Fanny was overwhelmed with panic. Wilhelm had left on 1 September and did not arrive until 18 September, laden with presents.

Fanny would have been better advised to worry about herself. On 27 July, she wrote to Rebecka: "May God protect me from falling so ill that I have to consult Schönlein. I won't do so for my hands, of which you have a very poor opinion if you think I can no longer write with them. The paralysis has almost left them; as for their weakness, it rather depends. I wasn't quite equal to the galvanizing, and now I have to try baths of aqua vitae. They've discovered, amazingly enough, that in Berlin where every other shop sells spirits, there's no crude distillery, and first of all I have to find or somehow obtain the thing."[28] This was just a hint of what was to come. These bouts of illness were so common that this one was not taken seriously enough— and besides, what could anybody do?

Pauline Viardot paid another visit to Berlin, and Rebecka, who was still in Freiburg, envied the Berliners: "Have you heard Viardot-Consuelo? This damned Sand woman, I think of her every time I pass a vegetable garden."[29] To which Fanny replied: "I can quite believe that you see Consuelo in every vegetable garden, but it's really too bad you can't see and hear the original model on stage. What a unique personality! And many of her characteristics have been portrayed very well; I recognize Consuelo when I hear her talk."[30] George Sand's novel appeared in serial form between 1842 and 1845, firing idealistic, prerevolutionary Europe with enthusiasm and adding to the renown of the singer who had provided the inspiration for its heroine.

On the night of 19 August the Berlin Opera burned down.[31] This splendid edifice, built in 1742 by the architect Knobelsdorff from plans by Friedrich II, was largely destroyed. Fanny spent most of the night awake, afraid that the fire would spread to the rest of the district and to Paul Mendelssohn's bank, among other things. How sad for Fanny to see her favorite theater disappear! It was rebuilt in 1844 by Langhans, but Fanny did not feel at home there: the pure rococo decoration had been replaced by a ponderous ornamentation in varying styles. Even though rococo was not Fanny's favorite, she always wanted stylistic unity and fidelity to a particular school to be maintained.

Felix returned in the autumn and conducted the first performance of his *A Midsummer Night's Dream* in the Royal Theater of Potsdam on 18 October. Naturally Fanny was present at this historic occasion, as were Felix's friends from Leipzig: Ferdinand Hiller, the violinist David, Gade, and a very young Hungarian violinist, Joseph Joachim, who was only twelve and "so gifted there was nothing left for David to teach him."[32] Much music was heard during the days preceding the performance. On the evening of the dress rehearsal, 17 October, Fanny sat next to Frau Tieck, whose husband had directed the production; Fanny was certainly unable to express her opinions of the seventeenth-century costumes Tieck had insisted on and which Fanny found most off-putting. But she was delighted by the music: "I have never heard an orchestra play so pianissimo!" she exclaimed.[33] When the famous March of Puck was over and the elves (thirty students from the ballet school) returned to the empty stage, it was "so beautiful one could weep, I tell you"—as Fanny wrote to her distant sister. Fanny attended the premiere the next day with Sebastian. Old Sara Levy was in the hall, and the balcony contained "two imposing rows of Mendelssohns and people they had brought. Paul declares that when Mendelssohn was called for, he stood up on the balcony most amiably, but no one paid attention."

At the end of October Fanny again revived the *Sonntagsmusik*, which she had discontinued for a year and a half, for reasons we do not really know. Was it from concern for their finances, since Wilhelm's paintings had not been sold; or was it that Felix's presence had a discouraging effect on Fanny? In any case, as soon as he returned from England, Wilhelm insisted that the matinées be revived. "And for the first time in a year and a half I had a musical evening yesterday, comprised of Felix's new cello sonata—in which Ganz managed to make a hideous blunder—my Faust piece, and Felix's alto solo with chorus, etc. It took a great effort for me to start giving these receptions again, especially for just one or two occasions, because I want to stop until the one in December, but Hensel wished it so."[34]

With his sociable nature, Wilhelm obviously enjoyed meeting people and had not learned to tolerate his wife's being inactive.

Thus, on 3 December, Fanny gave another matinée: "Yesterday, the final *Sonntagsmusik* of the year, which was very popular. I played Beethoven's trio in E-flat, and Felix and I played Beethoven's Polonaise, and the Entr'actes from *A Midsummer Night's Dream*, much to everyone's delight."[35] Felix worked incessantly and had composed his *Psalm 98* for the New Year, to be performed in the cathedral.

The musicales began again in February, this time at the prompting of Felix, "who had heard tittle-tattle, to the effect that he did not want music to be played here."[36] To be sure, Felix was a butt for all manner of gossip, but the Berliners must have wondered why his sister had stopped giving her musical receptions.

Early in February and inspired by the fine weather, Fanny opened her garden room to the public. "Felix had composed two very brilliant and pretty variations for four hands, which I watched being composed page by page on Saturday; I practiced them a little and they progressed very well." For the benefit of her little sister, she added this more personal digression: "I can see how young you are when you think that in another year or two we'll be too old to do the [Italian] journey again. When you're as old as I am, you won't be at all afraid of growing a bit older; now that I'm very close to being forty, I'm serious in thinking I want to be fresh and cheerful when I'm fifty. It will be just the same for you, and I'm far from giving up the idea of our all going on such a journey together."[37]

At the beginning of March, Fanny rehearsed *The First Walpurgis Night*, one of her favorite works by Felix. The soloists were not at all reluctant to sing with the chorus, and Fanny observed that "Decker, Auguste Löwe,[38] Bader, and Beer, our new bass, did wonders in the choir."[39] This preparation yielded good results, for the resulting *Sonntagsmusik* became almost legendary. Fanny had to admit as much to her sister, on 18 March:

Last Sunday we had what was, I think, the most brilliant musicale ever to see daylight, in regard both to the audience and the performance. If I tell you there were twenty-two carriages with their horses in the courtyard, and that Liszt and eight princesses were present in the room, you'll excuse me from giving a more detailed description of such splendor. In return, I'll describe the program to you: Hummel's quintet—a slight tumult among the fingers; a duet from *Fidelio*; variations by David played by the admirable little Joachim, who is not a child prodigy, but a prodigiously remarkable child, and Sebastian's close friend besides. Two lieder, of which Eckert's very fine *Lass die Schmerzen dieser Erde* (Leave the suffering of this world), which Felix and Decker performed from memory, was much applauded. . . . Then the "Walpurgis Night" which my audience had been eagerly awaiting for four weeks, and which went very well. We had three rehearsals, in which the singers had such fun they would willingly have had twice as many; Felix came to the last one, and was very pleased. I would really have liked him to accompany it, but he absolutely refused. Instead, he played the overture with me, adding a few notes in the difficult passages, either in the bass or the soprano; this resulted in a kind of improvised arrangement for four hands which sounded very good.[40]

Fanny Lewald was probably in attendance that day:

It was in the course of one of those matinées that I first saw and heard Felix Mendelssohn. Among those present were Henrik Steffens, Friedrich von Raumer, the artists Wach and Tieck, a princess from Dessau, the Radziwill princes and their families, Count Westmoreland, the English ambassador, two of Bettina's daughters, a daughter of Prince Karl of Prussia and her governess, Schönlein, and a further mass of people whose names were important or would become important later, such as the musician Joseph Joachim who was still a child at the time, and who played some very brilliant variations by David, accompanied by Mendelssohn.

The music had already begun when suddenly all eyes turned toward the door and a joyful smile lit up every face: a man who was still young appeared in the doorway of the room. He had a slender, mobile silhouette and entered noiselessly, head high, with brilliant eyes that had something surprising, even subjugating about them. This was Franz Liszt.[41]

Fanny Lewald, however, confused this musicale with the one in February, and mixed up the programs—which, even so, were of dazzling richness:

This matinée began with a quartet by Weber played by Frau Hensel, with the Ganz brothers and Felix Mendelssohn accompanying; next Frau Hensel and her brother performed his own Variations for four hands. Pauline von

Schätzel, then already married to the court printer Decker, sang an aria from the Creation with accompanying chorus; then, with a remarkable singer whose name, I think, was Bär, she sang several long scenes from *Der Templer und die Jüdin* [by Heinrich Marschner, 1795–1861, first performed in 1829 in Leipzig]; Felix Mendelssohn accompanied the singing at the piano, and at the end Mendelssohn played the above-mentioned Variations with young Joachim.

The matinées were nonetheless interrupted again, for Felix needed time and people, Fanny said, to perform *Israel in Egypt* on Palm Sunday. Among his other activities, Felix was in fact editing and leading performances of Handel's works. He needed a chorus of 450 people and a large orchestra, in addition to an organ. He also had to conduct the choral Ninth Symphony, besides composing and correcting his own works. Despite this intense activity, he could not with any degree of pleasure allow his sister to be pursuing an independent career in his territory.[42] Fanny, on the other hand, attended all his rehearsals and knew by heart the works he was conducting.[43]

Felix and his family left for Frankfurt in early April, to be with Cécile's family. Fanny was extremely busy in the garden, planting fruit trees and giving Walter Dirichlet an account of the family goat farm. On 23 June she gave the final *Sonntagsmusik* of the season, "which I want to conclude with Felix's male chorus *Wer hat dich, du schöner Wald* (Who, o lovely forest) with horns and trombones."[44] Nothing was expected of her, except to exist and enjoy the summer. "The nightingale is in full voice," she declared delightedly,[45] and if she missed Cécile's babies she was soon able to go and cuddle Paul and Albertine's firstborn, a little girl born at the end of May.[46]

CHAPTER TWENTY-EIGHT

Rebecka and Arnold: Two Mendelssohns During the *Vormärz*

The Dirichlets stayed longer than anticipated in Italy. Fanny expected them back at the end of August at the latest, for at Rebecka's request she had reserved an apartment for them at 18 Leipzigerplatz. Thanks to a corridor, the apartment had separate rooms—something Fanny marveled at, for her own home consisted entirely of connecting rooms.[1] But the summer came to an end, and still the Dirichlets had not returned to Berlin. An ailing Rebecka left Naples for Rome, where she was told she had jaundice. The Dirichlets' stay was extended in fortnightly increments, with the doctors continually promising a prompt recovery.

That autumn, Felix returned to Berlin to ask the king for a definitive release, with the proviso that he would remain at the monarch's disposal if the king had a precise commission for him. He was still a court musician, but now had permission to reside wherever he liked with a salary reduced from three to one thousand thalers. Felix left Berlin on 30 November 1844, after a final performance of *Saint Paul*. Fanny was saddened and disappointed by the result of these long negotiations. She had grown accustomed to the presence of Cécile and her children, and hoped they would all grow old together.[2] She was less sorry, in a way, to see Felix go than to lose the little world surrounding him—he was, after all, a migratory bird. Her sadness is reflected in her diary:

As for Felix, we shall actually see him almost as much as we do now, for if—as he expects—he comes back several times a year and stays awhile and is our guest, we shall gain more benefit from his presence than if he lives here but is absent for most of the time and peevish for the rest of it. But Cécile and the children are completely lost to us, and I am so fond of them. Felix is very pleasant again, and I find his playing more splendid than ever. All that pitiful dilettantism seems loathsome and contemptible when one perceives what true art is. If I don't give it all up, it's partly because I don't think myself so pitiful when Felix isn't there—on the contrary, I have a better opinion of myself—and partly because I don't want to upset my husband, who would be beside himself with rage.[3]

Despite all the affection he claimed to feel for his sister, Felix actually helped her less than Gounod. Why, at this time in their lives and at this stage of his career, could he not find words that would have encouraged her musical talents? For there could be no doubt that at the age of forty, she lagged irreparably behind him. Did he really need to crush her so completely, in order to fulfill his own artistic potential? Fanny seems not even to have a great desire to see him at this point. She "has a better opinion of herself" and feels better when he is not there. As in the past, Wilhelm is the "anti-Felix," and plays a stabilizing role.

After her brother's departure, Fanny did not have much time in which to be depressed about her fate: Rebecka finally admitted she was ill, that her jaundice signified an infectious disease and was not getting any better, and that she was pregnant. Dirichlet had come down with an ailment known as "Roman fever," and both had been conveyed to Florence—a journey that caused Rebecka pains she never liked to speak of later, having felt close to madness at the time.[4]

Women had no careers: it was so often necessary for them to attend to the sick, and the panic aroused by ever-threatening infections left them little time and energy to devote to anything besides their families. Fanny played nurse for a good part of her life. For a long time, society was content to let women work unpaid. When news of the Dirichlets' illness reached the Mendelssohns, Paul and Albertine's little daughter was critically ill. In these anxious circumstances, the Hensels nevertheless decided to go to the rescue of the unfortunate Dirichlets. The mathematician Carl Gustav Jacoby (1804–1851) agreed to cover Dirichlet's courses at the university and war college without seeking any compensation—his sole intention was to keep the two jobs open for his friend.[5]

The Hensels were due to depart sometime between Christmas and the New Year, but Fanny fell victim to a nosebleed that lasted for thirty-six hours without stopping, day or night. Thus they did not leave until 2 January 1845. Sebastian went with them, having promised to study during the entire journey so as not to lose a year at school. The little family took the train as far as Leipzig, then traveled in their own carriage drawn by post horses. Passing through Munich and the Brenner pass, they reached Florence on 19 January, to be met by a Rebecka so transformed by illness that they were seriously alarmed. Dirichlet's face was also disfigured by his fever. The Hensels rented an apartment with windows facing the Dirichlets' apartment, and life became more organized. Rebecka recovered quickly. Wilhelm, who had canvases to paint and was unable to find suitable models and costumes in Florence, was obliged to leave for Rome. Fanny rented a grand piano and Rebecka a more modest instrument, and the two sisters made music, an activity indispensable to their survival. Sebastian studied mathematics with Dirichlet—"one of my worst memories," as he later admitted. He did not fare much better in Greek or Latin. Still tired from his illness, Dirichlet had no pedagogical talent at all. As his son Walter would say later, he had progressed so far in mathematics that he had forgotten the basics.[6]

Rebecka's baby was expected in early April; it did not wait that long and a little girl was born on 13 February, so quickly and painlessly that everyone was stupefied. The baby arrived safe and sound almost at the same time as the doctor, whose appearance Fanny had awaited in a state of great anxiety. No one thought the child would be born alive, or that Rebecka would give birth so easily, since labor was usually a real torture for her. Alone to face this event, Fanny had been expecting the worst, yet everything turned out for the best. Rebecka had never recovered from childbirth so quickly and all her ailments disappeared as if by miracle. The infant's premature arrival created much work for its aunt, who had to find it clothes, write announcements of its birth, see that everyone was fed, and generally think of everything. At least the child's name had already been dictated by the circumstance: Florentina. A boy would have been disappointing—there were already so many little Mendelssohn boys![7]

"Fanny and Beckchen belong to each other," said their sister-in-law Cécile to Felix one day.[8] Mendelssohnians usually speak of the relationship each sister had with Felix, but in reality the relationship between the two of them was deeper, more durable, and more effective. In 1829 Wilhelm had already drawn Felix's two "otters" intertwined, and rather than belying this image of their youth, their lives only tended to confirm it. Rebecka was far less fortunate than Fanny: whereas the elder sister could, thanks to her music, make her way within the private world of women and on the borderline of public life, Rebecka suffocated at home. Her talents were not designed to remain under lock and key. Openly republican, she asked only to play a part in politics, as is proved by an event that took place in 1850. The revolutionary Gottfried Kinkel had been arrested after organizing a march against the arsenal of Siegburg; he was condemned to death, but thanks to the intervention of Bettina von Arnim (the prisoner's wife, Johanna, taught music to Bettina's children) the sentence was commuted to imprisonment in Spandau.[9] Kinkel escaped from Spandau with the help of Karl Schurz. It seems highly probable that Rebecka took the risk of delivering the money needed for Kinkel's escape. Karl Schurz stated that he received this sum from "the hand of a female relative of the famous Felix Mendelssohn Bartholdy." He met "a lady dressed in black, whose features I could just distinguish in the half-light. She was no longer young and not really beautiful, but there was great charm to her appearance." It is very possible this person was Rebecka, and the doubts existing on that score are too insubstantial to prove the contrary.[10]

There is no reason to think her marriage was not happy: Dirichlet was a kind and unpretentious man, even if his mathematics sometimes plunged him into silence. Thanks to him, Rebecka frequented a circle of university professors who suited her as well as the artistic world suited Fanny. Nevertheless, Rebecka had even fewer ways of expressing herself than her sister, and her numerous illnesses and nervous ailments would seem to indicate she suffered more and had no outlet for her feelings. Fanny and Rebecka shared the same destiny as women of great culture who were relegated to the home. They belonged to each other instead of belonging to their talents.

Florentina was christened on 12 March 1845, and everything was going so well that Fanny left for Rome to join her husband, enjoy her favorite city, and see her friend Charlotte Thygeson—only to find, when she arrived, that Wilhelm had fallen ill. The poor food and cold weather were held responsible. Once again, Fanny took charge of running the household in a healthy manner, complaining of the lack of vegetables in Italy. There was nothing but cauliflower, and the Hensels' Italian cook had no idea how to prepare it.[11] Wilhelm recovered and began painting again, and Fanny, as usual, rented a piano.

They returned to Florence on 20 May, passing through Perugia, and on 15 June the Hensels and Dirichlets set off north together. After leaving Pisa, the party followed the Italian coastline as far as Genoa, then turned inland to Milan, crossing the Alps via the Splügen pass. They then hurried on to Freiburg-im-Breisgau, where they were awaited by their great friends the Woringens; Felix and Paul also joined them for a grand family reunion that lasted six days. Next they followed the course of the Rhine to Mainz and Soden, and were welcomed there by Felix's family. Cécile was pregnant with her fifth child, Lili, who was born shortly afterward in Leipzig, Felix having resumed his position as head of the Gewandhaus Orchestra.[12]

This was Fanny's last major journey, and she and her family returned to Berlin on 2 August. Felix was now completely absorbed in the composition of his masterpiece *Elijah*, and whereas his life seemed to move forward with frenetic speed, Fanny's appeared to be reaching a point of equilibrium and fulfillment.

The Mendelssohns, however, could not remain indifferent to the social context: politics invaded every conversation. The word *Vormärz*, "before March"—that is, before the revolutionary days of March 1848—conveys the state of mind retrospectively deemed typical of these years in which people "felt" revolution coming. Likeminded people were drawn closer together; meeting Felix and Fanny in the restaurant of Bad Homburg on 17 July 1845, Varnhagen von Ense wrote in his diary: "I was delighted to meet them again. Being abroad illumines what is easily hidden at home: faithful and longstanding affection, based on long acquaintance and high esteem."[13] Varnhagen von Ense was a particularly dear friend of the Dirichlets, and he, of all their circle, came closest to militant activity. Fanny had less confidence in the republican ideal than did her sister. On the other hand, the absence of freedom was felt with equal frustration by the entire enlightened middle class. Even Fanny expressed bitter annoyance: "There is little to rejoice about in public life: an incredible passion for speculative swindling in the railways; the unspeakable wretchedness of the Silesian weavers which they're trying on all sides to remedy"; and, despite all these disorders, "the attempts of German universities to create humane and common relationships are punished by prison and the board of discipline; daily prohibitions; tentacular interventions by the government and police on all sides, except in the domains of public safety and morality."[14] A few months later she noted indignantly again: "God! What a lamentable edifice the Prussian state must be, if it really runs the risk of tottering each time three students constitute an association or three professors bring out a journal."[15] Fanny and her friends and kin were protesting against an authoritarian state that forbade individual liberties while protecting material gain at the expense of the poor.

In the nineteenth century the Prussian state did not control salaries or rents, and did not feel responsible for the wretchedness engendered by a barbaric capitalism.

There was another Mendelssohn whose existence is mentioned neither by Sebastian Hensel nor by biographers of Felix in the century following his death. This was Arnold Mendelssohn, born on 19 November 1817 in Neisse. Of the ten children born to Nathan Mendelssohn and his wife Henriette Itzig, Arnold was one of three who survived. He was thus doubly a cousin of the Mendelssohn Bartholdys: Nathan Mendelssohn, his father, was Abraham's youngest brother, and Henriette Itzig, his mother, was Lea Salomon's first cousin—a granddaughter of Daniel Itzig and the daughter of Elias Daniel Itzig and Marianne, *née* Leffmann.

Nathan and Henriette converted to Protestantism long before their marriage. The children of Elias Daniel Itzig were the first in the family to choose their religion: his elder son Julius Eduard received a Lutheran baptism in 1799,[16] and his daughters did so in the early 1800s.[17] Although a talented engineer, Nathan was the least wealthy member of his family, and so the rich banker Joseph helped pay for his nephew Arnold's medical studies. Arnold did valuable medical research, publishing an important work in 1845 on the relationship between the respiratory system and the circulatory and digestive systems. He practiced medicine in a hospital for poor people from Vogtland, in the weavers' district in Berlin. Being in permanent contact with poverty, he naturally developed social theories and socialist ideas. At the same time, he studied philosophy and soon came into contact with Ferdinand Lassalle.[18]

Lassalle had been introduced to Berlin society by Professor Boeckh, the friend and tenant of the Mendelssohns. Paul Heyse noticed Lassalle one day at one of Fanny's musicales: "One day I observed a man with chiseled features, extremely Jewish in appearance, whose countenance exhibited a forcefully authoritarian expression and cold irony. I asked Sebastian who was the owner of this astonishing face. He told me it belonged to Ferdinand Lassalle, a visitor introduced into the house by old Boeckh, who predicted a brilliant career in philology for him on account of his work on Heraclitus the Obscure."[19]

Lassalle acquired considerable influence over young Arnold Mendelssohn, who was seduced by the Hegelian rhetoric of this very young man with an answer to everything. Research of that era bore the imprint of Hegelian phenomenology, and in his own work Mendelssohn came to view illness not as a parasite but as a bodily phenomenon.[20] The two young men's relationship could have been confined to fascinating discussions on Hegelian dialectic and its effects on science, but in late 1845 Lassalle embroiled Arnold and his friend Alexander Oppenheim in the defense of Countess Hatzfeld. The countess was in the process of divorcing her husband, who wanted to despoil her totally. Oppenheim and Mendelssohn followed Count Hatzfeld's mistress, Baroness Meyendorf, to an inn, and stole from her a casket containing papers—for which mad deed they were obliged to take flight. Oppenheim surrendered to the police a few days later, but Arnold Mendelssohn, after traveling through England and Belgium, got as far as Paris where he asked Heinrich Heine for help. He stayed there until June 1847, becoming a student of Proudhon whose ideas he embraced completely. He contributed to the review *Spartakus*, edited by Gottfried and Johanna Kinkel.

On 11 September 1846, Varnhagen was still chatting gaily about this escapade in Fanny's drawing room:

At the Hensels' that evening; many people and a lot of music. I spoke at length to Boeckh, then had a serious discussion with Paul Mendelssohn about the new bank. Hensel and Dirichlet joined us and turned the conversation to the Hatzfeld story. Half jokingly, half seriously, I defended the three young men, comparing their action to that of Wilson, Hutchinson, and Bruce in freeing Lavalette. I discussed the idea of chivalrous behavior, throwing in the fever for dueling, and we had a very entertaining conversation, which greatly softened what had at first been a harsh judgment. Boeckh told us that Lassalle, who had approached him with a view to being admitted to the university, had spoken of new fragments of Heraclitus he claimed to have found; Boeckh viewed them with suspicion and that's why Lassalle never returned.[21]

Lassalle was definitely no longer in Professor Boeckh's good books.

Alexander Oppenheim, who went before the Cologne Assizes in November 1846, was acquitted of the charge of theft for personal gain: ascribed to a rich banker's son, the motive was plainly inconceivable. Arnold Mendelssohn then surrendered to the Prussian police on 2 July 1847, went before the Assizes, and was sentenced to five years of hard labor. No one could possibly have thought he would receive so harsh a punishment—especially after Oppenheim had been set free—or that matters would lead to so catastrophic a conclusion as a Mendelssohn being sent to prison by a court of law.

This event must have figured prominently in the Mendelssohn family's conversations, but those who survived Fanny and Felix made no reference to it in writing. We do know however that when Felix was returning from his final trip to England in 1847 he was stopped in Belgium on 11 May and had to give proof of his identity, having been mistaken for his cousin.[22] The general atmosphere smacked of rebellion and social dispute. As idealistic descendants of the eighteenth-century Enlightenment, convinced that scientific progress would lead to greater happiness for humanity, the Mendelssohns were very dismayed to see the misery engendered by the misuse of that progress, and the extent to which the rich managed to appropriate both authoritarian power and the conquests of science to strengthen their position.

Arnold Mendelssohn described how one day his first cousin Paul Mendelssohn-Bartholdy gave him a book by Lorenz Stein on socialism and communism in France and, observing his own luxurious room, remarked "I wonder what gives me the right to all that?" To which Arnold then replied: "Other people are beginning to wonder, too."[23] Paul, Arnold used to say, wanted to be a good man, and enjoyed making everybody realize how good he was. In Berlin, Arnold, who had a front-row view of poverty, could always count on the charity of his entire family, but he was revolted by their hypocrisy. His uncle Joseph was always ready to give him money and advice, yet when in 1844 Arnold asked for his help in founding a credit union so that the workers could take over their means of production—an idea Arnold would later study in more developed form with Proudhon— Joseph Mendelssohn retorted that such a form of production would never find a system of distribution. That did not prevent the injustice of the system from making itself felt on all sides, and it was becoming difficult to wear blinkers while simultaneously keeping a clear conscience.

Thanks to the intervention of Alexander von Humboldt, Arnold's five-year sentence of forced labor was commuted: he emerged from prison in 1849 and went into exile. He left Vienna, where he was suspected of taking part in the Hungarian revolt, and joined Hungarian refugees en route to Constantinople. He practiced medicine in Alexandrette, Aleppo, and Gazir. Pursued by the vengeful interference of the Prussian administration, Arnold placed himself under the protection of Lequeux, the French consul, and even thought of adopting French nationality. In October 1851, with the assistance of Lequeux and an Italian priest, he founded a hospital with twenty-two beds in Jerusalem, but they were forced to close it for lack of money. He crops up again in Rome, then in Tripoli after 1853. He died of typhus in May 1854 at Burjazid on the Persian border.[24]

Thus ended the existence of a Mendelssohn so thoroughly atypical as to have been carefully "forgotten" by his family. Yet his story deserved to be told; the letters he wrote his brother Wilhelm are now an important source of information for studying the Mideast as it was in the nineteenth century.

Fanny had just died when Arnold was arrested in July 1847. She knew only of the tragicomic adventures of this young man, whose story had created a sensation among the Berliners. Even if the Mendelssohns deplored the weakness of character of this too-easily influenced young relative, they could only be touched by his idealism and generosity. Without a doubt, Fanny felt concerned by Arnold's misfortunes. Yet the scandal implicated an entire family, all of whom wanted to be "models of moral conduct," as Wilhelm was to say about his wife, when lamenting her death.[25] Could one in the long term claim to be true to oneself while respecting despicable social rules? The ideals of the eighteenth century were disintegrating. Fanny would take her leave at a time when the notion that science would bring humanity peace and happiness was becoming questionable.

CHAPTER TWENTY-NINE

The First Publications

In this climate of revolt and social upheaval, Fanny decided to take the definitive step forward and begin publishing her work.

The garden had never been as beautiful as in the premature spring of 1846. Fanny enjoyed it all the more because its days were numbered:[1] there was some thought of selling this earthly paradise, perhaps to Count Pourtalès (1779–1861), master of ceremonies to the kings of Prussia, who lived as a tenant at 3 Leipziger Strasse from 1843 to 1850 with a retinue of nineteen people.[2] And the town, as it expanded, was threatening to cut new streets across the garden, showing not the slightest respect for the greater age of trees, nor for the fruits, and still less for the flowers.

For Fanny, everything was nonetheless going well and she felt very happy. She was also composing actively. She had just met a young man, the councilor Robert von Keudell, who, as she said in late July 1846, "keeps me breathless and in a constant state of musical activity, as Gounod used to do. He looks with great interest at each new thing I write and tells me if something is missing—and in general, he's right!"[3]

Robert von Keudell (1824–1903) came from a wealthy family and had embarked upon a diplomatic career; he was endowed with musical knowledge and talents that served him extremely well.[4] He possessed an excellent pianistic technique, "without being a virtuoso," as he put it,[5] and an excellent memory besides. He had devoted two years to studying music (1841–1842), concentrating on counter-point and Beethoven's sonatas. The two years he spent in almost daily contact with Fanny Hensel only added to his already firm grasp of the subject; thanks to this knowledge, he later became a close friend of Bismarck and his family. Bismarck, indeed, loved to hear music being played, saying it "spurred him in one of these two opposite direc-tions: the premises of war or those of romance."[6] Keudell had to rein in his own liberal ideas before the great statesman, but when ap-pointed ambassador to Rome in 1873 he played a role that was more artistic than political, and did not find another position in Berlin. He left the foreign service in 1887.

It was Keudell's influence that induced Fanny to take the decisive step, disobey the interdictions imposed by her father and brother, and publish her compositions. Her husband was still in agreement, Keudell was urging her to do so, and two publishing houses, Bote und Bock and Schlesinger, made her splendid offers: as a Berlin per-sonality and the sister of a famous musician, Fanny was a good prospect. Rebecka, who remained peevish and unsatisfied despite her good health and three children,[7] was living proof that the role of mother is not enough to fulfill a gifted woman. In any case, Fanny's maternal duties in regard to her sixteen-year-old son cannot have been very onerous by this time. The one remaining obstacle was, as usual, Felix. But had he repaid the confidence she had shown him when, as a little girl, she had ceded her superior position to him? On 9 July 1846 she addressed him on the subject of *Elijah*:

Once again an entire oratorio of yours is setting out into the world, and I don't know a note of it. When will it reach us? Actually I wouldn't expect you to read this nonsense now, busy as you are, if I didn't have to write and tell you something. Since I know in advance that you won't be pleased, I'll go about this very awkwardly. Laugh at me, if you like, but at the age of forty I'm as afraid of my brothers as I was of Father when I was fourteen—or rather, fear is not the right word, it's more that I wish to do right by you and everyone I love in every aspect of my life, and so when I know beforehand that this will not be the case, I feel *rather* uncomfortable. In a word, I'm be-ginning to publish. I have finally lent a well-disposed ear to Herr Bock's sincere professions of affection for my lieder, and to his favorable terms. And since I made the decision on my own initiative and cannot blame any-one in my family if annoying consequences result (friends and acquaintances have indeed been urging me for some time), then I can, on the other hand, console myself with the knowledge that I in no way sought out or occasioned the kind of musical reputation that might have brought me such offers. I hope I shall not disgrace you all, for I am no *femme libre*—still less, alas, *young* Germany. I hope *you* will in no way be bothered by this, for as you see, in order to spare you every possible unpleasant moment, I have proceeded entirely on my own, and I hope you won't think badly of me. If it succeeds, that is, if people like the pieces and I receive further offers, I know it will be a great stimulus to me, which I have always needed in order to create. If not, I shall be at the point where I have always been, and not be upset; and then if I were to work less, or stop working altogether, nothing would be lost by it either.[8]

Felix took more than a month to digest this letter. Fanny had considered every aspect of the matter and knew what she wanted, what she had always wanted. If Felix was displeased, and sorry he had never been able to help her, that was henceforth his problem. In remarking how afraid she had been of her father when she was fourteen, Fanny clearly indicates the importance of the letters Abraham had written her, asking her to make way for her brother; she also announces her intention of setting all her fears in perspective.

After careful thought, Felix eventually replied on 12 August with a letter that was somewhat ambivalent:

My dearest Fenchel, only today, just before leaving, do I, hard-hearted brother, get round to answering your kind letter and give you my professional blessing upon your decision to enter our guild. I give it to you now, Fenchel, and may you obtain satisfaction and joy from providing delight and joy to others; may you know only the pleasures of being a composer, and none of the miseries; may the public only send you roses and never sand; may the printer's ink never seem black or oppressive to you—in fact, I think there can be no doubt in the matter. Why did I not wish you this before? It's only because of the guild, so that I too could give you my blessing, as I now have.

The fellow-tailor
Felix Mendelssohn Bartholdy[9]

Fanny expected nothing more. On 14 August she wrote in her diary:"Felix has finally written to me and conferred his professional blessing in a very friendly way; I know that in his heart he doesn't like it, but I'm delighted that he's finally offered me a word of encouragement."[10]

It was to Felix's wife, Cécile, that Fanny sent her Opus 1, receiving in return the following letter: "Heartfelt thanks for the fine lieder which I so enjoyed—especially when Felix sang them to us quite nicely with his splendid voice. I did not, however, let him steal *Pale Roses* from me, even though I haven't sung it for more than a year; I consider it my song. Felix sang all the others, swearing revenge between each one. Mother says to tell you that she is delighted by them too, and not nearly as egotistical as Felix, who wanted to begrudge the world something so lovely."[11]

The family obviously knew the whole story. Fanny had already given Cécile a copy of *Pale Roses* (*Warum sind denn die Rosen so blass?*) in August 1838.[12]

And this was not the end of it! Fanny began by sending some figs and grapes from the garden, to plead her case, and enclosed another letter of announcement to her brother:

Why did I not address my lieder to you? I partly know the reason, and partly do not. I needed Cécile as a mediator because I had a kind of guilty conscience in regard to you. To be sure, when I consider that ten years ago I found it too late to publish and now I find it high time I did, it's all *rather* ridiculous, as is my long-held feeling of rebellion at the idea of beginning with an Opus 1 at my advanced age. But since you're so kind about it, I'm also going to confess how terribly self-important I've become, and that six four-part lieder are going to appear next, of which you scarcely know a single one. I would gladly have shown them to you, but you didn't come, and it doesn't work in writing. My Friday singers were happy to sing them, and sustained by the good advice at my disposal here, I took the trouble of making them as good as I was able. I shall take the liberty of sending Dr. Mendelssohn a copy.[13]

Fanny was laughing at her brother. Ten years earlier, it was Felix's unsympathetic attitude that had stopped her from publishing. Even in 1841, when full of enthusiasm for Josephine Lang's lieder,[14] she was glad to have discovered and appreciated them before finding out that Felix liked them too—otherwise she would not have known if she really did like them, or if she was simply echoing his thoughts.[15] Five years later, she could joke about it: Robert von Keudell had become more significant than the famous stranger, Felix Mendelssohn Bartholdy.

The fine weather, to which Fanny was always extremely sensitive, continued uninterruptedly that summer and certainly contributed to her good mood and energy. Rebecka was also feeling much better. Fanny wrote in her diary on 14 August:

The infinite well-being filling me this summer continues, as does the magnificent summer itself, and none of us has experienced one like it. This good mood is likely to make me selfish, for I have absolutely no wish to be disturbed in my well-being by some external worry, and often argue on the subject with Wilhelm, who has unfortunately retained from his sickness of last spring a nervous irritability that makes him ill at the slightest annoyance, or each time his pity is aroused, as occurs too often. The heat of the summer is doing him good too, however, but his flexibility at work has greatly diminished and he realizes this with some regret. Moreover, I am always working, and feel I am doing some things well; in harmony with the miracle of this splendid summer, this makes me inwardly and outwardly satisfied and happy as I have perhaps never been, except for a short time during our first visit to Rome.[16]

Robert and Clara Schumann were in Berlin that winter and got on very well with the family of their old friend Felix Mendelssohn; the Dirichlets made them very welcome, but it was with Fanny that Clara got along best, and her desire to become established in that city increased. "I have really taken a liking to Frau Hensel," wrote the famous pianist on 15 March 1847, "and feel particularly drawn to her musically; we are almost always in accord, and her conversation is always interesting. The only slight problem is that at first one has to get used to her rather abrupt way of behaving."[17] Clara had great admiration for Fanny's playing but did not accept her as a composer any more than she accepted herself: "Women as composers cannot deny themselves as women, and I say this of myself as much as of the others." Clara had hidden her considerable talent beneath her husband's bushel, composing fine works rather sparingly while Schumann was alive—for example, her Opus 17 trio for piano, violin, and cello—and not at all after he was dead. Her situation was the opposite of Fanny's, for Clara's father had intended his daughter to compose music and perform, rather as if raising a performing dog. Her refusal to submit to the destiny he planned for her may be viewed as a form of liberation from paternal authority. Fanny's path took her in the opposite direction, and both composition and publication were roads to liberty for her.

Despite their friendship, Fanny had some difficulty in truly accepting Robert Schumann's music. She heard a performance of *The Paradise and the Peri*, which was unfortunately so dismal that she wrote to Felix on 11 April 1846: "Peri quite impossible. I just can't acquire a taste for this Schumann."[18] Her approach to music remained very rigorous, and above all, devoid of sentimentality: that aspect of Romanticism was utterly foreign to her. Nor was she entirely convinced by Chopin's music. "I cannot deny that I find him too lacking in an important component—namely, power—to pass as a complete artist. His playing does not exhibit shades of grey, but shades of rose—if only it could bite a little! But he's a delightful man, and if you think his 'idylls' have given me no enjoyment, then either you're mistaken, or else I haven't expressed myself properly."[19] A little further on, she reveals the true substance of her opinion: "Does Chopin really have a feeling for scores by Handel, or music like *Saint Paul*? Haha, I don't think so." For Fanny, that said it all.

Sebastian recalled a Sunday musicale that Fanny and Clara shared between them. At once brilliant and comical, the evening was honored by the presence of the Radziwills.[20] The well-known singer Henriette Sontag, now Countess Rossi, wished strongly to hear Pauline Decker sing, but Decker had a cold and was in a bad mood and had decided not to open her mouth. Annoyed, Countess Rossi also opted for silence, so that Fanny and Clara had the whole evening to themselves. They were assisted by a very young singer, Melitta Berendt, who was astonished to find herself the star performer in the presence of two divas!

Johanna Kinkel was among the enthusiastic members of the *Sonntagsmusik* audience and has left a written record. Her opinion is all the more significant in that she was herself an accomplished musician:

Fanny Hensel's interpretive skills impressed me even more than the great voices I heard at her house. I was particularly impressed by her conducting. The spirit of a work was grasped in its most intimate texture, pouring forth to fill the souls of listeners and singers alike. A sforzando from her little finger would flash across our souls like an electric discharge, enrapturing us in quite a different way than a wooden baton tapping on a music stand.[21]

Fanny was in full possession of her art. Filled with the inner well-being acquired during the summer, she plunged into what was to be her masterpiece, a grand romantic Trio in D Minor for piano, violin, and cello. In four movements, it was not especially original in form. But Fanny endowed it with all her passion, animating it with lyrical phrases as broad and generous as the ideas of that time. In the first movement, which is in sonata form, she displays her mental rigor and the force of her inspiration; the second movement returns to the contrapuntal discipline that marks Fanny and Felix as students of Zelter and descendants of J. S. Bach; and the third movement is not a scherzo. Why would she need scherzos, when Felix wrote such good ones! No, the third movement is a lied, simple and direct, as her lieder always were. The fourth movement, in the form of a fantasy, suggests a Bach toccata with the bit between its teeth; after a grand, recitative-like phrase from the violin, it concludes with a clever reintroduction of the second theme from the first movement. The work's heroic side reminds us that Fanny, too, was a composer formed in oratorio and that for the Mendelssohns, religious inspiration could be transformed into Dionysian ardor.

She had composed the trio for Rebecka's birthday, 11 April. It was also to open her season of *Sonntagsmusik*, to be given in the garden room.[22] It met with great success.

The same day a *Landtag*, or Prussian Diet, finally assembled. Fanny, who belonged entirely on the opposition side, wrote in her diary: "Now politics is going to dominate the next period in time, and everything else will become impossible."[23] And she had almost reached the end of her diary when she concluded with these words: "Yesterday, the first scent of spring was in the air. It was a long winter, cold and full of snow, with famine and general misery; a winter filled with suffering. How can one possibly deserve to be among the few fortunate people in this world! At least I feel this keenly and with gratitude, and after I've had breakfast every morning with Wilhelm, and we both go to our respective work, then I feel my happiness with true emotion, thinking of the day to come and the day that is past."

Her compositions were appearing. Bote und Bock published *Sechs Lieder*, Opus 1 (1846); *Vier Lieder für das Pianoforte*, Opus 2 (1846), and some *Gartenlieder* (Garden Songs): *Sechs Gesänge für Sopran, Alto, Tenor und Bass*, Opus 3 (1847). Schlesinger then brought out her *Six Melodies for Piano* in two volumes, Opus 4 (1 through 3) and Opus 5 (4 through 6) (1847). She turned back to Bote und Bock to publish *Vier Lieder für das Pianoforte*, Opus 6; and *Sechs Lieder für eine Stimme mit Begleitung des Pianoforte*, Opus

7, dedicated to her sister. The opus numbers 6 and 7 appeared after her death.

In January 1847, critical reviews began appearing in the *Neue Zeitschrift für Musik*, the Leipzig paper that Robert Schumann had founded in 1835 and left in 1844. With the pedantic tone common to all the *Neue Zeitschrift*'s articles, the reviewer begins by remarking that the composer was a woman. The review of the Opus 2 appeared first, on 11 January 1847:

Of the four lieder presented here, whose outward appearance does not at all betray a woman's hand, but suggests an artistic study of masculine serious-ness, it seems to us that the final one is the freest and the most profound, whereas the others lack either a commanding individual idea, or else clear phrasing. We shall reserve a more detailed and general judgment until fa-miliar with other works by the composer.[24]

Clearly, the critic was amazed that the works were not entirely bad, but was obviously not going to grant a woman a smidgin of origi-nality. The same tendencies appear in the article on Opus 1 of 1 Feb-ruary 1847:

This volume of lieder is almost exactly like the one previously announced. As in the previous case, we here applaud the solid work, the correctness of the harmony, the elegant forms of the accompaniment—in a word, all the out-ward aspect; yet we are not gripped by the inner aspect, for we miss that feeling which originates in the depths of the soul and which, when sincere, penetrates the listener's mind and becomes a conviction. This is the sole re-proach that we can justly address to this work. Whoever is satisfied with a mu-sical representation that is outwardly correct will be entirely content here.[25]

The editor had no wish to be pleased, having seemingly decided not to allow himself to be touched by a woman's work, no matter how ir-reproachable it might be "outwardly." He is far from displaying the enthusiasm that Robert Schumann showed in 1837 for the lied *Die Schiffende*. Yet after all Felix's predictions concerning the "miseries of a composer" and the nonsense uttered in neighboring reviews, these papers are relatively encouraging. Fanny only needed more time for people to become convinced.

The following month, on 15 March, the review of her Opus 4 ap-peared, certainly penned by someone else:

The invention is neither striking nor new, but tasteful, pleasing, and free of that superabundance of feeling which is seemingly the dominant characteristic of our modern composers, though not when they are women.[26]

A woman who composed and published was like a trained monkey. No one would ever admit that she had individual creative power. If her music was full of feeling, she was accused of feminine sentimentality. If it was rigorously composed, she lacked inner depth.

On 14 May 1847 the review of the Opus 3 *Gartenlieder* was printed. The editor, who gave his name this time—Dr. Emanuel Klitzsch—compared them to other four-part lieder published at the same time. He began by praising lieder by Herr Hauptmann, before turning to Fanny's collection:

The lieder by Fanny Hensel, *née* Mendelssohn Bartholdy, stand out from many others of the same kind through their artistic concept, even if we find less individuality and discern in them the prevalence of a gracious, pleasant element rather than a powerful feeling drawn from deep conviction. The harmonic language is highly select and one cannot fail to recognize an artistic hand. All are bathed in a tender and poetic atmosphere, particularly no. 1 *Hörst du nicht die Bäumen rauschen* (Don't you hear the trees rustling) of Eichendorff and no. 3 *Im Herbste* (To autumn) by Uhland, in which we point to the central phrase *Ahnest du, o Seele, wieder* (Do you recognize, my soul) as being remarkably well-turned.[27]

Klitsch went on to tear apart the lieder by Wilhelm Herzberg.

In speaking of a lack of individuality and of an "artistic hand" one wonders if the *Neue Zeitschrift* supposed Felix had directed his sister. It scarcely matters: the articles in this journal express reservations about almost all the works reviewed, and Fanny knew very well that she would be criticized for being a woman. Criticism, we know, comes easily, and it would be interesting to hear compositions by Klitsch and other reviewers, the better to judge the "depths" of *their* souls. Apart from the "powerful feeling" which could not in any case emanate from a female pen, Fanny's work is credited with many qualities: it is rigorous, well-conceived, elegant, graceful, and evinces a fine harmonic sense. Certainly, it was worth continuing.

The week before this last review appeared, Fanny had suffered from violent nosebleeds, which had been assuaged by a new remedy.[28] On Friday 14 May 1847—the very day of the review—she made several social calls during the morning, returned feeling rather tired, and ate a hasty lunch. Instead of taking a nap, as was her habit, she immediately began preparing for the rehearsal of that coming Sunday's concert. She had her piano moved very near to the open door of the garden room and began rehearsing the choruses for *Walpurgis Night*, which was in the program.[29] It was very hot, and Fanny took off her shawl just as a fierce draft swept through the room. Suddenly her hands refused to obey her. Leaving the piano to another musician, Fanny went into a neighboring room to soak them in warm vinegar. "How beautiful it sounds," she said, listening as the rehearsal continued.[30] Thinking she had recovered, she tried to resume rehearsing, not wishing to send for a doctor to treat an illness she thought she knew well. But the paralysis returned, and this time became general. Recognizing her condition, Fanny said only: "It's a stroke, like Mother had." She then lost consciousness entirely, never to regain it. She died at eleven o'clock that same evening.[31]

Fanny certainly suffered from high blood pressure, and the hot and stormy weather of preceding days had probably exhausted her. The last few months had been particularly exciting, what with the meeting of the *Landtag*, the trio, her first publications, and her continuous activity. On her writing table was found her final lied, *Bergeslust* (Mountain Pleasure), composed the previous day to a text by Eichendorff. This lied is also one of her most joyful works, with a very rapid tempo. How her heart must have been beating as she wrote it! For the last time, Sebastian had watched her put the corner of a handkerchief in her mouth as she began composing.[32] That day she said to Wilhelm: "I'm happier than I deserve to be," to which Wilhelm had replied: "If you don't deserve to be happy, then who ever does?"[33]

The family's mourning was all the more painful for being so brutally sudden. That Sunday, in place of the concert, Fanny's coffin was put on view in the garden room, covered with flowers the Deckers had sent.[34] Wilhelm drew his wife on her deathbed, but was incapable thereafter of working in his studio. His final painting, a portrait of Friedrich Wilhelm IV commissioned by the Duke of Sutherland, remained unfinished.[35] Sebastian later went to live with his aunt Rebecka.

Felix was crushed—one might say, devastated—by this death, even more so than by his mother's death. He was incapable of returning to

Berlin for his sister's burial. This blow had smitten an exhausted man. Ever since the triumphal performance of *Elijah* in Birmingham on 26 August 1846, Mendelssohn had been unable to recover from the excessive fatigue caused by his creative activity. Robert Schumann, who saw him the following February, found him greatly changed. His travels and the incessant, vibrant activity he had pursued for years had overcome this man of thirty-eight. Did he, too, suffer from high blood pressure? The sudden deaths of his mother, father, and of his grandfather Moses had already given him cause to ponder the inherited family tendency. Fanny's death thus seemed to herald his own impending fate.[36]

He set off with his family to Baden-Baden, where he was joined by Paul, then on to Interlaken in an attempt to recover. Hensel joined them there. Felix composed a melancholy quartet in F minor and planned to start work on a series of large compositions. He had an oratorio in mind, *Christus*, to complete a trilogy, and an opera, *Loreley*, which he had promised to write for his favorite singer, Jenny Lind. In September he paid a short visit to Berlin and then returned to Leipzig. On 9 October he fainted at the piano, as Fanny had. Recovering, he prepared to depart for Vienna. In the meantime, he had given the prestigious Leipzig publisher Breitkopf & Härtel four opus numbers by Fanny: *Four Lieder for Piano*, Opus 8; *Six Lieder with Piano Accompaniment*, Opus 9; *Five Lieder with Piano Accompaniment*, Opus 10; and in conclusion the Trio for Piano, Violin, and Cello, Opus 11. All four appeared in 1850. On 28 October he had an attack that left him partly paralyzed,[37] then another on 1 November. He was still, however, able to converse with his brother Paul, who had arrived in haste. But on 3 November, after fearful headaches, he suddenly sat up in bed, cried out, and fell back on the pillow. Thereafter he remained unconscious for most of the time, declaring himself "tired, very tired" in response to Cécile's questions. He fell asleep until the following morning and died at twenty-four minutes past nine.[38] Once again, Hensel sketched him on his deathbed: it was 4 November.

His body was taken back to Berlin where he was buried beside Fanny in the cemetery of the Dreifaltigkeitskirche. Barely six months had separated their deaths.

The Circle Broken

The Mendelssohn family was henceforth broken and scattered, bereft of its center and its poetry. Sebastian did not become an artist. He fell seriously ill after his uncle's death and went to live with his aunt Rebecka as soon as he recovered. On 18 March the following year, when Sebastian wanted to join the barricade erected in front of his secondary school, the Dirichlets promptly locked him in his room. The next morning as he crossed the city, Sebastian saw scenes of devastation: corpses being removed on litters, his barricade overturned with dead bodies sprawled across it. The Dirichlets had saved his life. Imagine Rebecka's despair, if her sister's son had been shot because she had allowed him to go out! Sebastian lived through the period of madness that follows any revolution, graduated, and decided to become a landowner. He bought a property in Grossbarthen, in Eastern Prussia, and married Julie von Adelson (1836–1901) who, like Fanny, had converted in her childhood. The couple had five children.

The climate in East Prussia did not, however, suit Julie Hensel, who had contracted malaria,[1] and so the family returned to Berlin where Sebastian became director of the association for the city's markets. The administration of the German Building Company put him in charge of constructing the grand hotel Kaiserhof, which opened in 1875; Sebastian remained its manager until 1880. He was also director of the Deutsche Baugesellschaft until 1889. Ousted by a reversal on the stock exchange, Sebastian then withdrew into his private world, content to live as an enlightened connoisseur. Published in 1879, his book *Die Familie Mendelssohn* met with an immense success that lasted until World War I. Sebastian also wrote a biography of his professor, Carl Witt, and some stories for his children, which he illustrated himself. After Sebastian's death his elder son, Paul Hensel, published his memoirs under the title *Sebastian Hensel: Ein Lebensbild aus Deutschlands Lehrjahren* (Sebastian Hensel: Portrait of a Life during Germany's Formative Years).[2] And why indeed would a man of such pronounced artistic talent devote himself to farming and administration, had he not wanted to create a new Germany? Had he not wished to serve his country by demonstrating that Germans were not simply dreamers, but could also be practical? His cousin Walter Dirichlet, himself a gifted painter, also chose a career in agriculture.

Wilhelm emerged from his grief in March 1848 and, ever faithful to the royal family, went on serving it as bodyguard and general factotum. He assumed command of a troop of four hundred artists who banded together to form a battalion in the national guard. Once again Wilhelm was in his element, bearing arms. His interest in politics lasted beyond the revolution of 1848. Although not always taken entirely seriously, Wilhelm was always greatly loved on account of his kindness and good humor. His devotion to Fanny never wavered. In November 1861 he was mortally injured while trying to save the life of the victim of a traffic accident. Rushing to his bedside, his sister Luise attempted to convert him to Catholicism—in vain. Wilhelm remained faithful to the religion of his wife and his prince, and died on 26 November 1861, having remained a Lutheran from birth. He was buried beside the body of his wife, who thereafter rested between her brother and her husband. Wilhelm belonged to the race of beings who never throw anything away, and Sebastian spent three weeks sorting out his papers, which were in an indescribably chaotic state. He then spent years bringing order to a collection of more than a thousand portraits, and the countless letters that enabled him to write his book about the Mendelssohn family.

In 1851 Paul Mendelssohn-Bartholdy sold the house at 3 Leipziger Strasse to the Prussian government for the sum of 100,000 thalers. The government made it the seat of one of its parliamentary assemblies, the *Herrenhaus*, or high chamber, where the aristocrats sat. To make way for it, the garden house and concert room were demolished. For some time an attempt was made to save the yew trees in the garden—those final traces of a certain Berlin legend, the dream of a midsummer night. The house was demolished in 1898, and rebuilt in 1899 and 1903. It was spared by the bombs of World War II, subsequently becoming home to the German Democratic Republic's Academy of Science.[3]

After the death of the mathematician Gauss (1777–1855), Dirichlet took over his chair at Göttingen and went to live there with his family. Initially desperate at having to leave Berlin, Rebecka soon established a pleasant circle of friends and music lovers whom she "nourished with the crumbs of our past glory."[4] Dirichlet went to spend the summer of 1858 in Switzerland and came back with a heart condition. While he was still recovering, Rebecka died suddenly, as her brother and sister had done, on 1 December 1858 at the age of forty-seven. Dirichlet soon followed her, dying a few months later on 5 May 1859.

Paul had to live through these calamities. When Felix died, he took his sons to live with him, while Felix's daughters stayed with their mother at their grandmother's home in Frankfurt. Cécile died six years after Felix, on 25 September 1853. Paul also took charge of Rebecka's daughter Flora after her parents died. This curious caretaking arrangement, by which Felix's young sons were separated from their mother and sisters so soon after their father's death, led to some hostility, particularly between Felix's eldest son, Carl, and Paul, whose conservative ways the young boy found intolerable. Carl (1838–1897) became a historian, distinguishing himself as a specialist in Greek antiquity. He taught at the universities of Heidelberg and Freiburg and with his uncle Paul published one of the first volumes of Felix's letters, but this task occasioned family friction. Carl became mentally ill in 1874 and ended his days in an asylum.

Felix's second son, Paul (1841–1880), resisted his uncle's wish that he pursue a career in commerce, for he wanted to become a chemist. After serving in the army as an officer in 1866 and again in 1870–1871, he did in fact become director of an aniline factory. He, too, died very young. Carl and Paul's younger brother Felix only survived their father by a few years.

Felix's daughters married. Marie (1839–1897) married Victor Benecke and Lili (1845–1910) married Adolf Wach, with whom she had three sons and three daughters. Rebecka's second son, Ernst, died at the age of twenty-eight in 1868; her daughter Flora married

Wilhelm Baum, a union that produced two sons and four daughters.

After the death of Joseph Mendelssohn in 1848, the Mendelssohn Bank was managed by Joseph's son Alexander and his nephew Paul Mendelssohn-Bartholdy. It continued to thrive; their sons continued the tradition and were raised to noble rank, Franz von Mendelssohn (1829–1889) in 1888 and Ernst von Mendelssohn-Bartholdy (1846–1909) in 1896.

The name of Mendelssohn had undergone numerous transformations. Henceforth there would be both Mendelssohns and von Mendelssohns. Felix's sons took the name of Mendelssohn Bartholdy, without a hyphen (his daughters took their husbands' names); Paul's children kept the hyphen; and the descendants of Ernst were called von Mendelssohn-Bartholdy.[5]

Unlike his brother and his sisters, Paul Mendelssohn-Bartholdy suffered a slow and painful death, following a long illness of which the details are unknown.

The continuation of the Mendelssohn story is the saga of a prominent, extremely bourgeois family that retained from its forbears a great respect for art and science. It was thus unthinkable for them to portray their ancestors in any but rosy colors, mostly out of filial respect but also to solidify the social standing of the Mendelssohn name. Sebastian Hensel never mentions the latent antisemitism surrounding his parents and grandparents, and he enhances all the family relationships. The same year that *Die Familie Mendelssohn* was published, the Berlin historian Treitschke's remark that "Jews are our misfortune" also appeared in print. Academics such as Mommsen, Virchow, and the Mendelssohns' old friend Droysen protested against this slander,[6] but antisemitism was spreading virulently in every milieu. Sebastian could not dream of portraying Jews—especially converted Jews—as anything but angels.

The composer Arnold Mendelssohn (1855–1933), nephew of the doctor and son of his brother Wilhelm (1855–1933), once observed: "The Mendelssohn family's attitude to Uncle Arnold and Aunt Dorothea is typically Jewish: nobody must think of them."[7] But was this really Jewish, or merely bourgeois? Although Aunt Dorothea had scandalized her contemporaries, she was not definitively banished by her family and her country. People spoke and thought of her. It was only in the second half of the nineteenth century that efforts were made to euphemize everything "indecorous." After being dragged to the top of Mount Vesuvius, Fanny had written that once or twice she'd been so afraid her heart almost fell into her trousers[8]—actually adding, "had I been wearing them." Sebastian omitted this last sentence, which was too daring for the Victorian era.

Sebastian Hensel's account of his family ends with the deaths of his mother and his uncle in 1847, as if propagating a myth that had to be perpetuated indefinitely with a few beautifications and a few lies through omission. He had to demonstrate that a family that had emerged from the ghetto could be integrated into German society by following an absolutely perfect path. One of the more "perfect" elements in his narrative is Fanny's submission to her womanly destiny, even though she had possessed a talent recognized by all.

Presented in the context of patriarchal idealism, this family legend could perhaps be transformed into the story of a struggle against maternal omnipotence. Fanny gave up trying to express her talent, in favor of a more temporal power: what she really wanted, and eventually took, was her mother's place. Lea's death had less impact on the family than Fanny's death. Well might Wilhelm be devastated at losing her, for she had taken over everything. "All business dealings, running the house, managing the family fortune, my education—my mother saw to all those things," wrote Sebastian.[9] Alfred de Reumont, who had been a guest of the Hensels around 1845, was harsher in his criticism: "Fanny Hensel was not an agreeable person, and she dominated her good-natured husband—who did not lack talent as a painter and poet, but was forever forging puns—in a manner that could even be wounding. But she was full of wit and talent."[10] It is also possible to imagine a Fanny who in her heart of hearts wanted Felix to be guided by her thoughts and live the life she might have had. In this case omnipotence would reside in the idea of possessing the Other. Felix, of course, took flight once Fanny had given up her rights of seniority, but he did not keep his part of the bargain. He did not sustain his sister through his own life. This might explain his feelings of guilt when Fanny died—publishing several of her works after being so opposed to publication, before punishing himself through his own death.

Death took Fanny just as she was beginning to confront the outside world—just as she was emerging from the domain of subterranean maternal power. Felix, at this juncture, wanted to give up traveling and concerts in order to stay at home and compose. Fanny was not yet forty-two; Felix was thirty-eight. Their deaths, occurring so early in life, create a feeling of anguish, like a malediction. It would be terribly easy to say that Fanny died of happiness, or because she did not want to live through her happiness—or even that she died to punish herself for having pursued a forbidden activity. By that line of reasoning, Felix died of guilt—or of despair at having lost his shadow and his counterpart. The field of psychoanalytical interpretation is open to all manner of speculation. But the Mendelssohns were determinedly rational beings passionately in love with life and music. They did not seek out darkness and vexation; on the contrary, they kept themselves busy, enjoyed being alive, and always tried to see the better side of things.

This was especially true of Fanny. Despite the unjust oblivion to which her work has been relegated, her destiny would certainly have been far worse had she allowed herself to sink into torpor. She managed to forge a fine life for herself—an achievement she owed only to herself and to her own temperament and energy. The pleasures of action and creativity were things she actually experienced. She knew how to give, and how to make her loved ones happy. At the end of her life she had reached an enviable state of equilibrium and personal fulfilment, and that is more than can be said of Felix. Admittedly, she lacked public approbation, but that is a deficiency shortly to be remedied, for her works are emerging from the darkness. A growing number of German and American musicians—particularly female musicians—derive great pleasure from presenting to a delighted, astonished public an artist whose work will soon be famous. This book, originally published in French, is her first biography. Many things remain to be said about Fanny and her music, but others will have to say them and perform her work, so that she may live again through being interpreted and studied in many different ways. There is much ground to make up here, yet I am proud to have pointed the way, and it is my hope that I have made people love her. Now it is up to the public to approach Fanny's music and rescue it, at last, from the anonymity of her private life.

Notes

INTRODUCTION

1. Virginia Woolf 1929, 48f.
2. Elisabeth Badinter 1986.
3. When women were lucky enough to get an education, that is.
4. The intention here is not to establish a list of creative female composers and musicians. For that purpose, consult Patricia Adkins Chiti's *Donne in Musica*. 1982. Rome: Bulzoni.
5. Cécile Lowenthal-Hensel 1970.
6. Rudolf Elvers 1984, 11.
7. Unfortunately the paintings have all disappeared. We have only photographs or pencil sketches of them. The illustrations in this book are some of the pencil sketches.

CHAPTER ONE

1. Sebastian Hensel 1879, vol. 1, 1f.
2. *Juden in Preussen* 1981, 136.
3. Honoré Gabriel Mirabeau, "Sur Moses Mendelssohn, sur la réforme politique des Juifs," in *La Révolution française et les Juifs* 1968, vol. 1, 2.
4. Robert Badinter 1989, 65–74.
5. *Juden in Preussen* 1981, 86. Actual nickname in German was Sokrates der Aufklärung (Socrates of the Enlightenment).
6. Gotthold Ephraim Lessing 1982, 71f. (*Nathan der Weise*. First ed., 1778; first performance, Weimar, 1801, revised by Schiller).

7. Sebastian Hensel 1879, vol. 1, 37.
8. Heinrich Heine n.d., vol. 2, 373.

CHAPTER TWO

1. Carola Stern 1990, 100.
2. Carola Stern 1990, 327. It seems Dorothea translated Germaine de Staël's novel, *Corinne ou l'Italie*, although Friedrich Schlegel's name was given as editor and translator.
3. Friedrich Schlegel was the somewhat Bohemian brother of August Wilhelm Schlegel (1767–1845) who, with Tieck, Fichte, Novalis, and Schelling, formed the first wave of German Romantics. In 1803 Wilhelm became tutor to Madame de Staël's children and influenced her as she was writing *De l'Allemagne*. A better balanced man than his brother, he held a position at the University of Bonn after 1818. Just as it links the Humboldt brothers, posterity views the "Schlegel brothers" as having founded a form of Romanticism.
4. Sebastian Hensel 1879, vol. 1, 55.
5. Jean-Jacques Anstett 1975, 73.
6. Henriette certainly spent much of her time in Vienna at Fanny von Arnstein's house, but it has not been proved that she was Henrietta Pereira-Arnstein's governess. Had this been the case, it would certainly have been mentioned often in the correspondence between Henrietta Pereira-Arnstein (1780–1859) and her Berlin cousin Lea Mendelssohn, who was Henriette Mendelssohn's sister-in-law.
7. Karl August Varnhagen von Ense 1840, vol. 7, 127.
8. Christian Lambour 1986, vol. 6, 50.
9. *Juden in Preussen*, 108.
10. Cecil Roth 1943, 326.
11. The reception of the Huguenots, driven from France in 1685 when the Edict of Nantes was revoked, was very different: the Grand Elector was said to have sold his silverware to support them. See *Juden in Preussen*, 116.
12. *Juden in Preussen*, 80f.
13. *Juden in Preussen*, 130.
14. *Juden in Preussen*, 83.
15. Wilhelm Treue 1972, vol. 1, 34.
16. Sebastian Hensel 1879, vol. 1, 78.
17. The youngest and least famous of the Mendelssohn brothers, Nathan (1782–1852), was talented in technical matters; he became an industrialist, then a tax collector and administrative controller in Berlin.
18. In 1778 David Friedländer (1750–1834) and Isaac Daniel Itzig (1750–1806), Fanny Hensel's great uncle on her mother Lea's side, founded the

Jüdische Freischule or Jewish Free School, where Jewish children were taught western culture in German and Hebrew. See *Juden in Preussen*, 146.
19. Wilhelm Treue 1972, vol. 1, 32.
20. Wilhelm Treue 1972, vol. 1, 34.
21. Jacques Attali 1985, 38–39.
22. Sebastian Hensel 1879, vol. 1, 79. Lea's use of French and her florid, precious style are typical of the letters she exchanged with Henriette: Francophilia is everywhere apparent.
23. Sebastian Hensel 1879, vol. 1, 80.
24. Sebastian Hensel 1879, vol. 1, 42–43.
25. Alexander Boyd 1979, vol. 3, 10.

CHAPTER THREE

1. Stendhal 1962, 330.
2. Klaus Lindner 1981, 22.
3. The Grand Duchy of Prussia was situated further to the east. Its capital, Königsberg, is now known by the Russian name of Kaliningrad. Memel, now known as Klapeida, is in Lithuania.
4. Klaus Lindner 1981, 25.
5. Klaus Lindner 1981, 29.
6. Heinrich Friedrich Karl, Reichsfreiherr von und zu Stein (1757–1831), was a Prussian statesman who abolished serfdom in 1807 and was driven from power by Napoleon. He then became counselor to Czar Alexander I At the Congress of Vienna, he championed a German federal state, opposing Metternich.
   Karl August von Hardenberg (1750–1822)—Prince von Hardenberg after 1814—was also a Prussian statesman. Successor to Stein, he became chancellor in 1810. He shared Stein's determination to modernize the state, and introduced free trade, the secularization of the holdings of the clergy, and the emancipation of the Jews (1812). With Wilhelm von Humboldt, he represented Prussia at the Congress of Vienna. He lost his political influence after the Congress of Karlsbad in 1819.
7. Neu-Voigtland was added to the 102 districts.
8. *Juden in Preussen* 1981, 157.
9. Quoted by Hannah Arendt in *Rahel Varnhagen* (1986), 156.
10. To be sure, the Jews owed their emancipation to the French Revolution, but the Revolution had borrowed its ideas from Moses Mendelssohn via Mirabeau and Christian Wilhelm Dohm. Racism is not logical.
11. *Juden in Preussen* 1981, 176.
12. Hannah Arendt 1986, 163–164.

13. See Chapter 2 note 18.

14. Its ideas were revived later (1854, in Breslau, Jüdisch-Theologisches Seminar; 1872, in Berlin, Hochschule für die Wissenschaft des Judentums). See also *Juden in Preussen* 1981, 163.

15. Henriette Mendelssohn (1776–1862), née Meyer, sister of Recha's husband.

16. Felix Gilbert 1975, 79.

17. Carola Stern 1990, 265.

18. Wilhelm Treue 1972, 33.

19. Manfred Kliem 1990, 127.

20. Sebastian Hensel 1879, vol. 1, 95.

21. Ilse Rabien 1990b, 158–159.

22. Christian Lambour 1986, 77.

23. Cécile Lowenthal-Hensel 1981, 77.

24. Sebastian Hensel 1879, vol. 1, 82–83.

25. Eva Weissweiler 1985a, 15.

26. Sebastian Hensel 1879, vol. 1, 85f.

27. Varnhagen von Ense 1859, vol. 9.

CHAPTER FOUR

1. Hugh Macdonald 1988, vol. 2, 701.

2. Alexander Boyd 1979, 25.

3. Christian Lambour 1986, vol. 6, 55.

4. Felix Gilbert 1975, 33–34.

5. Carola Stern 1990, 305.

6. Willi Kahl 1949–1967, vol. 1, col. 1691–1693.

7. Sebastian Hensel 1879, vol. 1, 90–91.

8. Sebastian Hensel 1879, vol. 1, 97. I have deduced this from Sebastian's indication: *24 Bach'sche Präludien*.

9. Sebastian Hensel 1879, vol. 1, 98.

10. Christian Lambour 1986, vol. 6, 67.

11. Felix Gilbert 1975, 38.

12. Christian Lambour 1986, 67.

13. Eduard Devrient 1869, 14–15.

14. Felix Mendelssohn 1961, 31f.

15. Victoria Sirota 1981, 20.

16. Alexander Boyd 1979, 44. Letter of 14 October 1833 to Mary Alexander.

17. Christian Lambour 1986, 56. Letter of 15 August 1820. The song mentioned, "Friendship," is in a private collection.

CHAPTER FIVE

1. Martin Geck 1949–1967, vol. 14, col. 1208.
2. Marc Vignal 1985, 567.
3. Klaus Siebenhaar 1981, 446.
4. Georg Schünemann 1928, 138.
5. Nele Hertling 1981, 249.
6. Philippe Beaussant 1985, 383. Orazio Benevoli's authorship is now considered doubtful. The creator of this work had taken the baroque extravagance of polychoral style so far as to write a mass for fifty-two voices!
7. Nele Hertling 1981, 250f.
8. Nele Hertling 1981, 250f.
9. Georg Schünemann 1928, 140.
10. Nele Hertling 1981, 250f.
11. Georg Schünemann 1928, 148.
12. Gotthold Frotscher 1923–1924, 431–448.
13. Peter Nitsche 1980, 16–17.

CHAPTER SIX

1. Karl Mendelssohn Bartholdy 1974, 190–191.
2. Depos. Berlin Ms 3, Mendelssohn Archives, Berlin Staatsbibliothek Preussischer Kulturbesitz.
3. *Grundbass* is a musical term. Did Abraham use it intentionally? Sebastian Hensel 1879, vol. 1, 89–90.
4. *Calendrier musical universel* 1972, vol. 9, 2428.
5. Nele Hertling 1981, 261.
6. Eduard Devrient 1869, 20.
7. Jacob uses the term *Musikus*, which is more pejorative than *Musiker*.
8. Sebastian Hensel 1879, vol. 1, 93.
9. Compare Lea's letter in Chapter 3.
10. Felix Gilbert 1975, xvi.
11. Eric Werner 1980, 28, and Felix Gilbert 1975, xxxv.
12. Eduard Devrient 1869, 11.
13. Jane Austen 1981, 216.
14. Compare with the repulsive remarks made by Karoline von Dacheroden, Wilhelm von Humboldt's wife. After calling on Hinni Mendelssohn in Paris, Wilhelm von Humboldt wrote to his wife: "I called on her in Paris, for I never desert either my childhood friends or Jews." (Hinni was both these things.) Karoline von Humboldt replied: "You boast of never deserting the Jews, and that is the one fault I find in you. . . . In their degeneracy, their ma-

terialism, and the cowardice that stems from this materialism, the Jews are the disgrace of mankind." Henriette Herz and Henriette (Jette) Mendelssohn considered Karoline von Humboldt their friend and protector. The Humboldt brothers always did their best to conceal Karoline's racist sentiments, and on several occasions Alexander von Humboldt used his influence with the government to thwart discriminatory measures against the Jews. (In Felix Gilbert 1975, xxxvi. From *Wilhelm und Karoline von Humboldt in ihren Briefen*, vol. 5. Edited by Anna von Sidow. 209, 219–220.)

CHAPTER SEVEN

1. Karl Friedrich Schinkel (1781–1841) was a painter and architect and an essential figure in German art at the beginning of the nineteenth century. Thanks to his connection with Wilhelm von Humboldt and Chancellor von Hardenberg, in 1815 he became the secret engineer-in-chief of the Prussian government. He was responsible for several monuments in which the classic Prussian style of architecture is pleasantly combined with each building's practical, utilitarian aspect (the Schauspielhaus, 1818; the Altes Museum, 1822–1836; the Bauakademie, 1832–1836). He designed countless sets and costumes, both for theater and opera, that clearly favored the romantic Gothic style. (Klaus Siebenhaar 1981, 455).
2. Sebastian Hensel 1879, vol. 1, 106; Cécile Lowenthal-Hensel 1979b, vol. 3, 181f.
3. Sebastian Hensel 1879, vol. 1, 107.
4. Cécile Lowenthal-Hensel 1979a, vol. 3, 176.
5. The hill on which Schinkel erected a monument, in 1821, to the Wars of Liberation—a monument crowned by an iron cross—took the monument's name, Kreuzberg, later retained in the Kreuzberg district of Berlin.
6. Carola Stern 1990, 275.
7. Clemens Brentano (1778–1842), Romantic author and Catholic mystic, wrote novels and short stories. In 1801 he began a friendship with Achim von Arnim (1781–1831). The two took part in the activities of the Heidelberg Romantics (1805), and Achim married Brentano's sister Bettina (1785–1859), herself a socially committed writer from the 1830s on. In 1818 Clemens Brentano publicly avowed his attachment to the Catholic faith.

A Romantic poet and legal writer, Joseph von Eichendorff (1788–1857) studied in Heidelberg, where he met Brentano and the von Arnims in 1825. A Prussian civil servant between 1816 and 1844, he subsequently devoted himself to literature.
8. Sebastian Hensel 1879, vol. 1, 110.

Adalbert von Chamisso (1781–1838) was an expatriate French aristo-crat who moved to Berlin in 1796. He became a German Romantic poet close to E. T. A. Hoffmann, and undertook scientific research and travels.

The author Johann Ludwig Tieck (1773–1853) belonged to the Ro-mantic circle in Jena (1799–1800), along with Novalis, the Schlegel broth-ers, Schelling, and Fichte. A critic, dramatist, and novelist, he translated Shakespeare with August Wilhelm von Schlegel.

9. Gelobt sei Jesus Christus (Praise be to Jesus Christ).

10. Since 1821, Luise Hensel had been governess to Count Stolberg's chil-dren in Sondermühlen. See also Felix Gilbert 1975, 60.

11. Felix Gilbert 1975, 57f.

12. Compare Goethe's "Mignon": *Im dunkeln Laub die Goldorangen glühn* (Amid dark foliage glows the gold of oranges).

13. Eva Weissweiler 1985b, 20.

14. Cécile Lowenthal-Hensel 1979b, vol. 3, 189. Theodor Fontane (1819–1898), novelist and journalist, appeared at the barricades in 1848. He was famous for his *War Diaries* and his *Travels Through the Brandenburg March*.

15. *Mendelssohn-Studien*, vol. 3, end pages. Cécile Lowenthal-Hensel 1981, 26.

16. *Alter Fritz* (Old Fritz): popular nickname for Friedrich II.

17. Cécile Lowenthal-Hensel 1979b, 188.

18. Felix Gilbert 1975, 51.

19. Cécile Lowenthal-Hensel 1981, 106.

20. Sebastian Hensel 1879, vol. 1, 116. See also note 22.

21. Cécile Lowenthal-Hensel 1981, 14f.

22. Sebastian Hensel 1879, vol. 1, 115f.

23. An entirely different destiny fell to Fanny Lewald (1811–1889), a pio-neer of feminism. Governed by a despotic Prussian father, Fanny Lewald stopped attending her school for well-brought-up young ladies at the age of thirteen and devoted herself to more typically feminine pursuits such as sewing and the piano, for which she did not have Fanny Mendelssohn's inclination. Freed from marriage when she became a widow, she obtained her father's permission to publish thanks to the intervention of her uncle, the editor August Lewald, who without her knowing had had her letters pub-lished in the form of travel narratives. Her major works date from before 1848 and concern the education of women, Jewish emancipation, and the democratization of art and politics. In 1854 she married her second hus-band, a historian of art and literature named Adolf Stahr, with whom she was very happy. In Berlin she had a salon frequented by Gutzkow, Varnhagen von Ense, Berthold Auerbach, and Theodor Fontane. She lost interest in politics after 1848 but continued to write essays advocating equality for women in education and work, such as her *Osterbriefe für die Frauen* (Easter

Letters for Women) of 1863 and her *Für und wider die Frauen* (For and Against Women) of 1870. See also Renate Möhrmann 1985, 409–410. It would not have been to Fanny's advantage to leave her own house: the situation of other women of her social class was even worse.

CHAPTER EIGHT

1. See also Chapter 5.
2. Marcia Citron 1987, xlix; Rudolf Elvers 1984, 11.
3. Rudolf Elvers (1984, 17) points out that Felix's letters must have been strictly controlled by Lea whenever the boy wrote to a stranger, resulting in a rather affected style—*altklug*—as befitted a child prodigy.
4. Fanny calls Felix her son in other letters as well, a convention not unusual in their time—see Suzanne to Figaro!

Karl Begas (1794–1854) was a German artist who specialized in historical and biblical paintings.
5. A play on words involving *hoffen*, to hope; *Hofmeister*, major-domo; and *Hausmeisterin*, mistress of the house. Fanny is referring to herself, of course. At that time puns were an established feature of German culture. The Romantics' admiration for Shakespeare was certainly responsible in part, but we should not forget that repeated alliteration gives German Romantic literature its distinctive character and identity. Brentano's works are an unending series of alliterations (*Gockel, Hinkel, und Gackeleia*, for example), as are the librettos of Wagner's *Ring*. For a race in search of its identity, plays upon the sound and meaning of words have the added advantage of being untranslatable!
6. Fanny Casper, née Levin: possibly the wife of Dr. Johann Ludwig Casper (1796–1864), who wrote the libretto for *The Two Nephews*, a youthful composition by Felix.
7. Eva Weissweiler 1985a, 25f.
8. Rudolf Elvers 1984, 19.
9. Susanna Grossmann-Vendrey 1969, 16f.
10. *Der Mensch denkt und Gott lenkt.* (Man proposes and God disposes; literally, Man thinks and God directs.)
11. Compare with another letter in which Abraham expresses himself in the same terms, in Chapter 6.
12. *Gutissimo.*
13. Eva Weissweiler 1985a, 30f. When Fanny writes that the finale must be dated by Goethe's native city, she means that Felix should write on the music that it was composed in Weimar on that date.
14. Wilhelm Pfannkuch 1949–1967, col. 1078–1090.
15. Dirk Scheper 1981, 286f.

16. Rudolf Elvers 1984, 21. The Elephant is Weimar's oldest inn.

17. Undated manuscript, transcriber's handwriting, in the Goethe Museum in Düsseldorf.

18. Manuscript in the Staatsbibliotek Preussischer Kulturbesitz, Berlin. Sebastian Hensel (1879, vol. 1, 102) published it with changes.

19. Autograph manuscript, Mendelssohn Archives, MAMs34, 17–18.

20. Sebastian Hensel 1879, vol. 1, 102f.

21. Susanna Grossmann-Vendrey 1969, 17.

22. Sebastian Hensel 1879, vol. 1, 129.

23. Karl Mendelssohn Bartholdy 1871, 21.

24. Cécile Lowenthal-Hensel 1981, 43–44. Letter of 30 July 1823.

25. Cécile Lowenthal-Hensel 1981, 21, note 13.

26. Cécile Lowenthal-Hensel 1981, 43.

CHAPTER NINE

1. Christian Lambour 1986, vol. 6, 86. Letter of 4 August 1821.

2. Hinni: nickname of Henriette Meyer, wife of Joseph Mendelssohn.

3. Christian Lambour 1990, 176.

4. Aunt Jette this time, Abraham's sister.

5. Sebastian Hensel 1879, vol. 1, 132.

6. Susanna Grossmann-Vendrey 1969, 18.

7. Quotation from Goethe (Mignon in *Wilhelm Meister*).

8. Sebastian Hensel 1879, vol. 1, 122f.

9. Rudolf Elvers 1984, 251.

10. Ferdinand Hiller 1878, 29.

11. Susanna Grossmann-Vendrey 1969, 10f.

12. Rudolf Elvers 1984, 26.

13. Marianne Mendelssohn (1799–1880), née Seeligmann; Lea's niece. Married to Alexander, second son of Joseph Mendelssohn.

14. Sebastian Hensel 1879, vol. 1, 124f.

15. Jane Austen 1981, 82.

16. Christian Lambour 1990, vol. 7, 177. Benny Mendelssohn, the elder son of Henriette and Joseph Mendelssohn, embarked on several educational trips through Switzerland and Italy, beginning in 1820.

17. Cécile Lowenthal-Hensel 1981, 78–79.

18. Sebastian Hensel 1879, vol. 1, 123.

19. Biedermeier denotes a bourgeois style of art and living in Germany, Scandinavia, and various central European countries between 1815 and 1848. It may also have petty-bourgeois, philistine connotations. See Gunter Pulvermacher 1980, vol. 2, 695.

20. Sebastian Hensel 1879, vol. 1, 133.
21. Sebastian Hensel 1879, vol. 1, 128.
22. Mendelssohn Archives, Berlin MAMs 32, 44–45.

CHAPTER TEN

1. Sebastian Hensel 1879, vol. 1, 135.
2. Sebastian Hensel 1879, vol. 1, 136.
3. This sonata is mentioned in a letter to Felix of 29 October 1821 and quoted in Marcia Citron 1987, 371. According to Dr. Elvers the sonata is privately owned. See Rudolf Elvers 1975, vol. 2, 215–220.
4. Cécile Lowenthal-Hensel 1981, 128.
5. Eduard Devrient 1869, 19.
6. Eduard Devrient 1869, 10f.
7. Sebastian Hensel 1879, vol. 1, 137.
8. Sebastian Hensel 1879, vol. 1, 140.
9. Felix Mendelssohn Bartholdy 1888, 1–2.
10. C. Moscheles 1972, 93–95.
11. Felix Mendelssohn Bartholdy 1888, 3.
12. Malla Montgomery-Silfverstolpe 1912, 275–276.
13. Susanna Grossmann-Vendrey 1969, 15f.
14. Susanna Grossmann-Vendrey 1969, 21. Letter of 6 April 1825. "Ce garçon est riche, il fera bien, il fait même déjà bien, mais il dépense trop de son argent, il met trop d'étoffe dans son habit."
15. Eva Weissweiler 1985a, 36.
   André-George Louis Onslow (1784–1852), French composer of English origins who devoted himself to chamber music.
   Antonin Reicha (1770–1836), French composer and theoretician born in Bohemia.
   For the Mendelssohns, the word *Schuhu* meant "terribly critical."
   The "thirty-three variations" are the *Diabelli Variations* in C major, Opus 120.
16. By Johann Sebastian Bach, evidently.
17. Pierre-Alexandre Monsigny (1729–1817) composed comic operas. Sebastian Hensel calls him Montigny.
18. Sebastian Hensel 1879, vol. 1, 148–149.
19. *Jessonda*: opera by Louis Spohr (1784–1859).
   Alceste: opera by Christoph Willibald von Gluck (1714–1787).
   Samson: oratorio by George Frideric Handel (1685–1759).
   Sapupi was the Mendelssohns' nickname for Spontini.
20. Adolf Bernhard Marx (1795–1866), composer and music theorist.

21. Pierre Rode (1774–1830), French violinist and acquaintance of the Mendelssohn Bartholdys.
22. Eva Weissweiler 1985a, 39.
23. Eva Weissweiler 1985a, 43. The words in italics are in French in the original text.
24. Sebastian Hensel 1879, vol. 1, 150–151. The words in italics are in French in the original text.
25. Cécile Lowenthal-Hensel 1990, vol. 7, 141f.
26. Eric Werner 1980, 63.
27. Sebastian Hensel 1879, vol. 1, 141.
28. Cécile Lowenthal-Hensel 1990, 143.
29. Michael Cullen 1982, vol. 5, 48f.
30. Sebastian Hensel 1879, vol. 1, 155f.
31. Sebastian Hensel 1879, vol. 1, 152.
32. *Gartenzeitung*, 21 August 1826, 6. Mendelssohn Archives, Berlin.
33. Herbert Kupferberg 1977, 154.
34. Sebastian Hensel 1879, vol. 1, 154.
35. Quotation from *Faust*: "Und alles ist zerstoben."
36. Eric Werner 1980, vol. 2, 128.
37. Sebastian Hensel 1879, vol. 2, 262.
38. It is difficult to enumerate them, because three of Fanny's manuscript notebooks are privately owned. See also Rudolf Elvers 1975, vol. 2, 215–220.
39. *Die Hochzeit des Camacho* (Camacho's Wedding), Opus 10.
40. Sebastian Hensel 1879, vol. 1, 159
41. Sebastian Hensel 1879, vol. 1, 181.

CHAPTER ELEVEN

1. See Karl-Heinz Köhler 1980, vol. 12, 137.
2. Although Alexander von Humboldt states this to be so in one of his letters, Mendelssohn researchers have questioned the assertion. See also Peter Honigmann 1990, vol. 7, 39–76.
3. Later Dorothea Schlegel and Rahel Varnhagen.
4. On loyalty in friendship, see Chapter 6, note 14.
5. Sebastian Hensel 1879, vol. 1, 43; Cécile Lowenthal-Hensel 1981, 130.
6. Sebastian Hensel 1879, vol. 1, 181–182.
7. Sebastian Hensel 1879, vol. 1, 213.
   Philipp August Boeckh (1785–1867) was a longtime friend of the Mendelssohns, as well as their tenant. He was a philologist specializing in antiquity and had been a professor at the University of Berlin since its beginning.

8. Theodor Schieder, "Johann Gustav Droysen," in *Neue Deutsche Biographie*, vol. 4, 135.

9. Cécile Lowenthal-Hensel 1981, 91.

10. Therese Devrient 1905, 251–252.

11. *Juden in Preussen* 1981, 206.

12. *Juden in Preussen* 1981, 27.

13. Lea, wife of City Councilor Bartholdy.

14. Cécile Lowenthal-Hensel 1981, 86.

15. Sebastian Hensel 1879, vol. 1, 210.

16. Sebastian Hensel 1879, vol. 1, 213.

17. Johanna Kinkel (1810–1858), née Mockel, composed music, married Gottfried Kinkel in 1843, and took an active part in his revolutionary activities.

18. Cécile Lowenthal-Hensel 1981, 75.

19. Sebastian Hensel 1879, vol. 1, 210–211.

20. Sebastian Hensel 1879, vol. 1, 202.

21. Eduard Devrient 1869, 99.

22. In French in the original text.

23. Sebastian Hensel 1879, vol. 1, 210–211.

CHAPTER TWELVE

1. Herbert Kupferberg 1977, 158.

2. Michael Cullen 1982, vol. 5, 45–46.

3. Sebastian Hensel 1879, vol. 1, 212.

4. Giacomo Meyerbeer 1960–, 468.

5. Except in the theater, conductors did not stand with their backs to the audience at that time. Felix had his pianoforte (no question of using a harpsichord!) placed diagonally, between the two choirs. The first choir was thus behind him, but he was able to see the second choir and the orchestra. See also Georg Schünemann 1928, 161.

6. Sebastian Hensel 1879, vol. 1, 207f.

7. Georg Schünemann 1928, 162f.

8. Since 2 January 1827, the Singakademie had been installed in a large hall named after it. The need for this move had been apparent for some time, for the choir had become extremely important. King Friedrich Wilhelm III agreed to Schinkel's plans in 1821 (Schinkel's wife sang in the Singakademie choir), but the expense of the projected work and the various difficulties encountered by Zelter delayed construction until 30 June 1825. The Singakademie was deeply in debt but possessed the sole concert hall in Berlin worthy of the name, and rented it regularly for all manner of occasions (for

example, the course given by Alexander von Humboldt that Fanny attended). See also Nele Hertling 1981, 256.

9. Eduard Devrient 1869, 61–62. Concerning the gloves: Felix was short of pocket money, and Devrient lent him a thaler so that he could buy the yellow gloves of untanned leather needed to complement the attire of Bach's two devoted fans: blue frock-coat, white waistcoat, black silk scarf, and trousers. But Lea reproached Devrient for this ill-considered loan, claiming that Felix should learn to manage his affairs better: "One should not encourage young people in bad economic habits," said this attentive mother.

10. Forty years before, in the early days of the French Constituent Assembly—on 22 December and for some days after—Clermont-Tonnerre, Maury, Baumetz, and other speakers had proposed granting civil rights to Jews, Protestants, actors, and executioners. See also Robert Badinter 1989, 139f., and Jacques Hérissay 1922, 40f.

11. Martin Geck 1967, 36–39.

12. Georg Schünemann 1928, 162. The choir consisted of forty-seven sopranos, thirty-six altos, thirty-four tenors, and forty-one basses, including soloists.

13. Eduard Rietz (1802–1832), violinist and conductor, was one of Felix Mendelssohn's closest friends. He died young, of tuberculosis, and his death affected Felix deeply. His brother Julius (1812–1854), cellist and conductor, collaborated with Felix in Düsseldorf and then in Leipzig, and between 1874 and 1877 edited the composer's works.

14. Instead of C major.

15. Ferdinand David (1810–1873), violinist and a friend of Felix. He became leader of the Leipzig Gewandhaus Orchestra in 1836 and director of violin classes at the Leipzig Conservatory in 1843, the year it was founded.

16. Letter from Felix to his family, dated Hamburg, 14 April, containing instructions for the Passion: he wanted to try having the clarinets play in C an octave higher during the first chorale *O Lamm Gottes* (Lamb of God). See also Rudolf Elvers 1979, 60.

17. Same letter. On the *mich* of *der mich verräth* (he who betrayed me), Devrient was to sing C-double-sharp instead of C-sharp.

18. In the same letter, Felix asked if Devrient could preserve his score "from ink, glued paper, and red pencil: in short, de ore leonis" (from the lion's mouth). Apparently, Devrient did so.

19. Marcia Citron 1987, 385f.

20. Georg Schünemann 1928, 165f.

CHAPTER THIRTEEN

1. Georg Schünemann 1928, 166.
2. Fanny Hensel 1829–1834, 28.
3. Fanny Hensel 1829–1834, 32–34.
4. Fanny Hensel 1829–1834, 35.
5. Fanny Hensel 1829–1834, 36. Monday 13 April 1829.
6. Sebastian Hensel 1879, vol. 1, 264.
7. Cassiopea Records.
8. The C minor sonata has recently been edited by the Furore publishing house (fue 147), along with a sonata movement in E major, Allegro assai moderato, dated 1822. Autograph manuscripts in the Mendelssohn Archives, Berlin, MAMs 34, 66–76, and MAMs 32, 31–34.
9. Eva Weissweiler 1985a, 228–229.
10. Cécile Lowenthal-Hensel 1981, 27.
11. Felix Gilbert 1975, 76–77.
12. Eva Weissweiler 1985a, 60–61.
13. Eva Weissweiler 1985a, 80–83.
14. Eva Weissweiler 1985a, 54.
15. Fanny Hensel 1829–1834, 25.
16. Fanny Hensel 1829–1834, 27.
17. Fanny Hensel 1829–1834, 30.
18. Eva Weissweiler 1985a, 60–61.
19. Marcia Citron 1987, 396.
20. Sebastian Hensel 1879, vol. 1, 207. Letter to Klingemann of 22 March 1829.
21. Eva Weissweiler 1985a, 84–85.
22. To identify the characters, see legend for *The Wheel* (Figure 11).
23. Herbert Kupferberg 1977, 161.
24. Sebastian Hensel 1879, vol. 1, 302–303. Letter of 10 September 1829.
25. Compare with Schiller's *An die Freude* (Ode to Joy):
    Deine Zauber binden wieder / Was die Mode streng geteilt
26. Eva Weissweiler 1985a, 63.
27. Bodleian Library, Oxford, MDM c. 22.
28. Mendelssohn Archives, Berlin, Depos. Berlin 3.
29. Susanna Grossmann-Vendrey 1969, 32f.
30. Cécile Lowenthal-Hensel 1986, 12.
31. Rudolf Elvers 1984, 58.
32. Sebastian Hensel 1879, vol. 1, 271–272. Letter of 26 August 1829. Sebastian or Felix mistakenly wrote *Hören möcht'ich* instead of *Stören möcht'ich*.
33. Sebastian Hensel 1879, vol. 1, 243.

34. Beethoven, Trio in B-flat Major, Opus 97, "Archduke."
35. John Thomson in *Harmonicon*, 30 March 1830, 99, in Victoria Sirota 1981, 46.
36. Felix Mendelssohn Bartholdy, letter of 11 August 1829, Mendelssohn Archives, Depos. Berlin 3; Fanny Hensel 1829–1834, 49.

CHAPTER FOURTEEN

1. Eva Weissweiler 1985a, 91.
2. Sebastian Hensel 1879, vol. 1, 281–282.
3. Sebastian Hensel 1879, vol. 1, 298. Letter from Glasgow of 10 August 1829.
4. Fanny Hensel 1829–1834, 51.
5. Fanny actually wrote *am allerwenigsten* (all the less) instead of "all the more so," or "especially."
6. Sebastian Hensel 1879, vol. 1, 295–296.
7. Mendelssohn Archives, Berlin.
8. Michael Cullen 1982, 50.
9. Autograph manuscript published by Furore-Verlag, fue 124, Library of Congress, Washington D.C.
10. Fanny Hensel 1829–1834, 50.
11. The German transcription is unclear; possibly "on the blue sofa in the arms of your sisters."
12. Eva Weissweiler 1985a, 95f., Marcia Citron 1987, 429f.
13. Eduard August Grell (1800–1886), an organist and director of the Sing-akademie from 1853 to 1876.
14. Hensel's other sister, Minna (1802–1893), who was less fanatical than Luise.
15. *Polterabend*: "end of bachelor life." *Poltern* means "to kick up a noise." A peaceful *Polterabend* is thus a contradiction in terms.
16. Friedrich Philipp Wilmsen (1770–1831), the pastor who had officiated at Paul's confirmation.
17. Recha Meyer, Abraham's sister, a perpetual invalid.
18. Fanny Hensel 1829–1834, 51–52.
19. Therese Devrient 1905, 351.
20. Michael Cullen 1982, 49.
21. Sebastian Hensel 1879, vol. 1, 307.
22. In French in the original text.
23. Sebastian Hensel 1879, vol. 3, 248.

CHAPTER FIFTEEN

1. *Liederspiele.*
2. A youthful work, *singspiel,* composed in 1820.
3. Sebastian Hensel 1879, vol. 1, 301.
4. Opus 89, his last complete work for the theater. His opera *Loreley,* Opus 98, exists only in fragments.
5. Felix Mendelssohn Bartholdy 1909, 67.
6. Felix Mendelssohn Bartholdy 1909, 72.
7. Therese Devrient 1905, 313f.
8. Felix Mendelssohn Bartholdy 1909, 70.
9. *Les Deux Journées, ou Le Porteur d'eau,* known in English as *The Water Carrier,* an opera by Luigi Cherubini, dates from 1800. Born in Florence, Cherubini lived and composed in Paris under the Ancien régime until the Restoration, and was a famed director of the Paris Conservatory between 1822 and 1842.
10. Moritz Levy, according to Rebecka. (See also Felix Mendelssohn Bartholdy 1909, 67.) He seems to have been a friend of Abraham, possibly a banker, or perhaps a relation of Lea. (Marcia Citron 1987, 656.)
11. Felix Mendelssohn Bartholdy 1909, 72.
12. Felix's first light comedy, *Die Soldatenliebschaft,* was no longer considered.
13. Friedrich Ludwig Schroeder (1744–1816) was among the most significant eighteenth-century German actors (Berlin, Mannheim, Vienna). As a theater manager (Hamburg) and stage director, he played a major role in the German discovery of Shakespeare. See also Klaus Siebenhaar 1981, 457.
14. Moritz Ganz (1806–1868) and Leopold Ganz (1810–1869) were members of the Royal Orchestra of Berlin who took part regularly in Fanny's musical evenings. (See also Marcia Citron 1987, 646.) They should not be confused with Professor Eduard Gans (1798–1839), legal scholar and professor of law at the University of Berlin, who converted in 1825.
15. Felix Mendelssohn Bartholdy 1909, 68.
16. Rebecka took it upon herself to reproduce her sister's play on words, which is, of course, untranslatable: *Es war . . . Not an Mann-tius, darum geben wir Hermann Herr-Manntius* (We needed a man [*Mann-tius*] which is why we assigned Hermann to Herr Mantius). See also Felix Mendelssohn Bartholdy 1909, 68.
17. Therese Devrient 1905, 312–313.

CHAPTER SIXTEEN

1. Meyerbeer 1960–, 469.
2. Heinrich Heine n.d., vol. 5, 3.
3. The Russo-Turkish war lasted from March 1828 to September 1829.
4. The Parliament of Dublin had been abolished in 1800. The Irish question hinged as much on religious problems as on agrarian ones.
5. The English Parliament was passing the Catholic Emancipation Bill just as Felix arrived in London in April 1829.
6. Fanny Hensel 1829–1834, 15.
7. Manfred Hecker 1981, 123f.
8. Sebastian Hensel 1911, 3f.
9. In England, Caroline of Brunswick caused a scandal by wanting to be crowned at the same time as her estranged husband, William IV, in 1820. Public reaction favored the queen, indicating that the monarch's image should be that of a good family man. "Licentious habits were no longer acceptable. Marriage and family were fashionable." This accounts for the popularity of Queen Victoria and for Louis-Philippe's image as a middle-class king. See Catherine Hall 1985, vol. 4, 54–55.
10. The extra negative is in the original German.
11. Marcia Citron 1987, 425.
12. Sebastian Hensel 1879, vol. 1, 142.
13. Eduard Devrient 1869, 101.
14. Sebastian Hensel 1911, 29.
15. Cécile Lowenthal-Hensel 1981, 36–37.
16. Sebastian Hensel 1911, 13f.
17. Eduard Devrient 1869, 99–100.
18. Felix Gilbert 1975, 79. Letter from Hinni of 7 October 1830.
19. Felix Gilbert 1975, 144. Letter of 21 May 1847.
20. In 1824 Jacob Bartholdy waxed lyrical over the youthfulness of his sister Lea who, according to the portrait Wilhelm brought him, could not have been more than twenty-five! See Felix Gilbert 1975, 62. Letter of 31 January 1824.
21. Sebastian Hensel 1879, vol. 1, 307f.
22. Felix Mendelssohn Bartholdy 1909, 78. Friedrich Rosen (1805–1837) was an orientalist and a friend of Felix. Klingemann married his younger sister in 1845. (Felix Mendelssohn Bartholdy 1909, 36.)
23. Fanny Hensel 1829–1834, 62–63.
24. Fanny Hensel 1829–1834, 63.
25. Sebastian Hensel 1879, vol. 1, 198. Letter of 8 December 1828. Dirichlet was known to be rather reserved, but he adapted well to the Mendelssohn circle.

26. Therese Devrient 1905, 350.
27. Sebastian Hensel 1879, vol. 1, 388.
28. Gottlob Kirschner n.d., 749–750.
29. Sebastian Hensel 1911, 186. Carl Friedrich Gauss (1777–1855) was an astronomer, mathematician, and physicist.
30. Fanny Hensel 1829–1834; 4 March 1831.
31. Cécile Lowenthal-Hensel 1981, 76.
32. Marcia Citron 1987, 441.
33. Psalm 115 for soloists, chorus, and orchestra, Opus 31.
34. Peter Sutermeister 1979, 67–68.
35. Delphine von Schauroth (1813–1887): a pianist, later Delphine Handley. Felix dedicated his Concerto in G Minor, Opus 25, to her. Fanny would meet her in September 1839.
36. Sebastian Hensel 1879, vol. 1, 318–319. Letter from Munich of 11 June 1830.
37. Marcia Citron 1987, 434. Letter of November 1829.
38. Phyllis Benjamin 1990, vol. 7, 179f.
39. Fanny Hensel 1829–1834, 78; 26 May 1833.
40. Fanny Hensel 1829–1834, 78.

CHAPTER SEVENTEEN

1. Through Zelter's work, particularly.
2. Petra Wilhelmy 1989, 144f.
   Amalia Beer (1767–1854), née Wulff, was the mother of Jakob Liebmann Beer (1791–1864), who later changed his name to Giacomo Meyerbeer; and of Michael Beer (1800–1833), whose principal work, *Der Paria*, was a protest against intolerance.
3. Christoph Helmut Mahling 1980, 28f.
4. Fanny wrote *Männer* (men) and not *Menschen* (people).
5. Carl Möser (1774–1851) was artistic director (as we would now say) of the Royal Chapel and professor of the instrumental classes at the Royal Opera, the first level of the Berlin Conservatory. He arranged concerts with the opera orchestra and played chamber music. He had played in a quartet with Friedrich Wilhelm II, who was a cellist. See also Rudolf Elvers 1983, 33–34.
6. According to Berlioz, "The director-instructor of the military bands in Potsdam and Berlin . . . commanded a body of six hundred musicians." Berlioz used them for his concerts in 1841 and was delighted with them. In any case, he was referring mainly to the brass. See also Hector Berlioz 1969, 141f.

7. Fanny Hensel 1829–1834, 3–8.
8. Adolf Weissmann 1911, 180f.
9. Felix Mendelssohn Bartholdy 1882, 121. Letter of 22 February 1831.
10. John 16:21.
11. Felix Mendelssohn Bartholdy 1882, 297f.
12. Felix Mendelssohn Bartholdy 1882, 300. Friedrich Kalkbrenner (1789–1849), German pianist and composer, spent his entire artistic life in Paris and composed a vast quantity of salon pieces.
13. Eva Weissweiler 1985a, 221.
14. Fanny Hensel 1829–1834, 69; 1 January 1832.

CHAPTER EIGHTEEN

1. Rudolf Elvers 1984, 160. Letter of 15 June 1832: "denn ich habe lieb, was ich lieb hatte, nur noch mehr, und hasse vielleicht stärker, was ich nicht leiden konnte, und freue mich meines Lebens." (For I am even fonder of things I used to like, and perhaps hate even more strongly things I could not tolerate before, and am happy with my life.)
2. François Habeneck (1781–1849), French violinist and conductor. He led the Orchestre de la Société des Concerts du Conservatoire and brought Beethoven's symphonies to the Parisians. Berlioz mentions him often in his *Mémoires*.
3. Ferdinand Hiller 1878, 18.
4. Eric Werner 1980, 217f.
5. Like the critic Fétis, who had taken a dislike to him during his stay in London in 1829. See also Susanna Grossmann-Vendrey 1969, 35f.
6. It was said at the time in Berlin: "Only old Zelter doesn't weep at the news; he prefers to die of it." And Zelter bowed to the bust of Goethe with these words: "His Excellency naturally takes precedence, but I shall join him immediately." See Eric Werner 1980, 230.
7. Even Meyerbeer only succeeded in getting his opera *Robert le diable* accepted in an abridged version. The opera was first performed on 20 June 1832. See Adolf Weissmann 1911, 192.
8. Klaus Siebenhaar 1981, 454.
9. Adolf Weissmann 1911, 187. Eric Werner 1980, 256.
10. Letter to Klingemann of 4–6 February 1833. In Rudolf Elvers 1983, 34.
11. Marcia Citron 1987, 493. Letter of 8 March 1835.
12. Hannah Arendt 1986, 272.
13. Sebastian Hensel 1911, 185. Letter of 4 April 1855.
14. Herbert Kupferberg 1977, 154.
15. Fanny Lewald 1871, vol. 3 (Wanderjahre), 150–152.

16. Eric Werner 1980, 255–256.

17. What about Paul?

18. The correspondence of Goethe and Zelter between 1796 and 1832 was edited into six volumes by Friedrich Riemer. The first two volumes appeared in 1833 and the last four in 1834.

19. Jane Austen 1985, 210.

20. An allusion to the Wars of Liberation, during which Abraham and Joseph Mendelssohn had become wealthy, but they had also contributed to the war effort.

21. There are two possible readings of this phrase. Riemer's edition has *nicht beschneiden lassen* (to not have [his sons] circumcised), whereas the later edition of Geiger (Leipzig: Briefwechsel, three volumes, no date) has *etwas lernen lassen,* (to have him learn something). The latter version does not make much sense. See also Eva Weissweiler 1985a, 124.

22. *Eppes Rores,* Yiddish for *etwas rares* (something rare). Zelter employs the Yiddish expression ironically, with the result that he appears more vulgar than amusing.

23. Fanny's pen did not dwell gladly on vulgar intolerance.

24. Eva Weissweiler 1985a, 120f. Letter of 1 December 1833.

25. Johann Wolfgang von Goethe and Karl Friedrich Zelter 1833, vol. 2, 473: "Today in Heidelheidelheidelberg [sic] August Schlegel is marrying the quite charming daughter of Councilor Paulus's wife: I'm not at all pleased with him for this, for he's thrown in his lot with the old French-woman" (Madame de Staël). August Schlegel, Dorothea's brother-in-law, was tutor for many years to Madame de Staël's children and provided considerable assistance while she composed her famous essay *De l'Allemagne.*

26. Felix Gilbert 1975, 93–94. Letter of 9 November 1833.

27. Concerning Goethe's materialism, see also Thomas Mann 1947, 93f.

28. Fanny was probably thinking of the passage: "les sottises imprimées n'ont d'importance qu'aux lieux où l'on en gêne le cours; . . . sans la liberté de blâmer, il n'est pas d'éloge flatteur; . . . il n'y a que les petits hommes qui redoutent les petits écrits." (Follies that appear in print are only important in places where their circulation is impeded; . . . without the freedom to criticize, there can be no flattering praise; . . . only petty men fear petty-minded writing." Beaumarchais 1966, 303.

29. Eva Weissweiler 1985a, 140. Letter of 24 November 1834.

30. On the publication of *Goethes Briefwechsel mit einem Kinde* (1835), see also Milan Kundera 1990 and all the nasty things he had to say about the un-fortunate Bettina.

31. Marcia Citron 1987, 458. Letter of 27 February 1834. Duncker was the publisher of Goethe and Zelter's correspondence.

CHAPTER NINETEEN

1. Fanny Hensel 1829–1834, 89.
2. Rudolf Elvers 1975, 216–217.
3. Spelled both as Türrschmidt and Türrschmiedt. Possibly the daughter of August Türrschmiedt, who sang in the *Saint Matthew Passion*.
4. Marcia Citron 1987, 448. Letter of 23 November 1833.
5. *Semele*: opera by Handel that Felix had brought back from London. *Opferfest: Das unterbrochene Opferfest*, opera by Peter Winter (1754–1825), famous at that time. First performed in Vienna in 1796. Fanny had sight-read it for her Sunday concert, not having had time to rehearse it, and her audience had much admired her performance. They had been equally astonished to see her perform *Die Zauberflöte* from the orchestral score. (Marcia Citron 1987, 450. Letter of 1 December 1833.)
6. Fanny Hensel 1829–1834, 91; 10 January 1834. Kubelius was a musician who possessed an excellent ear.
7. Marcia Citron 1987, 451–452. Letter of 25 January 1834.
8. The Königstadt theater was founded at the request of Friedrich Wilhelm III, who wished to see a popular theater next to the Schauspielhaus. It opened on 4 August 1824, offering Viennese light comedies by Nestroy and Raimund, but also plays in the "dialect" of Berlin. The orchestra that accompanied the "couplets" provided musicians for the city's concerts. See also Dirk Scheper 1981, 291f.
9. Julius Amadeus Lecerf (1789–1868), composer and teacher at various private schools in Berlin between 1829 and 1843. See also Marcia Citron 1987, 656.
10. Overture in C Major, Fanny's sole purely orchestral work. This letter is the only one to provide a date for it, around 1832. Mendelssohn Archives, Berlin, MAMs 38, 39 pages.
11. Marcia Citron 1987, 468–469. Letter of 11 June 1834.
12. She wrote on page 103 of her diary on 3 July 1834: "It attained a perfection that will not be emulated for some time; Bader was particularly sublime, but all three of them swept each other along and their three fine voices formed an unforgettable torrent of sound."
13. In French in the original text.
14. The tenors Bader and Mantius and the bass, Busolt, belonged to the Royal Opera. Türrschmidt (who took part in the *Saint Matthew*) and Blano sang the alto parts in Fanny's choir.
15. Marcia Citron 1987, 493.
16. Sebastian Hensel 1879, vol. 1, 423.
17. Marcia Citron 1987, 470. Letter of 11 June 1834.
18. Marcia Citron 1987, 467. Letter of 4 June 1834.

19. A revolution in taste. (In French in the original text.)

20. In French in the original text.

21. Eva Weissweiler 1985a, 145–146f. Letter of 27 December 1834.

22. Marcia Citron 1987, 167. Letter of 2 January 1835.

23. Five cantatas for soloists, chorus, and orchestra that were never published.

24. Rondo brillant for piano and orchestra in E-flat Major, Opus 29.

25. We do not know which aria she is referring to; it either has disappeared or is privately owned.

26. Eva Weissweiler 1985a. Letter of 17 February 1835.

27. Virginia Woolf 1980.

CHAPTER TWENTY

1. Sebastian Hensel 1911, 14.

2. Fanny Hensel 1829–1834, 67; 4 October 1831.

3. Marcia Citron 1987, 447. Letter of 2 November 1833.
    Paul Heyse (1830–1914), poet, son of the Mendelssohns' former tutor Karl Heyse and his wife Julie Saaling.

4. Marcia Citron 1987, 450. Letter of 1 December 1833.

5. Sebastian Hensel 1911, 15. When she died, Fanny bequeathed her sisters-in-law sufficient money to ensure their independence: 300 thalers of annual income to each one, with the wish that they should live together, although this was not a condition of the will. If one of them died, the other was to receive 400 thalers of annual income. See also Felix Gilbert 1975, 146. Letter from Wilhelm to Luise of 28 May 1847.

6. Sebastian Hensel 1911, 15.

7. Marcia Citron 1987, 452–453. Letter of 28 January 1834.

8. Marcia Citron 1987, 471. Letter of 18 June 1834.

9. Sebastian Hensel 1911, 17.

10. Sebastian Hensel 1879, vol. 1, 385–386.

11. See also the beginning of Chapter 19.

12. Cécile Lowenthal-Hensel 1985a, 17.

13. Adolf Bernhard Marx 1859, vol. 2, 120.

14. Alexander Boyd 1979, 48.

15. Marcia Citron 1987, 484. Homeopathy was becoming acceptable; the idea that an illness could be treated with an infinitesimal dose of a remedy that caused symptoms in human beings similar to those of the disease had been recognized by Hippocrates and revived by Christian Friedrich Samuel Hahnemann (1755–1843).

16. Felix Gilbert 1975, 90f.

17. Heinz Knobloch 1987, 132. Varnhagen proposed in April 1834.
18. Marcia Citron 1987, 463.
19. Marcia Citron 1987, 467. Letter of 4 June 1834.
20. Heinz Knobloch 1987, 133.
21. As badly as possible. (In French in the original text.)
22. Marcia Citron 1987, 471. Letter of 18 June 1834.
23. Felix Gilbert 1975, 102–103.
24. Alexander Boyd 1979, 46. Letter of 7 April 1834.
25. Victoria Sirota 1981, 83. Letter of 21 July 1834 in Fanny and Sophie Horsley 1934, 97.
26. Marcia Citron 1987, 492. Letter of 8 March 1835.
27. Marcia Citron 1987, 496. Letter of 8 April 1835.
28. Marcia Citron 1987, 495. Letter of 8 April 1835.
29. Sebastian Hensel 1879, vol. 1, 398.
30. Victoria Sirota 1981, 85. Letter of 1 June 1835, Library of Congress, Washington D.C. *Les Femmes savantes*, play by Molière.
31. On the role played by sisters of famous men (Goethe, Thomas Mann, Musil, Nietzsche, Claudel, Chateaubriand), see Eugénie Lemoine-Luccioni 1976, 114–124.
32. Sebastian Hensel 1879, vol. 1, 401–402. Letter of 10 July 1835.
33. Annals of the Société libre des beaux-arts, vol. 4 (1836), 49–66.
34. Sebastian Hensel 1879, vol. 1, 402–403.
35. Giacomo Meyerbeer 1960–, 468. Letter of 7 July 1835.
36. Sebastian Hensel 1879, vol. 1, 403.
37. Sebastian Hensel 1879, vol. 1, 403.
Sarah Austin (1793–1867) was a writer and a remarkably good translator of German and French works (especially scientific ones). She was one of the Misses Taylor whom Felix had spent time with during his first visit to England in 1829. See also Cécile Lowenthal-Hensel 1986, 61.
38. Sebastian Hensel 1879, vol. 1, 406.
39. Sebastian Hensel 1911, 1.
40. Marcia Citron 1987, 497. Letter of 8 October 1835.
41. Cécile Lowenthal-Hensel 1981, 27. After Fanny's death, Minna went to join her sister in Cologne. Between 1851 and 1876 she took care of an orphanage; for this activity she was decorated with the Luisenorden ((Order of Queen Luise) in 1874 and earned a pension from the king in 1876.
42. Sebastian Hensel 1879, vol. 1, 422.
43. Franz Hauser (1794–1870), Czech baritone, sang at the Leipzig Opera from 1832 to 1835, then at the Berlin Opera during the 1835–1836 season, among other places. He retired from the stage in 1837, became a singing teacher in Vienna, and then in 1846 became director of the Munich Conservatory which had just opened; he left this position in 1864. See also Mar-

cia Citron 1987, 648–649.
44. Marcia Citron 1987, 502. Letter of 18 November 1835. Fanny included in the program *Liebster Gott, wann werd' ich sterben* (Dear God, when shall I die), BWV 8, and *Herr, gehe nicht ins Gericht* (Lord, go not to judgment), BWV 105.
45. Sebastian Hensel 1879, vol. 1, 423.
46. Sebastian Hensel 1879, vol. 1, 424.

CHAPTER TWENTY-ONE

1. Marcia Citron 1987, 505.
2. Felix Mendelssohn Bartholdy 1875, 114.
3. Rudolf Elvers 1979, 170. Letter of 15 July 1834. Elvers 1979, 191. Letter of 30 June 1836.
4. Marcia Citron 1987, 196f. Letter of 1 January 1836.
5. See also Chapter 16.
6. Marcia Citron 1987, 510. Letter of 4 February 1836.
7. Paul's first letter to the Corinthians, 14:34.
8. Rudolf Elvers 1984, 190. Letter of 28 March 1836.
9. Sebastian Hensel 1879, vol. 2, 8.
10. Sebastian Hensel 1879, vol. 2, 10.
11. Elise Polko 1869, 68–69.
12. Sebastian Hensel 1879, vol. 2, 10f.
13. Sebastian Hensel 1879, vol. 2, 11.
14. Sebastian Hensel 1879, vol. 2, 45–46. Letter of 15 June 1836.
15. Marcia Citron 1987, 513–514. Letter of 30 July 1836. In the original text, Fanny complains about being accompanied by *Alevin*, a French expression meaning "fresh fish"—beginners.
16. Marcia Citron 1987, 517. Letter of 28 October 1836.
17. Marcia Citron 1987, 521. Letter of 22 November 1836.
18. Sebastian Hensel 1879, vol. 2, 45.
19. Marcia Citron 1987, 529. Letter of 2 June 1837.
20. Letter of 7 March 1837; Mendelssohn Archives, Berlin, Depos. Berlin 3.
21. Felix Mendelssohn Bartholdy 1909, 214. Letter of 30 April 1837.
22. Marcia Citron 1987, 527. Letter of 13 April 1837. Fanny wrote *Der abermalige Unfall*, which suggests there were many.
23. Marcia Citron 1987, 529. Letter of 2 June 1837.
24. These lieder are in an album belonging to Cécile dated 1844, in the Bodleian Library, Oxford, MDM b. 2.
25. Marcia Citron 1987, 529f. Letter of 2 June 1837.

26. Sebastian Hensel 1879, vol. 2, 54. Letter of 5 October 1837.

27. Sebastian Hensel 1879, vol. 2, 48. Letter of 2 June 1837.

28. Sebastian Hensel 1879, vol. 2, 55.

29. Marcia Citron 1987, xlix.

CHAPTER TWENTY-TWO

1. Sebastian Hensel 1879, vol. 2, 53.

2. Sebastian Hensel 1879, vol. 2, 4; Marcia Citron 1987, 509. Letter of 4 February 1836.

3. Marcia Citron 1987, 246–247. Letter of 13 January 1838.

4. Marcia Citron 1987, 539. Letter of 15 January 1838.

5. Pieter Hubert Ries (1802–1886), violinist and composer from Berlin, member of the Königstadt theater orchestra in 1824 and of the court orchestra from 1825. See Marcia Citron 1987, 668.

6. Marcia Citron 1987, 539. Letter of 15 January 1838.

7. Sebastian Hensel 1911, vol. 2, 7.

8. Marcia Citron 1987, 549. Letter of 6 January 1839.

9. Marcia Citron 1987, 538. Letter of 15 January 1838.

10. Marcia Citron 1987, 539. Letter of 15 January 1838.

11. Marcia Citron 1987, 524. Letter of 2 February 1838.

12. Marcia Citron 1987, 524. Letter of 2 February 1838.

13. Sebastian Hensel 1879, vol. 2, 56.

14. Marcia Citron 1987, 545. Letter of 21 February 1838.

15. Letter of 12 February 1838; Mendelssohn Archives, Berlin, Depos. Berlin 3.

16. In French in the original text.

17. Letter of 13 November 1835; Mendelssohn Archives, Berlin, Depos. 3.

18. Victoria Sirota 1981, 91–92.

19. Marcia Citron 1987, 503. Letter of 18 November 1835.

   Camille Marie Pleyel (1811–1875), French pianist. Professor at the Brussels Conservatory from 1848 to 1872.

20. Sigismond Thalberg (1812–1871), a particularly acrobatic Swiss virtuoso. Gave concert tours in Europe and the United States after 1830. Considered Liszt's rival.

21. Sebastian Hensel 1879, vol. 2, 46.

22. Sebastian Hensel 1879, vol. 2, 47.

23. Sebastian Hensel 1879, vol. 2, 47.

24. Marcia Citron 1987, 549f. Letter of 6 January 1839.

25. Christoph Helmut Mahling 1980, 74f.

26. Christoph Helmut Mahling 1980, 72.

27. Zimmermann was a violinist who had revived Möser's quartet concerts. See Christoph Helmut Mahling 1980, 46.

28. Charles de Bériot (1802–1870), Belgian violinist and composer, husband of the singer Maria Malibran who was the sister of Pauline Viardot-García.

29. Sebastian Hensel 1879, vol. 2, 57.

30. Sebastian Hensel 1879, vol. 2, 57f.

31. Cécile Lowenthal-Hensel 1975, vol. 2, 206.

32. Cécile Lowenthal-Hensel 1986, 15.

33. Sebastian Hensel 1879, vol. 2, 65.

34. Felix Gilbert 1975, 122f. Letter of 22 September 1838 from Wilhelm and Fanny Hensel to Luise Hensel.

35. Sebastian Hensel 1879, vol. 2, 65. Letter of 9 October 1838.

36. Sebastian Hensel 1879, vol. 2, 70–71.

37. Cécile Lowenthal-Hensel 1986, 68.

38. Marcia Citron 1987, 555. Letter of 26 February 1839.

39. Marcia Citron 1987, 548. Letter of 14 December 1838.

40. Sebastian Hensel 1911, 18.

41. Today known as Swinovjscie, outer harbor of Szczecin (Stettin).

42. Sebastian Hensel 1879, vol. 2, 75.

43. Sebastian Hensel 1879, vol. 2, 74. Letter of 1 July 1839.

44. Yvonne Knibieler 1991, 362.

45. Napoleon of peace. (In French in the original text.)

46. Sebastian Hensel 1879, vol. 2, 78–79.

47. Sebastian Hensel 1879, vol. 2, 87.

CHAPTER TWENTY-THREE

1. Sebastian Hensel 1911, 20.

2. Sebastian Hensel 1911, 21.

3. Sebastian Hensel 1879, vol. 2, 88; taken from Fanny's diary. The architect Leo von Klenze (1784–1864) had been put in charge of building the "Valhalla."

4. Marcia Citron 1987, 561. Letter of 23 September 1839.

5. Sebastian Hensel 1879, vol. 2, 91. Letter of 27 September 1839. Hohenschwangau castle was the work of the architect Joseph Daniel Ohlmüller (1791–1795).

6. Sebastian Hensel 1911, 47–48.

7. Sebastian Hensel 1879, vol. 2, 92. Letter of 27 September 1839.

8. Sebastian Hensel 1911, 21.

9. Sebastian Hensel 1879, vol. 2, 96. Letter of 27 September 1839.

10. Sebastian Hensel 1879, vol. 2, 97. In French in the original text—had Fanny read Diderot?

11. Sebastian Hensel 1879, vol. 2, 99.

12. Sebastian Hensel 1879, vol. 2, 99.

13. Sebastian Hensel 1879, vol. 2, 100f. Letter of 13 October 1839.

14. Sebastian Hensel 1911, 24.

15. Sebastian Hensel 1879, vol. 2, 109.

16. Sebastian Hensel 1879, vol. 2, 107.

17. Sebastian Hensel 1879, vol. 2, 111, from Fanny Hensel's diary.

18. Sebastian Hensel 1879, vol. 2, 114, from Fanny Hensel's diary.

19. Sebastian Hensel 1879, vol. 2, 116f. Letter of 28 November 1839.

20. The Danish sculptor Bertel Thorvaldsen (1768 or 1770–1844) spent part of his life in Rome (from 1797 to 1819 and again from 1821 to 1838). Influenced by the German archeologist Johann Joachim Winckelmann (1717–1768), he became a leading figure of Neoclassicism.

21. Sebastian Hensel 1911, 22.

22. Sebastian Hensel 1879, vol. 2, 117. Letter of 28 November 1839.

23. Susanna Grossmann-Vendray 1969, 44.

24. Marcia Citron 1987, 562f. Letter of 1 January 1840.

25. Sebastian Hensel 1911, 47.

26. The painter Jean Auguste Dominique Ingres (1780–1867) spent many years in Italy. A student of J.-L. David, he won the Prix de Rome in 1801 and lived at the Villa Medici from 1806 to 1810. He settled in Rome until 1821 and then in Florence until 1824, returning to Rome as director of the Académie de France from 1835 to 1842.

27. Sebastian Hensel 1879, vol. 2, 118f. Letter of 18 December 1839.

28. Sebastian Hensel 1879, vol. 2, 120f. Letter of 8 December 1839.

29. Sebastian Hensel 1879, vol. 2, 126. Letter of 30 December 1839.

30. Sebastian Hensel 1879, vol. 2, 128. Letter of 4 February 1840.

31. Sebastian Hensel 1879, vol. 2, 131. Letter of 25 February 1840.

32. Marcia Citron 1987, 567. Letter of 4 March 1840.

33. Sebastian Hensel 1879, vol. 2, 138–139. Letter of 25 March 1840.

CHAPTER TWENTY-FOUR

1. Sebastian Hensel 1879, vol. 2, 139–140. *Reisetagebuch*, 5 April 1840.
   Horace Vernet (1789–1863) painted battles and scenes from Oriental life. Director of the Villa Medici from 1829 to 1835.

2. Sebastian Hensel 1879, vol. 2, 139–140.

3. Everything degenerates in human hands. (In French in the original text.) Sebastian Hensel 1879, vol. 2, 142–143. *Reisetagebuch*.

4. Sebastian Hensel 1879, vol. 2, 146–147.
5. The enormity of it! (In French in the original text.) Sebastian Hensel 1879, vol. 2, 156. *Reisetagebuch*, 3 May 1840.
6. Sebastian Hensel 1879, vol. 2, 145. *Reisetagebuch*.
7. Charles Gounod 1886, 101–102.
   Charles Gounod (1818–1893) was considered the pioneer of the "renaissance" in French music.
8. Sebastian Hensel 1879, vol. 2, 146. *Reisetagebuch*.
9. Sebastian Hensel 1879, vol 2, 146. *Reisetagebuch*.
   George (Ange) Bousquet (1818–1854), composer, music critic, and conductor; won the Prix de Rome in 1838. See also *Le Ménestrel* 1875, 324.
   Charles Dugasseau (1812–1885) was a student of Ingres. A landscape and genre painter and collector, he became curator of the museums of Le Mans and exhibited his work regularly in Paris between 1835 and 1878. (See also Michèle Bordier-Nikitine 1985, 300–329.) The Hensels did not really appreciate the school of Ingres.
10. Sebastian Hensel 1879, vol. 2, 153.
11. The Concerto in D Minor.
12. Sebastian Hensel 1879, vol. 2, 149–150. *Reisetagebuch*, 23–26 April 1840.
13. Sebastian Hensel 1879, vol. 2, 155. *Reisetagebuch*, 2 May 1840.
14. Sebastian Hensel 1879, vol. 2, 158. *Reisetagebuch*, 8 May 1840.
15. Sebastian Hensel 1879, vol. 2, 160. *Reisetagebuch*, 13 May 1840.
16. Charles Gounod 1886, 109–110.
17. Martin Cooper 1980, vol. 7, 580–591.
18. Marcia Citron 1987, 570. Letter of 10 May 1840.
19. Sebastian Hensel 1879, vol. 2, 161.
20. Susanna Grossmann-Vendrey 1969, 45–46.
21. Sebastian Hensel 1879, vol. 2, 166. Letter of 20 May 1840.
22. Sebastian Hensel 1879, vol. 2, 165–166. *Reisetagebuch*, 17 May 1840.
23. Sebastian Hensel 1879, vol. 2, 162.
24. Sebastian Hensel 1879, vol. 2, 173–174. *Reisetagebuch*, 30 May 1840. The phrase in italics is in French in the original text.
25. Sebastian Hensel 1879, vol. 2, 174f. *Reisetagebuch* and letter of 31 May 1840.
26. According to Hans Naef, the canvas that Ingres showed Fanny must have been his *Stratonice*, which he painted during his tenure as director. (See Hans Naef 1974, 19–23.) Ingres gave Fanny a drawing depicting Santa Francesca Romana, an early fifteenth-century saint who has since been designated patron of motorists. (Drawing is in the Mendelssohn Archives, Berlin.)

CHAPTER TWENTY-FIVE

1. Sebastian Hensel 1879, vol. 2, 183. Letter of 9 June 1840.
2. 20 May 1840.
3. Sebastian Hensel 1879, vol. 2, 180–181. *Reisetagebuch.*
4. Saint-Alban n.d., 30.
5. Sebastian Hensel 1879, vol. 2, 184f. Letter of 9 June 1840.
6. Sebastian Hensel 1879, vol. 2, 191. Letter of 9 June 1840.
7. Sebastian Hensel 1879, vol. 2, 188.
8. Pauline Viardot-García (1821–1910) was a great singer of the nineteenth century and the sister of Maria Malibran. She was a friend of Turgenev and the model for George Sand's *Consuelo.* An excellent teacher, she was also a composer and one of the richest personalities of her time.
9. Sebastian Hensel 1879, vol. 2, 189–190. *Tagebuch,* 8 June 1840.
10. Sebastian Hensel 1879, vol. 2, 195f. Letter and diary.
11. Sebastian Hensel 1879, vol. 2, 212. Letter of 11 July 1840.
12. Sebastian Hensel 1879, vol. 2, 213.
13. Sebastian Hensel 1879, vol. 2, 212.
14. Sebastian Hensel 1911, 26.
15. Sebastian Hensel 1879, vol. 2, 218f. Letters of 10 and 14 August 1840.
16. Sebastian Hensel 1879, vol. 2, 222. *Reisetagebuch,* 16 August 1840.
17. Sebastian Hensel 1879, vol. 2, 224. *Reisetagebuch,* 20 August 1840.
18. Sebastian Hensel 1879, vol. 2, 224f. Letter and diary, 24 August 1840.
19. Karl August Varnhagen von Ense 1861, vol. 1, 125; 2 May 1839.
20. Sebastian Hensel 1879, vol. 2, 228f. *Reisetagebuch*
21. Sebastian Hensel 1879, vol. 2, 230. *Reisetagebuch,* 25 August 1840.
22. Sebastian Hensel 1879, vol. 2, 232.
23. Sebastian Hensel 1879, vol. 2, 232. *Reisetagebuch,* end.

CHAPTER TWENTY-SIX

1. Heinrich Heine n.d., vol. 2, 173–175.
2. Karin Kiwus 1981, 374f.
3. Gert Mattenklott n.d., 141.
4. Johann Ludwig Tieck: see Chapter 7, note 8.
Jacob Ludwig Carl Grimm (1785–1863) and his brother Wilhelm Carl Grimm (1786–1859), founders of modern German studies and editors of popular legends and short stories.
Joseph von Eichendorff: see Chapter 7, note 7.
Bettina von Arnim, née Brentano: see also Chapter 7, note 7. After raising her eight children between 1815 and 1831, Bettina von Arnim began

publishing. Her book *Göthes Briefwechsel mit einem Kinde* (1835) was a sensation, as was the more politically committed *Das Buch gehört dem König* (1843). Bettina, who possessed multiple talents, was gifted in both music and drawing. She used her influence at court to defend the revolutionaries.
5. Sebastian Hensel 1879, vol. 2, 237.

Peter Cornelius (1783–1867), history painter and former Nazarene. Director of the Munich Academy between 1825 and 1841, he came to Berlin at the request of Friedrich Wilhelm IV to oversee the installation of frescoes in the entrance to the "Old Museum," the first museum in Berlin (opened in 1830). He then spent much time working on projects for the king: frescoes for a cathedral and a funerary monument—projects which came to nothing. See Cécile Lowenthal-Hensel 1981, 34.
6. Sebastian Hensel 1879, vol. 2, 267.
7. Karl August Varnhagen von Ense 1861, vol. 2, 355; Sunday 31 August 1844.

CHAPTER TWENTY-SEVEN

1. Ernst Raupach (1784–1852) lived in Russia from 1804 to 1822 and was professor of German literature and history at the University of Saint Petersburg after 1816. He returned to Berlin in 1824 and became one of the most fashionable authors of his time.
2. Sebastian Hensel 1879, vol. 2, 297. Letter of 5 December 1840.
3. Mendelssohn Archives, Berlin; MAMs 47. *Das Jahr: 12 Characterstücke für das Forte-Piano*. First published by Furore Verlag (Fue 138) with a price of 88 Marks, not a modest sum!
4. Marcia Citron 1987, 574. Letter of 28 September 1840.
5. Marcia Citron 1987, 578 and 303.
6. Henrik Steffens (1773–1845) was a Norwegian naturalist, philosopher, and poet who had moved to Berlin in 1832.
7. Paul Heyse 1912, 42–43.
8. Karl August Varnhagen von Ense 1861–1862, vol. 1, 385.
9. Boeckh lived on the ground floor at 3 Leipziger Strasse between 1840 and 1846, according to Cécile Lowenthal-Hensel 1981, 90.
10. Sebastian Hensel 1879, vol. 2, 257.
11. Marcia Citron 1987, 583. Letter of 13 July 1841.
12. Sebastian Hensel 1911, 14f.
13. Sebastian Hensel 1911, 15.
14. Sebastian Hensel 1911, 17.
15. Sebastian Hensel 1911, 27.
16. Sebastian Hensel 1879, vol. 2, 275.

17. Marcia Citron 1987, 584. Letter of 5 December 1842.
18. Sebastian Hensel 1879, vol. 3, 1–2. The passage in italics is in French in the original text.
19. Marcia Citron 1987, 599. Letter of 4 March 1845.
20. Robert Schumann 1987, vol. 2, 266, June 1843.
21. Otto Nicolai (1810–1849), conductor and composer. His best-known opera, *The Merry Wives of Windsor*, still appears constantly on theater bills in Germany. Nicolai founded the concerts of the Vienna Philharmonic Orchestra.
22. Sebastian Hensel 1879, vol. 3, 3.
23. Mendelssohn Archives, Berlin; MAMs 48, 16 pages; published by Furore-Verlag, Fue 146.
24. Victoria Sirota 1981, 114; mentioned in Michaelis 1888, *Frauen als Schaffende Tonkünstler*, 16.
25. Eva Weissweiler 1985a, 154. Letter of 24 November 1843.
26. Cécile Lowenthal-Hensel 1975, 208.
27. Cécile Lowenthal-Hensel 1975, 212.
28. Sebastian Hensel 1879, vol. 3, 12.
    Johann Lukas Schönlein (1793–1864) had been professor at the medical clinic in Berlin beginning in 1840 and doctor to Friedrich Wilhelm IV. He founded what was known as the natural historical school. See also Ilse Rabien 1990a, vol. 7, 299.
29. Sebastian Hensel 1879, vol. 3, 8. Letter of 15 July 1843.
30. Sebastian Hensel 1879, vol. 3, 12. Letter of 27 July 1843. The two sisters could be referring to this passage from *Consuelo* in which Porporina, after admiring the canon's "fine vegetable garden," contemplated his beds of rare plants in the morning and "sought in her mind for the connection between music and flowers. . . . For a long time the harmony of sounds had seemed to her to correspond somewhat to the harmony of colors." (George Sand 1991, vol. 2, 115 and 132.) A reference to a far less attractive vegetable garden than that cultivated by the musically minded canon occurs in the following volume, in a passage in which Matteus chatters on. (George Sand 1991, vol. 3, 247.)
31. Sebastian Hensel 1879, vol. 3, 21. Letter of 19 August 1843.
32. Sebastian Hensel 1879, vol. 3, 49. Letter to Rebecka of 18 October 1843.
    Joseph Joachim (1831–1907), one of the nineteenth century's most famous violinists; founded a quartet in 1869 and played often with Brahms, whose violin sonatas he was the first to perform.
33. Sebastian Hensel 1879, vol. 3, 50f.
34. Sebastian Hensel 1879, vol. 3, 72. Letter to Rebecka of 31 October 1843.

35. Sebastian Hensel 1879, vol. 3, 87. Letter to Rebecka of 5 December 1843.
36. Sebastian Hensel 1879, vol. 3, 114. Letter to Rebecka of 30 January 1844.
37. Sebastian Hensel 1879, vol. 3, 123.
38. Or possibly Sophie Löwe (1815–after 1860), a soprano at the Berlin Opera from 1836 who also sang oratorio.
39. Sebastian Hensel 1879, vol. 3, 122.
40. Sebastian Hensel 1879, vol. 3, 128.
41. Fanny Lewald 1871, 147f.

Christian Friedrich Tieck (1776–1851), brother of the writer, was a sculptor who had been influenced by the Jena group of Romantics (1801); then assistant director of the Academy of Fine Arts (1839).

Karl Wilhelm Wach (1790–1845) was a painter whose studio was situated on the Klosterstrasse next to the studios of sculptor Christian Daniel Rauch (1777–1857) and Friedrich Wilhelm Tieck; he, too, had been a assistant director of the academy since 1840.

Friedrich von Raumer (1781–1873), historian and professor of political science and history in Berlin from 1819 to 1869.

Radziwill: The history of this great family of Lithuanian Catholic princes is closely linked to the cultural history of Berlin. Prince Anton Heinrich von Radziwill (1775–1833) was an accomplished musician who composed some music for *Faust* that was performed in 1835 and caused a sensation in Berlin. Like his daughter Elisa (1803–1834), he took part in the famous *Lalla Rookh* in which Wilhelm Hensel distinguished himself. In 1837 his two daughters-in-law, Mathilde (who was married to Prince Wilhelm Radziwill) and Leontine, banded together with Marianne Saaling and Luise Hensel to form the Union of Women of Saint Hedwig for the Care and Education of Catholic Orphans. This union was needed to deal with the ravages of cholera in particular. Princess Leontine and her husband Prince Boguslaw maintained the Radziwills' tradition of hospitality. See Cécile Lowenthal-Hensel 1981, 59f. and 155.

42. Sebastian Hensel 1879, vol. 3, 129.
43. Sebastian Hensel 1879, vol. 3, 131.
44. Sebastian Hensel 1879, vol. 3, 168. Letter of 19 June 1844.
45. Sebastian Hensel 1879, vol. 3, 139. Letter of 30 April 1844.
46. Sebastian Hensel 1879, vol. 3, 163. Letter of 5 June 1844.

CHAPTER TWENTY-EIGHT

1. Sebastian Hensel 1879, vol. 3, 121. Letter of 2 March 1844.
2. Sebastian Hensel 1879, vol. 3, 194. Letter to Cécile of 19 November 1844.
3. Sebastian Hensel 1879, vol. 3, 192. *Tagebuch.*
4. Sebastian Hensel 1879, vol. 3, 197.
5. Sebastian Hensel 1879, vol. 3, 198.
6. Sebastian Hensel 1911, 46; 134.
7. Sebastian Hensel 1879, vol. 3, 214.
8. Sebastian Hensel 1879, vol. 3, 213.
9. Ingeborg Drewitz 1979, 97.
10. According to Rebecka's great-great niece, Dr. Cécile Lowenthal-Hensel, trustee of family secrets. See Cécile Lowenthal-Hensel 1981, 75.
11. Sebastian Hensel 1879, vol. 3, 215–216.
12. Sebastian Hensel 1879, vol. 3, 227f.
13. Karl August Varnhagen von Ense 1861–1862, vol. 3, 127; 18 July 1845.
14. Sebastian Hensel 1879, vol. 3, 150. Letter to Rebecka of 18 May 1844.
15. Sebastian Hensel 1879, vol. 3, 190. Letter to Rebecka of 4 September 1844.
16. See also Lea Salomon's letter of 1799 in Chapter 3.
17. Ilse Rabien 1990b, vol. 7, 153.
18. Ferdinand Lassalle (1825–1864) was a German socialist and lawyer who had been strongly influenced by Hegel. Undertook the defense of Countess Hatzfeld between 1846 and 1851. Joined forces with Proudhon and Marx and spent time in prison in 1848–1849. Embraced German unity and socialist ideas, thereby earning further years in prison. Revived the notion of an "iron law of wages" that was based on the work of David Ricardo and used it to formulate his own theory, "the brass law of salaries," which maintains that production costs reduce workers' salaries to the strict minimum needed to keep workers and their families alive.
19. Paul Heyse 1912, 45.
20. Arnold Mendelssohn was a student of Johannes Peter Müller (1801–1858), who was considered the founder of modern physiology and who opposed Schönlein's school of historical naturalism.
21. Karl August Varnhagen von Ense 1861–1862, vol. 3, 438; 11 September 1846.
22. Robert Schumann 1948, 55.
23. Felix Gilbert 1975, 156–157. Letter of Arnold Mendelssohn written from the prison to his father Nathan, 22 April 1849.
24. Ilse Rabien 1990a, vol. 7, 296–321.

25. Felix Gilbert 1975, 145. Letter from Wilhelm Hensel to his sister Luise, 28 May 1847.

CHAPTER TWENTY-NINE

1. Marcia Citron 1987, 612. Letter of 9 July 1846.
2. Michael Cullen 1982, 53–54.
3. Sebastian Hensel 1879, vol. 3, 233.
4. Günter Richter n.d., 560–561.
5. Robert von Keudell 1901, 63.
6. Robert von Keudell 1901, 63.
7. Marcia Citron 1987, 610. Letter of 22 June 1846.
8. Marcia Citron 1987, 611. Letter of 9 July 1846. Fanny used the English word *rather* and the French *femme libre*. In saying that she was not *young* Germany, she was making a pun on her age and the political movement, Junges Deutschland.
9. Sebastian Hensel 1879, vol. 3, 234–235.
10. Sebastian Hensel 1879, vol. 3, 234.
11. Marcia Citron 1987, 356, undated.
12. Autograph copy in Fanny's hand. Bodleian Library, Oxford, MS Margaret Denecke Mendelssohn c. 21, fol. 133, dated 18 August 1838.
13. Marcia Citron 1987, 613. Undated letter, probably written in late August 1846.
14. Josephine Lang (1815–1880), soprano and composer of lieder.
15. Marcia Citron 1987, 583. Letter of 13 July 1841.
16. Sebastian Hensel 1879, vol. 3, 244–245.
17. Berthold Litzmann 1920, vol. 2, 161.

Clara Wieck (1819–1896) was herself a child prodigy. Her father, who was also her piano teacher, was so against her marrying Robert Schumann that Clara and Robert had to appeal to a court of law to quash his opposition. Clara had six children with her composer husband, whom she married in 1840. After Robert's death in 1856, she had a brilliant career as a concert artist and teacher.

18. Marcia Citron 1987, 608. Letter of 11 April 1846.
19. Marcia Citron 1987, 498. Letter of 8 April 1835.
20. Sebastian Hensel 1911, 57–58.

Henriette Sontag (1806–1854) became famous in 1825 for her interpretations of Weber's *Der Freischütz* and *Euryanthe*. Raised to noble rank by Friedrich Wilhelm III in 1830, Countess Rossi abandoned the theater and gave concerts until 1849. See Klaus Siebenhaar 1981, 458.

21. Eva Weissweiler 1985b, 11.

22. Sebastian Hensel 1879, vol. 3, 245.

23. Sebastian Hensel 1879, vol. 3, 246.

24. *Neue Zeitschrift für Musik*, 26:4, 14.

25. *Neue Zeitschrift für Musik*, 26:10, 38.

26. *Neue Zeitschrift für Musik*, 26:22, 89.

27. Dr. Emmanuel Klitzsch, *Neue Zeitschrift für Musik*, 26:40, 169.

28. Sebastian Hensel 1879, vol. 3, 246.

29. Felix Mendelssohn Bartholdy 1909, 329. Letter of 3 June 1847.

30. Eduard Devrient 1869, 281.

31. Felix Gilbert 1975, 144. Letter from Hinni Mendelssohn of 21 May 1847.

32. Sebastian Hensel 1911, 104.

33. Felix Gilbert 1975, 144.

34. Sebastian Hensel 1879, vol. 3, 247.

35. Cécile Lowenthal-Hensel 1981, 20.

36. Eduard Devrient 1869, 282.

37. Eduard Devrient 1869, 284f.

38. Eduard Devrient 1869, 286.

CONCLUSION

1. Cécile Lowenthal-Hensel 1981, 30–31.

2. Cécile Lowenthal-Hensel 1981, 19–20.

3. Michael Cullen 1982, 70f.

4. Sebastian Hensel 1911, 198.

5. Gisela Gantzel-Kress 1986, 175.

6. *Juden in Preussen* 1981, 276.

7. Ilse Rabien 1990a, vol. 7, 295–296.

8. Sebastian Hensel 1879, vol. 2, 198.

9. Sebastian Hensel 1879, vol. 3, 247.

10. Cécile Lowenthal-Hensel 1981, 18.

Bibliography

Altmann, Alexander. 1973. *Moses Mendelssohn: Bibliographical Study.* London: Routledge.

Anstett, Jean-Jacques. 1975. Henriette Mendelssohn. In *Aspects de la civilisation germanique.* Travaux 12. Saint-Étienne: Centre interdisciplinaire d'étude et de recherche sur l'expression contemporaine.

Arendt, Hannah. 1986. *Rahel Varnhagen.* French translation by Henri Plard. Paris: Tierce. (Original ed., 1958. English translation from the German by Richard and Clara Winston, Harcourt Brace Jovanovich, Inc., 1974.)

Attali, Jacques. 1985. *Sir Sigmund Warburg, 1902–1982: un homme d'influence.* Paris: Fayard.

Austen, Jane. 1981. *Pride and Prejudice.* London: Penguin English Library. (First ed., 1813).

———. 1985. *Persuasion.* London: Penguin English Library. (First ed., 1818.)

Badinter, Elisabeth. 1986. *L'un est l'autre.* Paris: Odile Jacob.

Badinter, Robert. 1989. *Libres et égaux . . . : L'émancipation des Juifs sous la Révolution française (1789–1791).* Paris: Fayard.

Beaumarchais, Pierre Augustin Caron de. 1966. *Le Mariage de Figaro.* Paris: Gallimard (Livre de Poche).

Beaussant, Philippe. 1985. Les inventions italiennes du génie baroque. In *Histoire de la musique occidentale.* Edited by Brigitte and Jean Massin. Paris: Fayard/Messidor-Temps Actuels. 395–421.

Benjamin, Phyllis. 1990. Quellen zur Biographie von Fanny Hensel, 4. A Diary Album for Fanny Mendelssohn Bartholdy. In *Mendelssohn-Stu-*

dien: Beiträge zur neueren deutschen Kultur- und Wirtschaftsgeschichte, vol. 7. Berlin: Duncker und Humblot. 179–217.

Berlioz, Hector. 1969. *Mémoires*. Paris: Garnier-Flammarion. (First ed., 1870.)

Bordier-Nikitine, Michèle. 1985. Charles Dugasseau. In *Revue historique et archéologique du Maine*, vol. 5. 300–329.

Boyd, Alexander. 1979. Some Unpublished Letters of Abraham Mendelssohn and Fanny Hensel. In *Mendelssohn-Studien*, vol. 3. 9–50.

Calendrier musical universel. 1972. Vol. 9 (1788). Geneva: Minkoff Reprints.

Chiti, Patricia Adkins. 1982. *Donne in Musica*. Rome: Bulzoni.

Citron, Marcia. 1987. *The Letters of Fanny Hensel to Felix Mendelssohn*. New York: Pendragon Press

Cooper, Martin. 1980. Charles Gounod. In *The New Grove Dictionary of Music and Musicians*, vol. 7. Edited by Stanley Sadie. London: Macmillan. 580–591.

Cullen, Michael. 1982. Leipziger Strasse 3: Eine Baubiographie. In *Mendelssohn-Studien*, vol. 5. 9–77.

Devrient, Eduard. 1869. *Meine Erinnerungen an Felix Mendelssohn Bartholdy und seine Briefe an mich*. Leipzig: S. Weber.

Devrient, Therese. 1905. *Jugenderinnerungen*. Edited by H. Devrient. Stuttgart: C. Krabbe.

Drewitz, Ingeborg. 1979. *Berliner Salons*. Berlin: Haude und Spenersche Verlagsbuchhandlung.

Elvers, Rudolf. 1972. Verzeichnis der Musikautographen von Fanny Hensel. In *Mendelssohn-Studien*, vol. 1. 169–174.

———. 1975. Weitere Quellen zu den Werken von Fanny Hensel. In *Mendelssohn-Studien*, vol. 2. 215–220.

———. 1984. *Felix Mendelssohn Bartholdy: Briefe*. Frankfurt: Frankfurt Verlagsbuchhandlung. (First ed., 1979).

———. 1983. Über das Berlinische Zwitterwesen. In *Die Mendelssohn in Berlin: eine Familie und ihre Stadt*, Ausstellungskatalog no. 20. Berlin: Staatsbibliothek Preussischer Kulturbesitz.

Frotscher, Gotthold. 1923–1924. Die Aesthetik des Berliner Liedes in ihren Hauptproblemen. In *Zeitschrift für Musikwissenschaft*, vol. 6. 431–448.

Gantzel-Kreiss, Gisela. 1986. Noblesse oblige: Ein Beitrag zur Nobilitierung der Mendelssohns. In *Mendelssohn-Studien*, vol. 6. 163–181.

Geck, Martin. 1967. *Die Wiederentdeckung der Matthäuspassion im 19. Jahrhundert, die zeitgenössischen Dokumente und ihre ideengeschichtliche Deutung*. Forschungsunternehmen der Fritz Thyssen Stiftung, Studien zur Musikgeschichte des 19. Jahrhunderts Band 9. Regensburg: Gustav Bosse Verlag.

————. 1949–1967. Zelter. In *Die Musik in Geschichte und Gegenwart*, vol. 14. Edited by F. Blume. Kassel und Basel: Bärenreiter Verlag. Col. 1208–1215.

Gilbert, Felix. 1975. *Bankiers, Künstler und Gelehrte: unveröffentlichte Briefe der Familie Mendelssohn aus dem 19. Jahrhundert*. Herausgegeben und eingeleitet von F. Gilbert, Schriftenreihe wissenschaftlicher Abhandlungen des Leo Baeck Instituts 31. Tübingen: J. C. B. Mohr.

Goethe, Johann Wolfgang von. 1833–1834. *Briefwechsel zwischen Goethe und Zelter, in den Jahren 1796 bis 1832*. 6 vols. Edited by Riemer. Berlin: Duncker und Humblot.

Gounod, Charles. 1886. *Mémoires d'un artiste*. 3d ed. Paris: Calmann-Lévy.

Grossmann-Vendrey, Susanna. 1969. *Felix Mendelssohn Bartholdy und die Musik der Vergangenheit*. Forschungsunternehmen der Fritz Thyssen Stiftung, Studien zur Musikgeschichte des 19. Jahrhunderts Band 17. Regensburg: Gustav Bosse Verlag.

Hall, Catherine. 1985. Sweet Home. In *Histoire de la vie privée*, vol. 4. Introduction by Michèle Perrot. Compiled by Georges Duby and Philippe Ariès. Paris: Editions du Seuil. 52–87.

Hecker, Manfred. 1981. Die Luisenstadt: ein Beispiel der liberalistischen Stadtplanung und baulichen Entwicklung Berlins zu Beginn des 19. Jahrhunderts. In *Berlin zwischen 1789 und 1848: Facetten einer Epoche*. 123f.

Heine, Heinrich. n.d. *Sämtliche Werke*. 7 vols. Edited by Ernst Elster. Leipzig and Vienna: Bibliographisches Institut.

Hensel, Fanny. 1829–1834. *Tagebuch*. Mendelssohn Archives, Berlin. Fot. 8835.

Hensel, Fanny. 1994. *Songs for Pianoforte, 1836–1837*. Edited by Camilla Cai. Recent Researches in the Music of the Nineteenth and Early Twentieth Centuries. Vol. 22. Madison, WI: A-R Editions.

Hensel, Sebastian. 1879. *Die Familie Mendelssohn, 1729–1847, nach Briefen und Tagebüchern*. 3 vols. Berlin: B. Behr's Buchhandlung. Reprint 1994, Frankfurt: Insel Verlag.

————. 1911. *Ein Lebensbild aus Deutschlands Lehrjahren*. Foreword by Professor Paul Hensel. Berlin: Georg Reimer.

Hérissay, Jacques. 1922. *Le Monde des théâtres pendant la Révolution, 1789–1800: D'après des documents inédits*. Paris: Perrin.

Hertling, Nele. 1981. Die Singakademie im musikalischen Leben Berlins 1791–1851. In *Berlin zwischen 1789 und 1848: Facetten einer Epoche*. Ausstellungskatalog der Akademie der Künste 132. Berlin: Frölich und Kaufmann GmbH. 243–265.

Heyse, Paul. 1912. *Jugenderinnerungen und Bekenntnisse*. 5th ed. Stuttgart and Berlin: J. G. Cotta'sche Buchhandlung Nachfolger.

Hiller, Ferdinand. 1878. *Felix Mendelssohn Bartholdy: Briefe und Erinnerungen.* 2d ed. Cologne: Dumont-Schaubert.

Honigmann, Peter. 1990. Der Einfluss von Moses Mendelssohn auf die Erziehung der Brüder Humboldt. In *Mendelssohn-Studien*, vol. 7. Berlin: Duncker und Humblot. 39–76.

Hoock-Demarle, Marie-Claire. 1990. *La Rage d'écrire: femmes-écrivains en Allemagne de 1790 à 1815.* Aix-en-Provence: Alinéa.

Horsley, Fanny and Sophie. 1934. *Mendelssohn and His Friends in Kensington.* London: Oxford University Press.

Internationale Komponistinnen–Bibliothek. 1994. *Komponistinnen. Eine Bestandsaufnahme* (Women composers, an inventory). Edited by A. Olivier. 2d ed. Wuppertal.

Juden in Preussen. 1981. Bildarchiv Preussischer Kulturbesitz. Dortmund: Harenberg Kommunikation.

Kahl, Willi. 1949–1967. Ludwig Berger. In *Die Musik in Geschichte und Gegenwart*, vol. 1. Edited by F. Blume. Kassel and Basel: Bärenreiter. Col. 1692.

Keudell, Robert von. 1901. *Fürst und Fürstin Bismarck: Erinnerungen aus den Jahren 1846 bis 1872.* Berlin and Stuttgart: W. Spernan.

Kirschner, Gottlob. n.d. Dirichlet. In *Neue deutsche Biographie*, vol. 3, 749–750.

Kiwus, Karin. 1981. Universität. In *Berlin zwischen 1789 und 1848: Facetten einer Epoche.* Berlin: Frölich und Kaufmann. 353–376.

Kliem, Manfred. 1990. Die Berliner Mendelssohn-Adresse Neue Promenade 7. In *Mendelssohn-Studien*, vol. 7. 127.

Knibiehler, Yvonne. 1991. Corps et coeurs. In *Histoire des femmes en Occident*, vol. 4, le 19e siècle. Edited by Geneviève Fraisse and Michelle Perrot. Paris: Plon. 351–387.

Knobloch, Heinz. 1987. *Berliner Grabsteine.* Berlin: Buchverlag der Morgen.

Koch, Paul-August. 1993. *Fanny Hensel geb. Mendelssohn (1805–1847): Kompositionen* . . . Literatur und Schallplatten. Leipzig: Hofmeister.

Koehler, Karl-Heinz. 1980. Felix Mendelssohn Bartholdy. In *The New Grove Dictionary of Music and Musicians*, vol. 12. Edited by Stanley Sadie. London: Macmillan.

Kundera, Milan. 1990. *L'immortalité.* French translation by Eva Bloch. Paris: Gallimard.

Kupferberg, Herbert. 1977. *Die Mendelssohns.* 2d ed. Tübingen: Wunderlich Verlag. (Originally published in 1972 as *The Mendelssohns.* New York: Scribners.)

Lambour, Christian. 1986. Quellen zur Biographie von Fanny Hensel, geb. Mendelssohn Bartholdy. In *Mendelssohn-Studien*, vol. 6. 49–105.

————. 1990. Ein schweizer Reisebrief aus dem Jahr 1822 von Lea und Fanny Mendelssohn Bartholdy an Henriette Mendelssohn, geborene Meyer. In *Mendelssohn-Studien*, vol. 7. 171–178.

Lemoine-Luccioni, Eugénie. 1976. *Partage des femmes*. Paris: Éditions du Seuil.

Lessing, Gotthold Ephraim. 1982. *Nathan der Weise*. Stuttgart: Reclam. 71f. (First ed., 1778; first performance: Weimar, 1801, as revised by Schiller.)

Lewald, Fanny. 1871. *Meine Lebensgeschichte*. 3 vols. 2d ed. Berlin: Otto Janke.

Lindner, Klaus. 1981. *Berlin im Kartenbild: Zur Entwicklung der Stadt 1650–1950*. Berlin: Staatsbibliothek Preussischer Kulturbesitz, Ausstellungskataloge 15. 22f.

Litzmann, Berthold. 1920. *Clara Schumann: ein Künstlerleben, nach Tagebüchern und Briefen*. 3 vols. 7th ed. Leipzig: Breitkopf & Härtel.

Lowenthal-Hensel, Cécile. 1970. F in Dur und F in Moll. In *Berlin in Dur und Moll*. Berlin: Axel Springer Verlag.

————. 1975. Wilhelm Hensel in England. In *Mendelssohn-Studien*, vol. 2. 203–213.

————. 1979a. Wilhelm Hensels "Lebenslauf" von 1829. In *Mendelssohn-Studien*, vol. 3. 175–179.

————. 1979b. Theodor Fontane über Wilhelm Hensel. In *Mendelssohn-Studien*, vol. 3. 181–199.

————. 1981. *Preussische Bildnisse des 19. Jahrhunderts: Zeichnungen von Wilhelm Hensel*. Ausstellungskatalog. Staatliche Museen Preussischer Kulturbesitz. Berlin: Hartman and Company.

————. 1986. *19th Century Society Portraits: Drawings by Wilhelm Hensel*. Exhibition catalogue, Berlin. London: Goethe Institute.

————. 1990. Neues zur Leipziger Strasse 3. In *Mendelssohn-Studien*, vol. 7. 141–151.

Macdonald, Hugh. 1980. Marie Bigot. In *The New Grove Dictionary of Music and Musicians*, vol. 2. Edited by Stanley Sadie. London: Macmillan. 701.

Mahling, Christoph Helmut. 1980. Zum "Musikbetrieb" Berlins und seinen Institutionen in der ersten Hälfte des 19. Jahrhunderts. In *Studien zur Musikgeschichte Berlins im frühen 19. Jahrhundert*. Edited by Carl Dahlhaus. Forschungsunternehmen der Fritz Thyssen Stiftung, Studien zur Musikgeschichte des 19. Jahrhunderts Band 56. Regensburg: Gustav Bosse Verlag.

Mann, Thomas. 1947. "Goethe and Tolstoy." In *Essays of Three Decades*. New York: Alfred A. Knopf.

Marx, Adolf Bernhard. 1859. *Erinnerungen aus meinem Leben*. 3 vols. Berlin.

Mattenklott, Gert. n.d. Junges Deutschland und Vormärz in Berlin. In *Berlin zwischen 1789 und 1848: Facetten einer Epoche.* 139–146.

Meier, Jean-Paul. 1978. *L'Esthétique de Moses Mendelssohn, 1729–1789.* Paris and Lille.

Mendelssohn Bartholdy, Felix. 1875. *Briefe aus den Jahren 1833 bis 1847.* Edited by Paul Mendelssohn-Bartholdy and Carl Mendelssohn Bartholdy. 6th ed. Leipzig: H. Mendelssohn.

———. 1882. *Reisebriefe aus den Jahren 1830 bis 1832.* Edited by P. Mendelssohn-Bartholdy. 9th ed. Leipzig: H. Mendelssohn.

———. 1888. *Briefe von F. Mendelssohn Bartholdy an Ignaz und Charlotte Moscheles.* Edited by F. Moscheles. Leipzig: Duncker und Humblot.

———. 1909. *Briefwechsel mit Legationsrat Karl Klingemann.* Edited by K. Klingemann. Essen: Baedeker.

———. 1961. *Paphleis: Ein Spott-Heldengedicht.* Basel: Jahresgabe der Internationalen Felix-Mendelssohn-Gesellschaft.

Mendelssohn Bartholdy, Karl. 1871. *Goethe und Felix Mendelssohn Bartholdy.* Leipzig: S. Hirzel.

Mendelssohn Bartholdy, Karl. 1974. *Goethe and Mendelssohn.* 2d ed. Translated by M. E. von Glehn. London: Macmillan.

Le Ménestrel. 1875. Vol. 41. Paris.

Meyerbeer, Giacomo. 1960–. *Briefwechsel und Tagebücher.* Edited by Heinz Becker and Gudrun Becker. Berlin: W. de Gruyter.

Möhrmann, Renate. 1985. Fanny Lewald. In *Neue Deutsche Bibliographie,* vol. 19. Berlin: Duncker und Humblot.

Montgomery-Silfverstolpe, Malla. 1912. *Das romantische Deutschland. Reisejournal einer Schwedin (1825–1826).* Leipzig: A. Bonnier. 275–276.

Naef, Hans. 1974. Ingres, Fanny Hensel, et un dessin inédit. *Bulletin du Musée Ingres* 36 (December): 19–24.

Neue Zeitschrift für Musik. 1847. Vol. 26. Leipzig.

Nitsche, Peter. 1980. Die Liedertafel im System der Zelterschen Gründungen. In *Studien zur Musikgeschichte Berlins im frühen 19. Jahrhundert.* Edited by Carl Dahlhaus. Forschungsunternehmen der Fritz Thyssen Stiftung, vol. 56. Regensburg: Gustav Bosse Verlag.

Pfannkuch, Wilhelm. 1946–1967. Spontini. In *Die Musik in Geschichte und Gegenwart,* vol. 14. Edited by F. Blume. Kassel and Basel: Bärenreiter Verlag. Col. 1078–1090.

Polko, Elise. 1869. *Reminiscences of Felix Mendelssohn Bartholdy.* Translated by Lady Wallace. New York: Leypoldt and Holt.

Pulvermacher, Gunter. 1980. Biedermeier. In *The New Grove Dictionary of Music and Musicians,* vol. 2. Edited by Stanley Sadie. London: Macmillan. 695–697.

Quin, Carol Lynelle. 1981. "Fanny Mendelssohn Hensel: Her Contributions to Nineteenth-Century Musical Life." (D.M.A. diss.) Ann Arbor: University Microfilms International.

Rabien, Ilse. 1990a. Arnold und Wilhelm Mendelssohn: Zur Biographie zweier bemerkenswerter Brüder. In *Mendelssohn Studien*, vol. 7. 295–328.

———. 1990b. Die Mendelssohns in Bad Reinerz: zur Familie Nathan Mendelssohns. In *Mendelssohn-Studien*, vol. 7.

La Révolution française et les Juifs. 1968. Vol. 1. Paris: Edhis.

Richter, Günter. n.d. Keudell. In *Neue deutsche Biographie.* 560–561.

Roth, Cecil. 1943. *A Short History of the Jewish People.* Revised ed. Oxford: Phaidon Press.

Rothenberg, Sarah. 1993. Thus Far But No Farther: Fanny Mendelssohn's Unfinished Journey. *Musical Quarterly* 77: 689–708.

Sabean, David Warren. 1993. Fanny and Felix Mendelssohn and the Question of Incest. *Musical Quarterly* 77: 709–717.

Saint-Alban. n.d. *L'illustre musicien Charles Gounod.* Paris: Maison de la Bonne Presse.

Sand, George. 1991. *Consuelo.* 3 vols. Edited by Simone Vierne and René Bourgeois. Grenoble: Éditions de l'Aurore. (First published 1842.)

Scheper, Dirk. 1981. Schauspielhaus. In *Berlin zwischen 1789 und 1848: Facetten einer Epoche.* 273–300.

Schieder, Theodor. n.d. Johann Gustav Droysen. In *Neue deutsche Biographie*, vol. 4. 135–137.

Schünemann, Georg. 1928. Die Bachpflege der Berliner Singakademie. In *Bach Jahrbuch* 25: 138–171.

Schumann, Robert. 1948. *Erinnerungen an Felix Mendelssohn: Nachgelassene Aufzeichnungen.* Zwickau: Predella Verlag.

———. 1987. *Tagebücher.* Edited by Gerd Nauhaus. Leipzig: Veb. Deutscher Verlag für Musik.

Sirota, Victoria, 1981. *The Life and Works of Fanny Mendelssohn Hensel.* Unpublished dissertation, Boston University.

Siebenhaar, Klaus. 1981. Biographien. In *Berlin zwischen 1789 und 1848: Facetten einer Epoche.* 431–462.

La Société des beaux-arts. 1836. *Annales de la Société des beaux-arts.* Vol. 4. Paris.

Stendhal. 1962. *Correspondance, 1800–1821.* Edited and annotated by Henri Martineau and Vittorio del Litto. Paris: Gallimard, Collection de la Pléiade.

Stern, Carola. 1990. *Ich möchte mir Flügel wünschen: das Leben der Dorothea Schlegel.* Reinbeck bei Hamburg: Rowohlt Verlag.

Sutermeister, Peter. 1979. *Felix Mendelssohn Bartholdy: Eine Reise durch*

Deutschland, Italien und die Schweiz. Edited by P. Sutermeister. Tübingen: Heliopolis-Verlag Ewald Katzmann.

Toews, John E. 1993. Memory and Gender in the Remaking of Fanny Mendelssohn's Musical Identity: the chorale in *Das Jahr. Musical Quarterly* 77: 727–748.

Treue, Wilhelm. 1972. Das Bankhaus Mendelssohn als Beispiel einer Privatbank im 19. und 20. Jahrhundert. In *Mendelssohn-Studien*, vol. 1. 29–80.

Varnhagen von Ense, Karl August. 1840. *Denkwürdigkeiten und vermischte Schriften.* Vol. 7. Leipzig: F. A. Brockhaus. Vol. 9, edited by his niece Ludmilla Assing, 1859.

———. 1861–1862. *Tagebücher.* 7 vols. Edited by his niece Ludmilla Assing. Leipzig: F. A. Brockhaus.

Vignal, Marc. 1985. Les nouveaux courants musicaux de 1750 à 1780. In *Histoire de la musique occidentale.* Edited by Brigitte and Jean Massin. Paris: Fayard. 564–584.

Weissman, Adolf. 1911. *Berlin als Musikstadt: Geschichte der Oper und des Konzerts von 1740 bis 1911.* Berlin and Leipzig: Schuster und Loeffler.

Weissweiler, Eva. 1985a. *Fanny Mendelssohn: ein Portrait in Briefen.* Frankfurt am Main, Berlin, Vienna: Ullstein Taschenbuch.

———. 1985b. *Fanny Mendelssohn: Italienisches Tagebuch.* Edited by E. Weissweiler. Darmstadt: Luchterhand.

Werner, Eric. 1980. *Mendelssohn: Leben und Werk in neuer Sicht.* Zurich and Freiburg: Atlantis Musikbuch-Verlag.

Wilhelmy, Petra. 1989. *Der Berliner Salon im 19. Jahrhundert (1780–1914).* Berlin and New York: Gruyter.

Woolf, Virginia, 1929. *A Room of One's Own.* New York: Harcourt, Brace & World, Inc.

Published Compositions by Fanny Mendelssohn

INSTRUMENTAL MUSIC

Chamber music

Adagio for Violin and Piano. Rosario Marciano, ed. Furore, Kassel, 1989.

Piano Quartet in A-flat Major. Renate Eggebrecht-Kupsa, ed. Furore, Kassel, 1990.

Piano Trio in D Minor, Op. 11. Wollenweber, Gräfelfing, 1984.

String Quartet in E-flat Major. Renate Eggebrecht-Kupsa, ed. Furore, Kassel, 1988.

String Quartet in E-flat Major. Günter Marx, ed. Breitkopf & Härtel, Wiesbaden, 1989.

Translated and reprinted with permission from the German edition of *Fanny Mendelssohn*. Françoise Tillard. 1994. *Die verkannte Schwester. Die späte Entdeckung der Fanny Mendelssohn Bartholdy*. Munich: Kindler Verlag. See also: Internationale Komponistinnen–Bibliothek. 1994. *Komponistinnen. Eine Bestandsaufnahme* (Women composers, an inventory). Edited by A. Olivier. 2d ed. Wuppertal. Unfortunately, some of the titles listed are no longer in print.

Music for piano

"Abschied von Rom"; "Il saltarello romano," Op. 6, No. 4; "Notturno"; "O Traum der Jugend, o goldener Stern." In *At the Piano with Felix and Fanny Mendelssohn*. Maurice Hinson, ed. Alfred Publishing, Sherman Oaks, CA, 1990.

Two Bagatelles for Piano. Barbara Heller, ed. Furore, Kassel, 1988.

"Das Jahr," Twelve Character Pieces for the Pianoforte, vols. 1 and 2. Barbara Heller and Liana Gavrila Serbescu, eds. Furore, Kassel, 1989.

Songs for the Pianoforte, Op. 2; Pastorella, Op. 6. Bote & Bock, Berlin, 1983.

Four Songs Without Words for Piano, Op. 8. Eva Rieger, ed. Furore, Kassel, 1989.

Six Melodies for the Piano, Op. 4 and Op. 5. Lienau, Berlin, 1982.

Melodies, Op. 4, Nos. 2 and 4. In *Frauen komponieren. 22 Klavierstücke des 18.–20. Jahrhunderts*. Eva Rieger, ed. Schott, Mainz, 1985.

Melody for Piano, Op. 4, No. 2; Melody for Piano, Op. 5, No. 4. In *At the Piano with Women Composers*. Maurice Hinson, ed. Alfred Publishing, Sherman Oaks CA, 1990.

Prelude for Piano. Rosario Marciano, ed. Furore, Kassel, 1989.

Sonata in G Minor for Piano. Barbara Heller and Liana Gavrila Serbescu, eds. Furore, Kassel, 1990.

Sonata in C Minor; Sonata Movement in E Major. Barbara Heller and Liana Gavrila Serbescu, eds. Furore, Kassel, 1991.

Sonata in C Minor; Sonata in G Minor. In *Two Piano Sonatas*. Judith Radell, ed. Hildegard Publishing, Bryn Mawr, PA, 1992.

Three Pieces for Four-Hand Piano. Barbara Gabler, ed. Furore, Kassel, 1990.

Two Etudes; Two Untitled Piano Pieces; "Notturno"; "Abschied von Rom"; Allegro Molto; Andante Cantabile; "O Traum der Jugend, o goldener Stern"; Allegretto; Allegro Vivace. In *Ausgewählte Klavierwerke*. Fanny Kistner-Hensel, ed. Henle, Munich, 1986.

Music for organ

Organ Prelude. Elke Mascha Blankenburg, ed. Furore, Kassel, 1988.

VOCAL MUSIC

Lieder for voice and piano

Selected Songs: "Sehnsucht nach Italien," "Mignon," "In die Ferne," "Sehnsucht," "Anklänge 1," "Anklänge 2," "Anklänge 3," "Traurige Wege," "Auf dem See," "Liebe in der Fremde." Edition Donna. Düsseldorf, 1991.

Selected Songs, vol. 1: "Wanderlied," Op. 1, No. 2; "Warum sind denn die Rosen so blass," Op. 1, No. 3; "Morgenständchen," Op. 1, No. 5; "Nachtwanderer," Op. 7, No. 1; "Frühling," Op. 7, No. 3; "Die frühen Gräber," Op. 9, No. 4; "Die Mainacht," Op. 9, No. 6; "Nach Süden," Op. 10, No. 1; "Vorwurf," Op. 10, No. 2; "Abendbild," Op. 10, No. 3; "Im Herbste," Op. 10, No. 4; "Bergeslust," Op. 10, No. 5; "Die Schiffende," "Kein Blick der Hoffnung," "Der Eichwald brauset." Breitkopf & Härtel, Wiesbaden, 1994.

Selected Songs, vol. 2: "Traurige Wege," "Harfners Lied," "Dämmerung senkte sich von oben," "Über allen Gipfeln ist Ruh," "Wandrers Nachtlied," "An Suleika," "Suleika," "Ach, die Augen sind es wieder," "Fichtenbaum und Palme," "Nacht ist wie ein stilles Meer," "Ich kann wohl manchmal singen," "Im Herbst," "Anklänge 1–3." Breitkopf & Härtel, Wiesbaden, 1993.

Sixteen Songs. John Glenn Paton, ed. Alfred Publishing Co., Inc., Van Nuys, CA, 1995.

Songs, Op. 1 and Op. 7. Bote & Bock, Berlin, 1985.

Songs, Op. 9 and Op. 10. Breitkopf & Härtel, 1850.

Songs, in *Felix Mendelssohn-sämtliche Lieder*: "Das Heimweh," Op. 8, No. 2; "Italien," Op. 8, No. 3; "Sehnsucht," Op. 9, No. 7; "Verlust," Op. 9, No. 10; "Die Nonne," Op. 9, No. 12. Edition Peters, Frankfurt.

Works for chorus a capella

"Morgengruss," Op. 3, No. 4, for four-part chorus a capella. Breitkopf & Härtel, Wiesbaden.

Choral movements for four-part chorus a capella: "Abendlich schon rauscht der Wald," Op. 3, No. 5; "Drüben geht die Sonne scheiden," "Hörst du nicht die Bäume rauschen," Op. 3, No. 1; "O Herbst, in linden Tagen," "Schweigt der Menschen laute Lust." In *Chorbuch Romantik*. Möseler, Wolfenbüttel, 1988.

Choral movements for four-part chorus a capella: "Frühzeitiger Frühling," "Unter des Laubdachs Hut." Joachim Draheim, ed. Breitkopf & Härtel, Wiesbaden, 1989.

Choral movements for four-part mixed chorus a capella: "Schöne Fremde," "Es rauschen die Wipfel." Joachim Draheim, ed. Breitkopf & Härtel, Wiesbaden, 1990.

"Gartenlieder" for mixed chorus a capella, Op. 3. Furore, Kassel, 1988.

Secular a capella choruses of 1846 (vols. 1–5): "Im Wald," Op. 3, No. 6; "Lockung," Op. 3, No. 1; "Abendlich," Op. 3, No. 5; "Waldeinsam," "Morgendämmerung," "Seid gegrüsst," Op. 3, No. 3; "Komm," "Ariel," "Schweigt der Menschen laute Lust," "Morgengruss," Op. 3, No. 4; "Schöne Fremde," Op 3, No. 2; "Schweigend sinkt die Nacht hernieder," "Lust'ge Vögel," "O Herbst," "Schilflied," "Schon kehren die Vögel wieder ein," "Wer will mir wehren zu singen." Furore, Kassel, 1988.

Works for soloists, chorus, and orchestra

Hiob (Job), cantata for soloists, chorus, and orchestra. Conrad Misch, ed. Furore, Kassel, 1992.

Io d'amor, o Dio, io moro, concert aria for soprano and orchestra. Bote & Bock, Berlin, 1992.

Lobgesang, cantata for soloists, chorus, and orchestra. Conrad Misch, ed. Furore, Kassel, 1992.

Index

Fanny, Wilhelm, and Sebastian Hensel; Abraham, Felix, and Lea Mendelssohn Bartholdy; Rebecka Dirichlet, and Paul Mendelssohn-Bartholdy are not included in the index.

Paternal Genealogy

Moses Mendelssohn
1729–1786
m. Fromet
  Gugenheim

- Dorothea
  1764–1839
  m. 1. Simon Veit
     2. Friedrich von
        Schlegel
  - Jonas
    1790–1854
  - Philipp
    1793–1877

- Recha
  1767–1831
  m. Mendel Meyer
  - Rebecka (Betty)
    1793–1850
    m. Heinrich Beer

- Joseph
  1770–1848
  m. Henriette Meyer
  - Benjamin
    1794–1874
    m. Rosamunde Richter
  - Alexander
    1798–1871
    m. Marianne
       Seeligmann

- Henriette
  1775–1831

- Abraham
  1776–1835
  m. Lea Salomon
  1777–1842
  - Fanny
    1805–1847
    m. Wilhelm Hensel
    - Sebastian
      1830–1898
  - Felix
    1809–1847
    m. Cécile Jeanrenaud
    - Carl
      1838–1897
    - Marie
      1839–1897
    - Paul
      1841–1880
    - Felix
      (d. in infancy)
    - Lili
      1845–1910
  - Rebecka
    1811–1858
    m. Peter Lejeune
    Dirichlet
    - Walter
      1833–1887
    - Ernst
      1840–1868
    - Flora
      1845–1912
  - Paul
    1812–1874
    m. Albertine Heine
    - Ernst
      1846–1909
    - Gotthold
      1848–1903
    - Fanny
      1851–1924

- Nathan
  1782–1852
  m. Henriette Itzig
  1781–1845
  - Arnold
    1817–1854
  - Ottilie
    1819–1848
    m. Eduard Kummer
  - Wilhelm
    1821–1866
    m. Louise Cauer
    - Arnold
      1855–1933

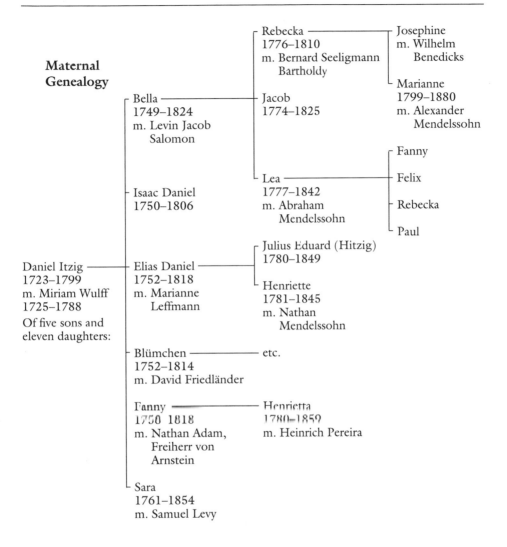

Maternal Genealogy

Daniel Itzig
1723–1799
m. Miriam Wulff
1725–1788
Of five sons and
eleven daughters:

Bella
1749–1824
m. Levin Jacob
Salomon

Rebecka
1776–1810
m. Bernard Seeligmann
Bartholdy

Josephine
m. Wilhelm
Benedicks

Marianne
1799–1880
m. Alexander
Mendelssohn

Jacob
1774–1825

Lea
1777–1842
m. Abraham
Mendelssohn

Fanny

Felix

Rebecka

Paul

Isaac Daniel
1750–1806

Elias Daniel
1752–1818
m. Marianne
Leffmann

Julius Eduard (Hitzig)
1780–1849

Henriette
1781–1845
m. Nathan
Mendelssohn

Blümchen
1752–1814
m. David Friedländer

etc.

Fanny
1758–1818
m. Nathan Adam,
Freiherr von
Arnstein

Henrietta
1780–1859
m. Heinrich Pereira

Sara
1761–1854
m. Samuel Levy

DATE